CW01431860

Greenhill
Books

Spies of the Bible

Rahab receives and conceals Joshua's spies (by Frederick Richard Pickersgill)

Spies of the Bible

*Espionage in Israel from the Exodus
to the Bar Kokhba Revolt*

by

Rose Mary Sheldon

Greenhill Books, London
MBI Publishing, St Paul

Greenhill
Books

Spies of the Bible
Espionage in Israel from the Exodus to the Bar Kokhba Revolt

First published in 2007 by Greenhill Books, Lionel Leventhal Limited, Park House,
1 Russell Gardens, London NW11 9NN
www.greenhillbooks.com
and
MBI Publishing Co., Galtier Plaza, Suite 200, 380 Jackson Street, St Paul,
MN 55101-3885, USA

British Library Cataloguing-in Publication Data

Sheldon, Rose Mary, 1948–
Spies of the Bible : espionage in Israel from the Exodus to
the Bar Kokhba
1. Guerrilla warfare – Middle East – History 2. Espionage –
Palestine – History – To 1500 3. Military intelligence –
Palestine – History – To 1500 4. Palestine – History – To
70 A.D.
I. Title
933'.05

ISBN: 978-1-85367-636-9

Library of Congress Cataloging-in Publication Data available

For more information on our books, please visit
www.greenhillbooks.com, email sales@greenhillbooks.com
or telephone us within the UK on 020 8458 6314.
You can also write to us at the above London address.

Edited and typeset by Wordsense Ltd, Edinburgh
Maps drawn by Derek Stone
Printed and bound in Great Britain by Creative Print and Design (Wales), Ebbw Vale

In Memoriam

Michael S. Harris
1944–2004

Incomparable teacher, host and friend

'The best portion of a good man's life is his little, nameless,
unremembered acts of kindness and love.'

WILLIAM WORDSWORTH

'Lines Composed a Few Miles above Tintern Abbey' ll. 33–5

CONTENTS

List of Maps   8
Chronology   9
Acknowledgements   11
Preface   13
Exodus and Entrance: Prolegomena to Biblical Research in the
    Twenty-First Century   21

PART I

1 The Book of Joshua   41
2 The Book of Judges   63
3 The United Monarchy   84
4 The Maccabean Revolt   99
5 Judith's Disinformation Campaign   112
Postscript: Spies in the Old Testament   117

PART II

6 The Jews Against Rome   129
7 The Jesus File   153
8 Israel's Last Stand – The Bar Kokhba Revolt   179
Postscript: Spying for Yahweh   200

List of Abbreviations   213
Notes   217
Bibliography   271
Intelligence Glossary   297
Index   299

MAPS

1 Sites Connected with the Conquest Narrative   43
2 Israel and Judaea   44
3 Battles in Northern Israel   66
4 Battle of Michmash   88
5 The Battles of the Maccabees   101
6 The Campaign of Cestius Gallus 66 CE   135
7 The Siege of Jerusalem 70 CE   143
8 Locations held by Bar Kokhba based on evidence
   from coins and documents   187
9 Roman Response to the Bar Kokhba Revolt   190
10 Judaea and Galilee after the Bar Kokhba War   193

CHRONOLOGY

Archaeological Periods

3500–2200 BCE	Early Bronze Age
2200–2000 BCE	Intermediate Bronze Age
2000–1550 BCE	Middle Bronze Age
1550–1200 BCE	Late Bronze Age
1200–1000 BCE	Iron Age I
1000–586 BCE	Iron Age II
586–538 BCE	Babylonian period
538–333 BCE	Persian period

United Monarchy

c.1025–1005 BCE	Saul
c.1005–965 BCE	David
c.965–928 BCE	Solomon (Yedidiah)

Major Events

930 BCE	Sheshonq I's campaign in Palestine
721 BCE	Northern kingdom of Israel invaded by Assyrian Empire. The Israelites are exiled and dispersed
700 BCE	Sennacherib takes Jerusalem
639–609 BCE	Reign of King Josiah
587 BCE	Siege of Jerusalem by the Chaldeans/Neo-Babylonians' destruction of the Temple. Some residents of the kingdom of Judah exiled to Babylonia
538 BCE	Babylon falls to Cyrus the Persian and the Jewish people are allowed to return to Jerusalem

515 BCE	The restored Temple is dedicated on the ancient site of Solomon's Temple
332 BCE	Persia conquered by Alexander the Great
323 BCE	Alexander the Great dies. Beginning of the Hellenistic period
301 BCE	Judaea becomes part of the Ptolemaic kingdom of Egypt
200 BCE	Judaea conquered by Macedonian kings of Syria, the Seleucids
167 BCE	Jerusalem is captured by Antiochus IV, who arranged for the offering of swine in the Temple: the 'Abomination of desolation'
166–36 BCE	Hasmonean Dynasty
164 BCE	Maccabees reconquer and purify the Temple
63 BCE	Romans under Pompey enter Jerusalem. Judaea becomes a client kingdom
37 BCE–94 CE	Herodian Dynasty
37–34 BCE	Reign of Herod the Great
4 BCE–6 CE	Reign of Herod Archaelaus
4 BCE–39 CE	Reign of Herod Antipas
4 BCE–34 CE	Reign of Philip
6 CE	Judaea becomes a Roman province. Revolt led by Judas of Galilee and Zadok the Pharisee
26–36 CE	Reign of Pontius Pilate
30 or 33 CE	Crucifixion of Jesus
41–44 CE	Reign of Herod Agrippa
44 CE	Judaea becomes a Roman province again
66–73 CE	Great Jewish Revolt
70 CE	Titus captures Jerusalem. Destruction of the Temple
73 CE	Fall of Masada
132–135 CE	Bar Kokhba Revolt
135 CE	Jerusalem destroyed and rebuilt as Aelia Capitolina. Jews forbidden to enter the city

ACKNOWLEDGEMENTS

THIS BOOK HAS BENEFITED immeasurably from numerous conversations with scholars and critiques by colleagues, so I have many debts to acknowledge. None of my research would be possible without the co-operation of the staff of the Preston Library at the Virginia Military Institute, who provided invaluable help with graphic design, inter-library loan and reference problems. Janet Holly on reference, the late Elizabeth Hostetter on inter-library loan and David Hess and Cathy Wells in Media Services have all earned my eternal thanks. The IT staff at the Virginia Military Institute, especially Bill Benish, solved several heart-stopping technical problems involving both hardware and software, as did my colleague from the Maths Department, Col. Thomas C. Lominac. Also at Virginia Military Institute I thank Penni Ticen for her illuminating discussions on the works of Mieke Bal. The late Michael Harris was always available for help with French translations and finding quotes. JoAnn Hartog and the staff of the Marshall Library must be thanked for their help with the use of the Friedman Collection.

Among my colleagues in the Washington, DC classical community, I must first and foremost thank Elizabeth Fisher of the Classics Department at George Washington University for her advice and kind hospitality on research trips. I cannot thank Elic Cline enough for being constantly available. He gave freely of his advice on many biblical topics and the current state of archaeology in Israel. The staff of the Library of Congress were always ready with advice and expertise about navigating their fine collection. Finally, I thank the Smithsonian Institution for allowing me to try out some of this material on the general public.

Without funding, much of this research could not have been done. The Dean's office at the Virginia Military Institute provided travel monies for trips to the Jewish and Middle Eastern Divisions of the New York Public Library, Harvard's Widener Library, the Andover Theological Seminary, the Richmond Theological

Seminary, and the Near Eastern Division of the Library of Congress. The Department of History at the Virginia Military Institute also provided travel money and software. At other Virginia institutions of higher learning, I must thank the staffs of the Leyburn Library at Washington and Lee University, and the Alderman Library at the University of Virginia.

I am indebted to readers who volunteered for the enormous job of reviewing the entire manuscript. These include Eric Cline of George Washington University, John D. MacIsaac of Mary Washington University, Aaron Schechtman of Monmouth University emeritus, and Ken Koons of the Virginia Military Institute. Jack Hershbell, emeritus of the University of Minnesota, applied his razor-sharp pen and wit to the manuscript and made this a much more readable text. All of these readers saved me from many of my own foolish mistakes.

Professor Yigael Sheffy of Tel Aviv University helped in locating materials in Israel. I thank Bishop John Shelby Spong for his advice on the midrashic approach and his constant encouragement. Professor Jack Cargill of Rutgers University helped me locate his insightful article on biblical history and western civilisation texts. I thank Sister Tabitha Jones, whose knowledge of scripture and of the English language have been of great help to me; I hope Aaron Franzblau would have been proud of us both. Andrea Berlin of the University of Minnesota helped with advice about articles from her book. As always, I am grateful for the comments of my students at the Virginia Military Institute, who always allow me to try new material on them and are generous with their insightful comments.

Finally, I would be remiss if I did not thank my husband Jeffrey Aubert, whose limitless patience helped me to overcome the frustrations of undertaking a project of this size, and made the celebration of its completion that much more joyful.

PREFACE

THIS BOOK IS CENTRED on a tiny strip of land, hemmed in on two sides by desert, and on one side by the Mediterranean – the land now known as Israel. It has, over the millennia, been plagued by almost continual warfare. Intelligence gathering played a large part in that warfare, as did deception, guerrilla operations and terrorist acts. Twentieth-century diaspora Jews have reclaimed the land of their ancestors, but the wars continue. As this book was being written, suicide bombers and Israeli counterattacks continued to drive up the death toll. An intelligence war is once again being waged in a land where, as I will demonstrate, intelligence wars have raged for three millennia. The need for human intelligence (HUMINT) has remained constant for any power that wishes to control the main land bridge of the eastern Mediterranean. Those who are familiar with modern intelligence operations in Israel may find eerily familiar scenarios in these chapters.[1]

Although respected as a book of both faith and history, the Bible has often been neglected as a source on military subjects. Paul Bentley Kern's *Ancient Siege Warfare* contains the startling statement that the 'Hebrews accomplished little of military significance', although he does admit that they left behind an historical source of unparalleled importance because the Hebrew Bible constitutes one of our longest and earliest records of warfare. He also points out that it contains descriptions of a wider variety of battles than any other ancient Near Eastern literary source.[2] Admittedly, siege warfare was not the forte of the Jews, nor was advanced technology. Martin Van Creveld, a well-known Israeli military historian, does not even discuss ancient Israel in his book *Technology and War. From 2,000 BC to the Present*.[3] Yet on the subject of military intelligence, I think Kern's judgement about ancient Israel's contribution should be revised, if not reversed.

Earlier studies have highlighted the great battles of biblical times such as Edward Longstreth's *Decisive Battles of the Bible* (1962) and General Sir Richard

Gale's *Great Battles of Biblical History* (1968). Yigael Yadin's *The Art of Warfare in Biblical Lands* (1963) discussed weapons and material culture, but he said very little about intelligence. More recently, this lacuna has been filled by Chaim Herzog and Mordechai Gichon's *Battles of the Bible* (1997, 2nd edn). Their book incorporates much discussion about intelligence on the battlefield. Eric Cline's *The Battles of Armageddon* (2000) covers military activities around the site of Megiddo and the Jezreel valley from the Bronze Age to the Nuclear Age, and his latest book, *Jerusalem Besieged* (2004), covers the 118 separate conflicts during which Jerusalem was besieged, attacked, captured, recaptured and destroyed. Finally, Richard Gabriel's *The Military History of Ancient Israel* (2003) surveys the wars from Exodus to the United Monarchy.

Yet surprisingly, no one has published a book solely on intelligence operations in ancient Israel, even though both the Hebrew and Christian scriptures are gold mines of information on intelligence activities.[4] Discussions have appeared in articles, conference papers and in smaller sections of books on warfare in the ancient Near East, but intelligence in the biblical lands has yet to receive a book-length treatment.[5] Nor has this material ever been combined with the intelligence history of later periods, as documented by Greek and Roman historians. For that reason alone, this book will be an original contribution to the debate.

There is a major methodological problem shared by many previous military histories of biblical battles that makes them either seriously outdated or ideologically slanted. Military historians, and even writers of general textbooks on the ancient world, often ignore the vast body of literary–critical biblical scholarship and archaeological evidence that has emerged in the last century.[6] Biblical scholars have long known that all the books of the Hebrew Bible, and the Christian scriptures also, were written long after the events they describe.[7] It is clear that the Bible is the product of multiple writers and editors involved in a complex literary process stretching over centuries. Biblical criticism, therefore, must be augmented by evidence from more than a century of modern archaeological excavations in Israel, Jordan and neighbouring regions. All too many military historians still base their narratives on a literal reading of the Book of Joshua; they use the so-called 'Conquest Model' as their conceptualisation and totally ignore the archaeological evidence and that fact that this model has been rejected by most historians of the ancient Near East in the last half century.[8] By dismissing available evidence, their arguments may become religious, not historical, and many even state their bias openly.[9]

When William F. Albright began his pioneering work in biblical archae-ology, excavations concentrated on uncovering large cities mentioned in the Hebrew Bible that confirmed the biblical story of the invasion of Canaan.[10] He believed that his work in archaeology had established an overwhelming number of material correspondences between the finds in Israel and the world described in the Bible.[11] Unfortunately for scholars who wish to take the biblical accounts at face value, the latest archaeological evidence does not agree with the story of Israel as traditionally told. By the 1970s, many archaeologists had shed the conquest model and Albright's interpretation, and looked instead to anthro-pological models to examine the human realities behind the biblical text. One can read the works of William Dever or the published papers of a 1991 Smith-sonian seminar to see a summary of current scholarship and realise that archaeol-ogy does not support the conquest model, or a literal acceptance of Joshua and Judges. When Mordechai Gichon attempted to defend the traditional view in the second edition of *Battles of the Bible*, he had to reach back for evidence from a half century before since most scholarly opinion had, in the meantime, gone in the opposite direction. Today, a literal reading of the campaigns of Joshua would not be accepted by many scholars – certainly no one in the mainstream of scholarship.[12]

What shall we do then with the account of Israel's history as related in Joshua, Numbers and Kings? Shall we dismiss it as a piece of 'pious propaganda' as some revisionist historians have suggested?[13] Shall we say that it contains no historical information whatsoever? Is there any substance to their claim that the history of Israel was 'invented' by modern Zionists in an attempt to deprive the Palestin-ians of their history?[14] This is a serious question, because if the revisionists are correct then some of the Western cultural tradition is based on a myth.[15] In this book, I have integrated the accounts of the Bible, the archaeological evidence and recent literary studies in an attempt to see what they tell us about the intel-ligence history of Palestine. Baruch Halpern has suggested: 'Behind the literary tradition [of the Bible] there must indeed be some sort of genuine historical memory.' Whether or not this is accessible to the text scholar, the archaeologist or the student of intelligence is another matter.[16]

The scope of this book includes intelligence activities as they were practised in ancient Israel from the entry of the Hebrews into Canaan to the expulsion of the Jews from Roman Palestine after the Bar Kokhba Revolt. There is insuffi-cient room to discuss every single military encounter of the Bible in detail, so I focus solely on intelligence activities carried out in ancient Israel over the span of a thousand years. While we cannot write the actual military history of the Late Bronze Age and Early Iron Age in Israel, we can at least create a reasonable conceptualisation of the nature of the culture in which these spy stories were told, and attempt to see why later authors chose to insert them into their historical accounts. What we can recover is at least the tradecraft (intelligence techniques) known to the writers at the time of scriptural composition, and we may then ascertain why these stories were included in the text and what military lesson, if any, the authors thought we might learn from them. We can also discern how such stories affected later Jewish writers and military commanders.

Certainly the authors of the books of the Bible were more interested in theology than history. Their first concern was faith, not espionage. History writing is a modern discipline, and when we look at the biblical material we are made painfully aware of its inadequacy for constructing a full picture of the past. Intelligence history poses an even greater problem, because intelligence activities are by their very nature secret. A spy who does his or her job well is never discovered. Only when they fail in some very public way, and their cover is blown, do we learn the results. I have argued elsewhere that the use of Livy as a source for early Roman intelligence history poses problems similar to those of using the Hebrew scriptures for early Israelite intelligence history. Many scholars consider Livy's narratives unreliable because he lacked military experience, he used miraculous events in his narrative, and he oversimplified events.[17] Livy and his sources, however, constitute the only evidence that shows how the Romans collected intelligence for their political and military needs between 756 and 264 BCE. If we reject Livy, almost nothing remains to be said about Roman conquests before 264, and it seems highly unlikely that the Romans carried out an aggressive foreign policy without collecting and using intelligence both on the battlefield and in the capital. We can fill in the story of the development of their intelligence capabilities by reading extant sources, and deducing what practices might have produced the outcomes as known. I believe the same is true with all the accounts used in this study. We certainly have to discount the miraculous events that are the preserve of the theologian rather than the historian, but I believe we can marshal evidence of the tradecraft possessed by both the writers of the Bible and those of later periods.[18]

Ancient religious sources should not be entirely ignored, especially where intelligence is concerned. In the ancient pagan world, religion and intelligence gathering were two sides of the same coin. This is also true of the biblical sources; intelligence at its oldest and most basic level consisted of religious revelation.

The belief that natural phenomena revealed the will of God or foretold the future is what connected intelligence and religious revelation. Consulting Yahweh or even the Witch of Endor was the biblical version of this phenomenon. As Allan Dulles observed:

> The earliest sources of intelligence, in the age of a belief in supernatural intervention in the affairs of men, were prophets, seers, oracles, soothsayers and astrologers. Since the gods knew what was going to happen ahead of time, having to some extent ordained the outcome of events, it is logical to seek out the divine intention in the inspiration of holy men, in the riddles of oracles, in the stars and often in dreams.[19]

War and religion were equally entwined. In the ancient Near East, war was portrayed as a sacred undertaking in which the honour of the national god was at stake. The writers of the Hebrew Bible had a similar conception of Israel's wars. The only difference was that the God of Israel was omnipotently transcendent and did not rise and fall with the fortunes of his people. In preparations for battle, Israel's dependence on God was always acknowledged. There were two primary moments in a military confrontation during which a leader would seek oracular guidance from God: before the mustering of troops, and just prior to the battle itself. This is true both of the Israelites and other Near Eastern peoples; they simply consulted different gods.[20]

Although none of the biblical authors was a trained historian in the modern sense, it has been suggested that there is too much sensible thinking about military topics in the Bible for the writers to have been totally ignorant of real combat requiring effective intelligence gathering. Malamat has written: 'Many of the biblical sources, when stripped of their theological varnish, do present a candid record of military lessons . . .'[21] The biblical authors claim to be preserving stories about people who fought these battles. Israelite commanders, especially in defensive engagements, display their superior knowledge of local geography. These stories often occur in places that still exist on the modern terrain of Israel and Jordan. We must determine, however, whether these battles took place where we are told they did, or if the writers knew of later battles at that same place and used those descriptions to project campaigns back into their own history. Military operations in Israel include examples of strategic and tactical intelligence gathering, battlefield stratagems, signalling, surprise attack, deception operations and clever use of tradecraft. A writer must be familiar with these techniques even if only to insert them into a fictional story.

17

One last question I explore in this volume is how we can compare the military accounts from the Hebrew Bible with those described by later Jewish, Greek or Roman sources of later periods. Are they less reliable? Are they reliable at all? Is there any consistency in the types of intelligence activities used by the Jews in their wars over a millennium? If they adopted the same techniques, then why do the Jews have so much success in the Books of Joshua, Judges and Kings, but so little success against the Romans?

The kinds of intelligence needed by the Jews altered with their changing political and military situation. Whether they were people who invaded or infiltrated Canaan, or people who separated from the indigenous population, there must have been military conflicts between Jews and their neighbours. When fighting as a small group against a larger military force, guerrilla warfare was an important part of their technique, as was using intelligence as a force multiplier (that is, something that makes an army seem larger or more effective than its numbers would imply). With the establishment of a monarchy, Israel had a standing army whose tactics and intelligence needs were different from those of more loosely confederated tribes. Later, as an occupied country under the Seleucid Greeks, the Jews again turned to guerrilla warfare under the Maccabees in an attempt to regain their independence. Under the Roman occupation, the Jews fought two massive but unsuccessful wars for independence, and intelligence activities played a large part in both of them.

The chapter headings of this book reflect the ever-changing intelligence needs of the Jews as their history unfolded. Chapter 1 discusses the thorny problem of the emergence of the Jews in the land of Canaan, and assesses the reliability of the battle accounts of Joshua. Its context is the Late Bronze Age (1550–1200 BCE) before new inhabitants (possibly Israelites) appeared in the hill country of Palestine. Chapter 2 describes Iron Age I (1200–1000 BCE), the period of the Judges, just before the twelve Israelite tribes united. The context for chapter 3 is the beginning of Iron Age II in the tenth century, and the text investigates the United Monarchy and the intelligence needs of David's kingdom. Chapter 4 covers the guerrilla wars of the Maccabees, and the discovery that a dedicated band of religious Jews could liberate a small country from a militarily superior occupying power. Chapter 5 highlights the story of the famous female undercover agent Judith, and her success against the Assyrian general Holofernes. Chapter 6 shows how imperial Rome maintained internal security in first-century Palestine and the ramifications this had for Jesus of Nazareth. Chapter 7 considers the First Jewish Revolt against the Romans and the intelligence operations of a war with a disastrous end for the Jews. Chapter 8 investigates the Bar Kokhba Revolt, in which the Jews attempted to gain freedom from the Romans for the last time, and in which they used superb intelligence gathering and relied on guerrilla operations. The Epilogue to each part of the book presents an analysis of what we may learn from intelligence operations conducted in the land of Israel first in the Hebrew scriptures and later in Roman sources and the New Testament.

Spies of the Bible is neither a narrative of military history of the Jews nor an attempt to insert anachronistic concepts into ancient material. The modern concept of intelligence and its appreciation is as much an anachronism in the biblical world as the modern technology used to collect it. Intelligence problems in all pre-modern societies, especially until the nineteenth century, were much simpler than their twentieth-century counterparts. By modern standards, all ancient intelligence organisations seem primitive. Speed in transmission, massive bureaucracies and technological means of collection of data by satellite and computers were unknown. Despite these limitations, the ancient world provides much evidence for intelligence activity. We must not assume that intelligence activities in all ancient societies were merely replications of one another. Each civilisation deserves to be treated separately, and Israel is no exception. Cultural differences among ancient societies made their approaches to intelligence very dissimilar. Monarchies do not operate like republics, nor do autocracies act like democracies. Furthermore, societies alter their intelligence practices as their needs change, from times of war to times of peace. The Jews used diffuse intelligence-collecting methods to build, defend and eventually recover their country. They could not have functioned without accurate intelligence and, perforce, an apparatus to collect it. Intelligence gathering is as much a part of statecraft as diplomacy, secrecy and propaganda.

I have discussed Roman intelligence activities in another book, *Trust in the Gods, But Verify: Intelligence Activities in Ancient Rome*. This companion volume studies a different culture that came into contact with the Romans. This clash of cultures resulted in an ongoing intelligence war. We will see that HUMINT has always been the basis for ancient intelligence gathering, and that basic notions behind the techniques of tradecraft have not changed much over the millennia even though the technology has.

Too often modern writers have tried to mine the past for nuggets of military wisdom it can teach commanders in the present. This is a dangerous pastime when it takes events out of their historical context or when it takes stories from the past and creates for them a context for which there is no firm evidence. This book is intended for intelligence professionals and military historians as well as general readers, to give them a more profound understanding of the problems of intelligence gathering in antiquity. Most readers do not have easy access to the many scholarly journals that publish the archaeological evidence or to the biblical criticism on which this study is based. Professional journals that require a knowledge of Greek and Latin, Hebrew, Arabic or Aramaic are not aimed at the general public. I have tried to pull together both the ancient and modern sources on intelligence in ancient Israel in an effort to show that these ancient spy stories are more than entertainment. They often describe real intelligence activities done by real people, and represent real problems faced by real armies. As Eric Cline's book on Armageddon has shown, even a modern military leader such as General Allenby could very well use the tactics of the Egyptian pharaoh Thutmose III as his model.[22] In a book of this size I cannot even discuss all of the spy stories, let alone list all of the secondary works; the bibliography alone would be a book-length treatment. I have tried instead to concentrate on some major incidents, battles and wars and to synthesise the best modern scholarship.

Neustadt and May once posed the question: 'What could the story of those ancients, armed with spears, propelled by oars, maintained by slaves, deprived of electronics, knowing nothing of air power, convey to men managing a modern war?' They believed that the tale taught us to 'think in time', that is, to make decisions based on evidence that is both cross-cultural and chronologically diverse.[23] This exercise will not work unless the evidence on which we base our vision is reliable and up-to-date. This synthesis of military intelligence, archaeological data and biblical criticism represents an effort to fill that niche.

EXODUS AND ENTRANCE

Prologomena to Biblical Research in the Twenty-First Century

BY THE HEBREW BIBLE'S own account, intelligence activities arrived in the Holy Land along with the Jews. In fact, intelligence activities had begun even before the Jews arrived. Without proper reconnaissance, not even Moses would have considered entering the land of milk and honey. To find out how best to go about conquering this new land, Moses sent out twelve spies. Numbers 13:1–20 provides the briefing Moses gave his reconnaissance team:

> Make your way up by the Negev, and go on into the hill-country. See what the land is like, and whether the people who live there are strong or weak, few or many. See whether it is easy or difficult country in which they live, and whether the cities in which they live are weakly defended or well fortified; is the land fertile or barren, and does it grow trees or not?[1]

This is a fairly standard list of requirements. It includes economic intelligence about the population and the agricultural possibilities of the land, as well as military intelligence about troop strength and fortifications.[2] The Jews had targeted the area of Canaan for invasion, and now they were collecting the intelligence necessary to make their conquest successful. Moses did not simply take the spies' word for what they found; he wanted hard intelligence, and so he instructed them: 'Go boldly in and take some of its fruit. It was the season when the first grapes were ripe.'[3] This episode has become the subject of many an artist's imagination. The spies heeded Moses' word and substantiated their report about the natural products of Canaan by bringing back samples of the rich fruit that grew there.

This reconnaissance mission has more to it than meets the eye. Moses sent out twelve spies, but not just any twelve picked men; he sent the head of each tribe. If he had really wanted a fair and impartial view of the nature of the land and the people of Canaan, he would never have sent out twelve political leaders;

he would have dispatched two or three technicians. From the religious point of view, Moses and Aaron did not need intelligence about Canaan. They believed they had the ultimate intelligence source – God – and they trusted him. The real purpose of the mission was, in fact, not only to find out what sort of land Canaan was but also to discover what sort of leaders these agents were. Were they strong and trustworthy? Most importantly, did they believe what Moses had told them about the Holy Land?

After the surveillance mission, even the spies were unable to arrive at an unanimous assessment of the situation. The majority report, given by ten of the spies, thought it unwise to enter Canaan. It was too powerful to defeat. The people were too big, too well armed, too strong and too numerous. The agents described the inhabitants as giants who made them feel like grasshoppers.[4] The minority report from Joshua and Caleb said that Canaan was there for the taking. We see clearly why it was important to have political leaders in agreement ahead of time. Fearful that the opinion of the minority report would ultimately prevail, the majority group 'spread an evil report of the land which they had spied out' and claimed it would eat up the children of Israel (Numbers 13:32). This description of an inhospitable land clearly and obviously contradicted their own earlier report (Numbers 13:27).

The disinformation campaign took its toll, and Moses soon faced a popular revolt against his leadership. The Israelites were condemned to wander in the wilderness for another forty years until a new, stronger generation of believers took over. Ten of the original spies died of plague, and only two members of the original group, Joshua and Caleb, were allowed to go into Canaan.[5]

This is a famous and seemingly realistic story of an intelligence mission preceding an invasion. Regardless of its verisimilitude, most scholars now believe it never happened. Can this be true? Are Moses' spies part of a fairy tale? In order to authenticate either this story or any other spy story in the Hebrew Bible, we must deal with two of the most intractable and controversial problems in biblical history. The first is: when and by whom was the Hebrew Bible written? The second is: what sources did the writers have, and do their scriptures describe events that actually happened? Even among the many biblical scholars who have written on the subject, there is still no consensus.[6] Yet, we cannot write about biblical battles or spies without taking into account textual criticism which, since the nineteenth century, has cast doubt on the veracity of the biblical accounts. Archaeological evidence over the last half century has added another source of information for reconstructing the history of Israel, and may help us to distinguish between the poetry of the biblical saga and the historical events and processes of the ancient Near East.[7]

The Exodus – Fact or Fiction?

The heart of the Hebrew Bible is the epic story that describes the escape of the Jews from Egypt and their arrival in the Holy Land. The story is a familiar one. Moses led the Jews out from the cities of the eastern Nile delta towards the wilderness of Sinai. After forty years of wandering, Moses brought them to the plains of Moab in Trans-jordan in sight of the Promised Land. He appointed Joshua to lead the people into Canaan and, by a campaign of swift conquest, he would take the land from its inhabitants. It is then that spies were sent to do the reconnaissance.

The problem with this traditional story, at least for the historian, is that no independent corroboration exists whatsoever. Certainly, immigrants coming down to Egypt from Canaan and settling on the eastern border of the delta regions is a well-known phenomenon. From earliest recorded times, Egypt was a place of refuge and security for the people of Canaan whenever drought, famine or warfare made their lives unbearable. The assertion by the Exodus and conquest traditions that Israel's origins were external to Palestine, however, is contradicted by recent archaeological discoveries. Rather than an invasion from outside, the evidence indicates an expansion of settlers into rural villages in the highlands and steppes of Palestine during the Early Iron Age by people who show a marked continuity in material culture with the Canaanites. Why would the biblical traditions draw such a radically different picture of their own origins? How are these traditions of external origin to be reconciled with the archaeological evidence of internal origins for the community?[8]

The archaeological evidence does not support a large exodus of Israelites from Egypt; there is not a single potsherd, structure, house or any trace of an ancient encampment. The archaeological record certainly provides no evidence for a force as large as six hundred thousand (two and a half million people if we follow the biblical text) surviving in a wilderness like Sinai for four decades. Modern archaeological techniques are quite capable of finding even the most meagre remains of hunter-gatherers and pastoral nomads all over the world, but they have not turned up a single trace of six hundred thousand wandering Jews. There is simply no evidence yet discovered for an Exodus in the thirteenth century BCE.[9]

Although sites mentioned in the Exodus narrative exist, they were usually occupied much earlier than the thirteenth century or in much later periods after the kingdom of Judah was established, and when the text of Exodus was set down for the first time.[10] They were unoccupied, however, precisely at the time they reportedly played a role in the events of the wandering Jews in the wilderness. The historical vagueness of the Exodus story, including lack of the pharaoh's name, makes it hard to date the text. This may be, however, precisely what the authors intended.[11] They were writing a story of an unorganised people united by a common experience and a common faith, under a strong leader who was guided by God. It was a story that might appeal to Israelites in any age.

The Conquest Model

If the Israelites did not arrive in the manner described in Exodus, then was Canaan conquered in battles as described in Joshua and Kings? The problems here are even greater. How could an army in rags, travelling with women, children and the aged, emerging after decades in the desert, possibly mount an effective invasion campaign? How did this unorganised rabble overcome the great fortresses of Canaan with their professional armies and well-trained chariotry, and what training could either side have had in military intelligence? Much as the archaeological record does not support the Exodus, it also does not support a lightning conquest by Joshua. The arrival of the Israelites may have been accomplished in stages rather than by a very quick campaign over several days in the thirteenth century. Interpretations about who the Israelites were and how they came to occupy Israel vary enormously.

The oldest theory for reconstructing the Israelite conquest of Canaan is drawn directly from the Hebrew Bible. The esteemed scholar William Foxwell Albright, known as the 'Father of Biblical Archaeology', defended a literal interpretation of the Book of Joshua from the 1920s until his death in 1971. This is now known as the 'Conquest Model'.[12] John Bright, a student of Albright's, wrote in 1959: 'The external evidence at our disposal is considerable and important. In the light of it, the historicity of such a conquest ought no longer to be denied.'[13] The conquest model took the biblical account in Joshua seriously, and the archaeological evidence known until the 1960s from sites such as Bethel, Debir, Lachish and Hazor seemed to corroborate the existence of military campaigns by foreign invaders of Canaan in the late thirteenth to twelfth centuries. Biblical scholars believed these foreigners were the Israelites.[14] The total absence of destruction levels at many of the key sites such as Dibon and Heshbon in Trans-jordan, and the lack of any occupational context for such destructions, seem to have been ignored or rationalised away by scholars still trying to salvage the traditional theory.[15] The leading Israeli archaeologist of his generation, Yigael Yadin, believed that his excavations at the great Upper Galilee site of Hazor in 1955–8 actually proved the historicity of Joshua 11:10–13 and its account of the fall of Hazor. Yadin still believed that archaeology broadly confirmed that at the end of the Late Bronze Age (thirteenth century BCE) semi-nomadic Israelites destroyed a number of Canaanite cities, then gradually built their own sedentary settlements on the ruins, and occupied the remainder of the country.[16] Similarly, in 1967, Paul W. Lapp, another student of Albright's, published a site-by-site survey of the archaeological evidence on the Late Bronze/Iron Age I horizon that supported the conquest model. He believed that the stratigraphic evidence pointed strongly to a destruction of nearly all important cities in the last half of the thirteenth century.[17] Few archaeologists today would make such a statement; the 'destruction horizon' is much more complex.[18] Even the name of the discipline 'biblical archaeology' has fallen into disrepute.[19]

By 1957, G. Ernest Wright, in his book *Biblical Archaeology*, acknowledged that the evidence had become somewhat problematic. But the real death knell for the conquest model came with the excavations at Jericho between 1955 and 1958, conducted by the respected British archaeologist Kathleen Kenyon. Although John Garstang had dug there in the 1920s, and uncovered a massive destruction of mud-brick city walls, which he dated to the fifteenth century, Kenyon used far superior field methods and showed conclusively that the destruction was part of the well-attested Egyptian campaigns that expelled the Asiatic Hyksos from Egypt at the start of the Eighteenth Dynasty. Kenyon further proved that during the mid- to late thirteenth century, when the Israelite conquest supposedly took place, Jericho was completely abandoned. There is not so much as a Late Bronze Age II potsherd on the entire site, nor is there any city nearby that might have been a candidate for such a destruction.[20] Similar problems arose at Ai, Gibeon, Debir and several other sites formerly thought to corroborate the biblical account. Archaeologists thus began to reinterpret the biblical account in the light of this fresh evidence, and many of them discarded the conquest model entirely.

Archaeologists have long since concluded that the Late Bronze Age destruction of various Canaanite cities is not attributable to one single event.[21] The few locations with datable finds present a much more complex picture of a process stretching over half a century, from 1200 to 1150 BCE. This decline appears to have paralleled the gradual reduction of Egyptian hegemony in the area established during the Eighteenth Dynasty and continuing until the reign of Ramses

III in the Nineteenth Dynasty.[22] The more recent approach is for scholars to see Israel's rise as part of the major changes that took place between 1400 BCE and 1200 BCE in the Middle East. These changes included a decline of the former great empires such as the Hittites, the Mitanni and the Assyrians, and the emergence of a new balance of power. The causes were varied, but the results were large migrations of regional populations and a disruption of ancient trading patterns. This larger historical context dovetails extremely well with the stories of the emergence of Israel in Canaan.[23]

In short, we cannot trace the destruction of Canaanite urban centres back to a single historical event. The devastation seems to be the result of various social and political forces, and conquests, the initiators of which cannot always be determined.[24] In the only case where agents of the destruction can be identified, for example Gezer, it was caused by the Egyptians. Several acts of demolition may be attributed to Sea Peoples, the sea-faring raiders who entered Egypt in the Nineteenth Dynasty. The settlement history after the destruction of Canaanite cities is even more complex. In Lachish, settlement was interrupted until the foundation of a new city in the early Israelite monarchy of the tenth century. At Megiddo, and at Aphek Gezer, settlement was continuous, although their inhabitants cannot be definitely identified through material remains. Ashdod, where settlement was continuous, was taken over by the Philistines in the later twelfth century.[25] It also seems certain that although the power and organisational structure of the Canaanite city-states were broken, and many Canaanite cities were destroyed immediately after the Egyptian withdrawal from the country in the late twelfth century, this 'conquest' is quite different from the biblical conquest tradition. The ruined towns are all located in the lowlands outside the territory where the Israelite monarchy was established, and their fall had no direct effect on the settlement in the highlands on both sides of the Jordan.[26] Furthermore, there is a definite continuity of Canaanite tradition displayed in the rebuilding of several cities. Volkmar Fritz summarised the situation well when he wrote: 'The Book of Joshua is of no historical value as far as the process of settlement is concerned.'[27]

Peaceful Infiltration

Archaeologists were not the only ones to doubt the validity of the conquest model. Even as early as the 1920s there had been a school in Germany that rejected the conquest model when it first appeared. Albrecht Alt and Martin Noth championed what came to be known as the 'Peaceful Infiltration Model', an alternative to the largely American conquest model that they thought was religiously fundamentalist.[28] This German school discarded the stories in Joshua, and concentrated on modern ethnographic studies of the sedentarisation of Middle Eastern pastoral nomads who wandered over long distances and who eventually settled down to become peasant farmers or townspeople. They compared this phenomenon to the biblical tradition of Israel's ancestors described in Genesis as wandering, tent-dwelling shepherds. From this they created the peaceful infiltration model, which suggested that those who settled the highlands of Canaan or western Palestine in the thirteenth and twelfth centuries were originally nomadic tribespeople of the semi-arid regions of trans-Jordan. Crossing the Jordan river on their annual trek in search of pasture and water, some groups had stayed on even longer each season in the cooler, well-watered, fertile hill country. Eventually they settled there and emerged into recorded history as the Israelites. Thus the Hebrews did not fight their way into the Sinai, but rather were part of a natural process of sedentarisation that has been going on in this region for millennia. In this view the only reconnaissance they needed was as shepherds looking for better pasture.[29]

The peaceful infiltration model has held sway with archaeologists for many years, and seems to offer a convincing modern, secular explanation for who the earliest Israelites had been, where they had come from, and how they had gradually transformed into a small-scale rural society with egalitarian ideals. Nonetheless, the peaceful infiltration theory has also come under attack. Critics argued that it was flawed by its dependence on nineteenth-century European misconceptions about Bedouin life. These misconceptions were based on the work of now out-of-date amateur ethnographers who knew little Arabic and who had observed local tribespeople only superficially. They had romanticised Bedouin life and failed completely to comprehend the real dynamics of sedentarisation.[30] Bedouin usually do not infiltrate or settle on their own initiative. Although drought, famine or adverse political conditions may compel them to settle, they often return as soon as possible to Bedouin life. In recent times Bedouin have been forcibly settled by urban authorities who considered them a nuisance and a hindrance to state control.[31]

The infiltration hypothesis failed to explain the fall of the Canaanite city-states, especially since the collapse of the Late Bronze Age culture presented no conditions for settlement. The peaceful infiltration model also did not answer the question of why the narrative in the Book of Joshua celebrates a massive, well-organised, lightning-quick military invasion of Canaan. It also does not explain where the extremely realistic spy stories came from, which seem to be the product of a very sophisticated military mind functioning from a strongly centralised position, rather than the creation of wandering nomads.

Revolting Peasants

In 1962, Albright's student, Professor George Mendenhall of the University of Michigan, published an article that rejected both the conquest and peaceful infiltration models.[32] He believed that Israel did not win against its neighbours because of superior military weapons or military organisation. He believed there was a religiously motivated internal revolution. He based his theory on the internal social developments in Canaan during the Late Bronze Age. He argued that city-states of Late Bronze Age Canaan were organised as highly stratified societies, with the king or mayor at the top of the pyramid, the prince, court officials and chariot warriors right below him, and the rural peasants at the base. The *apiru,* a group mentioned in the Tell el-Amarna letters, was apparently outside this scheme of organisation.[33] These *apiru* threatened the social order by creating a solidarity among a large group of marginalised people, thus challenging and eventually defeating the cities of Syria and Palestine. Mendenhall believed there had been a peasant revolt whose participants were united in their worship of the God YHWH. This new religious movement placed its faith in a single God who established egalitarian laws of social conduct and who communicated directly to each member of the community. The hold of the kings over the people was effectively broken by the spread of this new faith. The Israelite conquest was therefore accomplished without invasion or immigration, but occurred when a large number of Canaanite peasants overthrew their masters and became 'Israelites'. According to Mendenhall, the idea that the Israelites must originally have been nomads or a distinct ethnic group is mistaken.[34]

In 1979, this theory was modified by Norman K. Gottwald, another American biblical scholar, who expanded Mendenhall's theory in his book, *The Tribes of Yahweh*, where he theorised that Israel emerged out of Canaanite culture at the end of the Late Bronze Age as a revolutionary social movement. The remote frontier and forest regions became attractive to the members of this independence movement who had fled from the more heavily controlled and populated plains and valleys to establish a new way of life. Gottwald suggested that their settlement of this rocky and poorly watered region was possible because of technological developments: iron tools for hewing cisterns in the bedrock, and waterproof plaster for sealing cistern walls and terracing hilly slopes. Their tribal structure was their self-constructed instrument of resistance and means of decentralised self-rule. Gottwald argued that in their new home the Israelites established a more equal society with a means of production open to all.[35] His theory was rejected by many scholars because of his Marxist rhetoric and model of class struggle and peasant revolts.[36] Furthermore, there is no support for the revolt hypothesis given the archaeological evidence in the early Iron Age settlements in Palestine's hill country – the very groups which Gottwald and Mendenhall would see as revolutionaries.[37]

The revolution hypothesis also came under attack. Critics believed it was forced into too many laborious explanations of the conditions conducive to revolt and reorganisation without being able to give sufficient reasons for this development. Nor did it take note of recent archaeological finds. In the end, none of these theories – the invasion hypothesis, the infiltration hypothesis or the revolution hypothesis – has gained a consensus, probably because each has some weaknesses and some validity. The three approaches may not be mutually exclusive. There was some military activity involved in the story; there may have been fighting over territory and cities. There was migration and settlement, and there may even have been some peasant revolts.[38]

The Revisionists

The most radical approach has been taken by the literary theorists who have influenced the reinterpretation of biblical texts. Academics following the French post-modernist philosopher Michel Foucault, and who believe that 'all history writing is fiction', will be attracted to this revisionist school. The fundamental assumption of post-modernism is that no objective knowledge is possible, especially of a past only attested by texts. To them, texts are simply 'social constructs' that must be deconstructed and analysed in terms of the way language is used in them rather than in terms of what their authors intended to communicate. Since no knowledge of objective truth is possible in this view, texts can mean anything that we want or need them to mean. Post-modernism is particularly sceptical of 'meta-narratives' – that is, texts that make sweeping, universal claims to knowledge of a superior order. Indeed, the Bible is the dominant meta-narrative in the Western cultural tradition. To these scholars, it is not only proper to demythologise the Bible and to unmask its pretence to truth, but also absolutely necessary.[39]

The small and very controversial group of European biblical scholars in this revisionist school have been described pejoratively by others as 'minimalist'.

They believe that it is simply impossible to write a history of Israel based on the biblical texts.[40] These writers consider none of the military accounts historical, let alone the spy stories. In fact, they accept none of the Hebrew Bible as fact since it cannot be verified by any independent data. This trend began in 1992 with the publication of Philip R. Davies, *In Search of 'Ancient Israel'*. To Davies, 'Ancient Israel' was just such a social construct. Use of the Bible for the critical reconstruction of periods that it describes is precarious and only possible where there is adequate independent data. Without such external data, Davies believes it is technically impossible to write a critical history of ancient Israel.[41]

Other authors published in the Sheffield Academic Press have taken an even more extreme political stance. Keith W. Whitelam's book, *The Invention of Ancient Israel: The Silencing of Palestinian History*, not only claims that there is no ancient Israel but also maintains that modern scholars, especially pious Christians and Zionist Israelis, have invented 'ancient Israel'. Their intent, he argues, is to dispossess the real native peoples of the region, the Palestinians, from their history. This finally gave an overtly ideological and political agenda to the revisionists.[42]

Copenhagen became another university centre of the revisionist movement. It was there that Niels Peter Lemche wrote a provocative book in 1998 entitled *The Israelites in History and Tradition*. He espoused the radical view that the Hebrew Bible was not a document from the Iron Age, or the monarchical period, but was composed, not just edited, almost entirely in the Hellenistic era, the second century BCE.[43] In other words, it was a piece of pious propaganda stemming from the identity crisis of the Jews living in Hellenistic Palestine. They created a fictitious Israel to give themselves a legitimate history. Like Whitelam, Lemche was arguing that the story of ancient Israel in the Bible was a myth.

The most extreme revisionist is Thomas Thompson, an American now teaching with Lemche in Copenhagen. In 1999, he published his revisionist treatment of ancient Israel: *The Mythic Past: Biblical Archaeology and the Myth of Israel*. He will not even use the term 'Israel' for the Jews, but refers to the inhabitants as 'the population of Syria's southern, marginal fringe'.[44] This has caused his critics to label him anti-Israel, anti-Bible and nihilistic.[45]

Literalism versus Midrash

How do we sort out these competing views of the biblical accounts? Norman Gottwald has written: 'It is fairly easy to recognise that ancient commentators offered metaphoric or mythic constructions of the past to ground their understanding of the communities in which they lived.'[46] There is nothing particularly objective about Old Testament tradition. These stories were composed, not as histories but as books to inspire faith. They emphasise religion over fact. That is why some people have rejected them out of hand.

Between the two camps of believing literally or rejecting all, there is in fact a giant arena to explore. Literalism is not a benign alternative. As Bishop John Shelby Spong has pointed out: 'A literalised myth is a doomed myth.'[47] He argues that it is best to use a 'midrashic approach' when dealing with such texts. You do not ask midrash 'did it happen?' The proper question of the midrashic tradition is: 'What was the experience that led, or even compelled, the compilers of sacred tradition to include this moment . . . or this event inside the interpretive framework of their sacred past?' Midrash means that, when one enters the scriptures, one must abandon linear time. This is the 'interpretive envelope' in which all these stories, including the military ones, must be enclosed. To suggest that these texts should be taken literally is to place extreme limits on both their truth and their power.[48]

Behind every literary tradition there may be some genuine historical memory, but unfortunately it is not always accessible either to the textual scholar or to the archaeologist. Priests composing in the seventh century BCE could not have remembered what happened in the thirteenth century, and we do not know what facts or documents, if any, they had before them. The events behind the narratives cannot be rescued. The narratives do not permit us to claim that all these events occurred, nor do they permit us to date them or claim that all the events occurred to a single group, but details conform to some experiences in their past. If two centuries of biblical scholarship has taught us anything, it is that the biblical material must be evaluated chapter by chapter and sometimes verse by verse.

The Hebrew Bible includes historical, non-historical and quasi-historical materials that sometimes appear very close to one another in the text. The essence of Old Testament scholarship is to separate one from the other.[49] We cannot decisively prove or disprove anyone's thesis about the rise of ancient Israel, but rather we can show what the Israelites thought of their past, the kinds of stories they told about themselves, and the military skills they attributed to their ancestors. The same is true of the spy stories. We must ask ourselves what experiences the Israelites had that enabled them to write stories demonstrating such sophisticated tradecraft, and such a profound understanding of human nature and behaviour.

Who Wrote the Texts?

In assessing any ancient source, we surely must ask who wrote the text, and when was it composed. Martin Noth is generally credited with the idea that the books from Deuteronomy to 2 Kings were written as a 'unified and self-contained whole' by an author he named the Deuteronomist (hereafter called Dtr) historian. Noth theorised that Dtr wrote in the middle of the sixth century BCE. He compares Dtr's mode of composition to that of Hellenistic and Roman writers who used older sources to compose a history of the distant past. Later redactors added to the history in what Noth called a series of 'accretions'.[50] While some scholars have challenged his sixth century dating or modified his redactional theories, most scholars now take seriously his concept of the Dtr history.[51] Three major schools of thought have developed concerning the sources and redaction of the Dtr history, and they can be roughly divided into pre-exilic, exilic and post-exilic dating.

In a recent book, *The Bible Unearthed*, Israel Finkelstein and Neil Asher Silberman have brought together the biblical narrative and the archaeological evidence to argue that the Torah and the Dtr history were composed for the first time in the seventh century BCE, and were not just revisions of earlier documents.[52] They believe that much of the Hebrew Bible was the product of the hopes, fears and ambitions of the kingdom of Judah, culminating in the reign of King Josiah at the end of the seventh century BCE.[53] They argue that the historical core of the Bible arose from particular political, social and spiritual conditions and was shaped by the creativity and vision of a powerful religious reform movement that flourished in the kingdom of Judah in the Late Iron Age.[54] Although Finkelstein and Silberman believe these stories have some historical basis, the tales primarily reflect the ideology and the world view of later writers. In other words, we must view the biblical stories through the lens of a later period and reinterpret the events in a different chronological and historical framework.

Suggesting that the most famous stories of the Hebrew Bible did not happen as they are recorded is far from implying that ancient Israel had no genuine history. Rather than taking the Hebrew Bible as the unquestioned historical framework into which every particular find or conclusion must fit, the authors combine the archaeological finds and extra-biblical records, and make the biblical narratives part of the entire story. This certainly seems eminently more sensible than trying to fit the military narratives into the now-defunct conquest model. If Finkelstein and Silberman are correct, then what we have are military narratives from a much later time being inserted backwards into an earlier period by a seventh-century writer. The stories may be based on an earlier tradition, but they are contained in a document created in the seventh century BCE – five hundred years or more after the events they describe. What did the Israelites know about the Bronze Age, and what role did they think their ancestors played in it? The biblical writers were not concerned with the objective recording of details and processes of historical change as a modern historian would be. Nor was the Dtr historian concerned with historiography; rather he focused on the didactic use of selected historical traditions. The Dtr history records Israel's ideas about Israelite pre-history in the Bronze Age. The historical milieu for the conquest stories, therefore, is the political and military realities of the seventh century BCE.

Judah was always the poorer, weaker, more rural and less influential of the two kingdoms. It came to prominence only after the fall of Israel to Assyria in 722 BCE. Then as heir to the northern traditions, Judah determined which stories would become part of their national epic and how they would be interpreted. In order to unify the people of Judah and lead them on to these new conquests, King Josiah needed a unifying story. A board of priests acting as authors and editors was assigned to construct such a document, drawn from many diverse and conflicting traditions on which they could embellish and elaborate. Their intent was ideological as well as theological. They were not recording history in the modern sense of the word, but appropriating the past for use in their own present. The epic that they created was edited and added to in subsequent centuries to become the powerful saga we know today as the Hebrew Bible. It articulated a national and social compact for an entire people under God. According to Finkelstein and Silberman, we should show reverence for it, by treating it not as a miraculous revelation but rather as a brilliant product of the human imagination.

The story is told in two separate sections. The first contains the five books of Genesis, Exodus, Leviticus, Numbers and Deuteronomy. Its stories about Israel begin with their ancestors (known traditionally as the Patriarchs) and continue with the story of their sojourn and bondage in Egypt, the Exodus and the wanderings in the wilderness. They conclude with Israel poised to enter the Promised Land. The second part includes the books of Joshua, Judges, Samuel and Kings. It tells of the conquest of Canaan, the rule of the judges, the establishment of the united monarchy, the division of that monarchy, the destruction of the northern kingdom (Israel) by the Assyrians, the destruction of the southern kingdom (Judah) by the Babylonians, and the beginnings of exile in Babylon.

The use of archaeological evidence to reinterpret the Hebrew Bible may seem shocking to many readers at first. The search for the Patriarchs in the traditional era turns up nothing; archaeologists tell us Exodus did not happen as described; the violent swift and total conquest of Canaan is called a myth; and the picture of the judges leading tribes in battle against enemies is discarded because it does not fit the data. Believers in the glorious monarchy in Jerusalem are disappointed with this interpretation, because even though David and Solomon may have existed in the tenth century the new story sees them as little more than hill-country chieftains.[55] There was no golden age of a united kingdom, no magnificent capital and no extended empire – at least not in the tenth century. For obvious reasons, this is not the story people want to hear, but Finkelstein and Silberman show why Josiah's version of the story took its present form, and why it opens up alternative understandings of the stories. It also provides a more appropriate interpretive framework for discussing military exploits with their tales of espionage and treachery.

Each story from the past was used to reinforce a portion of Josiah's goals. In bringing together the Judean patriarch Abraham and the Israelite patriarch Jacob, the ancestor stories served well the needs of seventh-century Judah for a unified kingdom. The pastoral landscape of these ancient stories resonated with the way a large portion of the later Judahite population lived. The Exodus traditions also served this setting. The authors extracted stories about how some Israelites came to Canaan by migration, but turned it into a story of a glorious escape from Egypt and a triumphal entrance into the Promised Land.[56] Josiah's efforts to establish Judah's independence and reclaim territory of the destroyed kingdom of Israel, for example, were at variance with a revival of Egyptian power that encroached on Judah and Israel. The challenge of Moses to an unnamed Pharaoh mirrors Josiah's challenge to Pharaoh Necho II. Similarly, the conquest narratives fit the setting. Like Joshua, Josiah fought in Yahweh's name, and commanded his people to stay faithful and apart from the surrounding world. His agenda was a second conquest of Canaan.

David and Solomon also reflect the reign of Josiah, the sole legitimate heir of his dynasty. Like David, Josiah sought a united kingdom, territorial expansion, military conquests and the centralisation of cult and politics in Jerusalem. This seventh-century king could, in a sense, nullify the transgressions of Solomon and restore the glorious past that never was by founding it in reality in the seventh century.

The archaeology of Judah gives us insights into how the religious history developed. Judah was an isolated and sparsely populated nation consisting of local shrines, 'high places' for the worship of Yahweh along with many other deities. They were not monotheistic, but had syncretistic practices that prevailed even in Jerusalem. Demographic growth, social transformation and the desire for a unified land came only in the eighth century BCE and they were probably related to the struggle for national survival under the shadow of the Assyrian Empire. Sensing that syncretistic worship was a barrier to unification, certain religious circles in Jerusalem condemned the local Judean shrines as a Canaanite evil and pushed for something new – a Yahweh-alone region centred in Jerusalem. Ironically, they labelled this new religion the traditional one, and turned the traditional religion into a heresy. It was their work that prepared the way for Josiah's Deuteronomic reformation in the next century.

Josiah's violent death at the hands of the Pharaoh Necho II produced a problem for the Dtr's account. Obedience to Yahweh was supposed to save the ideal king, but it did not prevent Egypt's return to enslave the people of Israel. Even Egypt's defeat a few years later by Babylon did not save the Jews. By 587 BCE, the Babylonians had devastated Judah, from the outlying cities to the capital city of Jerusalem. Its aristocracy was exiled. These are the biblical and archaeological realities. The story, however, does not end here. To account for the violent death of Josiah and the total destruction of Jerusalem, the exiles revised their national saga to produce a second edition of the Dtr history.

The function of a national myth is to unite a people against their enemies. The xenophobia expressed in these texts towards non-Israelites, inhabitants of the lowlands, Canaanites, is clearly expressed. This, too, is a natural function of a national myth. Such myths exclude others, as do circumcision and dietary restrictions. In creating a story focused on liberation from slavery and on national enfranchisement in a particular region, ancient Israel was consciously erecting a paradigm. They were excluding Canaanites in order to set up the basic conditions under which their ethnic community could enjoy a sense of both separateness and independence. Using contemporary details (including battle descriptions and spy stories), the authors created a powerful saga that borrowed familiar landscapes and monuments for a seventh-century audience. Egypt of the Twenty-sixth Dynasty was expansionist, and hampered the fulfilment of King Josiah's dreams of empire. Images of the past and memories now became ammunition in a national test of will between the people of Israel and the pharaoh and his charioteers.[57]

The patriarchal narratives were thus woven together in the service of a seventh-century national revival in Judah. The story of the great power of God of Israel and his miraculous rescue of his people served a more immediate political and military end. This great saga of the new beginning and a second chance must have resonated in the consciousness of the seventh-century readers, reminding them of their own difficulties and giving them hope for the future. The story of Israel's exodus from Egypt was thus neither historical truth nor literary fiction. As Finkelstein says: 'It is a powerful expression of memory and hope born in a world in the midst of change.'[58] The confrontation between Moses and pharaoh mirrored the momentous confrontation between the young King Josiah and the newly crowned pharaoh Necho. To pin this biblical image down to a single date is to betray the story's deepest meaning. Stripped of its chronology, or even a link to a specific pharaoh, Passover becomes not a single event but a continuing experience of national resistance against an oppressive foreign power.

Spy Stories – Truth or Fiction?

Those who use the conquest model frequently do so not because the evidence supports their case, but for religious reasons – whether consciously or unconsciously. Not only have many military historians chosen to ignore the evidence of archaeology and literary studies, but some also actually brag about it.[59] My methodological assumption is that all evidence must be considered and, once the evidence is examined, the likely conclusion is that spy stories from the Bible were written half a millennium later than the events that they portray, and may in some cases be apocryphal. This will come as no surprise to scholars who have studied the textual problems of the Hebrew Bible for decades. As Yair Zakovich has written: 'Fire will not descend from the heavens nor will bears come out of the woods to punish our presumed irreverence.'[60] The Pentateuch may represent some traditions, memories, myths and local legends about the destruction of the Canaanite cities, but mostly they show how later generations viewed their past. The military operations described in Joshua, Judges and Kings show the Israelites using an indirect approach and avoiding frontal assaults or siege warfare. The biblical authors were not unaware of the role that intelligence played in their military operations, especially when they were operating with a smaller force. They particularly avoided straightforward encounters with chariotry in the open field. They resorted to tactics based on deception, feints, decoys, ambushes and diversionary manoeuvres – any guile to attain surprise in overcoming the enemy.[61] All these tactics rely on gathering accurate and timely intelligence.

The use of surprise attacks, guerrilla operations and even terrorist acts involves knowing where the enemy is, and what he is likely to do. In order to use surprise as a force multiplier, the Israelites needed to know where the enemy was and his capabilities in order to achieve their goal of conquering the land of Canaan, whether it was in the thirteenth century or the seventh BCE. Because these stories reflect such a sophisticated understanding of intelligence needs, tradecraft techniques and human motivation, our conclusion must be that they were composed long after Israel had a monarchy and a centralised government, and not in the thirteenth century by nomads wandering in the Sinai. If the stories were composed by people who had access to earlier accounts written by people with real military and intelligence training, we are unable to trace who they were and their accounts are not extant.

Part I

CHAPTER 1

The Book of Joshua

THE BOOK OF JOSHUA tells the story of a lightning military campaign during which the powerful kings of Canaan were defeated in battle and the Israelite tribes came to take possession of their land. It is a stirring war saga with heroism, cunning and bitter vengeance narrated with some of the most vivid storytelling in the Bible – the fall of Jericho's walls, the sun standing still at Gibeon, and the burning of the great Canaanite city of Hazor. Traditional scholars have accepted this account as a detailed geographical essay about the landscape of Canaan, and an historical explanation of how each of the twelve Israelite tribes came into its traditional territorial inheritance within the Promised Land. The Book of Joshua is not any of these things, and certainly it is not an accurate, detailed history of early Israel.[1]

If recent scholarship does not support the belief that the Israelites arrived as described in Exodus, neither does it back up Canaan being conquered in battles as Joshua and Kings relate them. The military problems seem as daunting as the historical and archaeological issues. How could an army of amateurs emerge after decades in the desert and mount an overwhelmingly successful invasion campaign against professional armies and well-trained soldiers? How could wandering Jews overcome the great fortresses of Canaan with an untrained army and no siege equipment? Furthermore, what could such wandering nomads know about the sophisticated intelligence techniques described in these stories?[2] There seems to be no choice but to reject the conquest model, because, just as the archaeological record does not support the Exodus, so it does not endorse a lightning campaign achieved over several weeks in the thirteenth century BCE.[3] Nor has any evidence of such events been found in the records of neighbouring cultures.

Many scholars now believe it is more likely that the early 'Israelites' were an amalgam of many different ethnic groups, and their arrival into Canaan occurred in stages over a long period of time by means of both military campaigns and transhumance.[4] There is no consensus among historians and archaeologists about how this occurred. Some believe the highland population of Iron Age I originated from the remnants of the Canaanite cities that had been destroyed.[5] Others think they came from the rural–nomadic population of the hill country.[6] Still others hold the view that the new settlers were semi-nomads who had a symbiotic relationship with the Canaanite city-states,[7] and settled in Iron Age I following the destruction of the Canaanite urban system.[8] None of these interpretations accepts the idea that there was a conquest. Even the biblical narratives themselves do not agree. The stories as they appear in Joshua seem to be a contradiction to the opening chapter in the book of Judges.[9]

If we consider the late composition of the Dtr history, then we must ask what a seventh-century author could have known about Bronze Age battles. Some scholars have argued that these battle descriptions are based on an earlier tradition that was then redacted in the seventh century BCE.[10] Others say they are descriptions of battles fought in King Josiah's time, that is, five hundred years later than the traditional date. In this latter view, the accounts were written by Israelites in the Iron Age reflecting back on the history of Egypt and Canaan and filled in with contemporary details. They are the Israelites' ideas about Israelite pre-history in the Bronze Age. We may legitimately ask why military accounts and spy stories played such a large part in the narrative. Most likely it was because the writer lived in a time of military conflict and he wanted to convey the idea of a victorious Israel, a people united, loyal and obedient to Yahweh, who guaranteed them success.[11]

Biblical writers were not concerned with the objective recording of military details or the process of historical change as a modern historian would be. The stories were told not because they had happened but because they could be used to provide hope in the present.[12] The historical milieu for the conquest stories is the political and military realities of the seventh century BCE. Individual stories were chosen not only because they recorded the taking of certain locations but because they also illustrated certain classic examples of success in warfare using intelligence operations. This is the only way of explaining, outside of a theological answer, how a smaller force succeeded so many times against a larger one.

Crossing the Jordan
The conquest stories make some sense geographically and strategically. If one wanted to conquer the Judaean heartland west of the Jordan, one needed to cross

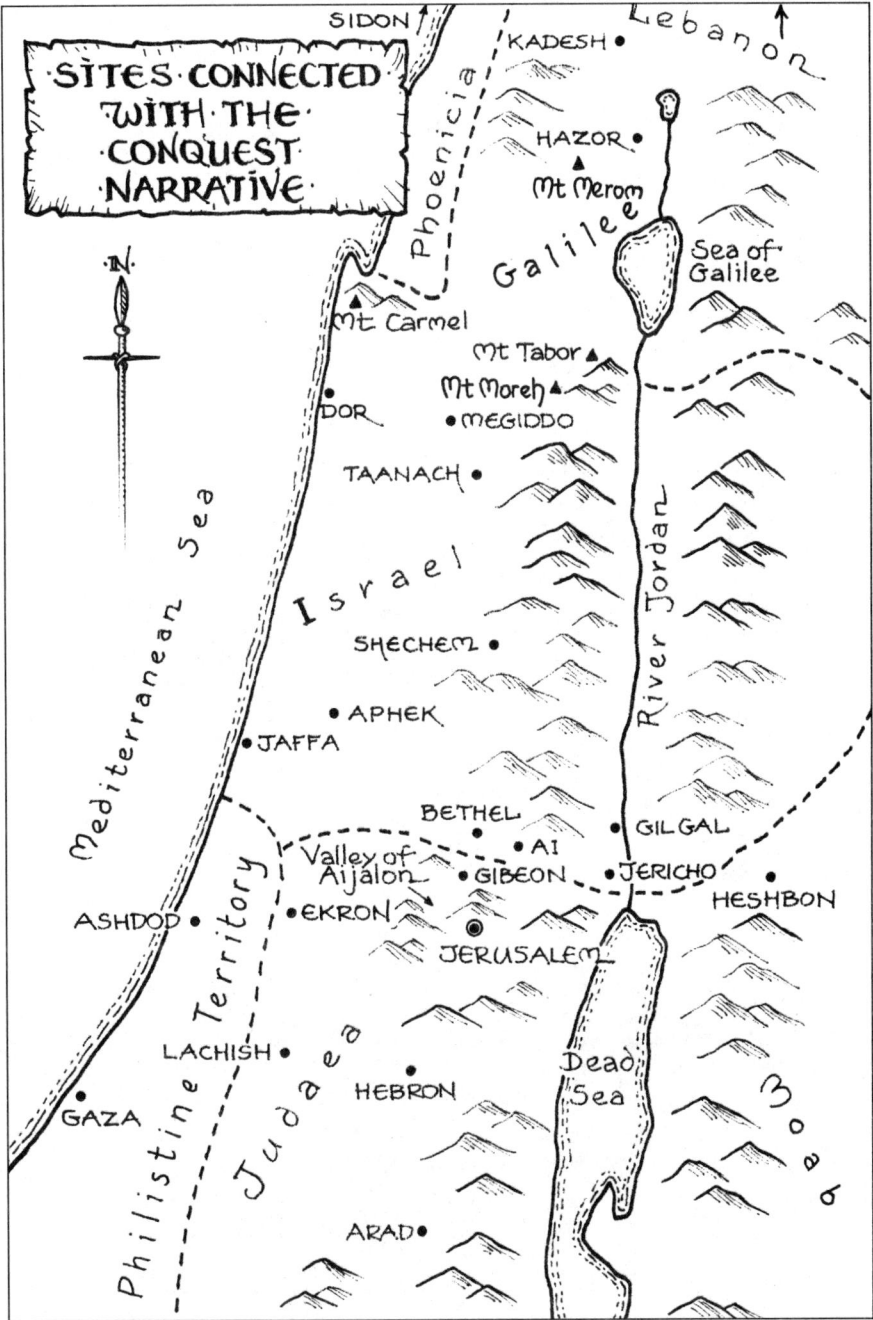

Map 1 Sites connected with the conquest narrative

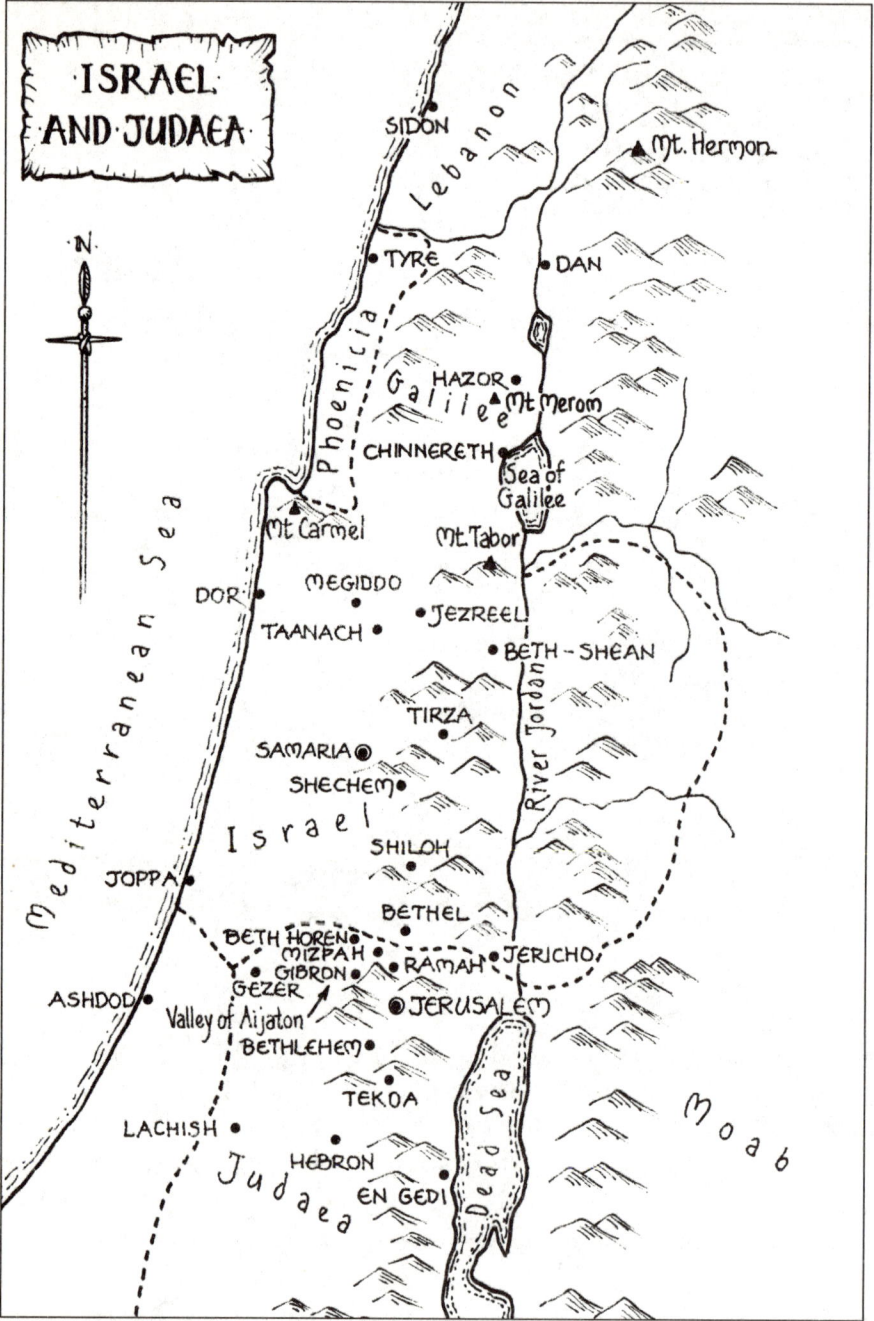

ISRAEL AND·JUDAEA

N

SIDON

Mt. Hermon

TYRE

DAN

Lebanon

Phoenicia

HAZOR

Galilee

Mt. Merom

CHINNERETH

Sea of Galilee

Mt Carmel

Mt. Tabor

Mediterranean Sea

DOR

MEGIDDO

TAANACH

JEZREEL

BETH - SHEAN

River Jordan

TIRZA

SAMARIA

SHECHEM

Israel

SHILOH

JOPPA

BETHEL

BETH HOREN

MIZPAH

JERICHO

GIBRON

RAMAH

GEZER

ASHDOD

Valley of Aijaton

JERUSALEM

BETHLEHEM

TEKOA

Moab

LACHISH

Judaea

HEBRON

EN GEDI

Dead Sea

Map 2 Israel and Judaea

the Jordan, establish a bridgehead west of the river, then gain a foothold in the mountains. From there, one would spread out from a secured base on the central ridge to widen the area of occupation and settlement. This is more or less the description we have in the Book of Joshua.[13] Certainly, the first thing a competent commander would do was send out a reconnaissance team to scout out the best crossing spot.[14]

How the crossing was achieved is another logistical problem that has puzzled scholars. Tell Damiyah, near the present Damiyah bridge over the Jordan, has been chosen many times as a good place to cross.[15] Once across the river, another problem presented itself. The city of Jericho blocked their path. The city was strategically located in the middle of the Jordan valley, close by a ford across the Jordan river. Blessed with an abundant supply of fresh water, its land is suitable for irrigation. Jericho is one of the earliest Neolithic sites, and has always produced an abundance of grain, fruits and vegetables. It is a natural way-station for travellers making the difficult journey across the Jordan valley before ascending the heights westward to Jerusalem, or east towards Amman. It has been described as the bread-basket of the West Bank. To capture this oasis meant the acquisition of a fertile base abounding in food and water, and control of the water source vital to holding the area.

Jericho loomed before Joshua as the first test of his command in the region. Jericho had to be conquered because it defended the eastern avenues of approach into the security of the mountainous highlands. Joshua knew full well the necessity of reconnoitring the area for hard intelligence, so he wasted no time in dispatching spies to Jericho. Josephus, the Jewish historian, writing c.60 CE, elaborated on the Bible story and concluded that by the time the spies reported back to Joshua they were 'well acquainted with the whole state of the Canaanites.'[16]

Rahab and the Safe House
Joshua's reconnaissance team introduces the story of the first safe house. Joshua sent two spies to reconnoitre Jericho. Unlike the story of Moses, Joshua told them only to view the land; there was no detailed briefing. Whereas Moses' spies were important leaders, these spies were chosen from among common people. Applying themselves to the mission, they infiltrated Jericho and found lodging in the establishment of a woman named Rahab. There has been much scholarly discussion over whether or not she was a prostitute. Since Rahab is a heroine in the story, the Jewish sources have always been favourable to her and present a sanitised version of the story that portrays her as an innkeeper. Josephus

followed this Jewish tradition. He had difficulties accepting the fact that, instead of completing their mission, the spies headed straight for the local bordello.[17] In later Hebrew usage, the word *zonah* means harlot, but some authorities have suggested that it is derived from the verb *zan*, which means to feed or to provide with victuals, and thus the connection with innkeeping.[18] The fact that Rahab had her own house, and did not live in the house of her father, husband or brother, suggests that she had a source of independent income.[19]

Given the number of sexually suggestive *double entendre* in the Hebrew, there should be no doubt about what the spies did at the inn, and attempts at distancing Rahab from harlotry undermines the literary intentions of the biblical writers since her profession provides an important part of the plot development.[20] Rahab's house may have served multiple purposes, and in any event she was in an excellent position to render intelligence to the Israelite spies.[21] Joshua's spies could gain valuable information about the countryside from travellers who, for whatever purpose, visited Rahab's domicile. Rahab says that Joshua's spies heard what the Israelites had done to the Amorites whom they utterly destroyed, and she says 'our hearts did melt, neither did there remain any more courage in many men because of you.'[22] This strengthened Joshua's conviction that the proper psychological moment for the attack on Jericho had come.

Meanwhile, the king of Jericho, who probably had his own sources of intelligence since he knew of the Israelite spies, sent men directly to Rahab's house to apprehend the infiltrators. Before Rahab's house could be searched, she cleverly hid the spies on the roof under the thatch, and after dark lowered them down the city walls by means of a rope. The grateful spies told her that if she did not betray them, when the Israelites took Jericho, she and all with her in the house would be spared. All she had to do was hang a scarlet thread in the same window from which she had lowered the Israelite spies.[23] Some have even suggested that Rahab herself leaked the information to the king in order to make the spies beholden to her and to spare her life in the upcoming invasion.[24]

She gave the king's men a cover story, saying that the Israelites had been there but had left the city by the main gate before sundown. Here the double meanings continue. When she answers 'yes, the men came to me', the implication is that the men had come to lie with her, but now they had finished their business and were gone. Had they simply come to find lodgings, they would still be there.

Her explanation was accepted as if her word was customarily trusted. The house was not searched, and the spies were not discovered. As far as agents go,

46

Rahab was both successful and lucky. When Joshua captured Jericho, he spared Rahab's life and that of her family as promised by the spies.

For a history written from a patriarchal perspective, and filled with role-stereotyping of women portrayed as men's possessions, how interesting that one of the Bible's great heroes is a women. Scholars of literary genres point out that the story type of 'the woman who rescues a man' is fundamentally a woman's story type, whereas the 'spy story' is entirely masculine. Here we have both: the woman is given dominance and the male spies look like worthless lackeys. The sexual element, an essential part of such stories, is toned down somewhat here because of the religious nature of the retelling. Inclusion of the bungling spies in the shadow of a Canaanite harlot produces an important link, however, with the story type. The lesson is that 'vain is the help of man' (Psalm 60:12) unless you are on the side of the Lord.[25] Rahab played a key role in the conquest of Jericho, and there is a theological reason for this choice. A foreign woman is one of only two persons named in the story – the other being Joshua. Rahab the foreigner recognised that Israel's God was the God who gave the land to Israel. Because she knew this, she dared to hide the Israelite messengers, and to lie to the messengers of her own king.[26]

Why was such a lowly woman chosen to represent Israel? As a prostitute she was on the margins of society, and her house, according to Joshua 2:15, was located right in the city wall. She lived not only in the social margins but also on the very physical edge of the city.[27] Israel too is portrayed as a people of lowest rank and as the ultimate 'outsider'. The Israelites were a unique people in the ancient world, forging a new religious movement centred around the worship of only one God. This was a new type of god – not a nature god, not an idol or an image but an ethical God. It is thus not unusual that, in the stories of the Hebrew Bible, we frequently see heroes and heroines who are lowly and outsiders. Israel was the ultimate 'other' – both in reality and in its self-perception. In its literature, therefore, heroic qualities are attributed to women and outsiders like Rahab. Her role also shows intelligence work as open to both genders.

Rahab becomes the first of many female agents to work for the Israelites.[28] This tale shows a woman caught in the virile game of war, with its masculine adventures in espionage, and succeeding. One woman seizes opportunity from the jaws of crisis and by a shrewd and assertive use of the unusual freedom inherent to her profession she saves both herself and her family.

Rahab's tale leaves much detail out of the story. How did the spies get into Jericho? Why did no one detect the foreigners? How did the king come to know of their presence? Because the ancient storyteller focused on dramatic effects and the theology, much of the actual intelligence work is left out. The Rahab story was probably not intended to show Joshua's cunning or military skill; the only information the spies delivered was the intelligence that the inhabitants of the land stood in terror before Israel. The statement: 'The Lord has put the whole country in our hands' (Joshua 2:24) is used continuously in the accounts of Israel's wars. A holy war cannot begin without assurance that the Lord gives his people victory. The spy story was placed in the Book of Joshua to show that the conquest did not begin until the will of the Lord had been determined. Once again, God is the ultimate intelligence source.

The Book of Joshua is framed by two spy stories, and the author seems to have intended that they be read together. Both sets of spies were given identical orders. In Joshua 2:1 they were told: 'Go, view the land especially Jericho.' Later, in Joshua 7:2, men are sent from Jericho to Ai with the command: 'Go up and spy out the land.'[29] The conquest of Canaan is based on intelligence, but it is not just territorial; it is also theological. You must side with Yahweh to win.[30] With its emphasis on Yahweh's will and miracles, nevertheless the Israelites still need to choose the proper techniques for achieving victory.

Did the Walls Come Tumbling Down?

Armed with intelligence provided by his reconnaissance units, Joshua then besieged Jericho. If his stratagem involved his knowledge of the city's defences and its defenders, we are unaware of it. His army marched around the city once a day for a week, and on the seventh day, the Torah says, the walls miraculously collapsed. Scholars have searched widely for a rational interpretation of what actually happened and how Jericho could have been taken.[31] The theological explanation with the trumpet hardly works for a modern, rational audience. Many a bizarre explanation has been offered. One suggestion was that the rhythmic trampling of the besiegers' feet while marching around the city made the walls unstable. Others posit a wall-shattering blast caused by a combination of trumpets and the outcry of the Israelite host.[32]

Archaeological evidence has been marshalled by some to suggest that the walls of Jericho in Joshua's time were in a rather negligent state of repair, and thus easily breached. The walls, so it is argued, were nothing more than the ruined ramparts of an earlier-stage fortification hastily patched up by the townspeople, who had not replaced them with a new defensive wall. Explanations of this type are nonetheless untenable or insufficient.[33] The easiest way to betray a city is to have traitors within open the gates. It is just as likely that some of Joshua's spies remained in Jericho and at the signal opened the gates of the city.

Many have wondered about the purpose of the Israelites marching around the city with the Ark of the Covenant. Herzog and Gichon have suggested a deception operation that lulled the enemy into a false sense of security by gradually accustoming them to manoeuvres.[34] Abraham Malamat argued that Joshua's ploy was a psychological device to lower the enemy's guard. He too suggests that the enemy was deceived and surprised by repeating the same 'field exercise' over and over until Jericho's defenders relaxed their vigil, and a decisive blow could be dealt.[35]

All these suggestions seem possible, but ultimately they are all untenable. The archaeological evidence conflicts with the biblical account and also seems to disprove it.[36] There was no strongly fortified Late Bronze Age city at Jericho for Joshua to conquer. Not only is there no sign of destruction in Jericho in the Late Bronze Age in the thirteenth century,[37] but there are also no destruction levels at Megiddo, Hazor or Gezer in the thirteenth century connected with the Israelites either.[38] The overall battle plan of the conquest simply does not fit the archaeological realities as they pertain to the thirteenth century. Such a battle plan might, however, fit the realities of the seventh century in the Iron Age. The Battle of Jericho was fought in territories that were the first target of King Josiah's expansionism after the withdrawal of Assyria from the province of Samaria. Jericho was the southeasternmost outpost of the northern kingdom of Israel.[39]

Joshua and Josiah seem to have had identical territorial goals. Joshua's expansionist programme and desire for annexation of the territories of the northern kingdom of Israel, especially the highlands, posed severe practical difficulties. The military challenge was daunting, and Josiah needed to prove to the population in the northern highlands that they were part of the great people of Israel who fought together with the people of Judah to inherit the Promised Land. The Book of Joshua was composed to express the great concern of the seventh century, namely unity of the Jews, only this time Joshua would succeed where Josiah tragically failed.

What did the Dtr historian use as a source for the conquest stories if an actual battle never occurred? There is actually another story of a walled city being attacked and walls tumbling down that Dtr may have adopted as a literary model. It comes from the Ugaritic tablets describing the legend of King Keret. In this Canaanite story, spies return from reconnaissance, and people begin to march around the city for six days. On the seventh day, there was a great shout, trumpets blared and the walls collapsed. Many scholars believe these events are too similar to the Jericho story to be a coincidence, and that the author of Joshua borrowed the story from a well-known Canaanite myth. The Israelites, in rewriting the story, may not only have been praising Yahweh but also have been mocking the chief god of the Canaanites.[40]

The scholarly search for a rational explanation for the conquest of Jericho will never bear fruit because the explanation is theological.[41] The story was meant as an object lesson on obedience for the Israelites. In Joshua's time, the people had observed the Laws of the Covenant, which were the central prerequisite for their possession of the land. In Josiah's time, on the other hand, the Israelites had not followed the laws. They had not eradicated all traces of pagan worship, nor had they stopped worshipping other gods to gain wealth through trade or political alliances. They had not faithfully followed the laws of purity in personal life, nor had they assisted their fellow Israelites who were destitute and enslaved by the Assyrians. In brief, the Book of Joshua offers a poignant juxtaposition of epic battles with a clear lesson. In the old days, the people of Israel followed the Laws of the Covenant with God to the letter, and so walls came tumbling down and earthquakes worked in their favour. In Josiah's day, however, the people had ceased to be a holy community, and thus they were punished with defeat. Although the deception operation for lulling the population of Jericho to inattention and making them susceptible to takeover makes perfect sense militarily, it is neither the technique offered by the Book of Joshua nor was it the explanation for Israelite success. That, as always, was attributed to Yahweh.

Battle of Ai

The next step in the story of the conquest of Canaan has the Israelites moving out of their base west of the Jordan and penetrating the Judaean mountains.[42] The pattern seems the same: reconnaissance done ahead of time, spies used to infiltrate the target area, then the use of surprise and speed to overcome the enemy.

The place guarding the ascent into the mountains was Ai.[43] Once again, the narrative begins with a spy story. Joshua dispatched a reconnaissance unit to 'spy out the region' (Joshua 7:2). Unlike the scouts' negative evaluation of Bethel, the intelligence reports about Ai were more optimistic. The spies gave Joshua the information he needed, but they also counselled that there was no need for the whole army to be involved in the attack. They told Joshua two or three thousand men could take the town (Joshua 7:3). The scouts seemed unaware of the great advantage that the city's defenders had in using their walls as a defensive barrier (Joshua 7:4).[44] Joshua, overconfident after repeated successes, adopted his scouts' suggestion. The result, in retrospect, was entirely predictable: the Israelites were overwhelmed by the army of Ai.[45] Their forces were chased away from the city and thirty-six Israelites were killed in battle (Joshua 7:5). Now it was the Israelites, not the Canaanites, who lived in fear.

The Bible explains the defeat not in military terms but in theological ones. The Israelites were punished because one of their number, Achan, had stolen booty (idols) and had hidden them with his gear (Joshua 7:21). Achan was equated with Israel, and God threatened that, unless the Israelites got rid of the banned material, they too would be banned. If Israel acted like Canaanites, Yahweh was saying, they would be treated like Canaanites and destroyed. Achan must be ejected before Israel would win, and so they stoned him to death in the Valley of Achor. He and his possessions were then burned, and a heap of stones was raised over the ashes.

Regardless of the reason, Joshua had to deal with the tactical drawback of the first defeat, which had affected his men militarily and psychologically. Not only had the Israelites lost faith in their prowess, but the myth of Israel's invincibility had been broken, too (Joshua 7:9). Added to this, the flagging spirits of their opponents had been strongly revived.

Undeterred, Joshua renewed his attack almost immediately, making the natural self-assurance of the victors the basis for setting a trap for the inhabitants of Ai. The plan would require excellent intelligence, timing, speed and surprise, and the participation of all of Joshua's forces. His complex, multi-phased operation relied on a deception plan that may be classified as a 'feigned retreat'. The Israelites would have to get the garrison at Ai out of its stronghold (Joshua 8:3). Joshua would achieve this by a head-on assault similar to the first abortive attempt followed by a simulated flight of the main force of Israelite troops. Prior to this assault, however, a detachment of picked troops would have been inserted behind the city under cover of night, so as to capture the city once it was deserted by its defenders.[46] Joshua would trap the pursuing enemy between his main force and the force that had captured the city. Finally, a strong blocking force had to occupy a position straddling the approaches from Bethel to prevent any outside assistance from reaching Ai.[47] Zero hour was at daybreak.

The army, led by Joshua, moved to its location in front of the city. When the enemy came out to pursue him, he and his force pretended to retreat (Joshua 8:6). The defenders, sensing another easy victory, pursued the 'fleeing' Israelites, leaving their city unattended. When the defenders were well drawn off, Joshua quickly went up the adjacent slope and flashed his spear (the pre-arranged signal), whereupon the hidden assault force rushed the almost abandoned defensive positions in the city and immediately set them on fire (Joshua 8:8).[48] Ai's defenders, who had pursued the Israelites, saw the smoke and turned to aid their burning town.

The rising smoke was also the signal for Joshua's 'fleeing' force to reverse their direction. They turned and attacked Ai's defenders who were struggling to return to the city's protective walls. Before the pursuers could recover their wits, they were attacked simultaneously from the rear by the capturers of Ai. Though it is not explicitly stated, the blocking force probably joined the mêlée by charging down the slope on the desperate and still-bewildered citizens of Ai, whose fate was now sealed.[49] They were completely trapped, and in later generations it was said that not a single soul escaped the ensuing rout.[50] The king of Ai was taken alive and presented to Joshua; the population of the city was slaughtered (twelve thousand), and Joshua burned Ai to the ground (Joshua 8:17–19). The king of Ai was hanged from a tree, and at sunset was buried at the gate of the city under a large pile of stones (Joshua 8:29). By military standards it was a brilliant campaign. By historical standards, it is a story with no corroboration.

Archaeology and Ai

As with the story of Jericho, there are major discrepancies between the archaeology and the biblical account of the taking of Ai.[51] The large mound called Khirbet el-Tell has been identified by scholars as the biblical Ai. Its location on the eastern flank of the hill country northeast of Jerusalem just to the east of Bethel matches the biblical description. The modern name el-Tell is more or less the equivalent of the ancient name Ai in Hebrew. There is, moreover, no alternative Late Bronze Age site anywhere in the vicinity.[52]

Between 1933 and 1935, Judith Marquet-Krause carried out a large-scale excavation at el-Tell and found extensive remains of a huge Early Bronze Age city, dated over a millennium before the collapse of Late Bronze Age Canaan. She brought to light a massively fortified Early Bronze Age city-state, with monumental temples and palaces, all destroyed sometime around 2200 BCE. After scant reoccupation in the early second millennium BCE, Ai appears to have been entirely deserted from c.1500 BCE until some time in the early twelfth century BCE. Thus it would have been nothing more than ruins in the late thirteenth century BCE. Not a single pottery shard or any other indication of settlement there in the Late Bronze Age was ever recovered. Marquet-Krause concluded that the conquest account in Joshua 7–8 was more legend than history.[53] Renewed excavation at the site in the 1960s produced the same conclusion. Like Jericho, there was no settlement at the time of its supposed conquest by the children of Israel. Between 1965 and 1972, Joseph Callaway, an American archaeologist who had studied with Kathleen Kenyon, reopened the investigation. He confirmed Marquet-Krause's results. To his credit, he acknowledged the excavation of Ai as 'a major blow to the conquest theory'.[54]

There still exists, however, a small circle of scholars who attempt to make an archaeological case for military conquest of the sort described in Joshua, and they usually do it by redating the supposed conquest on the one hand and revising the archaeological chronology on the other.[55] Two of the most articulate spokespersons for the very small minority of scholars who still accept the conquest theory are John Bimson and Bryant Wood.[56] The vast majority of scholars, however, agree that there is a large discrepancy between the archaeology and the biblical account of the battle at Ai.

Perhaps a solution may be found by changing the date instead of the location. We do not know the full extent of Josiah's conquests, but Finkelstein has suggested that the Battle of Ai, like Jericho, was fought in territories that were the first target of Josianic expansionism after the Assyrians left Samaria. Jericho was the southernmost outpost of the northern kingdom of Israel, and Bethel was the much-hated cult centre of the northern kingdom and a focus of Assyrian resettlement for non-Israelite peoples. The region flourished after the Judahite takeover, and the northern temple at Bethel was completely destroyed by Josiah.[57] To give his story of the capture of Ai an aura of authenticity, the Dtr author used military elements from a more recent battle and transplanted it into an older story. The conquest story of Ai, therefore, did not emerge from an authentic historical memory of the event, but rather from the reworking and adaptation of a conquest story of a much later date.[58]

Gibeon and the Battle with the Amorites

Joshua formed an alliance with Gibeon that set the stage for the next battle and its accompanying intelligence operations.[59] The Gibeonites, besieged by the Amorites, sent a messenger to Joshua's camp at Gilgal. Joshua realised that they were the key to retaining his newly gained position of strength along with his foothold in Cis–Jordan, and he decided to come to their defence. To neutralise any enemy spies or observers, he began his twenty-four-kilometre march from Gilgal to Gibeon quickly and stealthily, and reached Gibeon with his force intact and without being observed. The wooded and sparsely settled terrain probably gave them ample cover, which Joshua used to allow his warriors time to rest and to make final preparations for battle (Joshua 10:6–7).

Once Joshua's forces were in place, his reconnaissance team would have seen the Amorite allies in the process of besieging Gibeon, and their camp or camps were probably situated not far from one or another of the springs and wells in the valley.[60] Amorite intelligence, on the other hand, must have been lax because they did not have an inkling of the presence of a large enemy force in their rear. They had neglected to send out effective screening parties to warn of any unexpected hostile movement in that area. With the intelligence edge, Joshua was able to achieve complete surprise. The downward gradient of his line of assault also gave his troops additional impetus and penetrating force. Once the attack began, the Amorites had to deal with the surprise Israelite attack behind them and the renewed strength from the battlements of the besieged city of Gibeon. They broke and fled in utter confusion.

The route of their flight was along the Beth Horon pass – the major gateway to Judah (Joshua 10:11).[61] The Israelites pursued them. This would have been quite a feat of strength considering there had been an approach march of twenty-four kilometres over a steep ascent of more than 580 metres, which took all night, a battle soon thereafter and then the pursuit itself. They gave the Amorites no rest until they were totally dispersed. Once the Amorites had been chased through Gibeonite territory, they were pelted with stones by the locals, although Joshua says the stones came from God (Joshua 10:11). Herzog and Gichon try to meld the military possibilities with the theological and suggest a hailstorm – a not uncommon occurrence in the Judaean mountains.[62]

Archaeology and Gibeon

What does one make of this tale of the Gibeonites and the battle? Excavations at the mound in the village of el-Jib, north of Jerusalem, which scholarly consensus identifies as the site of the biblical Gibeon, revealed remains from the Middle Bronze Age and from the Iron Age, but none from the Late Bronze Age. Archaeological surveys at the sites of the other three Gibeonite towns of Chephirah, Beeroth and Kiriath Jeaarim revealed the same picture. None of these sites includes any Late Bronze Age remains.[63] The problem is therefore that we do not have a Gibeonite city during the time that Albright, Malamat and Yadin place the event. Excavations at Gibeon by James B. Pritchard in the 1960s produced a small amount of Late Bronze materials in some reused tombs, but no evidence of a city dating to that period.[64] An extensive surface survey of Khirbet Kefire – probably biblical Chephirah of Joshua 9:13, one of the Hivite cities allied with Gibeon – provided no evidence of a thirteenth-century city either.[65]

Nadav Na'aman has described the Battle of Gibeon as a 'battle report devoid of any concrete details'.[66] And yet, there are those who still believe it to be historical.[67] Once again, the solution may be to change the date, not the location. The story of the Gibeonites who had 'come from a far country' and sought to make a covenant with the invading Israelites (Joshua 9:3–27) may reflect the adaptation of an old tradition to a seventh-century reality. Expanding northwards into the area of Bethel after the retreat of Assyria, Judah faced a problem of how to integrate descendants of the deportees brought by the Assyrians from afar and settled there a few decades earlier. The mention of Avvim in this area in Joshua 18:23 recalls the name Avva – one of the places of origin of the deportees listed in 2 Kings 17:24. Especially crucial in the Josianic era was the question of how to absorb those who were sympathetic to Judah into the community. The old story of the Gibeonites provided an 'historical' context in which the Dtr historian could explain how this might be done.[68]

In addition to the non-historical character of the conquest tradition in the Book of Joshua, we might add the Battle of Gibeon to the list of those events that did not occur in the thirteenth century. The author, no doubt, described this battle in the light of the reality of his time. He was well acquainted with the sites and the topography of the area. He simply composed narratives that appeared outwardly authentic by borrowing outlines from concrete events that had taken place in the history of Israel. Some scholars have suggested that the story is a reflection of the historical episode of David's second battle against the Philistines near Gibeon.[69] The Dtr author selected five major Judaean cities, parallel to the number that took part in the Battle of Gibeon, all of which were located on ancient ruined tells (archaeological mounds) and were conquered in the course of the Assyrian campaign against Judah. By way of a stereotypical battle report, he linked the five cities to a continuous line of march that followed the general course of an historical campaign conducted along this line. As realistic as it may seem, the episode is fictitious and has nothing to do with the Late Bronze Age.[70]

Conquering the Galil

The last area captured by Joshua, according to the biblical account, was in Galilee. There is much controversy over how the Israelites took possession of the sparsely settled mountain lands. According to the biblical account, Joshua left central Judah and his people fanned out in all directions into the central mountain massif and its western foothills and then into Galilee itself. We are told that Joshua smashed the alliance of all the northern Canaanites headed by Jabin, king of Hazor, the foremost city in the area. The battle occurred at the Waters of Merom.[71]

It has been suggested that the event revolves around a surprise attack set up because of advanced intelligence collection. The choice of the Valley of the Waters of Merom as the concentration point for the Canaanites and their allies seems to have been a logical one. It would be an excellent staging area for their combined offensive to oust the Israelites from their possessions west of the Jordan, and especially to stop them from infiltrating Galilee. The major axes of communications in Upper Galilee all converged on the central ridge of Mount Merom, and from this pivot the roads radiate in a compass of 360 degrees all over the countryside. By concentrating on Merom, therefore, the allied forces from all over Galilee could meet at a common, central crossroads. Moreover, they would be able to direct their offensive in whatever direction they thought fit, which in itself would make pre-emptive defensive measures by Joshua difficult.[72]

The Waters of Merom campaign is also interesting militarily because it is the first biblical account to mention the war chariot. The charioteers were the Maryannu, who formed a privileged caste of warriors in Canaanite society.[73] In the same way that it was impossible for a smaller force of Israelite tribal contingents to meet the Canaanite infantry on open ground in a set battle, so too it would have been impossible for such a force to meet the Canaanite chariots head-on. A smaller Israelite force would have had to rely on the use of intelligence to achieve a tactical surprise that would provide the force multiplier. Joshua had to wrest the initiative from the enemy by quick action. While the Canaanites prepared for the offensive, Joshua needed a counterstroke that would catch them off balance before they could deploy their chariots on more open ground.

Joshua decided to surprise the Canaanites while they were encamped in the narrow gorge of the Merom brook (Joshua 11:5). This setting was ideal because there was no space for the Canaanites to deploy their chariots, and this would make their fighting vehicles a burden rather than an advantage. The need for time to get armed and arrayed has always been a weakness of mounted and wheeled troops. If the horses were unharnessed either before or after watering, the chariots would be a hindrance. Harnessed but frightened, the horses might even endanger the close ranks of foot soldiers. With the chariots thus neutralised and temporarily out of action, Joshua charged down the adjacent slopes and won another complete victory (Joshua 11:7–8). Surprise was achieved by both stealth and speed, and by knowing where the enemy was while keeping their own location a secret.

Herzog and Gichon believe the line in Joshua 10:12 that says: 'Sun, stand still at Gibeon, and thou Moon in the Valley of Aijalon . . .' reflects an actual situation where, in the early morning, the setting of the moon in the west over the Aijalon valley can still be seen while the sun rises in the east over Gibeon. The Israelites might have realised that, since they were attacking from the east, the enemy would have been blinded while facing them. Others have suggested a total solar eclipse.[74] All these explanations show an attempt to read into the text what is not there. The author is simply giving an example of God intervening on the side of Israel. The sun needs to stop in its course in order to lengthen the day so that Israel could take vengeance on its foes.[75]

The Waters of Merom – The Archaeology

The northern campaign as described in Joshua 11 is divided into two literary units: the Battle of the Waters of Merom (Joshua 11:1–9) and the conquest of Hazor and the other northern towns (Joshua 11:10–14). The presentation of both campaigns is similar: a detailed description of the coalition formed to fight Israel is followed by divine assurance to Joshua, a surprise attack, a decisive victory in battle and then the taking of the northern towns.[76] The account of the Battle of the Waters of Merom and that of the Battle of Gibeon are closely related in their structure and phrasing, and in their concept of the 'Yahweh War'.[77] Both accounts contain the motif of the total conquest brought about by one decisive victory, suggesting that both narratives were composed with the same literary and theological pattern, apparently by the same author.[78]

The biblical narrator mentions Hazor as head of the anti-Israel league in both the wars of Joshua and of Deborah (see chapter 3), and names Jabin as Hazor's king or military chief in both of these instances. The king of Hazor's place at the head of the coalition and the emphasis on the destruction of his city can be attributed to the historical memory of the primacy of the kingdom of Hazor among the Canaanite kingdoms. Finkelstein believes that the references to Hazor recall its reputation in the distant past as the most prominent of the Canaanite city-states, when Hazor was the most important centre of the kingdom of Israel in the north and a main regional centre of the Assyrian Empire with an impressive palace and a fortress.[79] Hebrew inscriptions do not even appear there until after its destruction by Jeroboam II c.800.[80]

There are also several elements common to the campaigns of Joshua and David: victory by a surprise attack of the Israelite infantry against an enormous foreign army whose backbone was chariotry, and its elimination by hamstringing the horses. The Dtr author may have once again used a known historical episode as a model for his narrative, adapting it to the new topographical arena. The location of the battlefield simply has to fit the main intent of the author, which was to demonstrate that conquering the whole region required only a single victory over the Canaanite coalition. A battle between Canaanite forces and a certain 'Israelite' group at the Waters of Merom may have occurred in early Iron Age I, but if so we are unable to reconstruct it from extant sources.[81] Finkelstein believes that this model too came from the seventh century in the reign of Josiah. He believes that the northern territories in the Book of Joshua correspond to the vanquished kingdom of Israel and later Assyrian provinces that Judah believed were the divinely determined inheritance of the people of Israel soon to be reclaimed by a 'new' Joshua.[82]

We do not know who destroyed Hazor and the other Canaanite centres. The kings of the four cities of Hazor, Aphek, Lachish and Megiddo are reported to have been defeated by the Israelites under Joshua. However, archaeological evidence shows that the destruction of those cities took place over a span of more than a century. Possible causes include invasion, social breakdown and civil strife. No single military force did it and certainly not in one military campaign.

Joshua's Wars
John Van Seters, the distinguished scholar of biblical studies, has observed that: 'Nowhere had modern historiography, in its reconstruction of the history of ancient Israel, experienced a greater sense of frustration than in its attempts to come to terms with the accounts of military conquest in the Book of Joshua.'[83] At best, the use of archaeology to document the various episodes has produced conflicting results. Certainly, excavation has not shown a pattern of destruction of cities in the late thirteenth and early twelfth centuries.[84]

The literal explanations of the origins of the conquest stories have been rejected in light of the later date of composition, the lack of archaeological evidence for a military takeover, and the inability of one hundred years of biblical scholarship to reach a consensus over the sources of the story. Some, like Alt and Noth, believed that most of the conquest narratives in the Book of Joshua emerged as local etiological sagas (stories that explained origins) that were later incorporated into the national, all-Israelite history. Others, like Finkelstein,

Na'aman, Thompson and Lemche, believed they were stories composed from scratch as a history of Israel (although the authors disagree on the date of composition).[85] They all agree, however, that the biblical accounts are descriptions of later battles used by the Dtr historian to describe earlier time periods for which he had no evidence. Dtr sometimes used conquest stories and campaign reports from other near eastern cultures as models for his descriptions.[86] John Van Seters recognised that the presentation of the episodes in the conquest account had striking resemblances to descriptions of military campaigns in Assyrian royal inscriptions. Since there were examples of such inscriptions in the capitals of both Israel and Judah, the later author of Deuteronomy would have had access to such documents.[87] The account in Joshua conforms to the same pattern found in Assyrian royal inscriptions; these include a march beset by obstacles (the crossing of the Jordan), the capture and execution of foreign kings (the five kings of Judah in Joshua 10:22ff.), and coalitions of princes coming together to withstand the invasion (Joshua 11).[88]

The spy stories were also written much later than the events that they portray, and may in any event be apocryphal. They show how later generations viewed their past, and they make their ancestors seem aware of the role that intelligence played in military operations, especially if one had the weaker force. Since many of the spy stories follow a set pattern, some have suggested that there may even have been a 'spy report' as a literary genre.[89] All military invasions are preceded by a reconnaissance. The Rahab story has the spy story preceding the invasion, then shows one group, symbolised by the king of Jericho, resisting and being destroyed while the other group, symbolised by Rahab, welcomes the invaders and is spared.[90] This is just the sort of Yahwistic propaganda typical of the Dtr historian. Notice also that Joshua, the leader of the group, has the first proper name in the Bible to contain the name Yahweh in it. The result of the conquest was the establishment of a Yahweh confederation in the hill country, which we know, through the archaeological evidence, did not occur until much later.

A main purpose of the Book of Joshua is to report how Israel actually entered Palestine. It is a schematisation of the taking of the land of Canaan. The campaigns are divided into three major advances – one to the south (Jericho), one to the central region (Ai) and one to the north (Hazor). Each campaign represents how this area might have been conquered militarily. The geography as described in Joshua and Judges is a purely utopian idea which cannot be explained either by the real ethnic settlement of the tribes or by the real political development of the kingdom of Israel.[91] No amount of chronological juggling or interpretation of the stories has overcome these difficulties. Rather than treat them as factual accounts, we should look at these stories as ancient conceptual models that served as the basis of the Israelite consciousness that Canaan had been 'inherited' by force. The author had a close and authentic intimacy with the land, its topography, demography and military realities, including the use of intelligence.[92] These are realities, however, from a later age.[93]

Dtr began with a tradition about the migration and conquest of the aboriginal inhabitants of the land, and then interpreted this tradition in terms of a great military campaign using the model offered by the Assyrian royal inscriptions. His historiographic method was to write past history in the form and style of contemporary historical texts. The basic genre of Joshua 1–12 is a campaign report. The spy stories are theological and didactic tales that depend on and embellish the Dtr narrative. Similarly, the Jordan crossing is a *topos* of the military campaign scheme introduced by the Dtr historian. The etiological elements in the story do not come from older oral traditions, but reflect the technique of the writer who embellishes his account with numerous monuments and place names to give his history a certain credibility.[94]

Following Finkelstein's argument, there is no need to associate archaeological ruins of the end of the Late Bronze Age with a conquest narrative written 600–700 years later. It is more likely that the author designed these stories in light of the reality of his own time and that, since he was well acquainted with the sites he describes, he was able to compose narratives that appeared outwardly authentic. To add to the veracity of his narratives, the author also borrowed the military descriptions of current events or recent history to supplement his material.[95] The Dtr historian did not have any records from Israel's earliest period, nor did he follow oral traditions. The invasion of the land of Canaan by Israel under Joshua was his own invention.

Spies in Joshua

The Book of Joshua gives a mixed picture of the importance of spies in warfare. It in no way implies that spies are always successful. Intelligence must be handled properly. Moses sent spies to gather intelligence in Canaan, but the majority of the people panicked when the spies brought back a negative assessment (Numbers 13:1–33, 21:32; Deuteronomy 1:22–3). Skilful reconnaissance provided opportunities for surprise in warfare and brought victory (Judges 7:10–11; 1 Samuel 26:6–7). Faulty reconnaissance cost Joshua and his people the element of surprise (Joshua 7:3, 8:1) and disobedience cost them victory at Ai (Joshua

7:1, 2–5, 10–12). In the book of Joshua, intelligence gathering was a dangerous enterprise that produce mixed results. In the end, however, it was always the support of the Lord, not clever reconnaissance, that brought them victory.[96]

In summary, no evidence supports the conclusion that any battles were fought by Joshua, or that conquest was the way the Israelites entered Canaan, or that any of these events occurred in the thirteenth century BCE. The Dtr author's overwhelming message is that the Land of Israel had been conquered as a national operation, initiated and guided by the Lord and carried out by the twelve tribes under the leadership of Joshua. M. C. Lind refers to Joshua's spies as 'Yahwistic propaganda agents'.[97] The history is always subordinate to the theological doctrine. Real factors, such as the number of soldiers or the type of weapons, are of no consequence, nor is the disparity in strength between Israel and its adversaries.[98]

The Israelites did come to inhabit these areas at a later date, and militarily Judaea may have been taken piecemeal with methods that are described in the biblical texts as we have received them. Faced with the challenge of defeating a larger Canaanite enemy or any enemy, a smaller Israelite force would probably have relied on reconnaissance and espionage to locate the enemy and to bring back information on their troop strength, methods of fighting, their troop dispositions and their intentions. Whoever planned these campaigns had a clear strategic insight, whether it was one commander or a conflated story of successive campaigns. The choice of objective, the use of intelligence and the results suggest that the Israelites relied heavily on advanced intelligence and speed to achieve surprise and ultimate victory. These stories demonstrate a highly developed sense of leadership and military assessment; they also suggest a later date when the Israelites were not just one generation away from a migratory existence but rather were a people who had occupied this geographical region for some time, knew where and when to strike, and how to use its geography to best advantage.[99]

This interpretation does not rule out military campaigns in the Late Bronze Age. If military conflicts occurred between the Israelites and the more numerous and much better-armed Canaanites, then intelligence operations would have played a very large role in the Israelite operations. If the Israelites were the weaker force in any of their battles, good intelligence gathering would have enabled them to undertake ambushes and surprise their enemies as a regular part of their warfare. All the battles in Joshua contain elements of ruse or surprise attack. Tactically, ambush is a very murderous form of battle that exploits surprise to its maximum.[100] That Israelite invasions were always preceded by excellent reconnaissance is indicative of good military procedure and common sense.[101] The two principal tactics employed by the Israelites were covert infil-tration to neutralise a city's defences, and enticement in order to draw a city's defenders out into the open.[102] The taking of Ai is an example of the latter technique. As for covert infiltration, it may very well be that the story of Rahab reflects the real method used to take cities such as Jericho. Such an intelligence mission has a realistic and secular ring about it that is quite out of line with the rest of the story.[103]

The use of surprise attacks, guerrilla operations and even terrorist acts involves knowing where the enemy is, and what they are likely to do. Much of Israel's geography lends itself well to guerrilla fighting and ambushes, then and now. The ambush was well suited to areas of rough ground broken by ravines and dry river beds that impeded the manoeuvrability of enemy chariots. In sum, if the Israelites wanted to use surprise as a force multiplier against a larger army they needed accurate and timely intelligence to achieve their goal of conquering the land of Canaan, whether it happened in the thirteenth century or the seventh.[104]

CHAPTER 2

The Book of Judges

THE BOOK OF JUDGES[1] presents an extraordinarily rich collection of thrilling war stories with tales of individual heroism in the battles between the Israelites and their neighbours.[2] The book covers Israel's history from Joshua's death to the rise of the prophet Samuel. An array of heroes and heroines called 'judges' emerge from these stories to save the Israelites from their enemies, and they use numerous stratagems that relied on accurate and timely intelligence for successful execution. Again, as in the stories about Joshua, the reader is struck by the sophistication of the techniques used by a supposedly tribal people and their constant cleverness in luring their enemies into traps.

According to the traditional account, the judges oversaw the final and complete entrenchment of the Israelites on both sides of the Jordan.[3] The Dtr historian portrays the Canaanites as divided among themselves, unable to withstand the persistent pressure from the Israelites even when aided by the desert-fringe kingdoms of trans-Jordan that resented Israel's encroachment.[4] The Canaanites became compressed into ever smaller enclaves until they submitted to the Israelites. In the beginning of the Book of Judges, however, the plains, the coastal area and the Jezreel valley were still securely in the hands of the Canaanites, a people with superior weaponry, organisation and fortifications. The army of the Israelites, by contrast, consisted of warriors from individual tribes who were summoned to battle only in emergency. Its internal organisation was still determined by the tribes themselves since each clan and family sent their quota of warriors to battle.[5] Compared to the Canaanites, their numbers were smaller, their weapons inferior and their organisation minimal. In this situation, the Israelites would have to rely on their cunning and the use of intelligence to improve their chances of overcoming their enemies.

In the opening section (Judges 1:23), the tribe of Joseph attacks Bethel and captures it by a stratagem that echoes the story of Rahab in the Book of Joshua.

Spies were sent to the town where they saw a man coming out of the city from a postern gate (or possibly a secret passage) rather than the city gate, which could be seen by all. Yadin believed that the narrative suggested the existence of tunnels.[6] The spies said to the man: 'Show us how to enter the city, and we will see that you come to no harm.' So the man showed them how to enter the city, whereupon they put the city to the sword, but freed the man and his family.[7] Taking cities by subterfuge is certainly the fastest and most efficient way to overcome a citadel when one lacks siege equipment.

Political assassination was another type of clandestine operation used by biblical agents. In Judges 3:12–30 the Israelites are subject to Eglon, king of Moab, for eighteen years; it was a punishment for fraternising with the enemy. The Lord elevated Ehud, son of Gera the Benjamite, to the position of judge. Ehud, being left-handed, fashioned a thirty-eight-centimetre, two-edged sword that he carried on his right side under his clothes, where it would not be detected. The text goes into great detail because this was a special sword designed solely for this clandestine mission.[8] Ehud brought tribute to Eglon, and when he had finished presenting it he asked for a private audience. Once in Eglon's presence, he drew the sword and drove it into the very large belly of the corpulent Moabite king. The fat closed over the blade, and Ehud left it in. Then Ehud locked the doors and slipped out the back. When the servants approached, they assumed the king wanted privacy, but after a long time had passed they became suspicious. Using their key, they entered and found their master dead on the floor. Ehud and the Israelites then came down from the hills and seized the fords of the Jordan against the Moabites (Judges 3:28).

The Song of Deborah

The Song of Deborah[9] in the Book of Judges is considered one of the oldest passages in the Hebrew Bible.[10] It is a poem that describes a battle fought in the Jezreel valley by Israelite forces led by a woman. Deborah, the only female judge, stands out as a God-inspired fighter for her country's freedom and her people's survival. In many ways, she is like a Jewish Joan of Arc. In the art of strategy and tactics, she is an expert who provided both leadership and an example of unflinching valour.[11] Judges 5 is emphatic in its depiction of Deborah as Israel's chief military commander, and her use of deception operations resulted in an amazing victory for the Israelites.[12] Recent commentators have taken her epithet 'woman of Lappidoth' to mean 'woman of flames', an appropriate title indeed.[13] Her successful campaign is the only military victory over the

Canaanites recorded in Judges, and she did this at a time when the Philistine city-states were a powerful military confederation in the south.

God had once again summoned an enemy to oppress the Israelites for their disobedience. In Judges 4–5, the enemy is Jabin, king of Hazor, the largest Canaanite city in the region.[14] Jabin's military might is considerable. He has nine hundred chariots under the command of a general named Sisera, and he has ruthlessly oppressed the Israelites for twenty years.[15] The Israelite cities cry to God for salvation and, in typical biblical fashion, their cry is answered with the appearance of a heroic individual, in this case the prophetess and judge Deborah, who leads the loose tribal confederation of the Israelites with the help of the warrior Barak, one of the leaders from Kedesh in Naphtali.[16]

Deborah divided the Israelites into two forces: one under Barak, and one under herself. Barak resisted the idea of Deborah commanding a force by herself. Some authors see him as a wimp who will not leave unless accompanied by Deborah.[17] Others think he was being chivalrous and wanted to draw the prophetess away from danger.[18] Still others believe that Deborah shamed Barak into doing his manly duty.[19] We do not know their arrangement, but we have Deborah's famous reply: 'Certainly I will go with you . . . but this venture will bring you no glory, because the Lord will leave Sisera to fall into the hands of a woman.'[20] As we see later in the story, that woman will be Jael, not Deborah.

Although the antagonists are now set in opposition, the details of the war itself are among the most problematic in the Book of Judges. Although some historians have rationalised a complete and multi-phased battle plan out of the biblical description, the account has no exact location, and it is not clear whether one or two battles is being described.[21] The battle was supposedly fought in the Jezreel valley near the Kishon river at one of two possible locations – either at Tanaach, by the Waters of Megiddo (Judges 5:19) or on the valley floor somewhere between the Kishon river and Mount Tabor. It is clear that the Canaanites would have the advantage in a set battle since they had regular infantry that included armed pikemen along with nine hundred chariots.[22] Sisera's force was both superior and menacing with its large chariot force, which used these mobile platforms to carry infantry armed with bows and spears. Against such an army, a conventional line of infantry would be useless. The weight of a chariot charge would prove too much for a standing line of infantry unless they were armed with lengthy pikelike spears; such weapons were, however, unknown among the Israelites. Counterattack was useless because the chariots could retreat and manoeuvre at a much faster rate.

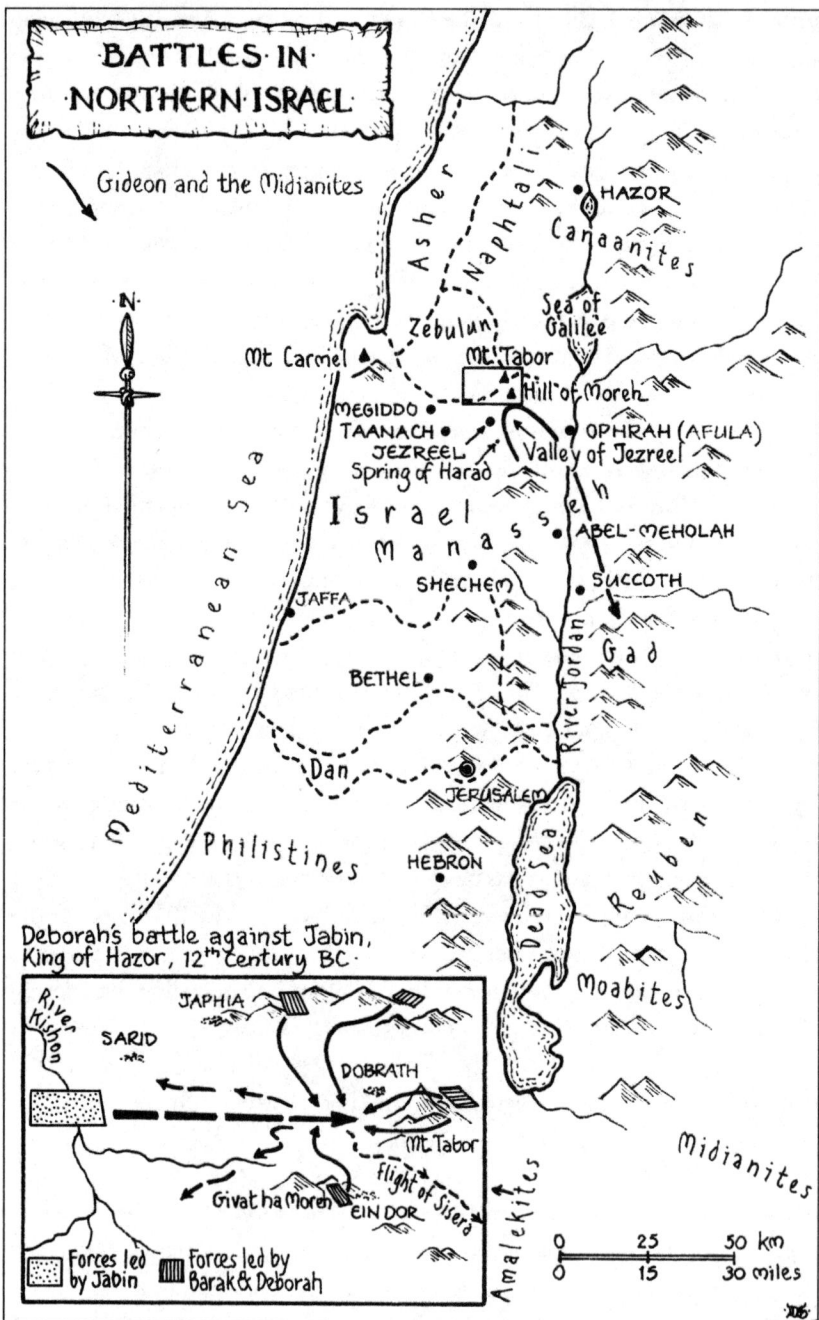

Map 3 Battles in northern Israel

Deborah met Barak at his home town of Kedesh in Naphtali, and from there they gathered the forces of the tribes of Zebulun and Naphtali. We do not know the location of this town, nor are we told why the tribes of Reuben, Gad, Dan and Asher did not answer the call.[23] A question arises as to where exactly in the Jezreel valley the Israelites went once they left Kedesh in Naphtali before meeting the Canaanites. The prose account of the story says that the Israelites marched to Mount Tabor, the poetic version makes no mention of Mount Tabor. This choice makes perfect sense, however, because Deborah probably knew that her first concern was to counteract the power of the chariot corps. Deborah's reconnaissance needed to scout out a battle area where the Canaanite chariots would be ineffective.[24] With advance intelligence and preparation, she could neutralise their obvious superiority. If she chose to concentrate her forces on Mount Tabor, she did so to position her tribal warriors on hilly ground, giving them more security against a Canaanite attack. It was an easily defensible base with a flanking position *vis-à-vis* hostile movement along the Jezreel valley, with excellent visibility in all directions. It also would have provided a perfect staging area for a surprise attack on an enemy encamped at the foot of the mountain.

Deborah's deception operation involved having Heber the Kenite leaking the position on Mount Tabor to the Canaanites in order to lure them into battle. Drawing the Canaanite chariotry to the lower slopes of Mount Tabor would have been a shrewd move, because once on the slopes the chariots would lose their manoeuvrability and their system of command.

Heber the Kenite was a good choice for Deborah's agent. He led a semi-nomadic clan that was allied to the Israelites. He faked his own defection, however, and planted intelligence with the Canaanites, pretending to give Sisera information on the concentration point of the Israelite forces.[25] It is clear from subsequent developments and the behaviour of Jael, Heber's wife, that Heber did this in collusion with Deborah.[26]

Sisera's men were assembled at the southern edge of the Jezreel valley near both Megiddo and Tanaach. Some have suggested their headquarters was at Megiddo, but this is no more than an informed guess.[27] When Sisera was given the bait and learned of the Israelite location, he reacted as predicted and collected his entire army to oppose Deborah and Barak. The two sides watched each other for days while Deborah waited for a rain that would turn the western Jezreel around the Kishon and its tributaries into a mire. A sudden downpour aided the Israelites and helped turn Sisera's defeat into a rout. The Song of Deborah tells how the Kishon river rose and swept away the enemy's horses and chariots in its torrent.[28] Even the heavily armed infantry became bogged down and hampered in its movements. The poetic version gives no further detail, but the prose account says the victorious Israelites chased the Canaanites back to their camp at Harosheth-ha-goiim and annihilated them.

With the Canaanite ranks in disarray, Sisera panicked, jumped off his chariot and fled on foot to the tent of Jael, wife of Heber the Kenite. Exhausted and probably frightened, Sisera sought refuge here because the house of Heber was not at war with the Canaanites. Hospitality was governed by rigid rules, and when Sisera was greeted by Jael he accepted her invitation to come in, thinking he was safe. When Sisera requested water to revive himself, Jael instead gave him milk that acted as a soporific and put him to sleep. Once Sisera was asleep, Jael grabbed a tent peg and a mallet, and drove the peg into Sisera's mouth (*raqaq*, nape often mistranslated as temple) thus severing his spinal column, leaving him to die a convulsive death.[29] When Barak arrived in hot pursuit, Sisera was already dead, and Israel had once again been saved by a woman. Many commentators have criticised Jael for being deceitful, a coward and an assassin. The usual morality had to be dispensed with in this type of operation.[30]

Deborah, the Battle and History

The story of Deborah is one of the most famous and oft-told stories of the Bible, and yet it stands in a contextual vacuum. We do not know its date, its location or the true identification of the enemy.[31] There is disagreement over which Israelite tribes participated. In Judges 4, Barak is the hero of the battle, but in Judges 5 he is only Deborah's second-in-command. Joshua 11:1–15 tells us that Joshua led Israel against the Canaanite alliance of Jabin, king of Hazor, who was armed with a huge army and a vast arsenal of chariots. That battle took place by a water source – but is the site the Waters of Merom? If Joshua captured and completely destroyed Hazor by fire and executed its king, why is Deborah fighting the same enemy within a generation?

Herzog and Gichon have produced an elaborate reconstruction of the battle in which they argue for a second Israelite force responsible for drawing the Canaanites into the desired area.[32] There is no indication in either the prose account or the poetic version that such a second Israelite contingent under an unnamed additional commander actually existed. As other commentators have pointed out, it is clear that the 'I' who drew out Sisera and delivered him into Barak's hand is the Lord rather than Deborah herself, contrary to Herzog and Gichon's suggestion.[33] While ingenious, their reconstruction is a work of imagination.

Scholars have written much about how the archaeological strata at the sites of Tanaach and Megiddo should be associated with Deborah and Barak's battle against Sisera. The excavators at Tanaach believed that the entire city was destroyed *c.*1125 BCE, followed by a large gap in occupation.[34] Neither the poem nor the prose version of the account mentions Tanaach's destruction after the battle, so it is a leap of faith to connect the two. Some archaeologists and historians argue that the entire event must have happened during a time when Megiddo was basically uninhabited, or it would have been mentioned in the story. Those who argue that Megiddo was Sisera's headquarters must find which occupation level was his, and a corresponding destruction level for the city after the battle.[35] Correlation between the observed destruction at Megiddo and the battle fought by Deborah and Barak is another leap of faith.[36]

This story, like all others we have examined so far, may come from the Dtr historian and serves as a national metaphor. This is a heroic narrative, not an historical description of a battle at Kishon. It was written to present the story of the death of Sisera at the hands of a woman. Jael, rather than Deborah, is chosen to represent the people of Israel, even though she herself is not an Israelite. Israel is: 'A nation on the margins, a nation struggling to get underway; a nation without the natural gifts that descended on the people of Egypt with the Nile, Assyria with the Tigris and Babylonia with the Euphrates.'[37] Israel is represented by lowly people like tent dwellers living on the margins of society. Jael is remembered as 'blessed above all women in tents' (Judges 5:24), a fitting heroine for Israel's national story and its collective destiny.[38] In the course of rescuing Israel, Yahweh took the honour of the victory away from a man who showed himself unworthy of it, and gave it to a woman. This is another example of the 'woman who rescues a man' theme we saw in the Rahab story. In both narratives there is the faint echo of the sexual component. Yael not only allows but even encourages Sisera to come to her, and at precisely the moment when he expects to reap pleasure he meets his end.[39]

In the story of Deborah, as with Rahab's story in the Book of Joshua, a lowly foreigner comes to represent Israel. The stories take someone from the margins of society and promotes that person to heroic status. As the incompetence of the spies in Jericho highlighted Rahab's capability, so Barak's glory was taken away by Jael. The success of the women comes at the cost of the male military heroes. Israel is identified not with the strong and the mighty, but with the weak and the lowly. The analogies between Jael and Rahab are designed to illustrate the surprising and unanticipated means through which divine providence operates.

Finally, both stories deal with wars between Israel and the Canaanites. When the definition of 'warriorhood' is broadened to include covert operations, women find a greater area of involvement in warfare.[40]

Deborah has been seen through many lenses. She has been perceived as the avenger of wrongs perpetrated against women, as a woman deferring to a man, as a model of co-operation between men and women, as a woman calling men to their responsibilities, as a womanly protector of her people, as a model of courage on the battlefield, and paradoxically as a model for women against war.[41] To this we should add woman as a commander who understands the use of intelligence and uses it to liberate her people from the oppression of King Jabin and the Canaanites. Wavell called Jael one of the 'early fifth columnists'.[42]

Dealing with Nomads: The Campaign of Gideon and the Midianites

Following defeat at the hands of Deborah and the Israelites, the Canaanite grip on the Jezreel valley was weakened. Now the Israelites could settle in the valley, but wandering nomadic tribes from the desert could enter it, lay waste to their crops or steal their resources. According to Judges 6:33–5 this is what the Midianites and the Amalekites did. Conflict has always existed between those who settle the arable land on the desert fringes, and the nomads. Palestine in the pre-monarchical period was perennially subjected to tribal *razzias*.[43] Especially in drought conditions, the tribesmen roaming the Sinai, the central Negev and eastern trans-Jordan had no alternative but to make inroads into the fertile country. The longer and more severe the drought, the more desperate the nomads became and the fiercer their raiding. Their aim was to occupy the large pasturelands in the arable areas for as long as they could along with their flocks and kindred.[44] In warfare, they had no permanent base from which to make military sorties, nor did they arrange themselves in strict military formations or even have definite plans of attack with clear objectives. These desert dwellers were able to harass the Israelites not because of their superiority in weapons and equipment but because of their vast numbers. They were frequently compared to an invasion of locusts (Judges 6:5, 7:12).

The Midianite enemy had armed guards for their cattle and camels, but they were not an organised military force. Their objective was to pasture themselves and their beasts on the unaccustomed plenty rather than to fight. To the nomads, it was like a gigantic annual picnic rather than an invasion, but to the Israelites it was a serious matter.[45] The scene suggests a wholesale invasion of northern Palestine by such nomads, driven possibly by a severe drought. Sometimes they are identified as Midianites and sometimes Moabites, which suggests this is another story without a firm chronology. There is also the obvious anachronism of having camels in the story, for which there is little evidence in this period.[46] In spite of this inconvenient detail, the nomads come galloping in on their swift dromedaries through Gilead, east of Jordan, penetrating into the Jezreel valley. Inspired by one of their kinsman, Gideon, the judge-leader of the clan of Aviezer, the northern tribes chose to fight rather than to retreat like their southern neighbours. Hearing that the vast nomadic host had encamped at the Hill of Moreh and around the Spring of Endor, Gideon decided to mount an offensive, and he succeeded in mobilising tribal contingents from Asher, Zebulun, Naphtali and Manasseh.[47] This is the background to the story of the campaign of Gideon. The Israelites turned to a local man from Ophrah (probably modern Afula), who planned the first night battle in the Bible.[48]

Gideon's deliberations while awaiting the concentration of his allied forces are unknown, but his main military problems are clear. He needed a way to neutralise the numerical superiority of the enemy, and a way to deal with their camel corps.[49] It would be foolish to lure the enemy into battle in daylight. The camel-mounted nomads could easily disengage and go around them for further looting, and if the Israelite line did not hold they could be severely mauled. Gideon's best chance was a surprise attack that would catch the enemy off guard and dismounted, and this meant a night attack. Gideon chose to use a small force of three hundred rather than the ten thousand who had remained after the 'fearful and afraid' had left. The number three hundred has many echoes in biblical literature and in history, but it is also true that a night attack would require a smaller force for success. This group had to be small enough to minimise the danger of noise and premature discovery.[50] Gideon chose his team in a very interesting way: he observed their habits in full daylight at the Spring of Harod, where they were open to attack at any time by the enemy. The enemy might have posted a guard on Mount Moreh and watched their every move.[51] The basis for the choice has been debated. According to some, the men chosen were those who remained cautious and drank lying down while lapping up water with one hand and holding their weapons in the other hand. If the enemy had prepared an ambush, these men would have been ready. They were the kind of men Gideon needed. Yadin says that those who would not get down on the ground were perhaps too fastidious for such a mission.[52] Those who lay down would also have made a smaller target. The important thing is that Gideon wanted only three hundred first-class men for this operation, and he controlled his internal security by knowing the trustworthiness of his own troops.[53] Meanwhile, the remainder of his men would be employed to block the flight westward of the surprised nomads, and to lure them into a vast killing field between Mount Gilboa, the eastern slopes of the Samarian ridge and the Jordan.[54] Those troops not engaged in the initial surprise attacks would swoop down on the retreating Midianites being driven on by Gideon's pursuit from the rear, and block the fords through the Jordan.

Raiding parties are swift and can cross terrain with great manoeuvrability; intercepting them has always taken two distinct forces.[55] The larger and less mobile force has to block the many possible ways of retreat, so that another smaller and more mobile group has the chance to pursue the raiders in the right direction. There is no lack of historical examples; for more than five hundred years this strategy was the basic concept of imperial Roman border defence on all desert frontiers.[56] Gideon's plan thus represents an archetype for a defence by settlers against nomadic raiders.

Having deployed his forces, Gideon decided on a personal reconnaissance of the enemy and its positions. According to Judges 7:10–14, only Purah, his personal armour-bearer, accompanied Gideon on this mission. This was a very dangerous and difficult operation for a commander to perform himself. Both of them had to infiltrate the enemy encampment and get close enough to listen to the conversations. Fortunately, the Midianites had a large noisy encampment, which made penetration by spies a bit easier. One wonders what kind of guard they had posted (if any), being so close to the enemy. Early in the evening, Gideon spied on the Midianite camp and listened to campfire stories. He overheard one of them relating a dream, and discovered that they were afraid of the Israelites and their new leader. Based on this intelligence, Gideon made his final plans.

Each soldier was provided with a burning torch hidden in an earthenware jar, and some carried trumpets also disguised in a similar way. The small force was divided into three parties that simultaneously approached the Midianite camp from three directions. Each company was to take a different side of the camp – north, west and south. This would push the Bedouin east, where the driving force would be the hammer, and the force sealing the approaches to the Jordan would be the anvil. On reaching the hostile perimeter, the men lay in hiding, waiting for the signal to assault. Gideon wisely waited for the change of the watches, and immediately after, before the new watch had adjusted its eyes and ears, he gave the signal to attack.[57] With a shout and blast of trumpets, the attackers broke the earthen vessels and probably threw torches at the tents of the nomads. Having split the force into three groups, it was important that none attacked early, and thus Gideon gave the signal himself. Between the lights, the breaking pitchers and the cry of the charging Israelites, the frightened men and beasts ran in panicked confusion, and finally dispersed in flight. As planned, Gideon's forces drove them into the gorge between the mountains and the Jordan river. The men of Manasseh had been alerted earlier to join with forces from Naphtali and Asher to harass and fall on the enemy in flight (Judges 7:23–4). Pursuing the Midianites and Amalekites across the Jordan river, Gideon called on reinforcements from the men of Ephraim who captured and killed Oreb and Zeeb, two Midianite army generals, and brought their heads to Gideon (Judges 7:25).

Gideon's surprise attack was an unqualified success, although even those who accept the story as factual concede that one hundred and twenty thousand enemy dead seems exaggerated. Gideon's successful attack included the same ingredients as the campaigns of Joshua: swift movement based on accurate intelligence about the enemy's location, strength and intentions. Offensive action was used to stage an unexpected assault. Gideon showed astuteness by attacking at night when his enemy was in no position to use their advantage – their mobile archers and pikemen. Gideon also added to his first tactical success pursuing and forcing a second, decisive battle on the retreating foe.[58]

From a military point of view, Gideon's decision to split his forces and to begin the attack with only three hundred men was a calculated risk. His decision was based largely on intelligence he had collected himself about the enemy's location, dispositions and morale. From inside the enemy camp, he had overheard the Midianites' doubts and worries and was thus able to conceive, on the spot, the details of his assault that aimed at playing on his enemy's superstitions and fears.

Clausewitz noted that night operations appear to be seductively easy, but are, in reality, very difficult to co-ordinate and execute. To be successful the attacker must know the complete layout of the defence. Unless the enemy is so close as to be in full view, full knowledge of his position will be incomplete. Such knowledge must be acquired from reconnaissance, patrols, prisoners' statements and spies, and it can never really be reliable for the simple reason that all such reports are inherently out of date. Yet, in this example, Gideon was able to pull off the surprise. His personal reconnaissance gave him intimate knowledge of the enemy camp, and he heard personal testimony from enemy soldiers, all gained just hours prior to his attack. His information was current, accurate and complete. Thus he met Clausewitz's criteria for proper surveillance of the battlefield. Clausewitz also quite reasonably notes that a night operation will not achieve surprise unless the attacker approaches the battlefield unnoticed. Gideon accomplished this feat by using a small force, personally leading them into positions he had reconnoitred, and concealing their movements by hiding the torches.[59] This battle was a perfectly executed attack that gets high praise from modern commentators.[60]

Gideon and History

The historical authenticity of the story of Gideon and his battle nevertheless has been challenged. The context of the Gideon story is a political and religious one from a much later date. Herman Gunkel says it has an atmosphere which is 'folktale-like', and he doubts that such an attack would be feasible.[61] One aspect of the Book of Judges that makes it so interesting is that, despite the Dtr historian writing in an effort to unify the worship of Yahweh, the practices of the people he describes resemble a polytheistic culture. Perhaps some of the tales were too well known to be altered with impunity.[62]

When Gideon was visited by an angel of God early in the tale, he was instructed to tear down his father's altar to Baal. When he does so, the towns-people threaten to put him to death for sacrilege. The people of Ophrah, including Gideon's own father, were worshipping Baal and the god's female consort Asherah. Gideon's own son Abimelech is later referred to as the son of Jerubaal, an alternative name for Gideon. The story may have been constructed by the Dtr historian to explain the rather embarrassing fact that one of the judges of Israel had a name honouring Baal. In the time of Josiah, the cults of Yahweh and Baal were rivals. Possessed by the spirit of Yahweh, however, Gideon/Jerubaal will lead his people against the tribes of the East.

Intelligence and religion are once more connected when Gideon goes to God for intelligence before the battle. He enquires of Yahweh if he will be victorious, and he uses a curious oracle. He lays a woollen fleece on the threshing floor, and prays that if he is to have victory the fleece will be wet with dew if left overnight, and that the ground around it will be dry. When this occurs, Gideon asks for even more confirmation by having Yahweh reverse the situation the next night.[63]

In sum, we encounter here the same Dtr historian who tries to reconstruct the remote past of Israel by telling stories that confirm his belief in the divine course of history. He used what sources he had, and included themes such as conflict and fighting between pastoralists and nomads, which were a common part of Israel's history. If this narrative actually preserves some remote echoes of battles conducted in these places in early Iron Age I, the battles do not lend themselves to reconstruction. It would not have been difficult for the author to use military events that took place later in Israel's history as models for his narrative. The military episodes he chose were entirely adapted to the new environment so that we cannot trace a direct linkage between the original story/tradition and its literary reflection.[64] Richard Gabriel has recently written that: 'One must be impressed by the degree of tactical sophistication and political skill with which Gideon carried out his war against the Midianites.'[65] This very well may be because the battle accounts are the product of a later age with a much more sophisticated understanding of intelligence operations.

The Rebellion at Shechem – An Inside Job

In the ninth chapter of the Book of Judges, Abimelech, son of Gideon, puts down a rebellion in Shechem by Ga'al ben Ebed, using one of the world's oldest stratagems – an agent placed inside a besieged city. Firstly, Abimelech placed a spy in the city in the person of Zebul, the city governor (Judges 9:30–3). Secondly, on the advice of this spy he organised a night advance on the city (Judges 9:34), dividing his force into four companies (Judges 9:35). He planned a surprise attack at dawn. The attack came just as Ga'al left the city, whereupon he fell into the Israelite ambush. The following day, Abimelech repeated his attack, but this time he manoeuvred some of his troops, now divided into three companies, behind the Shechemites, barring their retreat (Judges 9:42–9). With the bulk of the armed men of the city now dead or captured, the city quickly fell to Abimelech (Judges 9:45–9). An attempt to repeat the process at Thebes proved unsuccessful, because Abimelech was mortally wounded in the attack on the city. Certainly, this tactic was more successful than besieging a city would have been. Taking cities by siege was too time-consuming and wasted resources and manpower.[66]

Delilah – the Philistine Agent

In the Book of Judges, Samson is the twelfth and last judge of Israel. In Judges 16, he falls in love with a woman named Delilah, who has no real affection for him and actually works for his enemies, the Philistines. She becomes the paradigm for every other story of 'woman as spy and seducer'. Delilah is more complex and interesting a person than might be suggested by her reputation as a one-dimensional seductress. She was a most powerful weapon in the Philistine arsenal.[67]

We are left with very little information about who Delilah was. She is not identified by the name of her home town, nor through any male kinsmen.[68] She was an unattached woman, and such women are often depicted as seducers who lead good men astray. In a narrative that constantly gives genealogies and proper names, even the most basic information about Delilah is absent. She seems to have been rootless, and was an unusually independent woman who engaged in direct commercial enterprises with men and used her sexuality to tangible advantage.

The Philistines had had a few encounters with Samson already, and lost. Knowing Samson was in love with Delilah, they contacted her and offered her eleven hundred pieces of silver to find out the secret of Samson's superhuman strength.[69] The text never says Delilah was in love with Samson. As a secret agent, she displayed some integrity; she did not compromise her emotions, she simply used his. If she was indeed a Philistine, she might even be thought of as patriotic given the hostilities between her people and the Israelites.[70] Her strategy was bold, perhaps even foolhardy. She asked Samson directly: 'Tell me the secret of your great strength and how you can be tied up and subdued (Judges 16:6).

Delilah was thus very outspoken about her intentions from the start. She asked Samson how he could be dominated, and he responded in the third person: 'They can dominate me by . . .', indicating that he got the message. With that question, any sane man would have jumped up and left in a hurry, but Samson just lied to her: 'If they bind me with seven fresh bowstrings not yet dry, then I shall become as weak as any other man' (Judges 16:7).[71] The Philistines immediately supplied Delilah with seven fresh bowstrings, and she tied him up while several Philistines hid in an adjacent room. Once he was tied up, she cried out: 'Samson, the Philistines are upon you' (Judges 16:9). But, of course, he snapped the bowstrings and drove off his would-be killers.[72]

The appeal of this game of love for Samson seems to have been that he was playing an extremely dangerous game.[73] Instead of exercising more caution with his double-crossing lover now that she had shown her true colours, Samson continued with the charade. When Delilah asked him a second time how he could be captured, he lied again: 'If you bind me tightly with new ropes that have never been used, then I shall become as weak as any other man' (Judges 16:11). Delilah found new ropes and bound Samson with them – again with the Philistines hiding in the next room. When Delilah yelled: 'The Philistines are upon you Samson,' he snapped the ropes off his arms 'as if they were threads' (Judges 16:12) and defended himself.[74] An intimation of sadistic fantasy hovers over this story.[75]

Delilah whined that Samson had made a fool of her with *his* lies(!), and asked for a third time: 'How can you be bound?' Still into the game, Samson replied: 'Take the seven loose locks of my hair and weave them into the warp [of fabric on a loom], and then drive them tight with a pin, and I shall become weak as any other man' (Judges 16:13). So she once again lulled him to sleep, followed his instructions, and then announced the arrival of his enemies. Samson had no trouble freeing himself from her trap, although one wonders why the Philistines did not attempt to capture him while he slept.

Delilah's nagging approach – asking Samson the same question day after day – might seem weak, but it worked.[76] He finally broke down and confessed the truth: 'No razor has touched my head because I am a Nazirite, consecrated to God from the day of my birth. If my head were shaved, then my strength would leave me, and I should become as weak as any other man' (Judges 16:17). Delilah sensed that, this time, her lover had divulged his true weakness, so she contacted her Philistine handlers and told them to come at once – and this time to bring the money.

She then lulled Samson to sleep on her knees.[77] When, at her direction, a man stole into the room and cut the seven locks of his hair, she cried out: 'The Philistines are upon you Samson' (Judges 16:20).[78] He woke up confident and said: 'I will go out as usual and shake myself free' (Judges 16:20), not knowing his strength had left him. The Philistines seized him and gouged out his eyes and then brought him down to Gaza. There they bound him with fetters of bronze and set him to grinding grain in the prison.[79]

This was not the end of the story, of course. When the Philistines assembled to offer a great sacrifice to their god Dagon, they brought out their Israelite prisoner Samson 'to fight and make sport' for the Philistines. They failed to notice that Samson's hair has slowly grown back. With one last burst of strength, Samson pulled down the central pillars of the Temple, killing himself and several thousand Philistines. Perhaps he was releasing the pent-up frustration of having been conned by a superb Philistine agent.[80]

Samson and Delilah's Origins

Of all the episodes in the Book of Judges, the story of Samson and Delilah most often gets called 'mythical'.[81] In the Talmudic period, many suggested that Samson was not a historical figure; he apparently was regarded as purely mythological. The rabbis of the Talmud viewed this as heretical, and they refuted this view. Yet so many elements of the story are just not consistent with the history of the Israelites: for example, Samson kept his hair long because he was a Nazirite. 'Nazirite' is a word that refers to one who has taken a holy vow. Nazirites were not supposed to drink, visit prostitutes or come into contact with unclean things like dead bodies. Yet throughout the story when Samson was not drinking, whoring through Gaza or playing tricks on people, he was killing a large number of Philistines. How could he possibly have been a Nazirite? Even during the twenty years when Samson served as a judge of Israel, he never required the least service from any Israelite.

Samson was not a military leader going into battle like Deborah or Gideon. In fact, his story, despite its Sunday-school romanticism, is a story of failure. Even with his dramatic suicide, Samson did not succeed in keeping the Philistines at bay. In the opening of the Book of Samuel, the Philistines posed an even greater threat to Israel's existence.

The nature of Samson's revelation to Delilah as to why his strength lay in his hair seems to have been an invention of the author of Judges – a worshipper of Yahweh is intent on disguising the origins of the story of Samson. Because of certain resemblances, some scholars have claimed that the biblical account of the career and exploits of Samson are but a Hebrew version of the Greek myth of Heracles. Other scholars have seen the story as deriving from a solar myth.[82] In this view, the name Samson is derived from *shemesh*, 'sun'. Samson is the sun, and his hair symbolises the sun's rays. As long as Samson's hair was allowed to grow, his strength would increase. The sun hero, whose fiery locks represent his strength, is finally trapped when night (Hebrew *laylah* and thus De-lilah) wove his locks in a magic loom as he rested in the underworld, thus preventing him from rising. In this version of the story, Delilah's third attempt with the loom was the one that worked. The last attempt was added by a later author who wanted to identify Samson as a Nazirite.[83]

Delilah was a complex and resourceful woman, a heroine for her own people, who perpetrated an age-old ruse: using a man's love to destroy him. The religious overlay of the story disguises the pagan elements of this well-known myth and turns it into the ultimate story of love and betrayal.[84] Love is the only way to explain such otherwise stupid conduct. Why else would he reveal the secret of his hair to a woman who had already shown on three separate occasions that she would use such knowledge to destroy him? Samson never dreamed that she would stoop so low as to use the precious information against him. He played with fire at his own peril and became the dupe in a spy story. Seduction will never go out of style as a means of acquiring someone's secrets.

The Three Judges and Intelligence History

Judges contains an amazing array of leaders and minor characters, many of them women, acting as intelligence operatives.[85] All wars of the period of Judges are portrayed as defensive wars, indicating that Israel needed strategies to defeat a much more powerful enemy. An army was usually raised to deal with intrusions by an enemy, or the attempt of a more powerful neighbour to dislodge the Isra- elites. For example, in the case of the invasion of Moab (Judges 3:12–20), Ehud the Israelite assassinated the Moabite leader, Eglon, in Jericho and gathered an army from the hill country of Ephraim to expel the Moabite force from Israelite territory. There was yet no central authority to demand military service, as there would be later in the monarchy. Instead, troop levies were small, but efficient enough to score some victories.[86] Were these victories, however, historical?

Some scholars detect traces of an Old Testament literary form called the 'battle report', and they believe that these preserve traces of oral or even earlier written histories of the battles.[87] With the publication of *Der Heilige Krieg im Alten Israel* in 1949, Gerhard von Rad tried to summarise common characteris- tics in the accounts of warfare in Joshua and Judges: the blowing of a trumpet announcing the holy war; the naming of the army as the 'people of Yahweh'; the sanctification of the participants; the sacrifice of an offering and/or the consulta- tion of Yahweh.[88]

Von Rad believed that a religious practice known as the 'holy war' existed during the period of the judges and was sanctioned by the so-called 'amphict- yony', the twelve-tribe confederacy. He also believed a conquest festival cel- ebrated in later times re-enacted the above pattern, and that the description of warfare by later authors reflected this 'cult'. Von Rad's work inspired a consider- able literature both for and against his theory of 'holy war' in ancient Israel. Not all commentators agreed with him. Craigie, for example, believed that war was no more religious than sheep shearing.[89] Others have expounded on the idea of a 'Yahweh war', suggesting that it was not a cultic institution but rather an early form of warfare conducted in the name of Yahweh.[90]

In the end, the holy war arguments share two flaws. They create a picture of Israel's past in which Israel acts in concert, in accordance with strict religious customs, and with inevitable success over her enemies. These ideas, however, are the product of a monarchical way of thinking. They stem from an imperialistic ideology that is basically religious in character. In this context, war is always holy when fought by the protagonist, and an evil thing if waged by the enemy. It is 'holy' by virtue of the fact that it corresponds to the social values and ideology of the Israelite monarchy. This would be more characteristic of the time of King Josiah than the periods of either Joshua or Judges. Joshua and the judge-leaders are often seen anachronistically employing strategy and tactics more sug-gestive of a centrally controlled society, and with intelligence operations much too sophisticated for the thirteenth century BCE. Joshua especially is seen as the perfect warrior-leader of this unified society. He emerges as the man who most of Israel's kings would like to have been.

Manfred Weippert suggested that the miraculous feats of the 'holy war' char-acteristic of Israel's ancient sources resembled the same sort of narratives in the Assyrian annals. A god was the ultimate cause of victory. Israel always operated from a position of weakness and relied on Yahweh's miracles rather than on military superiority.[91] Such a source could have been drawn on by the author of the Book of Judges.

The same language and outlook are pervasive in the Books of Joshua, Judges and Kings, which are all most probably the product of the seventh-century Dtr historian. Characteristic of the outlook of the Dtr historian is the cultic and theological view of the Israelite community as a people destined to occupy and hold Canaan militarily provided only that it maintains its moral and cultic integrity.[92] The Dtr historian may have known that total conquest never took place; the Books of Joshua, Judges and Kings are full of evidence that Israel was not in control of large sections of the so-called Davidic state. The job of the Dtr historian was to portray a theme: Yahweh would leave Canaanites in the land to punish Israel for its illicit contacts with the Canaanites and their gods, and specifically to test Israel's faithfulness (Judges 2:21–2) or to train Israel in the arts of war (Judges 3:1–2).

The biblical account is, in some sense, a deception. It probably never hap-pened that way. Nor did the author have accurate sources to draw on for what happened six centuries before his time. The purpose of the Book of Judges was to inspire a contemporary audience with an understanding of its collective goal and provide an incentive, a reinforcement, to achieve in its own time what its forefathers had achieved in theirs. It suggests concrete action to unite and extend the Israelites as a people of the true faith. Side-by-side with this claim of total unity stood stories from Judges of disunity and parochial achievement.

In the Book of Joshua, the story is of pan-tribal, total territorial conquest aimed at cultic purity. In Judges, however, another sort of pan-Israelite out-look dominates, namely cycles of apostasies and foreign oppression. If the people of Israel remain apart from the indigenous population they will be rewarded.

Should they be tempted to assimilate, divine punishment will be swift and severe. Yahweh's message is clear and still they do not listen. Only the intervention of divinely inspired righteous leaders, called judges (*shophetim*), saves the people of Israel at least temporarily from losing everything. The Book of Judges provides the portrait of twelve such persons, one of whom was a woman.

Those who have studied the narrative structure of the Deborah–Barak story, for example, point out that 'the narrative positively demands the controlling intelligence of an author'.[93] The weaving of the complex interrelationships and subtle nuances could not have resulted merely from the haphazard collation of disparate literary units or a conglomeration of many centuries of folk narration. The story as it stands is not a folk account of the glorious victory of Israel over the forces of Sisera, nor is it a dramatic presentation of the military prowess under Yahweh of Barak or Deborah. The author has woven an intricate pattern of plot and theme, a structure in which the dominant theme is the inherent irony of the situation between the two men and the two women. It is not a quasi-historical account of Barak's battle against Sisera.[94]

Good leaders influence Israel to fulfil its covenant; bad leaders allowed them to go astray. The Book of Judges is filled with tales of the ongoing struggle with idolatry. As in the time of Josiah, there is an attempt to show what happens when the Israelites do not follow the laws of God. They are punished. This is not a real story of Israelite settlement. The Book of Judges, in fact, tells us very little about the day-to-day life of the Israelites.[95] Figures such as Samson are particularly ambiguous. Christian commentators saw Samson as the antichrist. To them he was a whoremonger, a murderer and a selfish warrior. He scarcely exemplified the virtues appropriate for a Nazirite. His slaughtering of innocent people did not fall into the category of self-defence during battle. Other Christian commentators saw him as a powerful negative example. Clement of Rome made Samson an *a fortiori* example of arguing for chastity![96]

Does the archaeological record support the biblical account? The settlement pattern of the Late Bronze Age in the Upper Galilee is not yet clear enough to know how close the biblical narrative is to the archaeological evidence. Tiny Iron Age I villages co-existed with the Canaanite cities over a long period, adapting various elements of their material culture. Since only a few sites in the area have been excavated, a full understanding of how and when these villages were established remains to be determined, but the pattern emerging so far does not seem to confirm the biblical accounts. Raphael Frankel discusses the settlement patterns for each of the areas of the hill country and in Galilee, and he has written:

The continuity of the material culture and the difference from the pottery of the central hill country do not correspond with the biblical narrative; neither do the description of common origins of the Galilee and central hill country tribes, nor with regard to some of the Galilean tribes originating in the central highlands.[97]

In Judges the battles with Israel's enemies are recounted but very little is said about the kinds of settlements the Israelites chose to establish and how they supported themselves. In the biblical account the Philistines come into prominence as the inhabitants of the maritime plain of Palestine from the time of the judges onwards. The tale of Samson suggests a close daily contact between Philistines and Israelites. The archaeological discoveries in the Shephelah, too, suggest close commercial and cultural relations with the Philistines. In Beth Shemesh, for example, which was an Israelite border city, a considerable amount of Philistine pottery has been found. The picture that emerges is that a Philistine takeover of the southern part of Palestine took place without any special difficulty so that the tribes of the southern hill country found themselves subject to the authority of the Philistine city-states.[98]

True information about the settlement of Israel in the Iron Age is lacking in the biblical story. One glaring anachronism is the presence of 'iron chariots' in the story of Deborah; scythed chariots or chariots with iron-tyred wheels were unknown before 700 BCE.[99]

Instead, the biblical story is a theological lesson about obeying God's commandments. The Book of Judges reflects considerable diversity in the premonarchical religion of Israel, and this is confirmed by archaeology. The author of the book had a rather idealistic view of religious conditions – the Levites led other tribesmen in the worship of Yahweh in ways that contrasted sharply with the idolatry of the Canaanites. Behind the editorial framework of the author, however, we find a far more complex situation. There is evidence of idolatry and human sacrifice. Along with the worship of Yahweh, the Israelites worshipped Azaezel and acknowledged other deities such as Chemosh. In the era of the judges, Israel lapsed from Yahweh and allowed the Canaanites to regain their strength and to harass Israel.

The moralising and centralising intent of the Josianic author gives the impression that people were morally more advanced under Joshua than in Judges, but in reality they were just as prone to idol worship. In Josiah's time, the critical provision of the law is prohibition of all forms of Canaanite worship and corresponding exclusive worship of Yahweh at an official central shrine in Jerusalem.

The community of Israel, as the seventh-century author views it, was under the command, militarily, of Yahweh from the beginning in its effort to destroy all the Canaanites so that not a shred of their religion could survive to tempt the Israelites to sin.

The stories in the Book of Judges seem to say: 'Our unity is basic and binding, and from time to time it may be plagued with open conflict. But each new generation must cope with the enemies who wish to annihilate us. It would be a great mistake to dwell on past accomplishments and fail to prepare ourselves for new struggles.'[100] The reason why the Book of Judges is written appears in Judges 3:2–3 and provides a hint of the military motivation of the stories. It says that the Lord wanted a means of testing the Israelites who had not taken part in the battles for Canaan. His purpose was to teach succeeding generations of Israel, or those who at least who had not learned in former times, *how to make war*. Intelligence lessons were an integral part of that lesson.

CHAPTER 3

The United Monarchy

THE ESTABLISHMENT OF THE Israelite monarchy[1] required a shift in both military tactics and the methods of intelligence gathering.[2] The socio-political system of the tribes was supposedly replaced by a kingdom centred on Jerusalem, yet the nature of that kingdom has been much debated. Once centralised, the Israelites were no longer outsiders trying to take control, but rather a kingdom trying to maintain control. According to the biblical account, King David succeeded in welding the Israelite tribes together with such strong national unity and cohesion that his reign is remembered in Jewish tradition as the first Golden Age of the Jewish people. Under David, the Israelites undertook wars of liberation and expansion. In a series of swift battles, he is said to have destroyed the power of the Philistines, and defeated the Ammonites, the Moabites and the Edomites in trans-Jordan. David ended his campaigns with the subjugation of the Aramaeans in the far north, and then returned to Jerusalem to rule over his kingdom. His empire, we are told, extended from 'the River of Egypt unto the great River of the Euphrates'. These aggressive wars of conquest began and ended with David. Warfare after David was mainly defensive or, if aggressive, represented an attempt to regain what had been lost.[3]

Revisionist scholars contend that this story is myth whereas literalists believe that the glorious empire of David and Solomon, as described in Samuel and Kings, actually did exist. Archaeological discoveries, or a lack thereof, dating to the tenth century have been used in attempts to prove or disprove whether a House of David existed at all. Did David's kingdom include an extensive empire and a magnificent capital?[4] Certainly control over a larger territory would have required a larger army, defended lines of supply, a regular maintenance of the army's efficiency through the supply of new recruits, and usable weaponry. It would have also needed a good intelligence arm and, not surprisingly, the stories of King David provide some interesting glimpses into his intelligence operations. Questions arise, however, as to when the texts describing these operations were written, and whether they describe intelligence operations that were contemporaneous with King David. Examination of these stories reveals little that is new. Rather they illustrate the same tactics and intelligence gathering as described in Joshua and Judges. The accounts feature the ambushing of small detachments, the use of surprise and speed based on intelligence gathering and knowledge of the terrain and, most importantly, victory attributed to divine intervention.

When writing about King David, scholars have often focused on his personality mainly because forming a coherent, detailed picture of David's military campaigns has been so difficult.[5] Yet the stories of the reign of David provide some of the most interesting examples of intelligence writing in the Bible, because his military career was so varied. As a fighter and commander in Saul's army, he led regular forces.[6] But when Saul saw him as a threat to the throne, David was forced to flee for his life and become a guerrilla leader.[7] David attracted to his side a motley bunch of followers including his brothers, his father's household and all those who were in distress, in debt or simply discontented (1 Samuel 22:1–2). As leader of an outlaw band on the run from the jealous King Saul, David acquired first-hand knowledge of guerrilla tactics both as hunter and as prey. David and his group helped shape the men who joined him in the wilderness into an exceedingly well-trained, victorious and deadly fighting force.[8] These men led adventurous lives in the Judaean wilderness. They hid in Philistine territory, were hired out to Achish of Gath for two years as mercenaries, and undertook border raids against nomadic tribes. They outwitted the bumbling Saul more than once, and learned about tricks as well as the lightning strikes necessary to neutralise nomadic raiders.[9] As the Bible describes it, David's skill as a warrior was the single most important factor in his rise to power (1 Samuel 19–20).

The Battle of Michmash

Most scholars of this period agree that it was the external element, the Philistine threat, that brought about the emergence of the monarchy. The Israelite tribes were pitted against a large, formidable Philistine enemy with an advanced military organisation.[10] The monarchy emerged in the territory of Benjamin because this was the area with the largest Philistine threat. The Battle of Michmash pass marked the beginning of the wars with the Philistines, which did not end until Saul's death.[11]

Under Saul, the Israelites were still a sacral union of tribes with no central government in the proper sense of the word. Saul's authority extended to only some of the tribes, and he made no effort to change the tribal organisation or to centralise the government. The army remained a tribal levy whose reliability was always in doubt.[12] Saul's monarchy did not see an immediate change in tactics, especially when fighting a larger enemy. The Israelites are portrayed in the Books of Kings as overcoming larger forces in the same way they overcame their enemies in Joshua and Judges, that is, by foreknowledge of the terrain, ambushes set up after effective intelligence gathering, and instilling panic into the enemy by the use of surprise.

Early in Saul's reign, Jonathan, his son and chief general, defeated a small Philistine garrison at Geba, which caused the Philistines to retaliate. The Philistines mustered their great army at Michmash with thirty thousand chariots, six thousand mounted cavalry and a large army that 'numbered like the sands on the seashore'.[13] Saul, in turn, mustered his army at Gilgal, and marched to Gibeah. The Philistines decided to draw him into a trap by surrounding him. They sent an army towards Ophrah, another towards Beth Horon and a third towards Zeboim in the desert, which was probably near Jericho. In other words they sent armies to the east and west to try to outflank Saul's much smaller army and draw him into the trap. Most of the men of Israel deserted to the hills once they heard that the huge Philistine army was coming. Saul's army of three thousand dwindled to six hundred (1 Samuel 13:15).

Jonathan was at Geba, separated from Michmash by a steep ravine.[14] He took his armour-bearer on a secret reconnaissance patrol north towards Michmash (1 Samuel 14:3–5). Jonathan's plan was to take the high ground. He told his armour-bearer that they would reveal themselves to the Philistine garrison. If the Philistines said: 'Stay where you are until we come to you,' that would be a bad sign because the Philistines would be fighting from the high ground. However, if they said: 'Come up to us,' then Jonathan would have the green light to take the superior position (1 Samuel 14:10). In the Hebrew Bible, 'going up' represents victory and 'going down' represents defeat. When the Philistines saw Jonathan in the ravine, they said: 'Come up to us, we have something to show you' (1 Samuel 14:12). In the same passage, Jonathan acknowledges that 'the Lord had put the Philistines into the power of Israel' and so he climbed up the cliff. As soon as he reached the top, he charged the Philistines, cutting them down with his sword. His armour-bearer behind him finished off the wounded. Jonathan killed about twenty men 'cutting across a half-acre field'

(1 Samuel 14:14). As he charged, terror spread through their ranks. The screaming of the Philistines that Jonathan and his armour-bearer hacked down created the sound of battle emanating from the cliff where nobody expected an attack. When the rest of the Philistine camp heard the screams, they panicked because they thought they were under attack. They could not see that it was only two men doing all this. Two men and God, however, were enough. God also pitched in with an earthquake that was enough to frighten anyone. The Philistines had Hebrew mercenaries with them in their army (1 Samuel 14.21), who now immediately switched sides and began killing their former allies, which further added to the confusion.

Saul's spies saw the commotion in the Philistine camp, and Saul recognised it as an attack from Israel. He immediately took a head count to find out who was missing and discovered Jonathan and his armour-bearer were gone. As the sound of battle grew louder, Saul proceeded with his army of six hundred and joined the Hebrews who were fighting with Jonathan. As the Philistines from Michmash began to scatter, the men of Ephraim, who had hidden in the hills in fear, suddenly got courage and attacked the column of Philistines as it marched west. This blind-sided the Philistines, who were not aware of any soldiers in the hills, so they ran southwest towards Ai, about five kilometres from Michmash. The Philistines also scattered to the east to Beth-haven. The Israelites had scored a victory over the Philistines, but not of the magnitude that would have been realised had Saul been able to lead the entire Israelite force against the enemy.

There are several problems with this narrative. It does not indicate why the Philistines increased their military presence in the Israelite territories, especially around Gibeah itself. The Philistine garrison may have been nothing more than a custom's post, a tax-collecting centre or just the local tribute official establishing his presence. We do not know why the Israelites attacked them.[15] The Israelite force was small to begin with and contracted further in size when many went into hiding and others defected to the enemy. How did Saul's force elude the Philistines when his troops were reinforcing Jonathan's? What was the purpose of the three flying columns of Philistines that left their camp? Why did the enemy commander divide his forces when he was being attacked? If they were reconnaissance units in force, why did they not detect Saul's reinforcements arriving at Geba? Was the force so small that they remained undetected or was Philistine reconnaissance that bad? More importantly, what should be made of the passage (1 Samuel 13:22) that indicates at the time of the Battle of Michmash neither sword nor spear was available to any of the soldiers; only Saul and Jonathan had

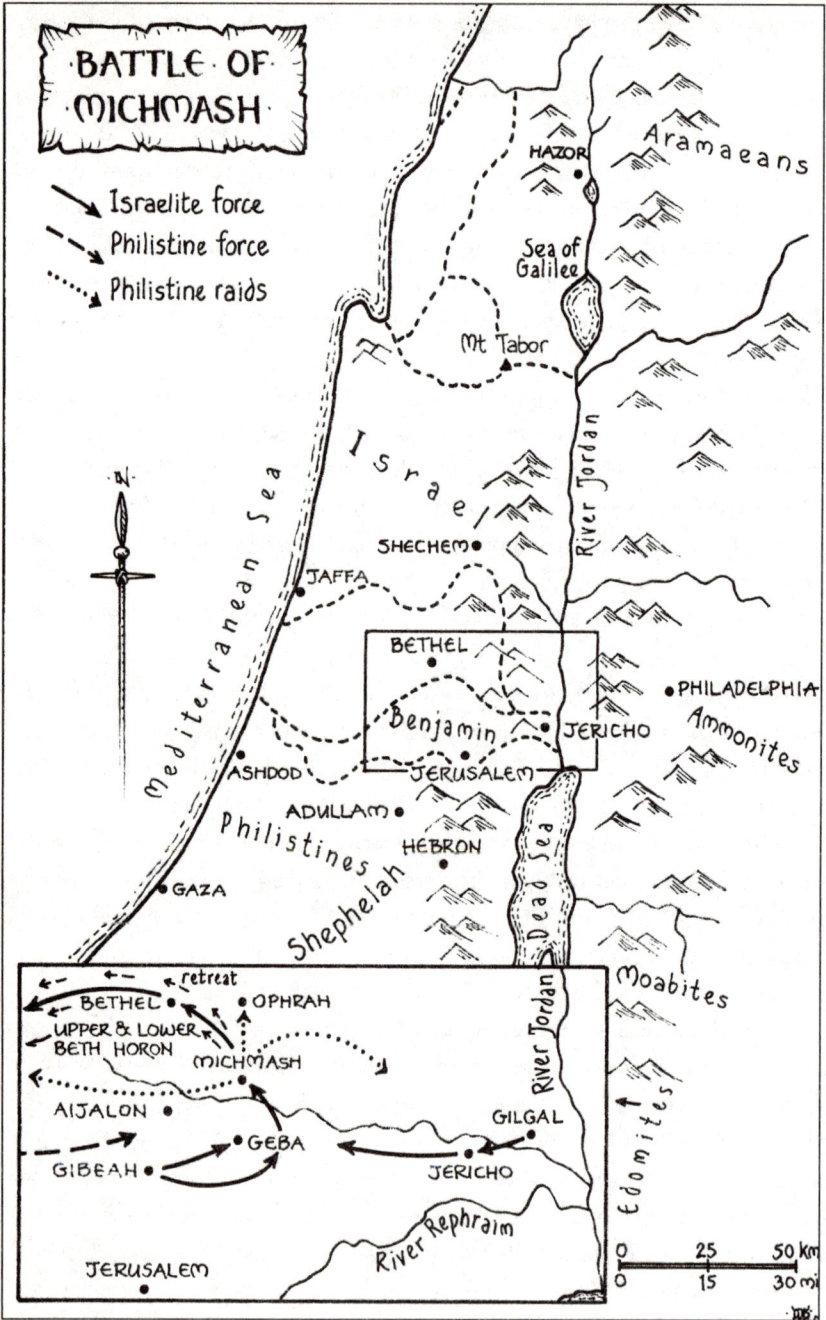

Map 4 Battle of Michmash

weapons. The Philistines had supposedly forbidden weapon-making among the Israelites (1 Samuel 13:19).[16] Is a surprise attack on the Philistine camp by only two men probable or even possible, especially when it is executed with only crude weapons? Why is it that after this small military achievement there is suddenly no Philistine presence in the hill country until after Saul dies at Mount Gilboa? Could the entire story have been a propagandistic account to emphasise Jonathan's courage and minimise Saul's contribution to the victory?

According to the text as written, the great victory at Michmash of an unarmed Israelite army over the Philistines was due to the heroism of Jonathan and his armour-bearer. Two men who obeyed the Lord set off the chain reaction that led to the Philistine defeat. Jonathan, who was in fellowship with God, took the high ground and won the Lord's victory. Jonathan recognised that the size of an army does not matter when God fights on its side.[17] Even after the battle when Saul's men were exhausted, Saul suggested they pursue the Philistines again, plunder them and kill everyone (1 Samuel 14:36). Rather than send out reconnaissance units, they turn to Yahweh for advice. When he did not answer, they abandoned the plan. Not even a night attack was undertaken without God's permission. Perhaps Yahweh voted against it since undertaking a major battle in total darkness seemed foolish in the extreme.

Long-winded discussions of the logistics involved in having the Israelites take advantage of the terrain they supposedly knew well do not make much sense when neither terrain, nor tactics, nor intelligence gathering had anything to do with the victory. It is possible for irregulars to score victories over much larger forces, and it has been done at this particular location.[18] It is equally possible, however, that the explanation for this Israelite victory is theological, and that the Dtr historian chose this location for his description of Jonathan's battle because many later battles had been fought there.

The Monarchy of David

After Saul's death, the men of Judah anointed David as their king with his capital at Hebron, while Saul's trusted general Abner installed Saul's eldest surviving son, Ishbosheth, as king over the rest of Israel. David continued his military triumphs, and consolidated Israel and Judah into one kingdom, and held them together by strength of arms. He subjugated surrounding clans and built a small empire in Palestine and its immediate environs.

As king, David established a strong strategic base by creating a new mobile army, with mercenaries and a chariot corps led by Joab.[19] By all descriptions, the

Israelite force seems to have been unusually varied. They had units of archers, spear and javelin men, and slingers. Tactics also changed radically under King David. While previously the Israelites relied on small forces and ambushes, once David had developed a strong strategic base he gave up guerrilla tactics. Although the Israelites now had a constantly armed force ready for immediate action under the command of a king, there seems to have been no great change in the methods of attack.[20] The Israelites remained the smaller force, and they relied on intelligence operations and ambushes for their victories.

In 2 Samuel 24:9, David took a census of young men of military age, suggesting at least the initiation of a system of compulsory military service.[21] According to the biblical account, the Israelites built fortified bases at places such as Hazor, Megiddo and Gezer. However, these sites, as we shall see below, may not be Davidic – and indeed may not even be Israelite.

Internal Security

The two Israelite camps of David and Ishbosheth spied on one another. There was always the danger that someone would turn double agent and try a penetration operation. In 2 Samuel 3:21, Abner's defection was a major coup for David in his bid for the throne of Israel. Abner's visit to David's camp incensed Joab, who accused Abner of only pretending to defect so he could spy on David. He asked David: 'What have you done? You know Abner, son of Ner. He came to deceive you and observe your movements and find out everything you are doing' (2 Samuel 3: 24–5). The text neither confirms nor denies whether he was a spy, but Joab took no chances. After speaking angrily to David, Joab invited Abner back to Hebron, and there he stabbed him in the stomach and killed him.[22] The assassinations of both Abner and Ishbaal ended the war abruptly, and David claimed Saul's throne.[23]

With David in charge of a united kingdom, intelligence continued to play an important part in Israelite military campaigns and the internal security of the Davidic kingdom. Even David himself never gave up spying. In his attempt to maintain his throne, David spied on his enemies, his subjects and even his family. In 2 Samuel 15, for example, David's son Absalom conspires to take the throne from his father. David's own counsellor, Ahitophel, fled the court and joined Absalom in Hebron, where he helped plan the coup. Absalom and Ahitophel were so successful that David was forced to flee Jerusalem. The Davidic administration appeared to be caught unawares by Absalom's revolt.[24] In 2 Samuel 15:10 Absalom sent spies throughout Israel to spread the message that: 'As soon as you hear the sound of the trumpet, then say, Absalom is King Hebron.' David's friend and advisor Hushai wanted to leave town with him, but David instructed him to wait in Jerusalem for Absalom. When Absalom reached the capital and joined Ahithophel, David's spies quickly undermined their revolutionary government.[25] Hushai learned that Absalom was planning to pursue David with twelve thousand men, and strike him down at night in the forest. Hushai not only sent a message to David informing him of this but he also bought the king time by convincing Absalom to put off the attack until the morning. This bit of infiltration allowed David to escape beyond the Jordan river, where he eventually regrouped and attacked Absalom (2 Samuel 17).

As David's men chased Absalom through the woods, Absalom's splendid hair was caught in a tree; he hung in mid-air while his mule went out from under him. David begged his men to 'deal gently with Absalom . . . for my sake', but Joab picked up three stout sticks and drove them into Absalom's chest. Joab's ten armour-bearers then surrounded Absalom 'and struck at him, and killed him'.[26] All monarchs need an internal security apparatus to protect their throne from pretenders. All too often those pretenders are members of their own families. David's spying saved his throne but broke his heart, or so he claimed. It has been suggested that Joab was actually following David's orders, and that is why he suffered no punishment for killing Absalom.[27]

Reconnaissance in the Field

David's ultimate source of intelligence always remained God. In 1 Samuel 30, he prayed to Yahweh and asked what he should do about the Amalekites who had raided the Israelite camps, and stolen their goods and women. David asked: 'Shall I pursue these raiders, and shall I overtake them?' And the Lord answered: 'Pursue them: you will overtake them and rescue everyone.'[28]

God's advice notwithstanding, David needed solid intelligence on the ground and so he himself went on a reconnaissance mission with six hundred men. They found an Egyptian in the field and took him captive. They fed him well and then asked him about the position of the enemy. The Egyptian gave them information and offered to guide them on the condition that they swore: 'By God . . . that you will not put me to death or hand me back to my master, and I will guide you to them.'[29] The intelligence given by this man enabled David's men to find the Philistine camp and stage a surprise attack. The Philistines were found 'scattered everywhere, eating and drinking and celebrating the capture of the great mass of spoil taken from Philistine and Judaean territory'.[30] David attacked at twilight and killed until the next morning. Only four hundred men on camels escaped; the Israelites recovered all the spoil and the captives.

The rise of the Israelite monarchy required accurate and timely intelligence, and yet this intelligence was not enough to allow the monarchy to survive. In the late eighth century, the Israelite kingdom came under Assyrian rule, and then in the early sixth century BCE the Judahites were sent into exile by the Babylonians. When they returned to their lands under the Persians, they were forced to accept the leadership of foreign rulers for several more centuries.

The Rephaim Valley Campaigns

Having been brought up 'through the ranks' David showed a keen understanding of the importance of building a professional military organisation and expanding and protecting Israelite territory. His military commander, Joab, was also a well-trained and experienced leader. The Hebrew Bible records several campaigns that illustrate how David and Joab used deception to achieve surprise during military operations.[31]

Philistine policy had always been to divide and conquer. Their strategic goal was to prevent the formation of a unified Israelite state. When David was anointed king of Israel, the Philistines immediately turned hostile and took steps to destroy his new regime. Their invasion may have been designed to kill or capture David, and to dismantle the monarchy and its army.[32]

David's operations in the Rephaim valley are mentioned briefly in two passages, and they include very little detail. The topographical and chronological difficulties presented by 2 Samuel are the common source of every commentary on the chapter and every book on the history of Israel. The biblical account suggests that David's knowledge of topography was critical to achieving tactical surprise, although where the battle actually took place continues to be debated.[33] We are told that the Philistine troops spread out into 'the lowlands of Rephaim', which many presume were south of Jerusalem. Tidwell points out that the term 'to spread out' is a military term usually associated with a specific type of military operation, namely a small-scale raid using small numbers of troops to strike swiftly and then withdraw.[34] Indeed the first battle seems little more than a skirmish. Chronicles 11:16 says David went out to the stronghold of Abdullam, a refuge in the Shephelah some twenty-five kilometres south of Jerusalem. David, therefore, would have occupied an excellent position to scout out Philistine movements, and to hit their flank or rear if they moved towards Hebron.[35] Since David's strength was in hit-and-run tactics, not siege warfare, this was a smart move. At Abdullam, he was better positioned to observe the Philistine advance as it moved up the valley and came into position around Rephaim. His own position was still unknown to the Philistines.

David's reconnaissance may have provided an early warning of Philistine activity, but the ultimate intelligence always came from Yahweh. David asked: 'Shall I go up against the Philistines? Will you hand them over to me?' Yahweh's response: 'Go up! For I shall indeed hand them over to you!' (2 Samuel 5:19–20). David thus attacked first and probably hit the Philistine army while it was still marching in column. The attack surprised the Philistines, who panicked and fled down the valley.

The Philistine commander, having been driven off, now assembled a larger force and came back a few days later. The outcome of the first battle may have confirmed the wisdom of defending Hebron from without, so that David reacted to the second Philistine incursion on Rephaim in much the same manner as the first.[36] The Philistines rallied their forces in the Rephaim valley for a second time (2 Samuel 5:22). David requested divine guidance that was provided in the form of a directive to employ a specific tactic: 'Do not attack now, but wheel around and take them in the rear opposite the mulberry trees [translated by the *NEB* as aspens]. As soon as you hear a rustling sound in the treetops, then act at once . . .' (2 Samuel 5:23–4).[37] David waited for the appropriate moment, and surprised the Philistines again.

In this second campaign, David's use of geographic intelligence enabled the Israelites to exploit the cover which the trees provided for their lightly armed fighters. David also used the wind patterns to achieve a surprise attack: he timed his attack so that the trees' rustling foliage would cover the steps of the stealthily approaching Israelites. This tactic enabled David and his forces to sneak up from behind, and defeat, the superior Philistine force in a complete surprise attack.[38]

These campaigns have been subjected to critical analysis and comment. There are topographical and chronological difficulties that compromise the authenticity of the stories found in the narrative of 2 Samuel 5. Did both encounters with the Philistines happen before or after David took Jerusalem? At least the first of them is presented as a reaction to the anointing of David at Hebron, but before his successful assault on Jerusalem. Even the location of the Rephaim valley itself is uncertain.[39] Not only has no universally accepted solution to these problems been found, but also most solutions that have been put forward are based on the assumption that the battles occurred in a place we can now locate, and that Samuel was written in the time of the monarchy (albeit with considerable adaptation and rearrangement to reach the present text). The only thing the text really conveys is the idea that two major clashes between David and the Philistines occurred, and that they had far-reaching political and military consequences for ancient Israel.

Some authors have noticed the close similarity in content and structure between the two Rephaim stories (1 Samuel 17–21, 22–5).[40] Both stories are short battle reports with a formulaic pattern:

(1) description of the troops, their location and the battle site;
(2) consultation of the oracle (collecting intelligence from Yahweh);
(3) battle tactics; and
(4) results and consequences.[41]

This has led some to suggest that the reality behind the stories is nothing more than a successful routing of Philistine raiding parties engaged in foraging for supplies for local garrisons or intent on destroying the harvested crops of the Israelites as they lay on the threshing floors or perhaps burning them in the fields. The three stories of 'military action' against the Philistines in these accounts are simply raiding parties.[42]

Other scholars suggest that the explanation for victory in the end is not tactical but theological. Yahweh, working through David, finally opened the way to the total fulfilment of the ancient promise of the land. This is how the Dtr author saw these events. It is obvious to many scholars that the biblical authors were rarely, if ever, motivated by a strict concern for historicity in what they wrote, and their methods of composition in stories such as these reveal the primacy of literary and theological goals rather than purely historical ones.[43]

Campaign against the Ammonites

The account of the Ammonite War in 2 Samuel 10:1–19, 12:26–31 provides a vivid description of military operations and seems to reveal a disinterest in religious ideas on the part of the author. This has led some scholars to suggest that the material came from an eyewitness account of the battle, adapted by a later editor.

One of the elements that makes this account seem authentic is that it portrays some of David's military and intelligence efforts as unsuccessful. In a fabricated story, David could always be made victorious. Instead, David's military commander Joab and his army were almost annihilated during an operation against Hanun, king of the Ammonites, because of inadequate intelligence.[44]

In this campaign, a Syrian–Ammonite coalition took the field to fight against the Israelites. Accounts in 2 Samuel 10 and 1 Chronicles 19 describe how Joab, without any knowledge of the location of enemy units, led his army directly towards Philadelphia (Amman), unaware that a large Syrian army with chariots had taken a position near Medaba, about forty kilometres southwest of Amman. The Syrians were on Joab's flank and in open terrain, which was favourable to their chariots. Once Joab realised what had happened, he bravely divided his army and assumed command of the force facing the Syrians. The other part of his army, under his brother's command, was directed to confront the Ammonites. Then, with the advantage of interior lines, Joab and his brother simultaneously attacked the Syrian and Ammonite armies, preventing them from reinforcing each other. 'By his brilliant leadership, lightning decisions and the offensive spirit', Joab defeated the coalition.[45]

Are These Really the Stories of Saul, David and Solomon?

For decades, archaeologists believed that the evidence uncovered in many excavations outside Jerusalem supported the Bible's account of a vast united monarchy. After all, the geographical descriptions seemed accurate, and some of the excavated Philistine sites showed evidence of destruction levels.[46] Whenever a Philistine city showed evidence of being attacked or destroyed, it was seen as David's handiwork. The dating of these sites, however, has come under closer scrutiny and levels that were once labelled 'Davidic' or 'Solomonic' are now being questioned.[47]

The most negative onslaught has come from the so-called historical revisionists Thompson, Lemche and Davies. For them, David and Solomon, the united monarchy of Israel, the battles and indeed the entire biblical narrative about the history of Israel are little more than an ideological construct produced by priestly circles in Jerusalem in Hellenistic times.[48] Even a more mainline scholar such as Jack Sasson has written, for example, that there is no independent confirmation of the kingdoms of David and Solomon from ancient Near Eastern sources.[49]

Archaeological evidence, albeit scant, does suggest that the kingdom of David existed. What is questioned is the extent or splendour of their realm. There seems to be a problem in finding remains of 'a glorious capital' in tenth-century Jerusalem. The directors of all four major excavations in Jerusalem died without writing final reports, which has made it difficult for scholars to evaluate the evidence on Jerusalem in the Late Bronze Age through to the Iron Age.[50] The archaeological evidence does not indicate the existence of a glorious capital in tenth-century Jerusalem, yet on the other hand the discovery of the Moab stone and the Mesha stele certainly suggest that the House of David was not the figment of someone's imagination.[51]

There is an interpretive middle ground between the literalists and the minimalists. No doubt the Dtr history was written by someone who wished to look back on the days of Saul and David as an ideological golden age. Whether or not this monarchy was as large, rich or powerful as they describe it may legitimately be called into question. For all their reputed wealth and power, neither David nor Solomon is mentioned in any extant Egyptian or Mesopotamian text. The archaeological evidence in Jerusalem for the famous building projects of Solomon is non-existent. No excavation of the nineteenth or twentieth century has turned up a trace of Solomon's fabled temple or palace complex[52] Certain levels and structures at other sites such as Megiddo, Hazor and Gezer have been attributed to Solomon, but their dating is far from clear, and the identification of these structures with a united monarchy in Israel has been severely challenged.[53]

Yet Jerusalem was not without its monumental buildings. Impressive finds from the Middle Bronze Age and from the later Iron Age suggest that it was an important capital, but at a much later date. The most optimistic interpretation of the tenth-century evidence, however, is that in David's time Jerusalem was a rather small town, perhaps little more than a typical hill-country village. The rest of Judah followed the same pattern; it encompassed perhaps twenty small villages and a few thousand inhabitants.[54]

To many scholars it now seems quite unlikely that this sparsely inhabited region could have been the centre of a great empire stretching from Egypt to Syria. There is no evidence in the archaeological record for the kind of wealth, manpower or level of organisation needed to create and maintain such an empire. Also lacking is any evidence of sizeable armies that would have been required for large conquests outside Judah.[55]

The size of David's army must have been small, and the society from which it arose pre-literate. Among all the Hebrew scriptures there is not a single instance of a written piece of communication used during battle. Communication must have been by messengers who transmitted the instructions of the commander-in-chief orally. The problems of oral messages and their fatal results in war are well known. Messengers forget or distort their messages, and sometimes bring them to the wrong people. Messengers can be attacked, captured or killed along the way. They do not have authority to urge the recipient to obey orders, nor do they have authority to change orders if something happens along the way to make a change essential. Because human voice was used to communicate with troops, it has been argued that it was better to have no more than one thousand men under the command of one officer. It is reasonable to assume that the standing force at the disposal of Israel's early kings comprised generally not more than two or three thousand men, and that its intelligence gathering capacity was minimal.[56]

Intelligence in Davidic Times

Intelligence in the period of monarchy should have had the same importance as in the period of Joshua and Judges. No matter how large or small the army, commanders needed intelligence to fight their battles effectively. The Dtr historian gives the same sense of realism in these battles that he did in the two other books. Battles were fought in places that really existed, and soldiers used tactics that may well have worked. Whether these events occurred during the early monarchy cannot be documented, and the chronology is severely truncated in some places. The biblical account is no more than an ancient conceptual model of how the monarchy was formed, and it depicts the Israelites' 'inheritance' and dominion over Canaan. To assure success, any of their warlike operations had to be preceded by intelligence gathering, and the stories of the monarchic period, like the stories in the conquest cycle, abound in spy stories. The accounts frequently mention reconnaissance units sent out prior to campaigns against regions or cities. As noted above, sometimes David himself performed this reconnaissance.

The battles in Samuel and Kings are also similar to those in Joshua and Judges. Ambushes are staged against small contingents, and, when a larger battle ensues, Yahweh intervenes and guarantees victory. Details are always missing about these forces and their manoeuvres. If ambushes were the supreme skill of the Israelite forces, then why at the Battle of Mount Gilboa did Saul permit the Philistines to go through the Carmel pass unhindered?[57] The Dtr author has not provided important details, but this has not stopped some military historians from filling in their own versions of these battles based on a modern commander's strategic judgement of what *should* have happened.

The victories in these accounts all seem to conform to a preconceived stereotype. The Israelites do not have chariots that could easily outrun a foot soldier. Yet the Israelites seem to be able to defeat huge hosts of Philistines with chariots, and then have the infantry run down the stragglers. Joshua's victory at the Aijalon valley and his pursuit of the Canaanite kings worked in the same way, as did Gideon's pursuit of the Midianites, and Saul's pursuit of the enemy at Michmash. Pursuits are not that easy. Troops become exhausted or they lose their discipline, as happened to Thutmose III's army at Megiddo, when it stopped chasing the enemy and started plundering its camp. When Saul ordered his troops not to stop to eat, this was probably from an awareness of what might happen if they did (1 Samuel 14:24). The Israelites not only fought constantly with the smaller force but they also attacked with a force that was so small that only a miracle could make success possible. The idea that two small units could decide the outcome of the Battle of Gibeon's pool would seem madness to a modern commander.[58] Yet with Yahweh's help battles can be won with crude flint weapons as at Gibeon's pool, or with none at all as at Michmash.

Another curious aspect of the stories of the monarchy is that so many of the battles are decided, as is the *Iliad*, by individual combat. The confrontation between David and Goliath is only the most well-known example, but the list of victories of champions given in 2 Samuel 23:8–39 shows only individual combatants. Individuals and small units of combatants are always guaranteed victory, because Yahweh like other Near Eastern gods guided the outcome.

The Dtr historian in the seventh century was fascinated by the memories of David and Solomon, and in the end his motivation is clear. He wanted to show that David's rise to power was not his own doing but strictly that of Yahweh. All during David's military exploits, he seeks oracles to ascertain God's will. In his descriptions of events, however, Dtr is projecting the Jerusalem of his own day – a relatively large city dominated by a temple to the god of Israel – back into the past.[59] The institutions he describes – the monarchy, the professional army, the administration – are all at a level of sophistication that far exceeded what existed on the ground in David's time, or indeed that of his neighbouring states. The Dtr has created a mythical golden age, and David is the hero who completes the unfinished job of Joshua, namely the conquest of the rest of the Promised Land. Finkelstein has described Josiah's powerful seventh-century vision of a national renaissance that brought the Israelites together and made them united in their worship of Yahweh.[60] This scenario is a theological hope, not an historical description.

CHAPTER 4

The Maccabean Revolt

THERE IS NO MORE fertile ground for espionage activities than a country occupied by a foreign power, and when resistance activity must be undertaken clandestinely. For much of their history, the Jews lived under the control of others, and they seldom rebelled unless provoked. When attempts were made to restrict the practice of their religion, however, the reaction was usually swift and violent. Just such a situation arose in the middle of the second century BCE when Judaea became a small province of the Syrian-based Seleucid Empire. Antiochus III had wrested the area of Palestine from the Ptolemies of Egypt in 198 BCE. When his son Antiochus IV Epiphanes came to power, he realised that Judaea was on the strategic route to the southern and eastern borders of his land.[1] Among his more unfortunate decisions was an attempt to unify the area by imposing Greek culture on its population.[2] King Antiochus believed that this would promote cultural coherence that, in turn, would generate allegiance to him and his rule. It turned out, however, to be a huge miscalculation.

Instead of unifying the Jews, the Hellenising of Judaea became a flashpoint for revolt. Either Antiochus, or a group of Jews acting under his authority, pulled down the walls of the Temple area, desecrated the Temple and looted its treasure.[3] Antiochus installed a Syrian garrison and fortified the citadel to defend the Hellenisers who supported him. He forbade all Jews to practise circumcision or to celebrate the Sabbath. In 167 BCE, he formally rededicated the Temple in Jerusalem to the supreme Greek deity, Olympian Zeus.

A revolt ensued, and it became a major struggle for religious liberty and independence. The methods of combat used in this war were surprise attack, guerrilla operations and many unconventional tactics that represented a complete departure from traditional practice of the time.[4] There are many details lacking in 1 and 2 Maccabees, and among these are the names and exploits of the spies and reconnaissance agents working on the Jewish side.[5] Even if we did not know their names, the outcome of the events suggest they existed because surprise attacks, guerrilla operations and insurgencies are impossible without them.

A careful reading of Daniel 2 and 1 and 2 Maccabees provides a sketch of the Maccabean Revolt and its aim, its beginning and its end. Many questions remain, however, and the sources will never answer them. None of the sources is contemporaneous with the revolt.[6]

Mattathias and the Beginning of the Revolt

When the Maccabean Revolt began in 167 BCE, no organised Jewish military force had taken up arms since Jerusalem had fought its losing battle against Nebuchadrezzar some four hundred years before.[7] This was not a revolt of trained soldiers, but rather a result of religious outrage among unnamed country folk.[8] The head of a priestly family, Mattathias, had left Jerusalem as a result of the paganism being practised there, and moved to his house in Modi'in.[9] When an officer named Apelles arrived in Modi'in with his troops, he erected an altar in the village. Before the assembled population, he ordered Mattathias, a Jewish priest, to sacrifice at this altar and to eat pig's flesh.[10] Mattathias refused. When a Jewish man in the crowd stepped forwards to the altar and tried to obey the order, Mattathias killed both him and Apelles. His five sons – John, Simon, Eleazar, Judas and Jonathan – led the villagers against Apelles' unit and destroyed it. Mattathias was forced to flee to the hills, possibly Gophna, northwest of present-day Ramallah, with his sons and some villagers, and there they started a resistance movement.[11] It has been argued that the Maccabean Revolt was primarily a peasant war, although some scholars stress only the religious motivations.[12] Certainly the country population was more conservative religiously and for them, faithful as they were to Yahweh, the idea of Hellenisation was a scandal. The Maccabean movement was above all a civil war, a religious struggle between orthodoxy and reformers. As the struggle progressed, however, the war would extend to the political oppressors as well.[13]

Troops from Jerusalem were sent to track down the rebels.[14] One group of Hasidim was massacred on the Sabbath, because its members refused to offer any resistance on that day.[15] From then on, Mattathias and his followers decided to fight on the Sabbath when they were attacked.[16] Another important consequence of this massacre was that the Hasidim, or at least a large number of them, now took the side of the Maccabees in the revolt, and this brought some reinforcements to the movement. Mattathias himself missed the remainder of the fighting since he died right at the beginning, c.166/165 BCE.[17]

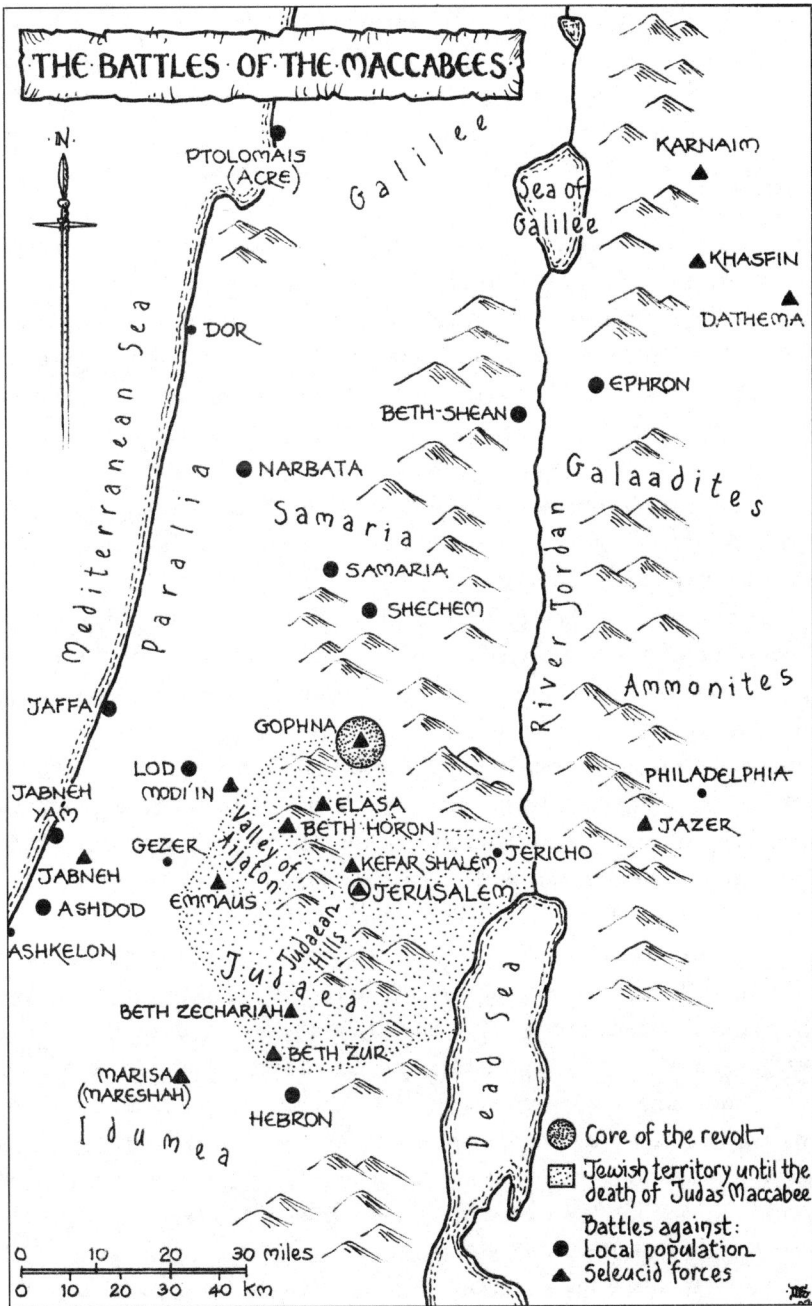

Map 5 The battles of the Maccabees

After the death of Mattathias, one of his middle sons, Judas Maccabeus, became leader of the rebels.[18] With several hundred rebel troops at his disposal, Judas spent a year training them in guerrilla tactics and planning their strategy. The large number of men he expected to recruit could not be permanently fed and sheltered in Gophna. They needed to establish bases close to their proposed actions in the different districts throughout rural Judaea. Each group would operate in its own region, and yet be ready to join another force for major action anywhere else. Volunteers proceeded to Gophna for training in small groups while their wives, children, parents and animals stayed behind to ensure a steady supply of food. Once trained, the fighters could return to their villages and blend into the countryside. They were self-sustaining guerrilla troops easily mobilised for small local actions. They set up secret lines of communication with other villagers in the countryside, and spread word of the revolt and the religious principles on which it was based. Soon they had an effective intelligence-gathering organisation and a growing people's militia.[19] These were the eyes and ears of the Maccabean intelligence system.

By the end of the first year, Judas and his force had set up clandestine supply depots through the countryside. His elaborate, if informal, intelligence system gave Judas full knowledge of the situation in Judaea and the region of Samaria to its north. They began offensive guerrilla activities against Seleucid patrols that they ambushed and often killed. These hit-and-run tactics were designed not only to disrupt the occupying forces but also to create an arsenal of professional arms for the Jewish rebels. Judas carried out wide-ranging attacks which soon made it impossible for the royal Greek mercenaries, stationed on the coastal plain, to move freely in rural Judaea. The Judaean hills gave the guerrillas protection, and an ability to evade the enemy. The weapons at their disposal were probably poor in the initial phases of the uprising, as they were armed with primitive farm implements and home-made weapons such as the mace and sling, or implements used by Jewish farmers to protect their flocks and crops from predatory animals.[20] Their most important source of military equipment became the spoils of war: weapons jettisoned by fleeing hoplites would serve the rebels well. Although the heavy armour would be a hindrance to a guerrilla fighter, the swords and helmets could be reused.[21] Their most important weapon, however, would be advance intelligence about the intentions and movement of the Seleucids.

Judas analysed his situation, and instinctively enumerated the elements that could be put to work in his favour. On the one hand the Seleucids enjoyed overwhelming superiority in manpower and arms. They were well trained, well organised and tested in battle. Their ranks were composed of heavy and light infantry, heavy and light cavalry, chariots and elephant units. Their weapons were swords, javelins, spears, bows, slings, ballistas (stone-hurling engines) and battering rams. On the other hand, Judas realised that the Seleucid troops were trained for set-piece battles in conventional fighting form. If the Seleucids were trained in conventional warfare, then the response to them must be unconventional warfare. If the Syrians were trained to fight by day, then the Jews would fight by night. As Mao Tse-tung expressed it thousands of years later, the Jews would operate like fish in water.[22] Judas' fighters came from the local populace in the villages and could blend back into the population and disappear. Every one of them would have to be an intelligence agent as well as a fighter and patriot.

As Judas' activities increased, entire areas of the countryside came under the effective control of the Maccabees, and the Seleucid garrison in Jerusalem was cut off. Aware of the deteriorating situation, and the fact that the Maccabees were gaining an upper hand in Judaea, Apollonius, the governor of Samaria and commander of Antiochus' forces in the region, decided it was time to respond.[23] In 166 BCE, Apollonius moved his forces from Samaria southwards to Jerusalem. Judas, however, realised the advantages gained by not allowing the enemy to dictate the field and style of battle. The Seleucid's advantage would be on flat, open ground, so Judas decided to attack in a narrow valley. If he attacked while they were marching, the Syrians would be neither prepared for battle nor able to assume the formations in which they had been trained to fight.[24] As he was advancing along the direct route that passes the Gophna area, a small Jewish force was lying in ambush waiting for him.[25]

The exact site chosen by Judas is unknown, although Nahal-el-Haramiah has been often suggested. It was five or six kilometres east of Gophna, where the route southwards from Samaria entered a narrow valley that continues uphill for more than a kilometre.[26] Judas, whose spies watched the enemy and their approach, divided his force into four groups, and they all took up their positions. One unit sealed off the southern end of the valley; the second unit acted as the main attacking force on the eastern side of the pass. A third unit would attack the enemy from the western side of the valley, while the fourth was held a short distance north of the main attacking unit, ready to seal off the northern entrance of the valley and thus close the trap.[27]

Predictably, the Seleucid force marched into the Maccabean trap. The murderous assault from both hills eliminated their leader Apollonius.[28] The Seleucid troops were completely trapped, leaderless and fighting under conditions for which they had never been prepared. The entire force was destroyed, and the Jews captured all their weapons and equipment. We are told that Judas took the sword of Apollonius, and used it in his campaigns for the rest of his life.[29] Because of his ability to think 'outside the box', and his excellent intelligence on the enemy's movements, Judas scored a major success that had an electrifying effect on the population of Judaea. He was accepted as a national leader, and more volunteers rushed to join his forces.[30]

The Battle of Beth Horon

Antiochus realised that a serious situation in Judaea had just got worse, and so he dispatched his general Seron to the area early in 165 BCE. Rather than fall into the trap that had led to Apollonius' death, Seron took the coastal road thereby avoiding the Gophna region and providing a safer approach march.[31] On reaching Jaffa, Seron turned inland and advanced eastward past the site of the present-day airport of Lod, and reached the foothills of Judaea. His force was only twenty-four kilometres, or one day's march, from Jerusalem and the nearest Seleucid garrison. He hoped to join up with that garrison and to fan out across Judaea in a punitive expedition that would destroy the Maccabean Revolt and crush all Jewish resistance. This was a good plan, but Judas' spies were busy unravelling it even before it became operational.[32]

Judas' reconnaissance men determined that Seron planned to approach Jerusalem by way of the Beth Horon pass, a location that has seen many historical battles.[33] The Romans were ambushed here twice by the Jews during the great Jewish War of 66 CE (see map 7, p. 142). This was the site that Judas chose to set up his next successful ambush.

As always, Judas was quite outnumbered, yet he took his small force of men into the hills above the pass, where they waited for the four thousand Syrian troops.[34] A passage in 1 Maccabees describes the apprehension with which the Jewish forces, entrenched in the Judaean hills, viewed the approach of this huge force across the valley of Aijalon. Judas' plan was similar to that used in his previous encounter with the Seleucids. By means of superior intelligence gathering and surprise, he would ambush the advancing forces in terrain that would neutralise the enemy's advantage in organisation, numbers and weapons. He would not be able to trap the entire enemy force as he had done with Apollonius' troops, because this time the Seleucid forces were too large and they were marching with wide gaps between their units. Their column was more than a kilometre long so that an attempt to bottle up the entire column would have meant dispensing with the element of surprise, which Judas was unwilling to do. Where exactly the ambush was sprung is not known, but it is curious that the Seleucid troops would have entered such a narrow pass without sending patrols out to check for ambushes.[35]

Seron's forces set out at dawn for what they believed was their last day's march before reaching Jerusalem. From the hills, Judas' spies noted how the Seleucid forces advanced slowly up the ascent to the Beth Horon pass, weighed down by their heavy equipment. As the Seleucid vanguard approached the site of the ambush, Judas' men charged and caught Seron, who was riding at the head of his troops.[36] This enabled them to eliminate the enemy commander early in the battle, which had a serious effect on the morale of the Syrian troops. With their leading formation decimated and Seron dead, the second formation turned and fled towards the coastal plain, leaving more than eight hundred of their own dead on the battlefield. Judas claimed another victory, more equipment was captured, and morale among his men was boosted yet again.[37]

The Battle of Emmaus

These initial successes probably resulted from the presence of very few Seleucid troops in the country, and those who were there had no experience in coping with guerrilla warfare in the hills. Seleucid intelligence seems to have underestimated the Maccabean threat.[38] The Syrian leadership probably saw the Judaean rebellion in its initial phase as nothing more than a minor disturbance, inspired by a small band of local zealots. The gradual transition from local action to major military operations of a wider scope afforded Judas sufficient time to train his men and gather intelligence. During the initial phases of the revolt, Antiochus IV was in the East, where he was concentrating all his attention on a war with the Parthians.[39]

By the autumn of 165 BCE, approximately six months after the campaigns against Apollonius and Seron, Judas' successes began to register with Antiochus' government. Once it became clear to him that he was fighting a major rebellion, he pulled out all the stops for the next offensive. He ordered Lysias, his representative in the capital, to annihilate the Jews and settle their land with strangers.[40] This seems an exaggeration. The real purpose was probably not extermination but a counterinsurgency operation against the rebels. Lysias sent three Syrian generals – Ptolemy, Nicanor and Gorgias – and a force of twenty thousand men to quash the revolt.[41] They established a base camp in the Ajalon valley near

Emmaus, and developed operations against Jerusalem from there.[42] According to 2 Maccabees 8:11, the Seleucids were so confident of their victory that, before the battle, they offered Jewish slaves for sale at the price of ninety to the talent. Slave merchants supposedly showed up at Emmaus with large quantities of gold and silver, and with chains in anticipation of carting away the losers.

It is a compliment to Judas that the Seleucid general Gorgias tried to imitate his tactics. He planned to lead a force into the Judaean hills under cover of darkness, surprise the Jewish camp and destroy Judas' forces. He assumed that Judas would not expect a night attack because this was not the way the Seleucids generally fought. Gorgias moved into the hills with five thousand infantry and a thousand cavalry troops.[43] Unfortunately, his actions were based on assumptions, and not on reconnaissance.

Judas' spies were too well informed to allow themselves to be ambushed.[44] Judas designed his own plan based on surprise, and he took advantage of the complacency and overconfidence of the Seleucid force. Judas employed a ruse to draw Gorgias' contingent deeper into the hills of Judaea and away from the main body of the Seleucid force. According to Josephus, he built large bonfires to make it seem as if a large force were encamped there, and under cover of darkness he and his men withdrew from the camp leaving only a rearguard of two hundred men.[45] When Gorgias' men attacked the phoney camp, they found it almost empty, but observed that the rear guard was withdrawing. Mistaking this for the main force escaping, Gorgias pursued the Jews who moved into the main valley leading up to Jerusalem, known today as Shaar Hagai (Bab el-Wad).[46] As Gorgias' forces advanced up the valley, the units Judas had stationed there in advance attacked them. The trap was sprung.

Judas next attempted an attack on the Seleucid base camp at Emmaus, where the majority of troops and cavalry were still positioned. Unfortunately, the Seleucids for once had their own spies who alerted their army, which formed up for battle in a phalanx on the plain. Judas could no longer attack the camp by surprise, so he dealt with the Seleucid forces in his usual unconventional way. Since they would expect to be attacked on the front, he assaulted them from the side, and used small groups to infiltrate their ranks and engage them in hand-to-hand combat. The phalanx disintegrated. A second Jewish force took the camp by surprise, and when stragglers returned there they too were killed.[47] Although both sides attempted to use indirect methods and surprise attacks, the winner was the side that could use its intelligence to the best advantage, and better manoeuvre in the rugged and intricate terrain.

The Battle of Beth Zur

The Battle of Beth Zur[48] had a similar disastrous outcome for the Seleucids.[49] This time Lysias himself set out from Antioch with sixty thousand infantry and five thousand cavalry determined to avenge the previous defeats.[50] He would not take the routes used by his predecessors for fear of an ambush by Jewish forces. He headed for Jerusalem, but did not go into the Judaean hills. Rather he marched southwards along the coast to Ashkelon, and then turned inland towards Marisa (Mareshah) and finally to Hebron. The last stretch went through Idumea, where the population was hostile to Jews but friendly to the Seleucids. They set up camp at Beth Zur, a Judaean border fortress some nine kilometres from Hebron.[51]

Judas knew that a direct assault on Lysias' forces was out of the question. Consequently, he sent out his reconnaissance men to find a terrain whose topographical features could be exploited to offset the enemy's numerical superiority. His reconnaissance team chose an area immediately north of Beth Zur, probably near what is today Khirbet Beth-heiran.[52] The route was narrow, on high ground and bisected at many points by wadis and ravines with excellent cover for ambushing forces. Judas sent his men to the site to occupy the slopes surrounding the route. Judas once again divided his ten thousand men into four groups.[53] When the Seleucids entered the defile, the Jews attacked from the surrounding ravines and high ground, from both front and sides. The ambush was a success. After routing the Seleucid army, Judas' force pursued the retreating army back to its base camp, but before the Jews could assault the camp the Seleucid forces had hastened back to the coast. It was the most serious defeat that the Seleucid army, led by Lysias himself, had suffered at the hands of the Maccabees.[54] The road to Jerusalem was open.

Judas and his men marched to Jerusalem, entered the Temple, removed all the profanities and reconsecrated it. On the 25th day of Kislev (c.15 December) in 164 BCE, the Temple was rededicated.[55] The Talmud relates a miracle that followed when oil sufficient for one day burned in the candelabrum for eight. Had it not been for Judas' extremely capable intelligence staff, there might not have been a Hanukkah.[56]

Techniques of Success

The same techniques of intelligence gathering that were used to stage surprise in the Hebrew scriptures continued to give the Jews success in later periods. Guerrilla warfare had won them independence and religious freedom, and the events celebrated in the Hanukkah festival continued to inspire the Jews to believe they could triumph against all odds. The success of the Maccabees would, however, be the last successful war the Jews waged against foreign occupiers, and their brief independence under the Hasmonean Dynasty would quickly come to an end.

In 163 BCE, Judas Maccabeus laid siege to the Acra (citadel) in Jerusalem; the siege however was unsuccessful. Judas' guerrillas had neither the expertise nor the means to capture a fortress. The besieged called on the Seleucids for reinforcements, which soon appeared under the command of Lysias, forcing Judas to break off the siege of the Acra. There was an encounter at Beth Zechariah, south of Bethlehem, between the troops of Lysias and those of Judas, whose force was defeated.[57] His brother Eleazar was killed in the fight. Lysias captured Beth Zur and advanced on Jerusalem, where Judas had retreated. Now it was Judas who was on the defensive and besieged by the troops of Lysias. Only the withdrawal of Lysias for political reasons saved the Maccabees.[58] Judas reached an accord with Lysias, knowing of his eagerness to wind up his Judaean campaign because reports were coming in that his adversary, Philip, had gained control of the capital city of Antioch.[59]

The lessons learned from these campaigns are many: all guerrilla warfare presupposes a basic inequality between the contesting parties, and guerrillas must make optimal use of intelligence to stage their hit-and-run tactics. Topographical factors are all-important because staging an ambush requires intimate knowledge of the terrain. Broken terrain and mountainous areas often allow clandestine fighters to reach their objective under suitable cover. Fighting under cover of darkness is risky, and also requires knowledge of the terrain. The Judaean mountains and the adjacent desert area were ideally suited to the secret struggle of the Hasmoneans. The Jewish partisans enjoyed the advantage of knowing the territory. Unlike the Syrian enemy, they were extremely familiar with the terrain.[60] Because the Judaean topography favoured the insurgents rather than the tactics of the Hellenistic armies, the Jews had an advantage. In order to unleash their deadly force, the regular hoplite armies needed open space not available in the broken hills of Judaea. Maccabean guerrillas, on the other hand, could emerge from every possible corner, deliver an unexpected blow and disappear as swiftly as they had come. Their initial objective lay in the destruction of the invader's combat strength, not in the conquest of towns and territory. Only when this first goal had been reached, did a second phase of the war begin.

Guerrillas cannot survive without the active sympathy of the local population. The more Jews that sympathised with the Maccabees, the more success the Maccabees had. Another important element was the intelligence supplied to the underground fighters. At some point, terrorism becomes the next stage. One must intimidate the occupying power and create a general atmosphere of insecurity. The Maccabees pulled down altars, raised troops, burned towns, circumcised children and other activities that created a sense of impotence on the part of the authorities.

Once they had overcome the Syrians enough to establish a secure base, the Maccabees liberated other areas and created a legitimate status from which they could make a treaty with Rome. At no time, however, did the Jewish army exceed the status of a partisan force. With the limited means at their disposal, they did not strain their forces beyond the feasible, and never lost sight of the fact that it was always an unequal contest. Through strict discipline, they never allowed their fearlessness to deteriorate into foolhardiness, or their fighting to become mere plundering. Only under Judas' brothers and successors was a fully fledged regular army established. By avoiding open, head-on confrontation with a superior force, the Maccabees waged a successful guerrilla war of liberation.

As long as the Jewish command adhered to guerrilla techniques and did not adopt the regular military doctrine of the Syrian invaders, they could find an advantage in their physical environment; when they tried besieging cities or meeting the Syrians in open warfare, they lost. Surprise and speed served the Jewish forces much better than force. Two circumstances, however, would change drastically with the result that these tried-and-true tactics would become ineffective. Internally, the Jews constantly fought among themselves over which religious faction would lead them. Externally, a new world power was about to make its appearance on the scene – the Romans. When Judas Maccabeus made contact with the Romans and negotiated a treaty with them, it fit well with Roman policy of maintaining client kingdoms, which kept the Jews safe for more than a century.[61] When Jewish independence was crushed under Roman domination, however, it would mean open warfare with a power the Jews could never hope to defeat.

The Maccabees and History

The stories from the Hasmonean period are sometimes different from those in the Hebrew Bible because historical writing had become known to the Greeks of the Hellenistic world. The stories continued to reflect biblical themes, and the actions of the major characters were patterned after biblical examples. Indeed they encouraged their readers by appealing to biblical precedents. Their restored form of worship was based on scripture. Yet, although the author of

1 Maccabees wrote his book in Hebrew, taking as his model the 'historical' books of the Hebrew Bible, especially Samuel, there are significant differences: prophecy is absent from the narrative, and so are miracles or any direct supernatural intervention.[62]

In contrast to the highly emotional account in 2 Maccabees, the author of 1 Maccabees wrote a sober narrative. Mattathias, Judas, Jonathan and Simon are portrayed as rebels against an unjust government. They are guerrilla warriors and men of action; they are models of this-worldly activism who champion religious freedom and national independence. None of the sources was eyewitness to the battles, yet they seem to have drawn on some sources that may have been. In short, the author feels obligated to write an historical narrative of some accuracy while maintaining the biblical themes of the past.

Although the Jews were victorious against a larger force, it must not be assumed that a clever use of spies was the magic bullet that solved all the military problems of the Jews. Larger forces were at work, and the Jewish victories need to be put into that perspective. There is a difference, for example, between the initial goal – getting rid of objectionable worship in the Temple – and the ultimate goal of political independence for the Jews. One reason for their eventual defeat was the concentration of power in the Maccabean dynasty. Although such a concentration might have facilitated centralised intelligence collection, it also led to rule by a family who monopolised political, military and religious power, and who fell victim to the same dynastic struggles that plagued the Seleucids and the Ptolemies. The struggles came to an end in 63 BCE, when the Roman general Pompey settled a Hasmonean family dispute about who was to be the successor to Salome Alexandria.

Not all of Israel supported the Maccabean Revolt. Even though 1 Maccabees tends to equate the Maccabean movement with Israel, and to dismiss other Jews as 'lawless men', it is clear that there were several parties besides the Maccabees. The course of the revolt was neither smooth nor quick. Judas and his band enjoyed dramatic initial military successes, probably due to their familiarity with the land and its people. The capture of the Jerusalem Temple and restoration of the Temple service solidified the movement and gave it credibility. The symbolic significance of Maccabean control of the Temple must have been very powerful. It is still powerful – so much so, that modern readers assume that the revolt reached its successful conclusion with the dedication of the Temple.[63]

The ancient sources tell a different story. There were further attacks against Judas and Jerusalem, defeats in battle, and deaths. Just as it is difficult to pinpoint the beginning of a revolution, it is also hard to know when one is over. A successful revolution results in a stable government and a normalisation of civil life. Revolutions, however, often sow the seeds of their own destruction. One such seed was the reliance on Rome as a protector. Though the Romans were eager to make treaties, they were slow to follow through on them unless it suited their own interests. The treaties between Rome and the Jews created an official link between the two peoples. This official link suited both parties in the short run. The Jews now had a powerful protector against the Seleucids and the Ptolemies. The Romans got a client state in Judaea, and a foothold in the Middle East.[64] The course of the revolution had been anything but straight. It was not the guerrilla warfare and the intelligence edge that brought victory in the end, but the political skill of Jonathan and the alliance with the greater power of Rome.

CHAPTER 5
Judith's Disinformation Campaign

IN CONTRAST TO THE accounts we have just discussed, the Book of Judith seems a completely fictional story created in the Hasmonean period. Although it is set in a certain place and time, it is not history but an exciting story with a moral.[1] The author was primarily interested in arousing emotions such as humour, fear and fascination in his readers. With elements such as God, sex, death and espionage, how could it fail to excite people both young and old, learned and illiterate, in every place and time?[2]

Women have always engaged in espionage, and, in fact, the major motif running through this book is 'the hand of a woman'.[3] Stories of undercover agents appear in the Hebrew scriptures and from the Apocrypha.[4] Judith herself has been described as 'perhaps the strongest of any woman in the Hebrew Bible'.[5] By the acts of Judith, Israel was freed from its enemies. Not only was the author of the Book of Judith a strong woman like Deborah and Jael, but she was also probably familiar with Judges 4 and 5 and used them as models.[6] All three women act in accordance with Yahweh's will and save Israel.

Judith's story begins with the Assyrian king Nebuchadrezzar sending his general Holofernes to punish various vassal peoples, including the Jews of Judaea, who had failed to aid him in a recent war (Judith 2:14–3:10). Historically, Nebuchadrezzar was a Babylonian king who conquered the Assyrians as well as the Israelites. The author of Judith, by making Nebuchadrezzar an Assyrian, created a composite enemy out of Israel's numerous foes. On Israel's side is the spy Judith, who acts on behalf of her occupied people. Her greatest weapons were her beauty, which she used as a diversion, and her clever use of disinformation.

In the story, Nebuchadrezzar's general Holofernes ravaged nations from Nineveh to Damascus and then swept down the Mediterranean coast towards Jerusalem with an army of one hundred and twenty thousand infantry and twelve thousand cavalry. The Jews of Jerusalem resolved to resist. They told the residents of the small mountain town of Bethulia to block the passes to the city.[7] In retaliation, Holofernes seized Bethulia's water supply in the hope that this would force the city to surrender without a battle. After thirty-four days, the water supply within the city was exhausted, and the Bethulians told the town leaders they would have to surrender within five days.

News of the surrender plan reached Judith, a widow living in austere retirement (Judith 8:1ff.). She sent for the leaders of Bethulia, and berated them for not trusting in God. She promised them that she herself would achieve deliverance from the enemy within five days. Without hearing the details of her scheme, they agreed to it and then departed. Judith prepared herself by praying and by putting on the adornments that she had laid aside after her husband's death. She took a single maidservant, a bag of clean (kosher) food, and headed off to the Assyrian camp (Judith 10:4).

When she arrived at the Assyrian lines, the guards were taken with her beauty.[8] Nevertheless, they interrogated her. Where did she come from? Where was she going? She gave them a good cover story: she was a daughter of the Hebrews fleeing because her people were about to be given up to the Assyrians. She wanted to be conducted into the presence of General Holofernes to tell him how to win all of the hill country without suffering any casualties. The brevity and shrewdness of her response shows her cleverness. Instead of acting like two helpless young women caught in the middle of nowhere, in the dead of night, surrounded by rough Assyrian soldiers, she and her servant kept their wits about them. Judith was not unnerved by their rapid-fire interrogation either, and in order not to be detained or abused by the soldiers she made them an offer they could not refuse. She assured them that she had reliable, inside information that assured risk-free success for the Assyrians if only she could get this information to the general. A prudent soldier would neither have delayed, nor abused, such a messenger.[9] Her plan of disinformation had begun. The soldiers bought her story, and not only took her to Holofernes but they also offered her advice on how to succeed with him. They gave Judith a contingent of one hundred men to accompanied her to Holofernes' tent (Judith 10:17).

Judith caused quite a stir in the Assyrian camp when she arrived with her military escort. People gathered in a crowd to see her, and were so stunned by her beauty that they failed to realise just how effective such a women could be as a spy, decoy or disinformation agent. Holofernes greeted Judith with assurance that no harm would come to her. She, on her part, reassured him that she could bring the Assyrians victory because the Jews had sinned by appropriating first fruits and tithes intended for God alone; God would thus deliver them up to their enemies. She was lying, but Holofernes was so attracted by Judith's beauty that he was taken in by her simple plan. Judith was in the presence of a man who had the power of life and death over her. Yet she conducted herself masterfully, and lied through her teeth. Holofernes may have been dazzled by her beauty, but the reader is taken rather by Judith's courage and cleverness. Holofernes invited her to his table, gave her wine and meats and showed her his silver vessels, but she rebuffed his overtures. Some commentators have noted the contradiction in ethics here – that Judith would have refused to eat non-kosher food but had no problem lying to him without a twinge of conscience. This may have been part of her cover story. She had to portray herself as someone who was so scrupulous about religious observance that she would betray her own people if they ignored such prohibitions. [10]

Judith stayed in the camp three days, and left only to pray and bathe. Although pre-dawn praying is not prescribed in the Hebrew Bible, Judith announced to Holofernes that she would go nightly into the valley to pray. He may have assumed she was collecting intelligence on the Jews so that he might attack them at an opportune moment. Her going out and praying while still dark also set up both an established pattern with the guards, and an escape route for her final exit (Judith 13:7, 10).

On the fourth day, Holofernes could not contain his desire to see Judith, so he arranged a feast at which only his servants would be present. Since he intended to seduce Judith, the fewer witnesses the better. Judith agreed to come on the condition that she be allowed to eat her own food that she had brought in her now-familiar bag. She dressed up again, came to his tent and sat herself beside Holofernes on a sheepskin. Judith had absolutely no intentions of getting into Holofernes' bed, but there is little doubt that she created an entirely opposite and deceptive impression. [11]

The critical moment arrived when the servants departed, leaving the spy and the general alone together. His excitement caused him to drink heavily ('much more than he had ever drunk in any one day since he was born' (Judith 12:20). If ever a man acted in a manner prejudicial to his own interests, it was Holofernes. Had he remained reasonably sober, Judith's task would have been far more difficult; indeed she would have been in great danger. Instead, he lay helpless on his couch. Judith was playing a dangerous game for high stakes, and she planned and prepared admirably. She was too intelligent to leave the biggest risk to chance. She must have known a certain amount of information about Holofernes: his drinking habits and his weakness for women. Her source of information may have been Achior. He was the ruler of the Ammonites, and while in the Assyrian camp he may have moved among the members of Holofernes' staff, where the foibles of the commander were common gossip among the subordinates. Judith was successful because she was aware of the fundamental requirements on which every deception scheme depends, namely knowledge of the target. Her intelligence on Holofernes was accurate.

The withdrawal of the servants and other military people played into the Judith's hands. Calling on God for strength, she took Holofernes' sword from above his bed and with two blows cut off his head, which she then put in a bag carried by the servant waiting outside (see cover art). The two left the camp as though to pray, in their usual manner, and escaped to Bethulia.

The people of Bethulia hung Holofernes' head from the wall early the next morning, and then made a sortie, taking the Assyrians by surprise.[12] Holofernes' servant, Bagoas, assumed his master was still asleep in bed after his assignation with the Hebrew woman, and would not have disturbed him during the night. When he tried to rouse his general, he found him dead. Deprived of their leader, the Assyrians were completely demoralised. A great many of them were massacred by the Bethulians, while the rest fled in panic. They were pursued north towards Damascus, and their deserted camp was sacked. The high priest Joakim came in person from Jerusalem to bless Judith. The book ends with Judith, this very pious agent, dedicating her share of the spoils to God. She remained a widow until her death at the age of 105, and her land remained at peace throughout her long life.

The story of Judith contains lies, deceits, *double entendre*, assassinations and seductions. Judith was not a military figure; she was not armed; nor did she fight with anything but disinformation. She represents Israel overcoming its enemies.[13] Unlike Delilah, her deception was for a good cause. She worked alone, and the survival of the Jews was uppermost in her thoughts. She was as righteous as a secret agent can be.

The Book of Judith is regarded as fiction by most scholars. It was deliberately written as an exemplary moral tale, and its historical and geographical anachronisms and inconsistencies offer glaring evidence of this. It was a consoling story written to address the concerns of the Jewish people in the second century BCE.[14] Some scholars see the book as an amalgam of texts with allusions to other women in the Bible: Miriam, Deborah, Jael, Sarah, Rebekah, Rachel, Tamar, Naomi, Ruth and Abigail. It amounts to a panegyric of these biblical woman. Some see her beheading of Holofernes as a parallel to David's decapitation of Goliath. She is not only a David redivivus of sorts but also a feminine Judas Maccabeus. The parallel with Jael is notable. Judith and Jael both beguile generals and win their trust in order to destroy them. Some commentators, however, believe that Judith should not have deceived Holofernes, let alone killed and decapitated him.[15] They are embarrassed at having to praise a deceitful murderer, ignoring the fact that deception and assassination are often the stock in trade of the espionage business. Other commentators portray her as the archetypal androgyne, a combination of soldier and the seductress.[16]

Many authors have portrayed this one-woman campaign against the Assyrians as an example of how a woman who is intelligent, beautiful and resourceful could not fail. But deception, no matter how carefully calculated, nearly always involves risk. Judith's story has its place in the history of deception because she achieved success by observing the principles on which such an operation depends: preparation, security, credibility and support.[17] Along with the risk, there is also the need for flexibility. If things go wrong, it should be possible to stop the plan imperceptibly or switch to a new plan unnoticed – one which also covers the original deception and the intentions behind it. Judith's plan was flexible enough up until the moment she killed Holofernes. Thereafter, she was in appalling danger until she was safely home inside the walls of Bethulia. If Bagoas or any Assyrian officer in the camp had come in at the wrong moment, he would have immediately killed her and her maid without the least compunction.

During the Hellenistic period, spy stories remained the stock in trade of biblical writers, for two reasons. First, they had a wealth of material to draw from in the Hebrew scriptures. Writers could make points about morality by comparing heroes of the past with heroes of the present. Second, as long as Israel was an occupied territory or fought against a superior enemy, the only way to defeat a more powerful force was to trick them, surprise them, deceive them or otherwise use intelligence operations as a force multiplier. Unless God intervened with a miracle, as he did frequently in the Hebrew scriptures, guerrilla warfare and intelligence operations were the only sensible course of action.

POSTSCRIPT TO PART I
Spies in the Old Testament

FINDING SPIES IN THE Hebrew scriptures is not difficult. Deciding on whether they are historical figures or simply characters in a rousingly good spy story is quite another matter. A significant problem is that only one literary source exists – the Hebrew Bible itself. The text has been studied by biblical scholars, literary critics, scholars of form-criticism and tradition-history, historians of the ancient Near East and the history of religion, and there is still no scholarly consensus. Those who accept the text as documentary evidence do so for religious reasons, not because the texts have been substantiated. Biblical texts are not even consistent with each other. In Joshua, for example, there is a picture of conquest, but in Judges there is another picture indicating that the conquest was by no means total and that much peaceful infiltration occurred along with piecemeal conquests. We know that the writers and editors of the Hebrew texts schematised remarkably. The texts feature a host of partisan distortions, inconsistencies and inaccuracies.

The Pentateuch seems to reflect historical events, and yet there is so little corroborating evidence to support such a claim. How did this document come to be written? What motivated its authors, and what were they trying to say? For whom were they written? There are too many questions, too few answers. Possible solutions will continue to emerge. Certainly the answers that scholars have proposed cover a broad historical, religious and political spectrum. If the Hebrew scriptures are the work of the exile or post-exilic period, it may be the collective memory of a people in exile trying to recast ancient traditions into a national history.

The solution to the problems of authorship, dating and intent is complicated by another historical question: how did the Israelites come to inhabit the Holy Land? The great French biblical historian Roland de Vaux described the emergence of Israel in Palestine as 'the most difficult problem in the whole history of

Israel', and he was not exaggerating.[1] Indeed, the last half century has witnessed an intense and often polemical dialogue as three major reconstructions of the evidence have vied for centre stage: the conquest model, the peaceful infiltration model, and the peasant revolt model. Adherents of the conquest model – for example, W. F. Albright and his students G. E. Wright and J. Bright – have argued that archaeology had demonstrated the essential historicity of the biblical narrative.[2] They were the last mainstream scholars to accept the conquest model, a view that has been all but discarded by the remaining investigators except for some military historians such as Mordechai Gichon and Richard Gabriel.

Abraham Malamat has spent as much time as any military writer being concerned with the history of ancient Israel, and even he realised that the conquest model had to be discarded. He conceded that the Old Testament was a literary creation written for purposes quite other than historical reporting. He described it as an 'ancient theoretical model' depicting the conquest of the Israelites.[3] But even Malamat was never precise on his use of the socio-political term 'Israel'. He wanted to give an impression of a country with centralised leadership, a deep sense of national purpose and a strategic military doctrine, including intelligence gathering, all attributed to Joshua. These concepts do not fit into the historical realities of the twelfth century. To create such a unified view of the past, one needs a unified present. The conquests of Joshua required that the army have: a clear and generally agreed on strategy with an idea of the conquest of Canaan; a central system of command, control, communications and intelligence, under the leadership of one person; and a clear motivation shared by all, namely a national all-Israel policy. All these things are characteristic of the monarchy under Josiah, or at least according to the people who later wrote about his reign.

The problem with the authors who follow the conquest model is that they have the *Sitz im Leben* wrong. When Mordechai Gichon wrote 'all agree that the Bible narrative reflects exactly conditions and the material background of its age', does he mean the age of the battles or the age of composition?[4] The context for these stories is not the twelfth century, but the seventh or sixth. The literary texts were probably created by the so-called Dtr historian, and he was probably using contemporary military examples to explain the Israelite takeover of Israel.[5] The Dtr author did not have enough evidence about Israel's ancient past to create an accurate historical narrative. The stories themselves create the impression of a couple of victories over opposing coalitions, a number of armed skirmishes and raids, and the capture and destruction of many cities, all against a curiously unclear historical and territorial background. Occasional vividness of detail does not mean that these texts comprise what Norman Gottwald called 'a coherent temporal-territorial representation'. The same is true of the spy stories that are very often generic and have no distinct reference to time and place.

Israel's View of Israel

The Israelite view of their own history portrays them as a marginal and oppressed people (whether of Canaanite origins or not) who entered Palestine (or rose up from within) and became a people with a national consciousness who wrote the history of their own origins. The Israelites themselves chose to see their history as a continuous military conquest. Does this allow modern historians to think they can write an accurate military history of themselves? Unfortunately, the answer to this question is 'no', since the stories cannot be corroborated. The evidence suggests that Israelite history included armed conflict with its neighbours, and that much of this conflict, especially in defensive wars, required intelligence gathering that made possible tactical surprise, deception, covert operations, insurgency and terrorism. Even Norman Gottwald, an opponent of the conquest theory, has admitted: 'There is truth in the conquest model in that there was some military activity that occurred.'[6] Most historians would also agree, however, that the Dtr author was not working from eyewitness accounts.

The premonarchical period in Israel may have been preliterate, and some scholars suggest there were no texts until the time of David and Solomon, when writing was introduced for administrative purposes. They believe it was only in the eighth to seventh centuries that Israel entered the realm of written history, when literacy spread in the kingdom of Israel and Judah. With no written records before the monarchy, and oral traditions that are not traceable, it is hard to say what the Dtr author could have factually known about Israel's past. Nor was this so-called 'historian' motivated by the same notions of 'objective' historiography that characterise current historical writing. The best that ancient authors could do was to gather the accounts of Israel's beginnings, which were probably legendary and sagalike, however much they might contain 'refractions of actual events'.[7] These stories were sometimes used by the Dtr historian out of their proper context, and were blended in with the reality of Israel later in the monarchy.

The purpose of the Dtr historian in writing his history was both political and theological. In times of turmoil, people tend to create narratives of historical consciousness in order to provide themselves with a sense of collective identity. They explain who they are, and describe their origins and their perception of their destiny, especially in periods when chaos poses a most potent threat.[8] The Dtr historian produced just such a narrative. He related a story of the assertion of power through violent conquest. This does not mean, however, that it should be seen primarily as a national battle epic or a xenophobic polemic, though there are such elements in the story. Rather, those who wrote the texts used the rhetoric of warfare and nationalism as an encouragement and as a threat aimed at their own population, to encourage them to submit voluntarily to the central authority of 'a government struggling to organise itself and create its own ideological framework of inclusion'.[9] The theology of the Dtr history always controls the text. The ideological purpose of writing early Israelite history was to bind the people of Yahweh together by nourishing their common identity at points of critical shared interest. Their goal was not so much to record the past as to use the past to reinforce desired tendencies in the present.

The suggested datings for the Pentateuch range from the tenth century (the time of the united monarchy) to the late Hellenistic period.[10] When did the young nation need a national history to legitimise its existence? Some have suggested it was the end of the seventh century BCE in the time of Josiah. This theory has many adherents including Israel Finkelstein, who suggests that Josiah was trying to restore the Davidic Empire – a dream that arose from the political situation of his age. The whole population of Judah and the former northern kingdom would have been ready to unite under a shared national ideology. With their newly written 'national history', the author managed to fashion a common historical tradition that both legitimised the rule of the Judaean kings over a unified Palestine and justified the costs of their military build-up. The stories included daring feats of strength and also clever stratagems to trick the enemy and bring victory. A strict monotheism conforms better to a seventh-century date and Josiah's cult-reform mentality. This date also explains why so many traditions from the northern part of the country survived and were incorporated into this new national history. The northern kingdom no longer existed, but the southern kingdom took over its intellectual heritage and used it in its project to annex the north. A Josianic date also explains why so many literary genres of Mesopotamian origin survived in the Hebrew Bible, especially the custom of writing annals which was borrowed from the Assyrians. This is especially true for the books of Deuteronomy, Joshua, Judges, 1–2 Samuel and 1–2 Kings, which all related in one way or another to Josiah's reforms.[11]

Other scholars have advanced arguments for a later date. The recurrent reference to migration may refer to the sixth century, and so to the Babylonian exile.

In exile the people grasped desperately for hope amid hopelessness. They satis-
fied their yearnings by writing Israel's early history. If Israel had once flourished,
it might rise again. In this document, Israel celebrated its golden age, and Israel
could find its roots and define its national identity so as not to be absorbed
by the Babylonian masses.[12] The prose form in the Pentateuch, however, seems
unusual for a sixth-century context. It was a form of narrative that the Greeks
developed in the sixth and fifth centuries, and which became even more popular
in the Hellenistic and Roman periods. John Van Seters, for example, holds to the
exilic dating of the narrative, yet he knows the Greek format well and suggests
that the models were earlier Greek historians, such as Hecataeus of Miletus, who
were active at the beginning of the fifth century. At the same time, he compares
the writing to Babylonian ideas of history.[13] In reality, we know next to nothing
about early Greek historiography. Yet we are familiar with much of the historiography from Herodotus to the Roman historians. Niels Peter Lemche believes
the Pentateuch belongs to the same genre as those later works, and that borrowing from these models would have been more characteristic of the Persian or
Hellenistic period, when the Greek and Eastern worlds came into contact. It was
in this environment that the authors of the Hebrew Bible may have used Greek
historiography as a source of inspiration. Lemche believes historiography proper
seems unlikely to have been part of Palestinian literary culture prior to the Hellenistic period. Both 2 Maccabees and Josephus were fully within the tradition
of Greek historiography, in striking contrast to Hebrew prose narrative.

War in the Hebrew Bible – Past Research

Much of the scholarship on warfare in Israel has ended up in dead ends because
the research was done by historians and archaeologists who accepted the conquest model or discussed the military themes only as literary motifs. The very
terminology of divine warfare is a literary phenomenon which, by its nature, is
ahistorical and has developed over time.[14] None of the literary research brings us
any closer to the reality of warfare in ancient Israel. All of the research on 'holy
war', 'Yahweh war' or 'divine war' is literary in nature, and much of the work
on the ancient Near Eastern parallels is a catalogue of terminology or primarily
of antiquarian interest. A more fruitful approach would be to redefine the issue.
Instead of looking for ancient institutions or a theology of war, we should look
to the Dtr historian for the relationship between violence, political power and
rhetoric in the text.[15] This is why we find that the motifs of divine war were
popular in the Davidic kingdom, where they were influenced by other Near

Eastern literatures. Yahweh as warrior became a particularly prominent theme in the prophets of Josiah's time and later.[16]

As Eric Hobsbawm has shown from a non-biblical context, 'traditions' that appear to be old are often quite recent in origin and are sometimes even invented.[17] Biblical traditions may be very much like this. Stories may have been adapted and interpreted over a long period of time, but then were written down and made relevant to different circumstances. Such traditions are usually developed during periods of rapid social transformation, when the social patterns for which the 'old' traditions have been designed are destroyed.[18] The Dtr historian used older traditions for a seventh-century audience. His recounting of stories such as the Exodus, the conquest narratives and the stories of the judges was most likely a self-perception by a later community retrojected into an earlier time. There are many examples of this in other world cultures – a tradition of a humble origin, great wars of conquest, the creation of a total egalitarian society and a new political structure.[19]

Ancient battles served a purpose in explaining the existence of sites now in ruin or how the people of Israel came to live in certain places. Events are introduced, and according to the editors' emphasis condensed, transposed or even deleted. War stories in the period of judges, for example, were concerned with the preservation of the order of the old covenant community. The pattern of apostasy–judgement–deliverance is repeated in story after story about the defence of the community against aggressors who are almost always portrayed as 'kings', that is, the embodiments of centralised and organised power. The stories repeat the fundamental theme of the underdog surviving against the odds. The poorly armed but cleverly led army of Barak outwitted the more powerful Canaanites; the once powerful Canaanite general was slain at the hands of a woman. Gideon's relatively small band set the stronger invaders into confusion and panic. The Samson story pits the hero against thousands of Philistines. These stories are an apologia for a tribal order, a testimony to the validity of that order and a legitimation of it. The preservation of the tribal order, the covenant community, a new experiment against the existing systems represented by the Philistines and Canaanites, is portrayed as created entirely through defensive wars. On no occasion in Judges is Israel the aggressor; it is merely a defender of its own borders. These stories are sagas. They originated in the oral tradition of the tribes, and were eventually incorporated into the framework of the Dtr history.

The outcomes of battles were dictated by Yahweh, who used seemingly insignificant characters to achieve his ends. Rahab, for example, plays a role in the military plot of Joshua, just as Jael plays a role in Judges. Her story gives notice that sometimes Yahweh's will is accomplished not by the glorious institution of divine war or by military superstars, but by the quick thinking, perceptive faith and decisive action of the lesser players in the drama: an alien prostitute, a nomadic housewife, a migrant farm worker from Moab, a pious widow named Judith. Intelligence operations work that way. Even the most insignificant persons can perform valuable services if they are in the right place at the right time.

The range of intelligence operations in the Old Testament is certainly impressive. Abraham Malamat believes that the Books of Joshua and Judges remain unique in the literature of the Ancient Near East because of the number and variety of stratagems employed.[20] Yet, although spies appear in every military encounter as a means of determining the enemy's intentions, the reliance on God is the ultimate intelligence source that never goes away.

We may never be able to reconstruct the military history of early Israel because of the lack of extra-biblical sources and the controversy over the date and authorship of the Old Testament itself, but we have been left with some of the most memorable and archetypal espionage stories in Western literature. Moses' list of reconnaissance requirements remains classic, Delilah is the quintessential female agent, Judith the greatest covert operator and Jael the perfect undercover assassin. Nor does the religious slant of the material preclude the use of intelligence. Indeed, as we have shown, one of the first religious acts performed by the Hebrews was to consult God before every battle for intelligence on the enemy to enhance their chances of success.

What Could the Ancient Israelites Have Known About Intelligence?

Whether the Israelites were nomads or city dwellers, whether they migrated into Israel or rose from within Palestine, whether they were Canaanites or an ethnically different group, conflict arose between them and their neighbours. When such conflict resulted in military confrontations, intelligence gathering became their first priority. The clever use of stratagem in the biblical stories has caused eminent military historians such as Abraham Malamat, Mordechai Gichon and those who follow them, such as Richard Gabriel, to suggest that there must be a core of historical reality to these accounts, even though details and numbers are exaggerated and whole accounts are recounted through a theological lens.[21] There were surely military elements to Israel's emergence in Canaan and this must be part of any synthesis. Even accepting this assumption, however, does not make it possible for groups of wandering tribesmen to take major walled

Canaanite cities such as Jericho. Military events cannot be treated in isolation. It is not enough to describe the event and fit it into the conception of what a modern commander might have done. As accurate as the geographical descriptions in the Hebrew Bible sometimes are, chronological problems persist. Unless combatants can be placed on the battlefield at a certain time, the accounts are not authentic history but rather simply a theoretical model of what might have happened. Miraculous events cannot be part of the historian's solution to how something apparently unachievable was accomplished.

Part of the reason why there are so many spy stories in the Hebrew Bible is that both their geography and military situation dictated the use of good intelligence for Israelite survival. Certain places on earth, by nature of their geography, seem destined to be perpetual fields of battle. By its location between the civilisations of Egypt and Mesopotamia, Israel has always been an area flanked by military behemoths. Whether the Egyptians attacked the Hittites, or the Hittites wished to pare away a few Egyptian tributary states, Palestine was caught in the middle. It lay between the rich province of Roman Egypt and its legions in Syria. Invaders going around the eastern end of the Mediterranean Sea must pass through this narrow, elongated strip of land, and thus the pass at Megiddo has often been the path of invasion from the north. Because it is a natural land route from Eurasia to Africa, Palestine has always been a corridor leading to other regions of wealth and power.

Another reality of ancient Israelite warfare was that the Israelites usually dealt with threats to its interests defensively. In not one single case was there a frontal attack in daylight in these narratives. Instead, because they were essentially outclassed militarily, the Israelites employed stratagems. They used decoys and ambushes, night attacks and surprise attacks, spies and infiltrators. They took advantage of topography in a remarkably realistic way. A sense of weakness and a threat to their survival would convince almost any leader of the Israelites to adapt those measures necessary to guarantee the survival of the state. Clever stratagems, deception operations and surprise attack would thus remain an essential part of their warfare.

Writing Military History

Why have military historians, even more so than other historians, been so reluctant to benefit from the last fifty years of research in archaeology or biblical and literary criticism? Legends, much more than historical or archaeological evidence, have exercised a great power over the minds of people. Towards the end of his life, the great poet Johann Wolfgang von Goethe witnessed the emergence of a new historical criticism, particularly in classical and biblical studies. As a poet, he felt that humanity was being impoverished by these harping critics, who 'through some pedantic truth displace something great which is of superior value to us'.[22] Goethe was disconcerted by the work of scholars such as Berthold Georg Niebuhr, who challenged the veracity of the Roman narratives on Mucius Scaevola and Lucretia. Goethe exclaimed: 'If the Romans were great enough to invent such stories, we should at least be sufficiently great to believe them.'[23] To discard a Roman legend is hard enough; when a legend appears as a religious belief, its rejection may be considered a sin by pious Christians and Jews.[24] Legends and miracles have the additional virtue of facilitating the harmonisation of obvious contradictions in the biblical sources that defy purely rational explanations. Real history, on the other hand, is messy.

Writers who follow the conquest model have a one-dimensional view of Israel's history, and have produced an argument that is reductionist. Complex problems such as those involved in the emergence and transformation of Israel often need centuries to work out. Only recently has it become possible to sketch a broad overview of the settlement patterns and social relations from the third millennium BCE onwards in Palestine, or to synthesise the vast archaeological literature that exists on the subject. To think it can be explained away with a few battle descriptions and spy stories is naïve.[25]

In the next part we turn to a time period when both the invention of history by the Greeks and other sources about Israel are available. The story of Israel's unbroken string of victories will end in the age when wars are no longer guided by a divine hand, and writers with no theological agenda write about Israel's wars, their military defeats and their intelligence operations.

Part II

CHAPTER 6

The Jews Against Rome

VICTORY UNDER THE MACCABEES remained in the memory and celebrations of the Jews.[1] Their hard-won independence, however, was lost in 6 CE when the Romans declared Judaea a procuratorial province.[2] A rebellion broke out led by Judas of Galilee and Zadok the Pharisee. Although the Romans crushed the rebellion decisively, the insurrection went underground and continued until 66 CE, when a full-scale rebellion broke out.[3] The collaborationist historian Josephus would suggest that the Great Jewish War was shallowly rooted, unnecessary and criminal, but in fact all levels of society participated, from the aristocracy downwards. The Jews had the same motivations in this war as they had in all their other wars: territorial sovereignty, financial independence, and political and religious freedom.[4] Social, economic, nationalistic and religious factors plus the abrasive government of various Roman procurators all played a part in causing the struggle; no one factor was supreme.

In these struggles for independence, the Jews, deprived of their national army, were forced once again to resort to guerrilla operations and terrorist activities. Why had the Jews become so desperate? Was Roman rule that bad? Was it worse than in other occupied provinces?[5] Was there a movement that could be labelled 'Jewish nationalists' or were these groups just made up of religious fanatics?[6] What drives a province to take on an emperor with twenty-five legions? Since no rebellion is truly spontaneous, there must have been political and social reasons for this unrest. Mass discontent and dissatisfaction usually exist before leadership and a movement emerge.[7] The pre-war period shows a progressive deterioration of the relationship between the various Jewish groups and the Romans. Relative peace and co-operation disappeared as a breakdown of law and order in the countryside occurred, as well as disorder in Jerusalem. The Jews suffered from many of the ills displayed by native populations under foreign occupation. They were overtaxed and lost their land as more areas were incorporated into the large estates of the upper classes.[8] There was enforced urbanisation and a disintegration of village life and their native élite, as well as exploitation, agricultural dispossession, mounting debt by the landless, and the recognition that their ruling class was getting richer but were unconcerned with the fate of the vast majority of the Judaean population. These rich Jews were simply well-fed collaborators. Successive messianic prophets promised apocalyptic deliverance, while a radicalisation of a critical mass of the population caused new revolutionary groups to be formed.[9] What made the Jewish élite begin the war is also a complicated issue, but it seems that they were not able to control this rising tide of Jewish unrest, and eventually the upper class was forced to throw in its lot with the people.[10]

Terror Before the Revolution

There were many different revolutionary activities running concurrently between the Roman takeover of Judaea in 6 CE and the Great Revolt of 66 CE. Indeed the descendants of Judas and Zadok of Galilee, who had started the revolution of 6 CE, continued their struggle against Roman oppression. The one underground group that was agitating against Roman rule and Jewish aristocratic collaboration during the 50s CE was the Sicarii . The leaders of this clandestine party were Menachem and Eleazar ben Yair, the grandson and nephew of Judas of Galilee. Josephus called their movement the 'Fourth Philosophy', because he placed this group after the Pharisees, the Sadducees and the Essenes.[11] Their slogan 'No king but God!' made it clear that they were religious Jews who believed anyone who acknowledged Caesar as master was a traitor. Judas and his followers attacked the Romans and any Jews who supported or co-operated with Roman rule.[12]

The Sicarii are well documented; they are mentioned in fifteen passages in Josephus' *Jewish Wars* and in his *Antiquities*.[13] He calls them Sicarii after their favourite weapon – the Roman dagger or *sica*. These men were assassins who carried daggers under their garments for purposes of assassination. Unable to engage in open warfare with either the Romans or the Jewish ruling class, these 'dagger-men' resorted to terrorism and assassination to get rid of their opponents. Their three-fold programme included kidnapping, assassination of key collaborators, and plundering or destruction of the property of wealthy and powerful Jews, all of which required timely and accurate intelligence gathering. These acts of terrorism were the natural weapons of insurgents, and such techniques depended on maintaining secrecy. Their approach was particularly well suited to the struggles of an occupied people, since the normal means of military action were closed to the Jews.

The Sicarii were an urban phenomenon. They operated in the heart of the holy city of Jerusalem, even in the Temple. They moved in public places and in broad daylight, yet their identities were unknown. No one knew who the assassins were, and they could lead normal public lives in the city. The Sicarii may have numbered in the hundreds, or even a couple of thousand at most, but hardly more. Their security was excellent and thus we do not know their identities. Historians, generally speaking, only get to know about such secret operations when someone's cover is blown in a particularly spectacular way. Such terrorist bands depend on tight security, because as their numbers increase so does the difficulty of maintaining secrecy. All we know is that their leadership had a political consciousness, and their likely membership was probably the intelligentsia of Jerusalem.[14] Although the Sicarii may have been concerned about social justice for the common people, as a group they seldom provided any genuine popular leadership for a mass movement. This is consistent with their being a small conspiratorial group that lacked a power base among the people.

Their weapon – discriminate terrorism – was more politically symbolic and oriented towards gaining allies rather than defeating the Romans. Although we have no direct evidence, the Sicarii may have been motivated primarily by the calculation that they could provoke counterterror from the Romans and gain more allies from victims of the resulting government repression.[15] There is no doubt, however, that the terrorist strategy of the Sicarii helped precipitate the revolt of 66 CE. It certainly created a strained atmosphere in Jerusalem. For leading men of the ruling class, death in a crowded public place was an immediate, daily danger.[16]

Zealots, Bandits and the Urban Mob

Another group formed during the revolt were the men Josephus called 'Zealots'. There has been much confusion over the term since popular writers and even older scholarly works often use the term 'Zealot' for lumping together all anti-Roman forces as if they were one united party.[17] This approach has fallen out of favour in more recent scholarly literature that seeks to define more clearly who the participants in the revolution were.[18]

Zealot as the name of a party occurs fifty-one times in Josephus' *Jewish Wars*.[19] He used the term Zealots for the aristocratic party established by Eleazar ben Simon after a provisional government had been established in Jerusalem following the first Jewish victory over the Romans.[20] This was the party that stopped the sacrifices to Rome and thus began the revolution. According to the traditional view, this party drew in peasants fleeing to Jerusalem as the Romans swept south from Galilee. The Zealots were thus a religious group of pious Jews led by the priestly party in Jerusalem, who championed the cause of the common people.

More recently, R. A. Horsley and J. S. Hanson suggested that the Zealots rose from the common people, and saw them as separate from the priestly party. They believed that the Zealots were groups of social bandits as defined by E. J. Hobsbawm, in his book *Primitive Rebels*.[21] This kind of banditry is a rural phenomenon and endemic to peasant societies; it is a consequence of economic stress and social dislocation.[22] These bandits lived by robbing the well-to-do, that is, merchants, government officials or landlords. They depend on the goodwill and protection of local peasants, and although they practised armed robbery for a livelihood they usually did not commit murder unless forced into a fight. Such bandits were well known to the peasants and officials who attempted to capture or kill them. For this reason they retreated to hideaways after striking. Some believe Josephus' descriptions of *lestai* (bandits from the Roman period) fit this basic pattern.[23] Many Jewish brigands were anti-Roman because they hated tax collectors and landlords supported by Rome, but most were not ideologically motivated at all. Like the word 'terrorist' in contemporary political vocabulary, 'bandit' is a relative term. One man's terrorist or bandit is another man's 'freedom fighter' or 'hero'. Those whom the Romans denounce as bandits included real malefactors as well as a few real revolutionaries.[24] Their goal was to make money, and they did not care much whether travellers and villagers whom they robbed were Jews or Romans.[25]

If such banditry escalates in scope and focuses more deliberately on a political goal it can evolve into guerrilla warfare. The banditlike warfare that Josephus describes and the popular messianic rebellions that broke out at the death of Herod in 4 BCE show the similarity in tactics between bandits and guerrillas.[26] Brigandage increased significantly in the countryside after Agrippa's death in 44 CE, and this sort of activity formed another facet in the social background for the revolt. Between 52 and 56 CE, a Roman veteran colony was planted at Acco-Ptolemais and a military road was constructed from the Syrian capital to the new colony. Josephus does not say that this was in anticipation of new troubles, but these Roman moves were obviously a security measure.[27] Banditry became epidemic in the years of unrest preceding the war, and once war broke out many bandit groups joined the revolutionary cause.[28]

In Horsley and Hanson's view, the Zealots were not a religious sect or a philosophy that advocated violent resistance to Roman rule. They were not the intelligentsia who championed the common people. The Zealots *were* the common people, who, when they became victims of Roman violence, took what may have been the only course of action available to them in their circumstances. Because they were from villages in northwest Judaea, they formed guerrilla groups in the countryside when the Roman reconquest of the country made their traditional way of life impossible. Then, as the Romans advanced, they fled to Jerusalem, formed a coalition and called themselves Zealots. They were a relatively small, but highly militant and effective party that played an important and determined role in the defence of the city, and was finally involved in its destruction.[29]

There is one other group agitating that the Horsley and Hanson hypothesis does not take into account. These are the urban rebels who were an important element in the pre-war activity in Jerusalem. These were the mobs aroused by Florus' raid on the Temple treasury in 66. T. L. Donaldson has described them as first among the supporters of Ananus, who resisted the Zealot takeover, but later as a group that found the priests too moderate and became a rebel faction. He traces their history throughout the war.[30]

There will probably never be total agreement among scholars on the exact nature of each group since we have no evidence outside that of Josephus. His upper-class mentality and apologetic *tendenz* make him a biased source on the interests and activities of the common people.[31] We know there were many anti-Roman groups agitating, but these bands were often too fluid and unorganised for there to be any history to trace.[32] We also recognise that the factions did not always co-operate with each other. Josephus certainly knew that the Zealots were a totally different group from the Sicarii. They were involved at different times and in different places during the Jewish Revolt.[33] As Jonathan Price points out, the war was fought by a wide variety of groups or parties whose animosity for one another often surpassed their collective animosity for the Romans.[34]

The Outbreak

The sharply repressive measures taken by the Roman procurators against terrorists, brigands and the urban mob simply bred more terrorist acts. The Sicarii helped to create an extremely unsettled situation ripe for more widespread popular rebellion. The chief priest collected a bodyguard around himself like private storm troopers, and this only egged on the assassins. The high priestly families and leftover scions of the royal family argued among themselves and quarrelled with their Roman overlords. Under the procurator Gessius Florus (64–66 CE), everything got speedily worse. When taxpayers fell into arrears, Florus raided the Temple treasury demanding 102,000 denarii 'for Caesar's needs'. He marched on Jerusalem with an army, determined to impose his will on this increasingly disorderly province. Instead of bringing the city to heel, he sparked a riot and a revolution. The urban mob foiled Florus' attempt to reinforce the small garrison in the Antonia fortress, which dominated the Temple. The Jews filled the narrow streets and blocked them off with improvised barricades, then lined the roof tops from which they hurled spears, stones and tiles. The Roman commanders quickly abandoned their attempt to march through the city, and pulled back into the palace on the western hill. Florus was massively outnumbered by the crowds of angry Jews, and made no second attempt to reach the Antonia fortress. He left a token force of five hundred men as a symbol of imperial power, and left the city.

Open hostilities commenced in the summer of 66 CE. Eleazar, second in command to the high priest himself, proclaimed that sacrifices at the Temple would no longer be accepted from any foreigner. This meant the twice-daily offerings to Rome and the emperor would be discontinued. In Rome's eyes, Eleazar's announcement was an act of rebellion. Menachem and the Sicarii allied themselves with the priestly revolutionary party, and for one brief moment at the beginning of the war the diverse and antagonistic elements within the Jewish population came together. It would not last long. Menachem made a spectacular arrival into Jerusalem like a messianic king and attempted to take control of the capital. He accepted the surrender of the Jewish soldiers of Agrippa II in his palace, while the Roman cohort retreated into the strong tower of Herod's palace.[35] In an act that permanently split the leadership, however, Menachem murdered Eleazar's father, the high priest Ananias. Eleazar responded by attacking Menachem in the Temple, where he murdered him and most of his men.[36] Eleazar allowed the Romans to move out of the towers under promise of safe conduct, but he later broke his promise and slaughtered all but the commander.[37] Menachem's surviving men took refuge on Masada, where they did little of importance for the rest of the war until the site was taken by the Romans in 73 CE [38]

The absence of a unified Jewish leadership is obvious from the beginning, and the revolt had little planning, co-ordination or shared intelligence. Although many groups resented Roman rule, the aristocratic party felt it had as much to fear from the more revolutionary elements targeting the upper classes as they did from the Romans. The removal of Menachem at this critical juncture, however, had disastrous consequences for the resistance movement. The influx of Zealots into Jerusalem blocked the mediating strategy of the priests, who

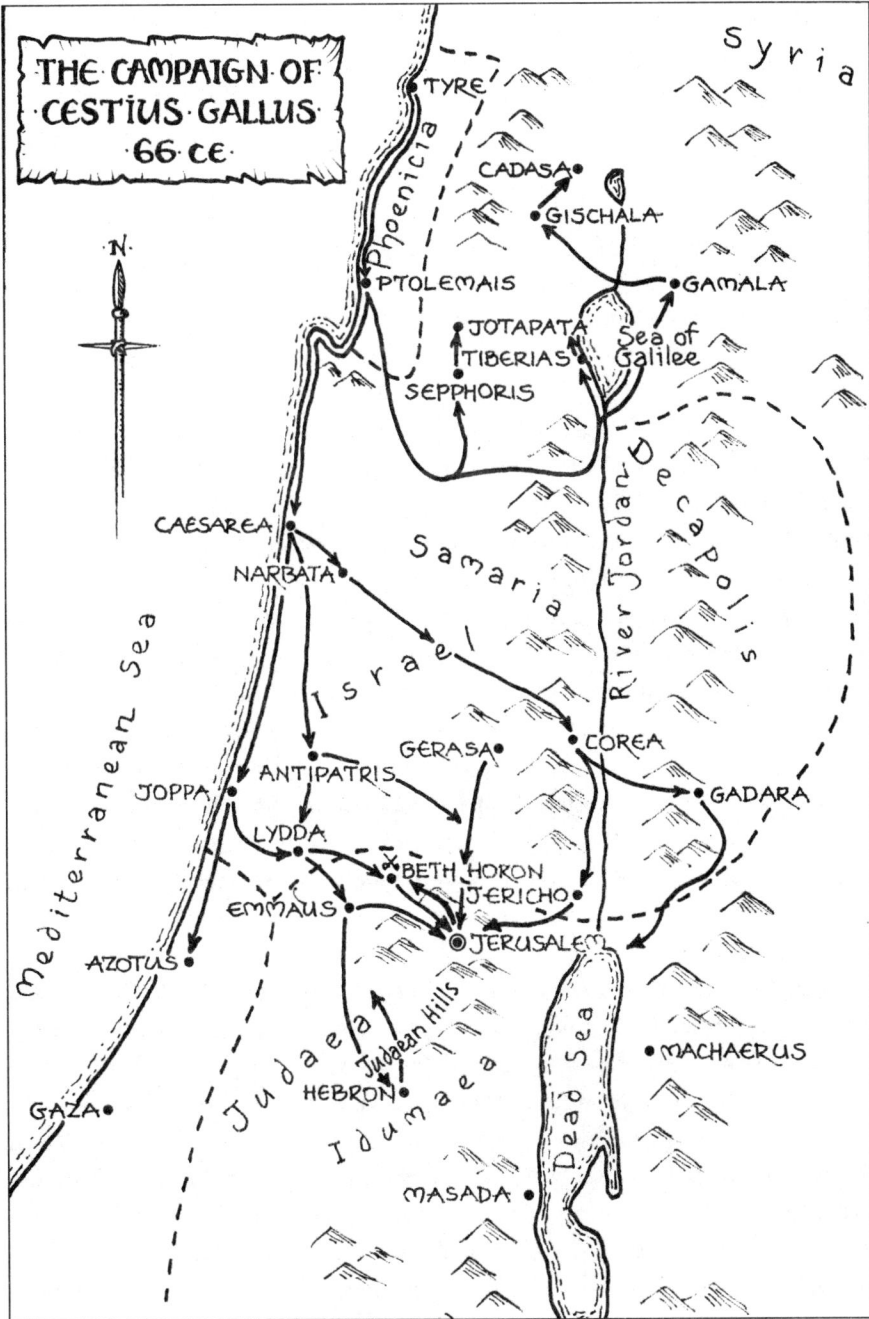

Map 6 *The campaign of Cestius Gallus 66* CE

sought a negotiated end to hostilities with the Romans. Instead of combining their forces under a unified command, the leaders of the various groups competed for power, which created only confusion and dissipated their strength. It also meant that there was no one group collecting and analysing intelligence against the Romans.

The Romans on the Defensive

When the procurator Florus realised that the revolt was beyond the control of his own forces, he reported to his immediate superior, Cestius Gallus, governor of Syria, who commanded a legionary army. A Roman military tribune named Neopolitanus was sent by Cestius to assess the situation and report back. We do not know what intelligence he brought, but Cestius' response was to lead a force himself and put down this provincial uprising before it developed into a major war.[39] Fortunately for the revolutionaries, the Roman response was not swift. Cestius took almost three months from the outbreak of the revolt to concentrate his forces for a punitive expedition to Judaea.[40] In the autumn of 66 CE, he moved south with an army of thirty thousand.[41] Although the composition of the expeditionary force was largely routine, auxiliary troops were added for special operations. If Cestius had advanced information, he would have known that the special character of the Judaean terrain, along with the guerrilla tactics of his opponent, necessitated augmenting the infantry with specialised units.[42] Archers were the best defence against weapons like the sling, the javelin and the bow, and thus a large contingent of archers, both foot and mounted, were supplied by local allies.[43] If Cestius had any intelligence on the size and location of the Jewish forces, he would have discovered that, apart from a few thousand organised rebels spread in many bands over Judaea, there existed no regular military forces in the entire province.[44] This may explain why the Jews missed so many opportunities to hinder the movement of the Roman army by ambushes and surprise attacks before they reached Jerusalem.

Cestius' advance through Galilee and Samaria was almost unopposed – evidently the Jewish rebels had been unable to arrange even for the fortification of towns north of Jerusalem. The army burned and destroyed its way down the coastal road before swinging east to the capital. The devastation of the Jewish settlements along the Roman line of advance was a deliberate policy designed to frighten the population into submission and to ensure that enemy activity in the rear and along the lines of communication did not have a supportive civilian base.[45]

After subduing Galilee, Cestius took the main road from the coastal plain to Jerusalem. After passing the Beth Horon ascent, he advanced into the mountains as far as Gabao, about ten kilometres from Jerusalem, where he encamped overnight.[46] Cestius had had no serious encounters yet, and since he probably considered the Jews incompetent he was careless. The next day, in order to speed his advance, he departed from the customary order of march. Instead of keeping his baggage train well in the middle of the marching column, he allowed it to move separately, many hours behind the main body.[47] Standard reconnaissance procedures seem to have been ignored; there is no mention of flank guards or securing the defiles and high ground that commanded the road by appropriate advance detachments and screening forces.[48] He would pay dearly for his mistakes.

Battle in the Upper Beth Horon

The Jews, meanwhile, did their own reconnaissance on the hills that bordered the road from Gabao to Jerusalem. Undetected by the enemy, they lay in wait for the advancing columns. According to Josephus, they attacked the Romans just as the legions were deploying from marching columns into battle formations, and before these were consolidated.[49] Advanced intelligence and surprise attack were the Jews' most effective strategies. The vanguard of the Roman force was attacked near Gabao, while, in the rear, most of the baggage and beasts were captured by Simon bar Giora during the ascent via the Beth Horon road. This is the first we hear of this revolutionary leader, who will become important later in the war. The distance of eight to nine kilometres between Upper Beth Horon and the neighbourhood of Gabao accords more or less with the length of a Roman marching line and indicates that the attack was launched simultaneously at Gabao and Upper Beth Horon.[50] The Roman losses were far greater than those of the Jews: 515 against 22.[51] They also lost many of their baggage mules – a loss that affected later developments. The Romans were saved from total destruction largely because the Jewish attack lacked a high level of co-ordination and because of their own high standard of battle drill. The forward columns, which had not been particularly heavily engaged, managed to disentangle themselves and wheel around to relieve the main body. Cestius then retreated to his camp at Gabao.

Cestius knew he could not continue without proper logistical support, and so he broke camp and moved towards Jerusalem, setting up a new camp on Mount Scopus. Four days later he invaded the outlying parts of Jerusalem and started a siege of the Upper City and the Temple. The arrival of the Romans brought together the feuding Jewish factions long enough to mount a common defence of the Holy City. Then a puzzling thing happened: Cestius lifted the siege after only six days. Even now historians have no idea why.[52] He may have circled about the city, assessed the number and intensity of the defenders, and decided to go back for more troops and heavy siege machinery. His intelligence perhaps told him that there would be no quick victory, and that the coming rains would slow his supply wagons. There may also have been logistical difficulties. Almost two weeks had elapsed since the ambush at Beth Horon, and the large Roman army certainly suffered from a shortage of supplies by this time. Much of their baggage had been captured by Simon bar Giora, and each legionary carried only three day's rations.[53] The early loss of baggage, heavy Jewish resistance and the lack of agriculture in the area must have made it imperative for Cestius to withdraw almost immediately.

While the bulk of the army retreated back to the camp at Mount Scopus, where it spent the night, the Jews used this time to occupy the hills between Scopus and Gabao. There seems to have been no Roman attempt to secure the road, and thus Jewish guerrillas harassed the Roman army the next day. The army finally reached Gabao with difficulty, with further loss of its baggage and many casualties among whom were senior officers.[54] Cestius decided to give his men a two-day rest at Gabao. Unfortunately, this also gave the Jews additional time to occupy the passes at Beth Horon. News of the previous successes spread and brought out more Jews from the countryside to join in the attack.[55]

Battle of Gabao

Did the Romans use the two-day respite at Gabao to reconnoitre the Jewish blocking positions and find an alternative route?[56] Evidently not, because Cestius led his men back into another ambush. The exact location of the ambush is uncertain; he may actually have been trying to take an alternate route to avoid Jewish guerrilla action. If this was his intention, the plan did not work. The legions once again did not perform their basic reconnaissance duty by sending a detachment to the hills commanding the road, in order to secure their line of march. Crossing such terrain is always a gamble, but, having been ambushed there once before, the Romans might have been a bit more cautious. The Roman army was ambushed by a large and determined force of Judaean insurgents.[57] While one group of Jews went ahead and barred their egress, another drove the rearguard down into the ravine. The main body of the Jews lined the heights above the narrowest part of the route and bombarded the Romans with arrows. The Roman cavalry was especially vulnerable and could not charge up or down the slopes to pursue the enemy. Roman catapults captured in previous battles were now used against the Romans. The Roman commander had to sacrifice his rearguard, abandon his heavy equipment to extricate the rest of his forces and struggle back to Syria. Weapons, money chests and many war machines fell to the rebels. Cestius had lost six thousand more men.[57]

The Jewish military victory over the Twelfth Legion gave new hope to the extremist cause in Jerusalem, and much of Judaea and Galilee were now leaning towards revolution.[59] The Jews had won the battle at a relatively small cost. Many pacifists and collaborators were driven out of the capital. The Jewish rebels, through tenacity, surprise attack and other guerrilla tactics, had defeated a Roman legion and its powerful support elements. But the Romans were not about to let go of Palestine – their vital strategic link between the rich provinces of Syria and Egypt. Many Jews still believed a war with Rome was suicidal and counselled so. When news of the defeat reached Nero, he did not choose a nego-tiated settlement with the rebels. The emperor appointed a veteran commander, Vespasian, to prepare a new campaign. In 67 CE, Vespasian was dispatched with sixty thousand men; he was joined by his son Titus, who marched a legion from Alexandria.[60] Nero believed it was the carelessness of his commanders rather than bravery of the enemy that was responsible for the disaster.[61] No guerrilla army, no matter how well trained, could hold out against his legions for long.

The Campaign in Galilee

While awaiting the second Roman invasion, the Jewish priestly revolutionary party organised its government and prepared a defence. It assigned commanders to each district of the country; most of those commissioned were not military men but priests. Their task was to prepare the country for war in anticipation of negotiations with, or hostilities against, the Romans. The best-known general was Josephus, the historian, who was sent to Galilee.[62]

The campaign in Galilee demonstrates Jewish tenacity, the clever use of stratagems and many deceptive tactics and guerrilla operations. It also illus-trates the main weakness of the Jewish plan: any battle with Romans from a fixed position was little more than suicide. Josephus spent six months feuding with local leaders, while trying to discipline a fractious population that had lit-tle desire to fight. He fortified key locations, raised and trained an army, brought local brigands under his command, and intimidated towns in the district to fight on the Jewish side. Josephus had no military or administrative experience, nor was he temperamentally suited to co-operative leadership, and his ultimate failure was predictable, because the Jews in Galilee tried to fight the Romans using conventional tactics from behind city walls.[63]

The Roman army appeared in summer 67 CE. Vespasian quickly secured the Galilean plain; the fortress at Jotapata was the only stronghold that gave the Romans any trouble.[64] The Jews used all the ruses of guerrilla warfare to fight back against the Roman siege. They made sallies every day while pillaging whatever fell in their way and burning the rest.[65] They attempted to deceive the Roman generals as to the scarcity of water in the city by hanging their clothes dripping wet over the battlements.[66] They procured supplies of food by sending men out at night camouflaged in dog's hides who then crawled on all fours through an unguarded ravine.[67] They broke the force of the battering ram by throwing out bags filled with chaff over the gates.[68] They threw boiling oil on Roman soldiers,[69] and boiling fenugreek on the boards of the scaling ladders to make them slippery.[70] But Roman siege tactics could not be resisted for long. One morning a deserter told the Romans that the exhausted guards were asleep. The Romans made good use of this intelligence. Titus led a commando unit which scaled the wall, dispatched the watchmen and opened the city for the waiting cohorts. The fortress was overpowered, with many civilians killed or enslaved. The fortified hilltop town had held out for almost seven weeks before capture by Roman assault. A surprise counterattack even wounded Vespasian.[71] The siege, while a display of ingenuity by Jewish fighters, also showed the utter hopelessness of their tactics against a conventional force. Josephus surrendered rather than commit suicide, and when brought to Vespasian he predicted that the general would be emperor of Rome.

Only three strategic centres were left to rebels in northern Israel: Gischala and Mount Tabor in Galilee and the precipitous fortress town of Gamala in the Golan.[72] The Romans first attacked Gamala, by storming the walls and forcing an entrance into the city. They encountered such bitter resistance that they were compelled to retire with very heavy losses. They forced their way in a second time and succeeded. More legionaries lost their lives to rocks hurled and boulders loosened by the defenders of the city than to sword or arrow wounds. The Jews tricked the Romans into chasing them on rooftops that were primed to collapse,[73] but the Romans countered with a ruse of their own that drew defenders into a tower that they had secretly undermined.[74] Once Gamala was taken, Mount Tabor fell to the detachment sent there,[75] and Titus took Gischala with a detachment of a thousand cavalry.[76] The rebel leader, John of Gischala, eluded Titus' deadly net and escaped to Jerusalem, where he continued the rebellion.

Jewish Factionalism

Bitter factional quarrels in Jerusalem made it almost impossible for the Jews to organise a vigorous resistance. The priestly aristocratic party was devastated politically by the ineptness of its military efforts in Galilee.[77] Its major leaders were murdered or executed in treason trials, and the Jews were left with no leadership strong enough to negotiate with the Romans. The extremists seemed to be in complete control of Jerusalem. John of Gischala arrived there in autumn 67 CE, supported by a contingent of Galileans, and he tried to take command. He turned on the Zealots, ousted their leader and brought them under his control. As allies, he enlisted the Jews of Idumaea and initiated a reign of terror that purged the city of many factions opposed to the revolution or those they deemed not Jewish enough. An even more revolutionary faction then emerged led by Simon bar Giora, a native of Gerasa in Trans-jordan. His radical social programme drew much support from freed slaves. Simon had taken advantage of the cessation of hostilities to gather around himself a crowd of supporters with whom he overran the southern parts of Palestine, robbing and plundering wherever he went.[78]

The Romans allowed the Jews in the capital to wear themselves out trying to kill one other while they reconquered territory as close as Jericho. After a winter break, Vespasian resumed operations in spring 68 CE, and by early summer he had pacified the entire countryside. Only Jerusalem and some of the isolated fortresses, such as Machaerus and Masada, remained in the hands of the rebels. Everything seemed set for an immediate attack on the capital, but in June 68 Vespasian learned of Nero's assassination. The death of this emperor meant that Vespasian's commission as general had expired, and accordingly he discontinued his military activities. He obtained his recognition as emperor from the Senate and the troops in the West in December 69, and he entered Rome in early 70 CE. He left his son Titus to finish the Jewish campaign.

If the second half of 69 CE was one of great turmoil and anarchy in Jerusalem, it was equally chaotic in Rome. While the throne of Rome remained disputed, the Jews might have made diplomatic overtures to save both Jerusalem and the Temple. Vespasian may have welcomed such a compromise, which would have spared him a costly war, although whether he would have granted Judaea any sovereignty is another matter. The tragedy is that Judaea was simply without proper leadership. The factions within the Judaean people busily fought each other on behalf of their ideologies, and there was nobody in Jerusalem who could exert sufficient influence to unite the people for the good of their country. If the

Jews sincerely believed they had any chance of defeating the Romans militarily, they should have taken advantage of the situation in Rome during the civil war between Nero's death and Vespasian's accession. Instead, many of them deserted to the Romans and brought the enemy needed intelligence about the factionalism in Jerusalem.[79] They did not even harass Roman troops with more guerrilla actions. The leaders just sat in Jerusalem waiting for Titus' attack. Simon bar Giora controlled the upper city and a great part of the lower city; John of Gischala held the Temple Mount, and Eleazar and the Zealots held the Inner Court of the Temple. John tried to stir up Parthia against Rome and to get help from the Babylonian Jews while he prepared supplies and fortified against the inevitable Roman invasion. Sadly the rival bands burnt each other's precious food supplies and greatly diminished their chances of survival against the impending Roman threat. So much grain and provisions were destroyed in this fighting that when the Roman siege began in earnest in 70 CE a famine soon broke out.[80]

The Siege

The siege of Jerusalem illustrates the relentless quality of Roman engineering warfare, and the futility of Jewish tactics. The Jews fought well; they used their guerrilla tactics wisely and effectively and their use of intelligence was superb. They succeeded in impressing even the Romans with their tenacity, but they did not succeed in defeating them.

In spring 70 CE Titus assembled his full army to march against Jerusalem. In all he had about sixty thousand cavalry and infantry, while the Judaeans had a combined force of about 23,400 men.[81] Jewish guerrilla operations began immediately. While the Tenth Legion prepared its camp on the slope of the Mount of Olives, the Jews launched a surprise attack that nearly routed the entire legion. It was only through Titus' personal intervention that the legion was brought to stand its ground and repulse the attack.[82] Another group of Judaeans burst from the Women's Gate, pretending to flee and asking for peace. The Roman believed these people were surrendering and fleeing from their leaders, and the Romans advanced to rescue them. But when the Romans reached the gateway between the towers, they were surrounded and attacked by the supposed 'refugees'. The defenders in the nearby towers pelted the Romans with stones and other missiles. When the Romans retreated, the Judaeans pursued them northwards as far as the tomb of Queen Helena.[83]

Jerusalem was fortified by three walls which were breached by the Romans in turn. After reprimanding his men for being taken in by Jewish tricks, Titus

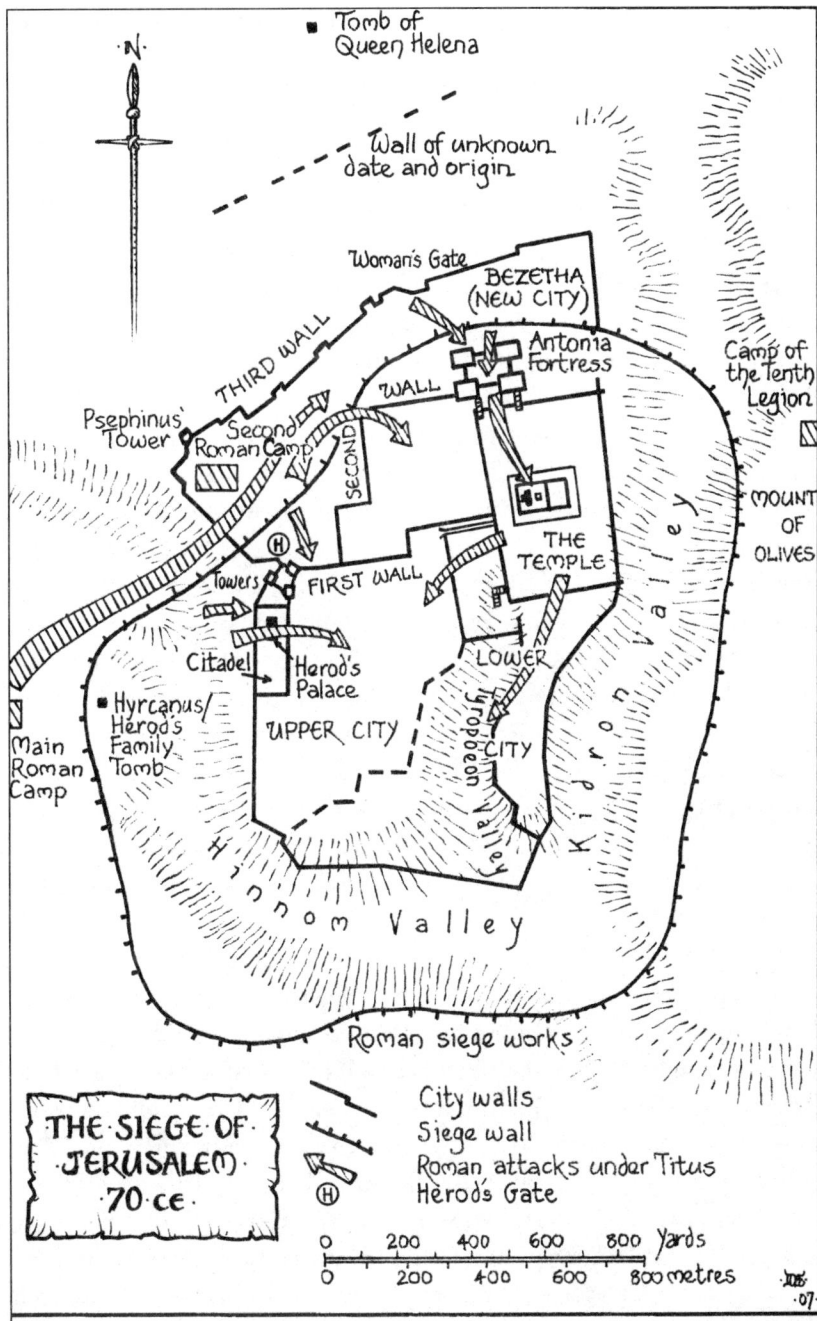

Tomb of
Queen Helena

·N·

Wall of unknown
date and origin

Woman's Gate

BEZETHA
(NEW CITY)

THIRD WALL

WALL

Antonia
Fortress

Camp of
the Tenth
Legion

Psephinus'
Tower

Second
Roman Camp

SECOND

MOUNT
OF
OLIVES

Towers

FIRST WALL

THE
TEMPLE

H

Citadel

Herod's
Palace

LOWER

Hyrcanus/
Herod's
Family
Tomb

UPPER CITY

CITY

Main
Roman
Camp

Tyropoeon Valley

Kidron Valley

H i n n o m   V a l l e y

Roman siege works

THE·SIEGE·OF·
JERUSALEM·
·70·CE·

City walls
Siege wall
Roman attacks under Titus
Herod's Gate

0   200   400   600   800 Yards
0   200   400   600   800 metres

Map 7 *The siege of Jerusalem 70 CE*

began his siege of the third or outermost wall. The Jews attacked the Roman siegeworks with firebrands, and in this battle many on both sides were killed. Although Jewish audacity frequently outstripped Roman discipline, on the fifteenth day of the siege, 25 May, the battering rams broke through the third wall.[84] Titus now shifted his camp to a site within the third wall, to the so-called Assyrian Camp. He kept far enough back from the second wall to be out of range for the bowmen posted there. Five days after capturing the third wall, and despite fierce Judaean resistance, the Romans stormed the second wall on 30 May. Josephus says: 'No form of warfare was omitted.'[85] The Jews lured unsuspecting Romans into traps; they staged quick, fierce raids and charges, ambushed Romans and bombarded them with missiles.

Titus, with one thousand picked men, entered the New City. The Judaeans manning the second wall were forced to flee, and many Roman soldiers burst into the city through the break in this wall. The Romans encountered strong resistance inside. The Judaeans counterattacked from the upper gates as well as from the rooftops, and the Romans, confused by the maze of narrow streets and alleys, lost their bearing and were unable to find their way back to the second wall. Thus, although the Romans had temporarily gained possession of the second wall, the Jews eventually ejected them from it. The Judaeans considered this a great victory.[86] The Romans once again attempted to pour through the breach in the second wall, but the Judaeans blocked it and held the enemy at bay for three days. On the fourth day, however, the Romans succeeded in pushing the defenders back and regained permanent mastery of the second wall. They immediately razed the northern portion of the wall and laid plans for an assault on the first wall.

By mid-June the Romans launched an all-out attack on the towers north of Herod's palace and the fortress of Antonia. After seventeen days the Romans completed their earthworks and had their war engines poised to attack. John of Gischala bought the Jewish defenders more time by digging a tunnel out of the Antonia beneath the siegeworks and reinforcing it with wooden supports. He piled up firewood smeared with pitch in the tunnel, and set it on fire. When the wooden props were consumed, the tunnel collapsed and the Roman ramparts were burned up.[87] Two days later Simon bar Giora attacked the other siegeworks near the tomb of John Hyrcanus. He set fire to them and the battering rams, and also attacked the Romans. The Romans were amazed at the audacity and ingenuity of the Judaeans. They were appropriately depressed that all their labour had gone for nothing, and some even doubted an ability to take the town by siege. Some Romans even deserted to the Jewish side. Despite a food shortage in the city, the deserters were well received and amply fed.[88]

Before reconstructing new ramparts, Titus resorted to another device. He ringed the whole city with a stone wall to starve out the defenders. This was the only way to guard every exit, and not be exposed to sallies. The walls also put the Romans on even ground with the defenders in the upper city and in the Antonia tower. This task was completed in three days, and produced quick results. Much food had been destroyed during the internecine strife among the Jewish factions, and the new wall around the city now prevented any Jews from counterattacking or smuggling in food. The starving defenders lacked the strength to mount a counteroffensive or to destroy the new earthworks.[89]

Titus then built new ramparts. Because of the complete devastation of the surrounding district, the timber had to be brought from some distance away. The ramparts were completed in twenty-one days, and the relentless battering started. The wall was breached, and a storming operation began. The Romans brought up enough men to withstand any counterattack on their forward position, and they took the New City. Both sides dug in for the battle for the heart of the city. The defence of Jerusalem rested on the strength of this last wall and on Jewish success in close combat. John of Gischala's men took up the defence of the Temple area, while Simon bar Giora's forces manned the lines at the upper city.[90] The Romans renewed their assault towards the end of July. Simon bar Giora held fast, but the fortress of Antonia was taken and razed.

By midsummer of 70 CE, the Romans were just outside the sacred precinct walls. Earthworks were built by two legions, and in August their onslaught began. The battering rams were brought up outside the western hall of the outer court of the Temple. After six days of incessant battering of the wall, Titus realised that he would be unable to capture the Temple by frontal attack. Instead he had his troops set fire to the Temple gates. Titus let it burn for a day, then had the fire put out, and called a meeting to decide the fate of the Temple. Some of his adjutants argued that the Temple should be demolished; as long as it stood it would serve as a focal point for anti-Roman agitation. The rule of war in antiquity required that temples not be molested, but this temple had become a fortress. It was therefore a legitimate military target. On the following day, the tenth of the month of Ab, a Roman soldier acting against orders, tossed a torch into the sanctuary.[91] Flames shot up, raged out of control and destroyed the Temple. While the Temple was still ablaze, the Romans slaughtered all who fell into their hands: women and children, priests and commoners, young and old. John of Gischala and his men managed to escape into the upper city. The Temple had not yet burnt out before the legions set up their standards in the outer court, and hailed Titus as *imperator*.

After another month, the Romans captured the Upper City and Herod's Palace; only then did resistance cease. With great jubilation the Romans raised their standards in token of victory, and proceeded to plunder houses, and to slaughter everyone they met in the streets. At dawn on 26 September they set fire to the Upper City. By decree of Titus, all the people of Jerusalem were taken captive and its buildings were levelled to the ground. The three towers around which the Tenth Legion had camped were left standing, and the ruins of Jerusalem and its region were placed under the surveillance of this legion.

John and Simon had abandoned the towers, and tried to escape by means of the sewers. When the Romans tore up the ground to ferret them out, they discovered about two thousand corpses. Some had committed suicide or killed each other. Most had died of hunger. John of Gischala was at the point of starvation when found, and he surrendered. Simon, too, had been unable to burrow out of the city, and he surrendered. He was slapped into chains and imprisoned.

On his return to Rome in 71 CE, Titus celebrated a joint triumph with his father Vespasian. The enemy leaders, Simon bar Giora and John of Gischala, were led in the procession; Simon was later beheaded, and John was enslaved.[92] The relatively long siege of Jerusalem and the destruction of the Temple were memorialised on the arch of Titus. From a military perpective the ending could only have been a defeat for the Jews.

Masada

Although Titus' triumph in Rome marked an official end of the war, a few mopping-up operations remained in Judaea. The fortresses of Herodium and Machaerus were besieged and taken by Bassus, the governor of Syria. His successor, Flavius Silva, had the more difficult task of taking Masada. Silva concentrated the Legion X Fretensis and some auxiliaries against Masada for the final blow of the war. Eleazar ben Yair, the Sicarius, kept the attackers at bay for months. The rebel group, including women and children, numbered perhaps a thousand. They had supplies for ten thousand and could hold out if water lasted. Recent archaeological excavations have cast serious doubt on the events of the final stand, but both literary and archaeological sources confirm the magnificence of the site and the difficulty of besieging it.[93] The Romans built a ramp up one side of the plateau and placed a tower up against the wall of the fortress. But what happened thereafter remains conjecture. According to Josephus' account, all the Jews voluntarily died at the hands of ten chosen executioners, one of whom then slew his companions and himself. The dead were 960 in all; two women and five children alone remained alive, hidden in the underground caverns.[94]

Although the Sicarii were effective as terrorists, they never came to the aid of their brethren in Jerusalem during the war. When the Romans laid siege to Jerusalem, the Sicarii could have easily harassed them from the south. There was also no lack of caves from which the Sicarii could have waged guerrilla warfare against the Romans. They regarded an independent Judaean state not based on their own principles no less abhorent than a Judaea subject to Roman rule. The Sicarii, therefore, stood aside while the Romans defeated and crushed the state of Judaea. Nor did they fight at Masada. The Galileans in Gamala, on their part, had fought to the last man, and it took twenty-eight days for the Romans to capture it. If the traditional story about Masada is to be believed, the Sicarii did not kill so much as one Roman soldier. Masada was not captured, but fell to the Romans by an act of mass suicide.

Intelligence Does Not Win the War

The outcome of the revolt was intense brutality, slaughter and the destruction of the Temple. Intelligence was certainly not a deciding factor in a war where brute force was triumphant. There has been an ongoing debate on the cause of the war, and whether it was an accident of circumstance or a planned, communal enterprise.[95] What becomes clear is that the revolt was never a single event from the point of view of Jewish organisation or Roman response.[96] On the Jewish side, no group ever gained enough strength for a long enough time to control the entire state according to its own conception.[97] This is what made intelligence gathering and sharing so difficult. Yet one consistent factor on both sides was that Jewish leaders (united or disunited) needed intelligence about the other side. The war provides many examples of activities that required timely and accurate intelligence; the years preceding the war were filled with terrorist acts. In the years after the outbreak, however, the Jews missed countless opportunities to hinder the movement of the Roman army by ambushes and surprise attacks.[98] Once the outbreak occurred, guerrilla warfare, insurrection, terrorism, surprise, deception and conventional military action all played a part in the hostilities. In fact, groups were often defined in the sources by their choice of method as well as their ideology. These various factions did not result from a split in an originally unified movement. By lumping such groups together, scholars have minimised the differences between them and reduced their divisions to petty factionalism or infighting.[99] By focusing instead on their methods, we see more clearly that each group had its own history, motivation and *modus operandi,* making them unlikely candidates for co-operation. The climax was a full-scale war that culminated in a siege on the Jewish capital.

Rome's enemies had few choices in tactics in their revolts against Roman occupation. There was no state powerful enough to have a standing army anywhere on Rome's borders. Even Rome's most formidable external enemy, the Parthians, had no standing army but raised their forces from the private retinues of prominent nobles.[100] Constant power struggles for the Parthian throne nullified any effort to attack Rome. As internal threat, this left only the many divided ethnic groups around the empire that might aspire to winning independence by taking on the Roman Goliath. Many tried and many failed, but the Jewish Revolt made a lasting impression on the Romans and the Mediterranean world. What made the Jews fight an enemy they could never hope to defeat on an open battlefield? Moreover, what could they could hope to accomplish with the methods they used?

In analysing the Jewish war effort, it first becomes clear that they were waging two wars simultaneously. The outbreak of a revolt for independence from Rome led to a civil war, and for three and a half years these two wars raged side by side.[101] The war was begun with little advance planning, and was run by men such as Josephus, who were priests not trained military commanders.[102] Added to this, the divided loyalties and lack of a unified command did not result in success. Even the Talmud admits that the Second Temple was destroyed because of senseless hatred, and refers to the internecine strife among the Jews themselves.[103] There was no clear, firm leadership, and no direction. The war was a truly spontaneous, emotional outbreak that led to the revolt itself. Although the Jews fought fiercely, they were led into situations that were untenable. The cost was enormous. One-third of the Jewish population perished in this disaster. Josephus estimated that 1,200,000 Jews died during the siege, with 97,000 taken captive.[104]

The most fatal strategic mistake, however, was allowing the revolt to evolve into a siege on the capital. The tactics that worked best in a small war no longer sufficed once the conflict developed into full-scale open combat. The Jews had much more success in the earlier Maccabean Revolt and the later Bar Kokhba Revolt, when they fought as guerrillas not as regular troops. Judas Maccabeus demonstrated his genius as a guerrilla fighter by attacking the Syrian troops whenever he could ambush them. Unlike the Zealots, he did not wait for the enemy to come to Jerusalem. Had the rebels stayed in the Judaean hills and engaged the Romans in guerrilla action, they may have been able to bleed the Romans badly enough to render a negotiated settlement an attractive proposition, as the Germans had done in the Teutoburg Forest. The Sicarii did more damage to the Romans as terrorists and assassins than as field combatants. Very few cities could withstand the relentless attack of Roman siege equipment, or the full onslaught of a Roman legion. The groups that had the most success against Rome were those that did not attempt a head-on assault.[105]

The Jewish War was a contest between professional, well-led troops against a roughly trained and poorly equipped force. The Jews had neither a unified command nor a well-defined strategy of war; part of their hereditary leadership and countrymen either remained passive or collaborated with the enemy.[106] The best the Jews could hope for was a tactical use of guerrilla fighting that struck at the Roman weak points. One such weak point was the size of the Roman army when mobile. The average army on the march stretched between twenty-eight and thirty kilometres. In some cases it is estimated that the foremost troops entered the camp for overnight rest before the last of the troops were able to leave the site of the previous night.[107] This expansiveness became dangerous when it occurred on difficult terrain. Marches offered an opportunity for successful attack, and the Jews very wisely capitalised on this.

The greatest strength of the Roman army was also its greatest weakness. Incessant drill and iron discipline gave the Roman soldiers a sense of self-reliance and security that often betrayed them. Soldiers were taught the immediate and faultless execution of tactical manoeuvres by both the individual and the unit, and their immediate change according to the changing situation on the battlefield.[108] Any deviation from this pattern was discouraged. Even acts of valour, if carried out in excess or in contradiction to orders and regulations, were not only frowned on but also severely punished. Josephus writes: 'Among the Romans even a victory without orders given is held dishonourable.'[109] When suddenly confronted with the unforeseen, Roman troops were apt to lose their wits and panic. The defeat during the first sally on Jerusalem was a typical example: 'Men habituated to discipline and proficient in fighting in ordered ranks and by word of command, when suddenly confronted with disorderly warfare, are peculiarly liable to be thrown into confusion.'[110] When morale and belief in victory were high they succeeded, but troops often became demoralised when somebody changed the rules.

The Romans' overestimation of their own skill could be turned against them. This happened more than once in the Jewish War. At Jotapata the Romans were 'stupefied by their opponents' audacity', and did little to save the siegeworks, having been 'so sure that victory was already in their grasp'.[111] This is also true of the siege of Jerusalem: several examples show Romans suffering from fright and dejection when the battle went against them.[112] This was a tendency on which the Jews could capitalise. Cestius Gallus was routed because unforeseen and unorthodox conditions arose.[113] Even with the best intelligence, however, the Jews were not able to create enough of these situations. Once the Jews barricaded themselves into any fortress, the battle immediately shifted to a situation both familiar and favourable to the Romans.

Another weakness on the Jewish side was their lack of diplomatic support from outside the country. The only power strong enough to threaten the Romans were the Parthians. Yet the Parthians seem to have made no moves towards aligning themselves with the Jews, nor is there any report that they were even contacted. After the fall of Masada, some Sicarii fled to Alexandria, where they sought to rouse their co-religionists to assert their independence, but this was hardly a time to convince anyone to join a hopeless struggle. The Alexandrian Jewish community wished to remain uninvolved. Josephus says that they handed over six hundred of these 'dangerous fanatics' to the Roman authorities; they also tracked down and arrested others who had escaped.[114]

The Jews have been severely criticised by scholars for attempting to oppose Rome.[115] Clausewitz said that war is meant to achieve results.[116] It is not supposed to be waged on impulse, to vent fury or to manifest grievances. It is waged to reach a goal. What could the Jews have expected to achieve by such an ill-planned effort? Their goal was independence, freedom from Roman exploitation, and the right to practise their religion unmolested. Josephus complains that the Jews were led into this conflict by fanatics, when most of the country wanted accommodation with the Romans, but then Josephus was a collaborator himself.

The truth was that the revolutionaries came from diverse groups throughout the population. Even if the war was started by 'zealots' – people who were zealously religious – when the showdown came the whole nation became caught up in the life-and-death struggle between God's people and their enemies. Every patriotic Jew, whether Pharisee, Essene or Zealot, would be called on to give his full measure of service in that holy war, a war that would be characterised by unimaginable bloodshed and suffering.[117]

Jewish history, as recorded in sacred literature, was filled with inspiring models of impossible victories won under divine guidance. The Maccabees had confirmed this pattern set long ago by Joshua and Judges. As a religious war, it was fully expected that the righteous would suffer terrible casualties and and that there would be unprecedented distress and anguish before the final deliverance came. Casualties and suffering were but certain signs of ultimate victory if only Israel would remain faithful to the end. Among some there was certainly the expectation that God himself would intervene directly.[118]

This eschatological framework for the war is the one way we can make sense out of what is known about the closing days of the conflict. The emotional ties which influence people – such as religion and national feeling – were no less powerful in the ancient Near East than they are today in Iran, Iraq, Afghanistan, Bosnia or Armenia.[119] People fight for hearts and minds, not just territory. Passion is a most important element; true believers are (to themselves) indestructible. They must be certain that they will ultimately win in the end. The emperor Titus described the Jews as men 'with desperation as their only leader'.[120] Nor is it a correct assumption that messianic zeal or apocalyptic promises would affect only the less well-educated or underpriviledged fringe groups. The separation of politics and religion is a modern device and of little use in understanding ancient Judaea. The Jewish state, as described by Josephus, was a theocracy.[121] In contrast, the Romans saw themselves as cool rationalists: 'Incautiousness in war and mad impetuosity are alien to us Romans, who owe all our success to skill and discipline; they are a barbarian fault and one to which the Jews mainly owe their defeats.'[122]

More opportune timing might have helped the Jews achieve a limited goal. One objective of terrorism is to make the repression of it so costly that a government prefers to withdraw rather than continue occupation.[123] Had the Jews rebelled a few years earlier, while the Romans were fighting the Parthians, they might have succeeded with guerrilla warfare and extracted concessions from the Romans in return for their surrender. Nor, of course, had the Jews any way of anticipating the considerable advantage they would have had by waiting two years. Had the revolt begun after Nero's assassination in 68 CE, the odds of success would have been immeasurably better. By 69 CE the empire was mired in other events; the succession was vigorously disputed, and Gaul had risen in rebellion. These circumstances would have been much better for a revolt, but for the Jews the opportunity came too late. The Jewish rebellion against Roman *imperium* ended, as did other rebellions against Rome, in failure.

The Jews collected and used intelligence wisely, and employed guerrilla warfare with excellent results. But intelligence and surprise can only be a force multiplier, not a force equaliser.[124] An open conflict between a world power and a small province can only end to the detriment of the latter. The odds were simply too great to be overturned by anything but a miracle. The conflict proved once again the truth of the words written in the Augustan history: never pick a fight with a man who has thirty legions.[125]

CHAPTER 7

The Jesus File

WHAT WERE THE INTELLIGENCE needs in Judaea as seen from the Roman side?[1] Once the Romans had taken over Judaea and turned it into a province, their biggest problem was collecting intelligence about insurgents in order to keep the province peaceful and secure. Although we know Judaea rebelled openly in 66 CE, the period between 6 CE and the outbreak saw many subversive activities. Groups that wished to throw off Roman rule had to be tracked and rooted out.

Rome did not have a unified, centralised intelligence service in the early empire; rather, there were separate intelligence-gathering arms – some political, some military, some private – cobbled together by the emperor to keep himself informed about activities in his vast empire.[2] Most of the organisations Rome would develop were not fully formed until well after the first century CE. Our focus in this chapter is not the empire-wide strategic intelligence needed by the emperor in Rome, but the internal security requirements of one governor, namely Pontius Pilate. Like most Roman administrators, Pilate probably served as his own intelligence chief, and delegated tasks such as building up a spy network. His intelligence staff paid informers, and generally saw to it that Rome had eyes and ears in all places where rebellion might be hatching. How many people Pilate had at his disposal, or who his agents were, we will probably never know. Five serious disturbances happened during his tenure, and all were put down.[3] Such efficiency could not have happened without good intelligence resources.[4]

Spying in Judaea was a dangerous and complicated job. The province had a long history of rebellion against gentile occupation, and Pilate needed sources and information gatherers of many kinds, yet his resources were limited. Apart from his armed forces, he had his office staff (*officium*) but they were probably not very numerous. The regiments he commanded were concentrated in the capital, Caesarea, with a detachment at Jerusalem, the chief trouble centre. To these he could add the Jewish municipal administrators of Jerusalem, who found it in their best interests to co-operate with Roman authorities. On the lowest level were paid informers, Jewish quislings and any other opportunists who offered useful information.

To see how well this system worked, this chapter will examine a well-known historical figure normally not associated with spies: Jesus of Nazareth. The passion story is told in the four Gospels, although with considerable differences in details. There is no reason to question the essential history. The city authorities seized Jesus and handed him over to Pilate. Pilate had him crucified as a would-be messiah, 'The king of the Jews'. Since Pilate was governor of Judaea from c.26 to 36 CE, the crucifixion can be dated within that decade. The external framework of Jesus' life, therefore, is reasonably certain.[5] Yet, although the facts surrounding these events seem clear, the circumstances surrounding the facts are not. As one writer put it: 'Almost no aspect of Jesus' life is indisputable.'[6]

Viewing the events as they may have been seen by an intelligence professional provides insights into the motivation behind Rome's actions. From the Roman point of view, Jesus' activities posed an internal security problem. Seen in this context, the recorded circumstances can be viewed in a very different light. We can offer no additional evidence, nor any conclusive proofs, but we can create a plausible scenario based on the facts as we know them and arrange them against the backdrop of the security issues of first-century Palestine. A case can be made for Jesus' execution as a security risk to the Roman state. Whether this threat was real or imagined is irrelevant. The Romans made what they considered a shrewd political and military move for their own protection, and they based it on a file which they had built one piece of intelligence at a time.

The Carpenter from Galilee

Into the political maelstrom of Jerusalem in the 30s arrived Jesus, a carpenter's son from Galilee. What would an investigator working for the Romans have put into the hypothetical 'Jesus File' as background material? Jesus was a preacher. He was considered a healer and miracle worker. He drew large crowds that the Romans always considered politically dangerous. He had been called to his life's work by John the Baptist, and spent two years in Galilee teaching and healing. He had attracted the unfavourable attention of Herod Antipas, the ruler of Galilee, who had already arrested and executed John the Baptist on the suspicion of having revolutionary aims.[7] Jesus had alienated the principal Jewish groups in Galilee, and when this deprived him of widespread support it appears that Herod brought pressure on Jesus to leave the area. In Matthew 14:13, it is reported that he crossed the Sea of Galilee to a point outside Antipas' dominions into that of Philip, Herod's brother. Roman agents in Galilee could have contacted their Jerusalem colleagues to warn them that a troublemaker was on the way.

Any Jewish or Roman authorities observing Jesus might have placed him among a well-known social type of his time – a teacher and so-called miracle worker who had messianic claims, and whose followers were possibly involved in revolutionary activities.[8] Depending on one's sympathies, such men were alternately described as prophets, deceivers, brigands, rabble rousers, charlatans, revolutionaries or messiahs. What was there about Jesus, other than his reputation as a public speaker, that would have alerted the Roman authorities to him, and caused them to see him as a threat? His choice of disciples may have suggested his political leanings and his reasons for coming to Jerusalem. This question is of great importance, because even if Jesus himself was not a revolutionary his association with known political activists or troublemakers created the impression among the investigating authorities that Jesus was about to lead an insurrection. Much has been made of Jesus' associations with such men, although the conclusions reached are based on a bare minimum of evidence and much inference.

The first job of Roman intelligence was to know their target. Part of the image the Romans had of Jesus came from the people with whom he surrounded himself. Among his followers was Judas, identified in John's gospel as Judas, son of Simon the Iscariot. For centuries scholars have been baffled by this title, which has not been connected to any other name or geographical location (like Kerioth). Some have argued that 'Iscariot' is cognate with the Greek loanword for *sikarios*, a dagger-wielding assassin.[9] Another follower, Simon the Zealot, is referred to in the New English Bible as 'Simon the Patriot'. The King James version refers to 'Simon the Canaanite'. Both are translations for the Aramaic word for zealot, *qannai*, which is rendered into Greek as *kananaios*. So Simon the Canaanite was really Simon the *kananaios*, or Simon the freedom fighter.[10]

In John's Gospel, there is yet another Simon, Simon bar Jonas. He is generally taken to be Simon, son of Jonas, even though the man's father is elsewhere identified as Zebedee. 'Bar Jonas' is again possibly a mistranslation from the Aramaic word *barjonna*, which, like *kananaios*, means 'outlaw', 'anarchist' or 'zealot'. The designation for James and John Boanerges means 'sons of thunder'.

These epithets describe five of Jesus' companions – the last two given as his own designation of them. No actual anti-Roman action is hinted at, yet implicit in some of Jesus' parables is a reminder of the gross injustices under which Jesus' peasant audiences laboured. The distinct possibility thus exists that Jesus became a popular figure of a quite different sort than he is often portrayed. This is suggested by the fragment in John 6:15 that says Jesus knew 'they were going to come and carry him off to make him king',[11] or the statement in Matthew 10:34 that: 'I have not come to bring peace, but a sword' (*NEB* translation).

If Jesus had disciples such as Simon the Zealot, Judas the Sicarius and Simon the Freedom Fighter among his followers, they can hardly have been as placid and peaceful as later tradition maintained. The entire group may have been involved in precisely the kind of political and military activity of which Jesus was accused, tried and executed. The most important fact is not whether the charges were actually true but whether the Roman authorities were convinced they were true.

Scholars such as S. G. F. Brandon, Hyman Maccoby, Joel Carmichael, Richard Horsley and Robert Eisler have all argued that Jesus' alleged pacifism was invented by the Gospel writers to make him more acceptable to gentiles in the period after the crucifixion.[12] Some even argue that Jesus was an ardent nationalist in the mould of his fellow Galilean Judas of Galilee, who had staged the uprising in Rome in 6 CE (see chapter 6). To their ears, Jesus' talk of the 'kingdom of God' was an appeal to nothing less than the overthrow of the Romans and the establishment of a new, independent Jewish state.[13] Few scholars have accepted this portrayal of Jesus as some kind of guerrilla leader; most violently reject it. The Romans, however, may have drawn this conclusion about Jesus from his teachings, his compatriots and his symbolic entry into Jerusalem perhaps claiming some sort of earthly kingship. If so, it would have provided the Romans with all the justification they needed to treat him as a political threat.[14]

During an often politically volatile time of the year – the Jewish Passover – Jesus, the great apocalyptic prophet, the visionary teacher, the widely popular healer and exorcist, and the well-known troublemaker, headed for Jerusalem with his entourage. His reputation preceded him. If either the Jewish or Roman authorities had sources who alerted them to his approach, the Jesus File would continue to grow. The Romans needed answers. Why was he coming? Was he merely on a religious holiday in the capital or was there a political dimension to his arrival? Would he draw large crowds or spend a quiet holiday? The residents of Jerusalem were about to find out.

The Triumphal Entry into Jerusalem – A Public Declaration

Jesus and his disciples arrived from Galilee[15] on the sabbath preceding Passover.[16] They stayed in the village of Bethany, five kilometres outside Jerusalem. Jesus had attracted enough public attention in Galilee to warrant surveillance by the authorities, both religious and civil. The authorities in Jerusalem always feared the possibility of an uprising at the time of Passover. The city and the Temple area of Jerusalem could accommodate perhaps three to four hundred thousand pilgrims, and large crowds meant that the festival of Passover could be an occasion for civil unrest. Consequently, the Roman governor came to Jerusalem with extra troops at that time of year. Roman soldiers patrolled the roofs of the porticoes of the Temple, so that they could be on the lookout for trouble.[17] Known agitators were watched.

Finding Jesus would have been no trouble for either Jewish or Roman spies. His entry into the city was both public and well orchestrated for the maximum symbolic effect. Jesus entered Jerusalem on a donkey. At festival time, the pious were expected to make their journey into the holy city on foot, so that by riding Jesus made himself stand out. It is the only occasion in the Gospels when Jesus rides rather than walks. People welcomed him by shouting: 'Hosanna! Blessed is he who comes in the name of the Lord! Blessed is the kingdom of our father David that is coming' (Mark 11:9ff.). According to Matthew and Luke, they explicitly called him 'son of David' or 'king'.[18] If Mark's account of Jesus' entry into the city has any truth, we must assume that the crowds had been prepared for his entry. Without prior warning of an impending demonstration, it is hard to see why crowds should have gathered at all, or even greeted him this way. The triumphal entry, as it is depicted by all four evangelists, suggests that Jesus was greeted as a messianic and, by association, nationalistic figure.[19]

The religious symbolism of this demonstration seems obvious. Matthew 21:4 makes it clear that the procession was intended to fulfil the prophecy of Zechariah 9:9, which foretold the coming of the Messiah.

Rejoice, rejoice, daughter of Zion!
Shout aloud, daughter of Jerusalem;
for see, your king is coming to you;
his cause won, his victory gained,
humble and mounted on an ass . . .[20]

Given Jesus' familiarity with the Jewish Scriptures, there can be little question that he was familiar with this prophecy. And being aware of its meaning, he can hardly have fulfilled it unwittingly or through 'sheer coincidence'. Symbolic actions were part of the prophet's vocabulary. They simultaneously drew attention and conveyed information. The entry into Jerusalem can only have been made with the calculated design of identifying himself, very specifically in the eyes of the populace, with the expected Messiah – in other words, with the rightful king, the 'anointed one'. This much would have been clear to his Jewish observers. Their definition of *meshiach*, or messiah, was: 'A charismatically endowed descendant of David whom the Jews . . . believed would be raised up by God to break the yoke of the heathen and to reign over a restored kingdom of Israel to which all the Jews of the Exile would return.'[21]

Politically, he may also have been identifying himself with another of Israel's liberators: 1 Maccabees 13:50 records that Simon Maccabeus entered Jerusalem 'and purged the citadel of its pollutions'. He entered the city 'with praise and palm branches, and with harps and cymbals'. When he climbed on a donkey, perhaps Jesus was consciously imitating Simon.[22] The crowd expressed its feeling towards him by reciting the liturgy shared by the feast of Tabernacles and the Dedication of the Temple by Judas Maccabeus in December 165 BCE. If the palms mentioned by John were intended to recall the triumphs of the Maccabees this was because Jewish religion and Jewish nationalism were closely bound together. It was by such celebrations that the freedom of the Jews from foreign oppression in the past was celebrated and its memory kept alive.[23]

The triumphal entry was probably understood in a monarchical sense. The Gospels of Matthew and Luke state that Jesus was of royal blood – a genuine and legitimate king, the lineal descent of Solomon and David. Such a lineage would have conferred on him at least one important qualification for being the Messiah, or for being presented as one. He would have had a legal claim to the throne of his regal forebears, and perhaps, as has been suggested, *the* legal claim. The kingly dimension is overt in the crowd's shout: 'Blessed be the kingdom of our father David' (Mark 11:10). Some scholars have even interpreted Jesus' anointing in Mark 14:3–9 as a messianic anointing.[24]

For Jesus to perform an act long prophesied and expected of the rightful Messiah certainly reflects no diffidence on his part. He was quite brazenly staging a public spectacle – one for which he knew he would either have been stigmatised as an upstart or acknowledged as precisely what he claimed to be. Significantly enough, he is acknowledged by a populace fully aware of the symbolism of his action. But how could such an act not be fraught with political implications and consequences? It was an explicit challenge to Rome, an act of deliberate, militant provocation. The Messiah was regarded as a liberator. For Jesus to have been accepted as Messiah, it must have suggested to some people that he was willing to wield the liberator's sword. Although Roman spies might not have understood the religious nuances of this demonstration at first, they would certainly have reported the crowds. Any mention of the word 'messiah' by Jesus' followers or spectators viewing the scene should have alerted the Romans to a possible political threat.

Once the local Jewish authorities got intelligence of this demonstration their reaction would have been immediate fear. A would-be messiah could have caused civil unrest and possibly a major riot in the city, when tens of thousands of pilgrims were squeezed into the narrow streets. Jesus, riding into the city on a donkey, may have believed he was about to inaugurate a new religious age. The Romans, on the other hand, would have seen it only as the inauguration of trouble and used it as a pretext to exact reprisals from the Jews. It was thus necessary for the Jewish authorities to isolate Jesus, and to stop the troublemaking before the situation got out of hand. The haste with which both the Jewish and Roman authorities wished to try Jesus, and the need to get rid of him before the Feast, suggest that they knew of, or feared, some plot which was timed to take place during the Passover season.[25]

The stage was now set for an extremely confusing drama. Even the small circle of initiates close to Jesus may not have known what was going on. Of the twelve, some like Judas knew what was happening, while others seem to have been in complete ignorance as their 'king' mounted the donkey on that Sunday afternoon and rode into Jerusalem. An organised plot may have been afoot, and not all of them may have been informed about it. Scholars have made some extremely ingenious suggestions as to who might have been involved, but the truth is that no clear evidence exists for more than intelligent guesswork.[26] Even if Jesus himself was not involved in a paramilitary plot, some of his friends may well have been. Radical political and military groups may have planned an insurrection that provided Jesus with the 'props' for his proclamation. For them, he might have been the best leader they could find for a revitalised Jewry that drew together all classes and sects in opposition to the Romans. Or he might have been a sincere religious figure being used by more sinister forces. The Romans would not have made such fine distinctions.

Watching these events were the Sadducees, the upper-class priestly sect who administered the Temple, and they would have been quite happy to eliminate yet another cranky, sectarian development within Judaism that might endanger their state, their rule and their social position. The Romans, on their part, were perpetually worried that the Jews would prove ungovernable, as indeed turned out to be the case thirty-six years later when the Romans had to subdue them by a most terrible display of force.

Each Gospel has a slightly different version of what happened next. Although it is impossible to reconstruct Jesus' motives for behaving as he did in the last week of his life, it is important to remember that Jesus' public behaviour put him on a collision course with both the Jewish and Roman authorities who were monitoring his movements through their informants.

The Cleansing of the Temple

That Jesus' entry into Jerusalem was fraught with political implications became even more evident when he arrived at the Temple.[27] We are told by Mark that Jesus went to the Temple and looked around. If we believe that this is what he did, then part of his motive must have been to show himself to the public. Though a popular figure in Galilee, Jesus was not generally recognisable by sight in Jerusalem. There is no scholarly agreement whatsoever about the precise meaning of Jesus' next public activity within the Temple. Those who believe Jesus was executed as a messianic insurgent search for some political act for which he was executed. Jesus' 'cleansing of the Temple' fills that description for many authors.[28] In his attitude towards the Temple tax, Jesus seems to have shared the kind of sectarian Jewish thought found at Qumran, and the radical attitude to the Temple found among the revolutionaries of 66. The longing for a renewed and reformed Temple cult is linked with expectations of the destruction and restoration of the Temple.[29] Certainly the Synoptic Gospels all connect the cleansing of the Temple with the death of Jesus in an intimate way.[30]

According to Mark, Jesus 'overturned the tables of the moneychangers and the seats of those who sold pigeons' (Mark 11:15). He then said: 'My house shall be called a house of prayer,' but you have made it 'a den of robbers' (Mark 11:17). This is a phrase from Isaiah and Jeremiah.[31] Jesus also made a second and possibly a third statement about the Temple. The authors of the Synoptic Gospels attribute to him a prediction that the Temple would be destroyed,[32] and they attribute to his accusers at his trial the testimony that he threatened to destroy the Temple.[33] The threat comes up again, during the crucifixion scene as he hung on the cross. Onlookers taunted him: 'Aha! You would destroy the Temple . . . save yourself, and come down from the cross!'[34] Later, Stephen, an early Christian martyr, was accused of saying that 'Jesus of Nazareth will destroy this place' [the

Temple].[35] These various statements make it difficult to determine what Jesus' action in the Temple symbolised. Was it cleansing or destruction? If he intended destruction, was it a prediction or a threat? If a threat, a threat of what?[36]

The incident can hardly have been a minor affair. Nor could it have avoided violence. Neither moneychangers, nor bystanders, nor Jesus' own followers are likely to have stood idle or engaged in theological debate while loose coins rolled in all directions. Given the size and importance of the Temple, and the prominent role of the moneychangers, Jesus' overturning of their tables must have resulted in a full-scale riot. Nor could Jesus himself possibly have expected anything else. Here again he adopted a course of confrontation, one of deliberate challenge to established authority. Whatever did occur, the cleansing of the Temple disturbed the peace and must have drawn the attention of the Temple police, the Roman garrison stationed nearby in the Antonia fortress, who patrolled the flat roofs of the overlooking colonnades, and any nearby informers with eyes in their heads to see.

One could not challenge the Temple, even verbally, with impunity. A story from Josephus illustrates this. He relates how a certain Jesus, son of a peasant named Ananias, threatened the Temple in 62 CE, four years before the outbreak of the Jewish War with Rome. This Jesus stood in the Temple and cried out: 'A voice from the east, a voice from the west, a voice from the four winds; a voice against Jerusalem and the sanctuary; a voice against the people.'[37] Eventually some leading Jewish citizens arrested this Jesus and chastised him, but when he persisted in his threats against the city and Temple the rulers brought him to the Roman prefect Albinus, who had him scourged. Not only does this show what happened to those who made dire predictions against the Temple, but it also points to the political ties between the ruling authorities and the Roman prefect. Yet there was no execution. What then did Jesus do to get such a stiff sentence?

No actual seizure of the Temple precinct would have occurred without an act of violence or an armed force. Regardless of the location of the Roman encampments, or the details of Roman security measures, there is no way that Jesus or anyone else could have visited the Temple, had an altercation with the Temple police and priests – to say nothing of the Romans soldiers on duty – and infuriated the moneychangers purely as a result of his personal, spiritual authority, or could actually have held the Temple for any period of time.[38] Jesus could not have thought that he and his small band could hold the Temple area, or knock down its walls by themselves. Some scholars have actually claimed that Jesus held the Temple for two days, and occupied it with a force large enough to withstand the opposition of not only the Roman soldiery and the Temple police but presumably also of the many thousands of Jews who might be out of sympathy with the Galilean revolutionaries. This was all done with an armed force.[39] Surely such a military event would have generated more evidence.

That the Gospels provide little detail is not surprising. The early Christians did not want Jesus to look like a rebel or even a troublemaker. Christianity, they wanted to maintain, produced good and loyal citizens. The author of Luke had this as his central concern. He repeatedly blames everyone except the Christian apostles for the fact that wherever they went there was a certain amount of civil tumult. This probably explains why Luke's account does not include any threat against the Temple. Whether Jesus predicted that the Temple would sometime be destroyed, or made a threat himself, becomes moot because his enemies reported to the authorities that he threatened it. Evil intentions do not have to be read into their report. It is just as likely that Jesus said and did something that onlookers believed to be a threat, and that it genuinely alarmed them so they reported it to the authorities. In any event, their reports would have made their way into the Jesus File. Even if their accounts differed from one another (as eyewitness accounts often do), it was clear that Jesus said and did things that disturbed the Jewish authorities, and his actions had to be brought to the attention of the Sanhedrin.[40]

If Jesus was only saying what God intended to do, why arrest him? The two incidents that are kept separate in the Gospels, namely Jesus' actions against the moneychangers and his prophecy about the destruction of the Temple, were probably connected in the minds of the authorities. They realised that prophets who aroused crowds, and would-be messiahs or people who caused disturbances in Jerusalem during holidays, were a threat to the peace and might bring Roman intervention down on them. The question arises – why was Jesus not immediately seized by the Temple guards right there? Were his actions too ambiguous to be construed as directly revolutionary? He did not take anything. He did not burn or destroy records of indebtedness. He did not lead any force that could be viewed as a revolutionary army. He simply briefly suspended one of the economic functions of the Temple without taking advantage of the act. Soon after he left the Temple we presume operations returned to normal. He was not seized immediately, because either no one was sure of Jesus' intentions or he just got away.

The Jewish authorities believed that they were being challenged, and a challenge to the power of the Sanhedrin, especially in the form of interference with the keystone of the Judaean economy, could not go unnoticed or unpunished.

Luke's account makes it clear they put Jesus under surveillance: 'They watched for their opportunity and sent secret agents in the guise of honest men to seize on some word of his as a pretext for handing him over to the authority and jurisdiction of the governor' (Luke 20:20).

Who these 'secret agents' were we will never know. It was, however, not necessary to trump up charges against Jesus at all. The disturbance that he had caused was both public enough and threatening enough for the Jewish authorities to move against him. Having him followed might have been just a way to know his location until the authorities decided what to do with him.

The Last Supper

Jesus was at great risk throughout his stay in Jerusalem. In Luke 22:1–5 he seems particularly concerned with sharing this Passover meal with his disciples.[41] He made special arrangements for the place where he would share this meal with them, which he believed might well be his last. Details in Mark's account (Mark 14:12–17) suggest that Jesus had arranged for a safe house. The disciples knew nothing of the arrangements on the very day of the meal (Mark 14:12). Instead of giving them simple, straightforward instructions, Jesus chose two disciples and gave them very round-about directions on how to locate the safe house where the meal was to be held. Jesus told them to go into the city, where they would see a man carrying a pitcher of water. They were to follow him, and when he turned into a house they were to ask the question: 'Where is the room reserved for me to eat the Passover meal with my disciples?' This man would show them a large room upstairs, readied in advance. We shall never know who the man with the pitcher of water was, but he would have to have been very conspicuous if the disciples were to find him in the narrow crowded streets of Jerusalem. And since it was usually a woman's job to carry the water, this man might have stood out. We are not told who provided the money for the large guest-chamber. The poor generally ate out of doors during this festival. The story itself suggests that Jesus made arrangements to hold the meal secretly, possibly to avoid arrest before he completed what he had intended to do. The meal itself was unusual in other respects. For one thing, it was a males-only affair. Jesus may have guessed that the evening was going to end in violence and did not want his mother or his other female followers to be present.

Judas left the meal in order to betray Jesus. There have been any number of sentimental and fanciful explanations for why he would do this. They range from the Gospel explanation – that Judas was bribed by the high priest – to notions of his disillusionment with Jesus for political reasons. None of the explanations quite fits. If Judas were a revolutionary who expected Jesus to lead a great armed rebellion against the Romans, and now realised that no such rebellion was planned, he would hardly have gained anything from handing Jesus over to the authorities. It would certainly be dangerous for him if Jesus, under torture, revealed the names of his fellow conspirators. Another explanation might be that Judas had always been a Roman agent, a plant, who kept an eye on Jesus for the authorities and was now about to do his last official act – revealing Jesus' location to the arresting authorities.[42]

If, at the time of his arrest, Jesus was a notorious figure in Jerusalem because of his actions the previous week, it is strange that they needed Judas' help in identifying him. The only plausible sense in which Judas could have helped the authorities was in giving away Jesus' location in a crowded city on a dark night. This is why so many precautions were taken at the last supper, because it would have been the perfect place to arrest Jesus quietly, at night, and with a minimum of public fuss. Instead Judas betrayed the whereabouts of Jesus' post-supper rendezvous. He may have been an unwilling accomplice.[43] For example, he himself might have been arrested with Jesus while his other friends waited in the garden, and he might have been forced to identify Jesus. He may have been paid as an informer as the Gospel suggests, but we cannot rule out the possibility that Judas was a double agent working for the Romans right from the start.[44]

The Arrest

All four Gospels report that Jesus was arrested at night.[45] No gospel writer tells us in plain language the reason for the arrest, and each treats the scene differently so guesswork must be used once again to reconstruct the events.[46] At face value, the Gospel portrayals of the events at Gethsemane can perhaps best be described as a scuffle. Armed men were sent by the chief priests to arrest Jesus in secret; Judas was with them.[47] The Synoptic Gospels tell us that Judas kissed Jesus in order to identify him to the soldiers. Yet it is not certain that the disciples even knew that Judas had betrayed Jesus.

A small fight broke out, and much has been written about exactly how many weapons were present at this scuffle. Some scholars assert that at least a few of Jesus' disciples were carrying concealed weapons, as did the Sicarii.[48] Although it was generally forbidden to bear arms at Passover, Jews were permitted to act in self-defence. Matthew 26:52 says Jesus forbade armed resistance – admirable advice for a Roman subject, but a trifle late.[49] In Mark and Luke, Simon Peter drew his sword and struck off the ear of the servant of the high priest who had come to supervise Jesus' arrest.[50]

Much ingenious reconstruction has also been used in calculating how many men came to arrest Jesus in the Garden. Mark is vague and merely says a crowd (*ochlos*; Mark 14:43). Others have the image of between ten and thirty men: a Jewish functionary or two, some representatives of the high priest, a contingent of the Temple guard, perhaps one or more Roman officials, or perhaps a small unit of Pilate's soldiery.[51] In Luke they are the Temple guard (*stragegoi tou hierou*; Luke 22:52) and in John a 'cohort' under the command of a tribune (*speira kai ho chiliarchos*; John 18:3, 12). This would entirely change the scope and meaning of the events in Gethsemane. A cohort has a very exact meaning in Roman military terms: it was one-tenth of a legion – as many as six hundred soldiers. It seems implausible that Pilate or any other military governor in his situation would have dispatched upwards of five or six hundred troops to Gethsemane for the sole purpose of arresting one man – a solitary prophet who preached love and was attended by twelve disciples. Not only would it have been a ridiculous example of overkill but it would also have been an open invitation to civic disturbance. As one writer put it: 'What a compliment to the power of Jesus!'[52]

Whatever happened during the night-time scuffle, the soldiers found their man. Peter ran away into the darkness, as did Jesus' other friends and followers, and Jesus was left alone with his captors. The facts seem simple enough: Jesus was arrested at a secret, nocturnal assembly in which some of his men gave armed resistance,[53] and one of the high priest's servants was wounded in the fight.[54] Three Gospels portray Jesus' surprise at the size of the guard sent to arrest him. He asks them if they suppose that he is one of the *lestai* they should have arranged a full military arrest. As we have seen in the last chapter, *lestai* is a term that is often taken to mean 'social bandits' or revolutionaries who used brigandage against collaborators and occupying forces as a form of social protest.[55]

Why did the high priest or the Romans arrest Jesus? On the grounds of pure probability, the answer to this question would be that reported by the Gospels. Jesus' public acts seemed to provoke violence. In a flamboyant fashion, he staged public spectacles which implicitly asserted his claim as Israel's foretold Messiah. Some authors have suggested that these spectacles were acts of calculated provocation, which reflect an undisguised militancy or an obvious willingness to use force. Also, these incidents make it clear that Jesus had a sizeable following greater than his original twelve disciples.[56] What we can be reasonably sure of is that both the crowds he attracted and the messianic pronouncements worried the priests who controlled the Temple and the city of Jerusalem. The Temple was a centre of national as well as religious sentiment; and a long series of riots, revolts and wars would be waged to control it. Jesus was a threat to the peace.

The Proceedings before the Sanhedrin

All the Gospels agree that after his arrest Jesus was taken to the house of the high priest,[57] but what happened thereafter is highly disputed.[58] The accounts of the interrogations and 'trials' before the Sanhedrin and Herod seem to be dramatisations of uncertain events that were not witnessed by the disciples who, by their own confession, hid after Jesus' arrest. None of Jesus' family or friends was present while he was being interrogated, and the Gospels indicate that none of them spoke to Jesus before his crucifixion. Many scholars believe, therefore, that the Gospels must have invented the trial scenes, and that there is little in them that can be considered historical.[59] Discrepancies among the stories of each evangelist have formed the themes of many books.

Indeed there is much to be disputed. Assuming that Sanhedrin procedure in the early first century was the same as in 200 CE, a nocturnal trial would have violated Jewish law since the hearing occurred on Passover night, when leaving one's house was prohibited.[60] Some have cited a Mishna that clearly states that no trial that involved capital punishment could be held on the eve of the sabbath or on the eve of any festival.[61] The charges themselves do not ring true. Claiming to be the Messiah did not constitute blasphemy under Jewish law and, besides, condemnation for blasphemy was punished by the legally prescribed penalty of stoning, not crucifixion. The Jews would not have handed the offender over to the Romans, who never got involved in a Jewish religious dispute unless it turned into a security matter.[62]

It seems unlikely that Jesus was arrested and brought before the Sanhedrin because of any theological differences with mainstream Judaism, as represented by the Pharisees.[63] The range of legal or theological dispute between Jesus and others was well within the parameters of normal debate.[64] The trouble involved the realities of the political relationship between the Romans and the Jews. The Jewish aristocracy and Roman officials shared a common concern for keeping the peace, since both groups were dependent on the product of the peasantry.[65] Given the power structure in Jerusalem, the proceedings seem logical. The Roman prefect or procurator had to maintain domestic tranquillity and collect tribute; both tasks he turned over to priestly aristocrats headed by the high priest. The high priest was responsible for good order in Judaea, and especially in Jerusalem.

Caiaphas served longer than any other high priest during the period of direct Roman rule, which speaks well of his ability and diplomacy.[66]

If the high priest did not preserve order, the Roman prefect would intervene militarily, and the situation might end in violence against the Jews. So long as the Temple guards acted as the police force of the high priest and carried out arrests, and so long as the high priest judged cases, there was relatively little possibility of a direct clash between Jews and Roman troops. To keep his job, the high priest had to remain in control. His public trust as leader of the Jews obligated him to prevent clashes with the Romans. He had to represent the popular view to the Roman prefect, and lobby for non-interference in Jewish customs and traditions. In other words, the high priest was the man in the middle.[67] In many respects, the Romans held Jewish leaders hostage for the obedience of the Jewish people to the Roman state. Under these circumstances, in order to save their own lives, many Jewish leaders acted as informers against dissenters and revolutionaries among their own people. Even if the charges were a purely religious matter, the Jews were probably aware that, to Pilate, its significance was political.[68]

It seems unlikely that Caiaphas thought that Jesus was planning a military takeover. Had he thought this, he would have had Jesus' companions arrested too, and his followers would have been executed, as were followers of other prophets in later years that made the mistake of marching in large groups. The execution of only Jesus suggests they feared he would rouse the mob, not that he was leading a secret army. Caiaphas did not act because of theological disagreements. He was primarily (perhaps exclusively) concerned that Jesus might incite a riot, or that revolutionaries would use Jesus' actions as a springboard for their own activities.

What may have occurred was not a formal trial but a series of hurried unofficial examinations, after which Caiaphas turned Jesus over to Pilate with a recommendation for execution, and Pilate promptly complied.[69] The Gospel writers composed speeches to represent dramatically what they thought might have been said at this hearing, a common practice among ancient writers.[70] The author of John attributes to Caiaphas at the trial an entirely appropriate statement: 'It is expedient for you that one man should die for the people and that the whole nation should not perish' (John 11:50). The high priest was compelled to turn over the rebel to avert suspicion from himself as an accessory to the rebels.

We do not know how Caiaphas collected his intelligence on these matters, but it would be reasonable to think that after he learned of Jesus' assault on the moneychangers, but before he ordered his arrest, he sought and obtained further information about him to add to the Jesus File. What he passed on to Pilate probably included the information that Jesus thought he was the Messiah. It was Jesus' claim to be king, the manner of his entry to the city and his behaviour in the Temple that motivated the high priest to act. This is the way the Gospels describe the events, and this is a plausible explanation. Thus began Jesus' confrontation with the might of Rome.

The Trial of Jesus Before Pontius Pilate

One of the few things all the Gospels agree on is that the trial of Jesus before Pilate happened first thing in the morning.[71] Almost all else is open to interpretation.[72] From the perspective of Roman criminal justice, there is nothing unusual about the trial as described in the Gospels. A. N. Sherwin-White, for example, has argued that the trial resembled a typical Roman provincial procedure of the period.[73] He noted that Roman jurisdiction was discretionary and arbitrary. The governor was not bound by the criminal law of the Roman state, which applied only to Roman citizens and to Roman cities. The provinces lacked a criminal code; provincial trials were referred to technically as 'trials outside the system', or *extra ordinem*. This meant that the governor was free to make his own rules for the conduct of the trial. He could accept or reject charges, and fashion penalties as he saw fit. In practice, however, governors tended to follow the rules of the system with which they were familiar in Italy. Though they were not bound by law, they were heavily influenced by custom. Custom required that trials were held in public with the governor on his bench or tribunal, and that charges be made formally by interested parties (who acted as private prosecutors since there were no public prosecutors in the Roman world), and that the accused persons had an opportunity to defend themselves.

The chief priests took Jesus to Pilate, and in Luke 23:2 the charges are specified: 'We found this fellow perverting our people, and prohibiting the payment of tribute to the emperor, and calling himself "Christ" (that is) king.' Prohibiting the payment of tribute and claiming to be the Messiah amounts to political subversion.[74] Clearly, the high priest regarded Jesus as a political offender and refused to try him as such, so he was turned over to the procurator. If the high priest convicted a man for a political crime without the consent of the procurator he might have been held liable, especially if Jesus were acquitted and the high priest were charged with releasing a known subversive.

Pilate then questioned Jesus about his claims of royalty (Mark 15:2). For this kind of trial the regular 'accusation' made by the plaintiff was unnecessary;

the mere information of a delator sufficed and even that was unnecessary if Pontius Pilate's intelligence network possessed sufficient knowledge of an action or plot.[75] The offence of rebellion was a *crimina extraordinaria*, and when it included armed participants it was considered particularly aggravating circumstances. The mere formation of night assemblies (*coetus nocturni*) such as Jesus meeting with his followers on the Mount of Olives was a crime in itself. Such offences could carry a death sentence, and the punishment was left in the hands of a governor. The only truly peculiar aspect of Jesus' trial was that he made no attempt to defend himself; this was rare in Roman courts. In order to prevent any miscarriage of justice, and to assure the accused a chance to speak, the direct question about royalty was put three times to Jesus before his case was allowed to go by default. Hence it was correct technically in Mark and Matthew, as well as in John, when Pilate repeated his question to the silent Christ.[76]

For Pilate, Jesus' case was just one of the many trials of rebel leaders that a governor in his position had to judge. In Mark's narrative (Mark 15:7), it is revealed that a man named Jesus Barrabas had been guilty of a murder in 'the uprising', as had the other two *lestai* who were crucified alongside Jesus of Nazareth.[77] The Romans had not been slow to arrest the Jews involved, and Jesus was executed between two of them. Since Peter, James and John were not arrested by the Romans, there is reason to believe that Jesus' followers were not yet under suspicion. If they had been in any way implicated in a plot or armed insurrection against the Romans, we can be perfectly certain that they would have been rounded up and executed also. Whatever insurrection is referred to here, no account of it has been left. Some scholars have a suspicion that Jesus, albeit passively, may have stirred up greater popular Jewish fervour than the revisionist Gospels convey. References to such a revolt would have been removed from later accounts to separate Christians from any charge of being political revolutionaries, especially after the Jewish Revolt of 66–73 CE had been crushed.

Why did Pilate order Jesus' execution? Because the high priest had given him both the information and the charge on which Jesus could be eliminated as a threat to the state: Jesus had stirred up the crowds and claimed he was king of the Jews. Pilate's Roman sources would have confirmed this interpretation. Pilate understood that Jesus was a would-be-king without an army, and therefore he made no effort to track down and arrest Jesus' followers. He probably regarded Jesus as a religious fanatic whose fanaticism had become so extreme that it posed a threat to law and order.[78] Pilate's primary concern at this moment was to draw that delicate line between asserting his authority and exciting worse violence than he was attempting to quell. Pilate's only fear was that he was condemning a popular leader, the consequence of which might be a bloody uprising.

Matthew and John give a different account than Mark. They have Jesus condemned by the Jewish mob, against Pilate's better judgement. Pilate consults the crowd; he is portrayed as a weakling who gives in and has Jesus executed.[79] In these Gospel accounts, Pilate is no more than a bureaucrat, almost genial, unwilling to condemn Jesus, yet he is urged to do so by the seething malice of the chief priests and other Sadducean leaders. Some have even suggested, based on the Gnostic traditions, that Pilate was a Christian himself.[80] Such a distortion of history is all the more alarming since it has been an excuse for two thousand years of Christian anti-Semitism.[81] Dominic Crossan has remarked: 'The often repeated statement that the Jews rejected Jesus and had Him crucified is *historically untenable* and must, therefore, be removed from our thinking, and our writing, preaching and liturgy.'[82] Crossan might also have added movie screens. The only likelihood is that Jesus was condemned by the Romans and crucified, and it was done by a governor with a reputation for being 'unbending and callously hard by nature'.[83] This is a reality which the early Christian Church, fearful of persecution from the Romans, did its best to obscure in order to protect itself. The later Pauline tradition spread the idea that Jesus had been condemned by the Jews for blasphemy, not for plotting to destroy the Temple. It would have been a poor recruiting tool among the Romans to inform them they had murdered the Messiah.

There is a wide divergence between the Pilate of the Gospels and the tough, cruel man of the secular sources. Sources outside the Gospels present a less sentimental picture. The Jewish writer Philo, who was Pontius Pilate's contemporary, wrote an appeal to the emperor Caligula with a description of Pilate. Philo wrote that 'the briberies, the insults, the robberies, the outrages and wanton injuries, the executions without trial constantly repeated the ceaseless and supremely grievous cruelty' that marked Pilate's rule.[84] Some have suggested that Pilate crucified Jesus because he was afraid that his home government would accuse him of shielding a rebel. If Pilate's superior found fault in his administration of Judaea, it was not because of his weakness or lack of patriotism to the empire but his excessive severity in dealing with his subjects. It is likely that Pilate, as Roman prefect, played a more aggressive role in the trial of Jesus than the Gospels suggest.[85] In fact, Pilate was eventually dismissed from office because of large-scale and ill-judged executions.[86]

Pilate was no administrative neophyte when Jesus was brought before him, and his previous actions in Judaea had created a crescendo of Jewish reaction:

mass civil disobedience, active rioting, diplomatic intervention by letter to Rome, and finally an embassy to the emperor himself to plead the Jewish case. Pilate would not have been intimidated by a Jewish mob. In at least one case, his undercover agents mingled with a crowd so as to provoke them to riot in order to provide himself with an excuse to cut them down.[87]

Pilate knew the ways of both violence and subterfuge. He was, after all, regionally responsible for the world's most efficient fighting machine, the Roman army. We will never know the exact intelligence on which he based his decisions, but we may speculate that it did not take much to move him once the possibility of sedition had arisen.

As a Roman prefect, Pilate – and only Pilate – had the legal authority to inflict the Roman penalty of crucifixion in Judaea. Jesus was crucified under Roman law by a distinctly Roman form of punishment. The evidence, primarily from Josephus' accounts, appears conclusive, that from the beginning of Roman rule only insurgents, or those who passed for or were in sympathy with insurgents, were executed by crucifixion.[88] Crucifixion was a political punishment for a political offence, and it was always carried out by Roman authorities, not Jewish officials.

In all probability, Pilate received Caiaphas' charge, had Jesus flogged and briefly interrogated, and when the answers were not forthcoming he sent him to the cross without a second thought.[89] This evidence agrees with the sequence of events narrated by the Gospels. The stories of Pilate's reluctance and weakness of will are best understood as subsequently produced Christian propaganda. They are a kind of excuse for Pilate's action, which reduces the conflict between the Christian movement and Roman authority.[90]

How much Jesus was affected by the revolutionary currents of his time will never be known, but his death certainly resembled that of a Jewish nationalist. It was Rome's job to eliminate rebels however much they cloaked themselves in talk of God. Such rebels belonged on the cross – not in the hills of Galilee or on the streets of Jerusalem, and certainly not in the precincts of the Temple. Jesus' public agony, his helplessness and ultimately his failure would discourage other charismatics from dreaming dangerous dreams. It would discourage the populace from following would-be king-messiahs, the deluded weavers of a fantasy kingdom of God that would never come. For Pontius Pilate, a charismatic turned over by his loyal and competent Caiaphas would have been a welcome opportunity for a display of Caesar's might, and the efficiency of his own intelligence network.

The essential role that the chief priests played was that of intelligence gatherers. It was they who first saw Jesus, because of his Temple behaviour, as a messianic claimant. After an informal interrogation, they brought him to Pilate. If Roman sources corroborated this information, they have left no trace in the historical record. In the end, our main source independent of the Gospels – Josephus – summarises in one line what we know for a fact: 'On an indictment by leading members of our society, Pilate sentenced him to the cross.'[91] All four Gospels report that the inscription on the cross, in Greek, Latin and Hebrew, was the phrase 'the King of the Jews'.[92]

The *titulus* was a Roman method of publishing the reason for the execution, so that everyone knew why the victim was so punished.[93] Both the penalty of crucifixion and the written public announcement would indicate to all spectators that Jesus was put to death for a political reason. The primary responsibility for Jesus' death lay clearly with the Romans; they were the true masters of the situation. The discrepancies in the Gospels and the widespread prevalence of the depoliticised version of the story most of us are familiar with may be accounted for by looking at the world in which the Gospel writers had to survive in the first century CE. The earliest Gospel, that of Mark, was written after the Romans destroyed the Temple in Jerusalem in 70 CE.[94] The Romans had just put down a massive insurrection by the Jews, and were hardly in the mood to tolerate the followers of another insurrectionist that they had already executed.

There was no obscuring the fact that Jesus had been executed as a 'king' of the revolutionary type. In mockery, Jesus had been arrayed in regal robes during his trial, and a crown, albeit of thorns, had been placed on his head. He had been mocked as a 'king' both by the procurator's troops and by the crowd at the crucifixion.[95] The Gospel writers were anxious to exonerate Jesus of the accusation of having been a revolutionary, with the consequence that they presented him as a king devoid of all political meaning. Much more than Mark, the later Synoptic Gospels show many signs of a desire to erase from the record of Jesus' life any suspicion that he had been a pretender-king of the type common in his day. They stressed Jesus' pacifistic programme. Jesus taught his followers to turn the other cheek to their enemies, and to meet their unjust demands with more than was asked. They were to love their enemies, do good to them and pray for those who persecuted them.[96]

Even with this attempt to soften the picture, the truth emerges. The Synoptic Gospels contain the elements of a correct version of the procedure in a Roman provincial trial.[97] All four Gospels agree that the political charge was either a primary or the sole charge before Pilate. It was only the non-synoptic version of John that tried to insert a theological charge as well. John's narrative seems to be a conscious literary reconstruction, and only in this latest Gospel is found the account of the session of the Sanhedrin in which the Jews brought Jesus before Pilate to sanction his execution for an offence against religious law. This is represented as an alternative to the political charge that Pilate seems to reject. The Gospel writers thus took their material and used it not to write history but to write a religious tract. We can still detect a core of possibly historical material under this attempt at reinterpretation. The evangelists, especially John, elevated Jesus above attack by obscuring almost completely the man of Galilee and setting forth the Jesus of *kerygma* (Christian doctrine).[98]

Intelligence and Political Decisions

We now come back full circle to our original question. What was in the Jesus File? We certainly cannot write anything like a detailed intelligence report, in the modern sense, on a figure who is seen so fitfully and through such a strange lens as the Christian scriptures. By concentrating on the intelligence needs of the Romans, we can discern the outline of a case that attracted the attention of the Roman authorities and presented a security risk. Rome's immediate intelligence sources are clear – the priestly leaders of Jerusalem and Roman army personnel. What other undercover sources they may have used will remain unknown, as such intelligence resources often do.

An examination of Jesus' career as filtered through the eyes of the Roman administration shows that the intelligence they received caused them to have him arrested and executed. There will probably always be a dispute about the significance of Jesus' triumphal entry into Jerusalem, the cleansing of the Temple, the disciples' swords and the arrest of Jesus, the Barabbas episode and the trial or trials. No consensus is ever likely to be reached based on the available evidence. But the attitude of Jesus to the Temple as well as his sayings concerning social injustice had to bring him, sooner or later, into conflict with the authorities, whose task it was to maintain order and to whom any national movement appeared suspicious.[99]

Jesus was probably being watched from the very beginning of his public career. The knowledge that someone had been proclaimed king in Galilee at a huge gathering in the wilderness must have reached the ears of the Romans. Witnesses may have included individuals willing to sell the information to the Romans or Roman agents themselves. Then they heard, through the Jewish authorities or paid informants, that Jesus, the king of the Jews, had reached Jerusalem and that there had been a symbolic assertion of his kingship when Jesus rode into the city at the beginning of the week on a donkey. Jesus created a disturbance when he turned over the moneychangers' tables in the Temple. Reports by various agents were probably confused, as happens with all raw intelligence. We must not overlook the possibility that the agents exaggerated their accounts to make themselves look more important or efficient. Some of the intelligence may have seemed useful; some of it not. We are left completely in the dark as to how such intelligence was collated and analysed.

If Pilate had informers within the Jewish community, they would have told him that Jesus had quarrelled with the scribes and Pharisees about questions of ritual observance. Such news would hardly have interested Pilate, since the Jews were always quarrelling among themselves about religious questions, which to an outsider were wholly obscure. But the question of resistance to the state would not have been ignored. No doubt some versions of his miracles circulated and had been picked up by Roman agents, and this might have led to the charge that he practised magic.[100] Likewise, they had detected some talk of his kingship. The Gospel of John (6:15) says Jesus himself was afraid that the people might try to force him to become king. Even if this was what he least wanted, intelligence might have got back to the Roman authorities on what people were saying.[101]

The fact that Jesus had operated for some time in the wilderness with a large following was in itself suspicious. Men who attracted large crowds in the Judaean countryside, charismatic leaders who performed or promised miracles, practised magic and claimed kingship invariably met a violent end. Even in later Christian propaganda, Jesus is seen as a figure of this same social type.[102] Rome had established a clear and consistent policy of suppressing such movements and executing their leaders.[103] Into this pattern Jesus fits perfectly from the Roman perspective. Pilate behaved with the pragmatic ruthlessness displayed so consistently by Roman officials in their dealings with people like Jesus. Pilate would exhibit this harshness in other incidents of his governorship. His execution of Jesus was a purely Roman solution for dealing with a man who had been involved in seditious or potentially seditious activities.[104]

Those who engage in biblical conspiracy theories believe that Jesus was a political opponent of the Roman regime who used armed force to raise an abortive insurrection. According to these scholars, the Gospels were a huge 'cover-up' of this story. The feeding of the five thousand becomes an abortive insurrection.[105] Jesus' counsel to 'render unto Caesar what is Caesar's' was, to these scholars, a disguised call *not* to pay tribute.[106] The cleansing of the Temple was in reality a violent occupation by Jesus and his men, perhaps the very civil discord in which, according to Luke 23:19, Barabbas had been arrested.[107] We need not stretch the evidence this far. It is equally possible that Jesus' death resulted from poor intelligence or judicial error.[108] In a country like Judaea with a large percentage of the population falling below the poverty line, it would not have been difficult for the Romans to find what Mesopotamian sources refer to as 'a mouth willing to talk'.[109] What matters for this investigation is not the literal truth but rather how the situation appeared to the Roman administration. Even if Jesus were politically as innocent as the Gospels depict, he was not regarded as such by the Romans. For even if Jesus' message differed substantially from that of other popular leaders, one wonders whether the Roman administration, with what little intelligence it had, was discerning enough to recognise this.

Agents might have reported that Jesus had attracted huge popularity as a miracle-worker, healer, exorcist and magician.[110] It seems likely that unless Jesus had a large following he would not have been crucified, and the preaching of his resurrection would not have found such a ready and wide acceptance.[111] A report on such a man would have been very disturbing since military rulers do not like crowds, because they lead to insurrections. If it had been reported, rightly or wrongly, that among Jesus' followers were extremists, then Pilate would have arranged for the elimination of Jesus by whatever judicial means necessary. On the day of Jesus' execution, Pilate already had some Jewish patriots arrested and ready to die by crucifixion. To avoid any chance of rebellion or further disturbance, the Roman ruler would have had no hesitation in condemning all of them to death.

The two men allegedly crucified with Jesus are explicitly described as *lestai*, which, as noted earlier, could mean a social protester. Could it be that, like them, Jesus was a patriotic Jew who believed passionately in God's exclusive sovereignty over Israel and thought that he was commissioned to prepare Israel for its imminent enforcement? Though his attack was not directly against the Romans, it was against the Jewish hierarchy that collaborated with them; it was then understandable that he was executed by the Romans on a charge of sedition. Whatever Jesus' association with these rebels (and the entire truth will never be known), he was certainly crucified by the Romans as a political revolutionary.[112]

Jesus died no ordinary death, in no ordinary circumstances. There is no question that the Romans perceived Jesus as a military and political figure, and dealt with him strictly according to that perception. Crucifixion was a penalty reserved for transgressions against Roman law, and Rome would not have bothered to crucify a man who preached a purely spiritual message or a message of peace. Jesus was not executed by the Sanhedrin, which at best could, with permission, stone a man to death who had trespassed against Judaic law.[113]

Scholars who have suggested that the Romans executed Jesus by accident believe that he inadvertently got involved in a riot that had nothing to do with his teaching or plans. He was, along with others, summarily executed. Seen in this light, Jesus' death may have had little or nothing to do with his public activities.[114] But from the Roman point of view, Jesus' death was no mistake. Jesus' execution by the Romans on a charge of sedition may prove nothing about his true stance, but in the explosive atmosphere of the time removal of someone who, however innocently, might lead or act as a catalyst for a popular uprising was a natural and intelligible action. That only Jesus was executed and his twelve disciples went free shows that the Romans did not see him as a leader of a seditious group – or they would have killed all of them. There is no reliable evidence that he or his followers suffered any significant persecution before his last days in Jerusalem.[115]

When the Great Jewish Revolt came in 66 CE, it was neither sudden nor unexpected. The country had been smouldering for some time. Since the beginning of the first century, militant factions had become increasingly active. They conducted prolonged guerrilla warfare, raided Roman supply caravans, attacked isolated contingents of Roman troops, harassed Roman garrisons and wreaked as much havoc as possible. This was just the sort of activity Pontius Pilate was trying to control, and he saw Jesus as a leading participant or instigator of it.

Why the story was suppressed is explained by what happened to the Christians in the thirty-five years between the crucifixion and the Revolt. The Gospels were written at least a generation after the crucifixion, and after the Temple was destroyed.[116] All records were scattered and people's memories of events were blurred or modified by more recent occurrences. The revolt of 66–73 CE was a watershed, and interpretations of previous events were transformed in the light of it. Even after Jesus' death, widely different interpretations of who he was and what he stood for persisted. Just as it is unhistorical to speak of a monolithic 'Judaism' in the late Second Temple period,[117] so it is misleading to believe that 'early Christianity' was a unified movement.

Very soon after Jesus' death there were different movements of Jesus-followers or Christ worshippers in different locations, all with different understandings of

Jesus.[118] Some of his immediate followers and his family formed the Nazarene movement in Jerusalem, which did not detach itself from mainstream Judaism and presumably had no sense that their support of Jesus constituted founding a new religion.[119] This group mourned his failure to become Messiah as well as his failure to liberate the Jews; perhaps they continued their political activities. In any case, in 66 CE they threw in their lot with the rebels and were obliterated with them in 70 CE.[120]

This left Pauline Christianity as the dominant sect. Through the work of Hellenistic Jews, pre-eminently Paul, Christianity became a mystery cult that welcomed gentiles and presented Jesus to them as a divine saviour in entirely non-political terms. It was the survival technique of a persecuted minority. As representatives of a young Christian sect in a hostile Roman Empire, the evangelists could afford neither to recognise Jesus' revolutionary activities nor to lay the responsibility for his death on the Romans.[121] The consequence of this view was a reasonably favourable but probably incorrect portrait of Pilate. The Pauline Christians depoliticised the Gospels, and responsibility for Jesus' crucifixion was transferred from the Roman administration to the Jews.[122]

Pontius Pilate's role was radically reinterpreted, and he has suffered much criticism for his role in Jesus' death. But we must not hold him or his intelligence sources to too high a standard. From the time of Pompey until the outbreak of the Great Revolt in 66 CE, Judaea was a relatively unimportant place in the Roman world. The governors of Judaea were generally low-ranking officials, mere equestrians of little note, who consistently displayed a general lack of sensitivity, tact and knowledge of Jewish customs.[123] Pilate, the most famous or infamous of them, was probably neither a monster nor a saint, but rather just another Roman bureaucrat of the type. He carried out his duty for ten years without spectacular incompetence, but he was unable to avoid serious friction with his subjects. This worsened the relationship between Judaea and Rome, and thus Pilate played a small part in creating the conditions for the Great Revolt. Rome's carelessness in choosing or monitoring its administrators in Judaea cost dearly later, when the empire had to pay the price of putting down a major revolt.

From the point of view of Rome's immediate security needs, Pilate had Jesus crucified for justifiable reasons. All groups act in their own self-interest and self-preservation. In the context of the first-century occupation of Palestine, that meant nipping any revolutionary action in the bud. Like many decision makers, Pilate made a judgement on the basis of the intelligence he had at hand, even if it was fragmentary. Whether this threat to Roman security from Jesus himself was real or imagined is in some ways irrelevant. There may already have been an intelligence operation gathering information on a revolt concurrent with Jesus' actions (by Barabbas?), and Jesus simply got caught up in the net. The governor of Judaea made a political and military decision for the protection of his province. Like many modern decision makers, Pilate has become the victim of Monday morning quarterbacks who second-guess his judgement. He is not in an enviable position historically being known as the administrator who crucified the man who would become mythologised as the centre of a world religion. But neither Pilate nor any other Roman administrator, even with the best intelligence, could have known that their decision would have such worldwide repercussions, especially for the Roman Empire.

CHAPTER 8

Israel's Last Stand – The Bar Kokhba Revolt

THE LAST GREAT CONFRONTATION between Romans and Jews was the Bar Kokhba Revolt of 132–135 CE; it was also a turning point in the history of Jewish Palestine.[1] The conflagration would exhaust Jewish armed resistance to Rome, and change both the political and cultural landscape of the Holy Land. Jewish life would shift from a devastated Judaea to that of Galilee.

The leaders of this revolt could draw examples from the Hebrew scriptures, plus the Maccabean Revolt and the Great Jewish War of 66 CE, for their techniques. The Maccabean Revolt had been a stunning victory; the war of 66 was a devastating loss. What intelligence lessons had the Jews learned from these historical examples, and how would they use them in the latest revolt? What had driven the Jews to take on Rome a second time, and what convinced them that they could win? This last confrontation set up another intelligence war in which each side would try to get the advantage on its opponent. Was the ability to stay mobile and surprise or ambush the enemy enough to win a war? If it had worked for Joshua and Judas Maccabeus, would it work again for Bar Kokhba?

The Sources

The Bar Kokhba Revolt differed from the one in 66 in two ways: it had a brilliant leader, but it lacked an historian such as Flavius Josephus. Consequently, we know very little about the Bar Kokhba War in spite of its tremendous importance. The literary sources and the archaeological evidence do not allow us to describe the course of the war. The *Epitome* of Dio Cassius, abridged by the Byzantine monk Xiphilinius, is the only consistent survey of the revolt. This account forms the basis for every modern discussion, and its credibility has been evaluated on internal grounds and by comparison with other literary and epigraphical sources many times.[2] The biography of Hadrian in the *Historia Augusta* supplements Dio, but it is not considered a terribly reliable of source.[3] The last two decades have seen spectacular archaeological finds in the Judaean desert and Galilee, and these new materials supplement our knowledge of the revolt.[4]

The size of the Bar Kokhba coinage and the quantities of coins issued tell us something of the population of Judaea at the time of the revolt. The legends and symbols on them embody our only extant contemporary evidence on the values and objectives of the insurgents. The coin evidence speaks well to the motivations for the revolt, when the uprising declared itself 'for Jerusalem'.[5]

Between the Wars

After the havoc wrought by the *Bellum Judaicum* of 66, both sides tried to seek a renewed *modus vivendi* within the Roman provincial organisation. Matters progressed under Nerva to the point where the Jews began to hope for a rebuilding of the Temple destroyed in the final phase of the fighting in 70.[6] By the time of Trajan, however, it became clear that the Jews would not be able to live under Roman rule without suffering religious persecution.[7] Trajan's father was one of the three legionary commanders who served in the Great War under Vespasian's command, and the reputation of Vespasian and Titus as great generals was important to the new emperor.[8] Trajan's treatment of the Jews was a shock after the raised expectations of Nerva's reign. A revolt in the Jewish diaspora broke out in 115 or 116 CE, perhaps as a reaction to Trajan's campaign in Mesopotamia, or as some have argued because Trajan refused to let the Jews rebuild the Temple in Jerusalem.[9] Although no ancient source directly connects the diaspora revolt under Trajan with the outbreak of the rebellion in Judaea in 132 CE, it certainly serves as a backdrop for the Bar Kokhba era. It can be argued that the Roman leadership changed its attitude to the Jews because of these disturbances in the diaspora. New evidence that Judaea had become a consular province, and was assigned a second legion at the end of Trajan's reign, suggests that Trajan wanted to ensure that Judaea itself did not rebel.[10]

This was the situation that greeted Hadrian when he assumed the purple. The destruction created in the diaspora revolt was appalling, according to contemporary witnesses.[11] Hadrian's policy was not just reaction; he attempted to think through the Jewish problem and come up with a solution that would end the rebelliousness once and for all. While on his provincial tour of 128–130 CE he visited Judaea and put into operation what Martin Goodman has called his 'final solution'.[12] He wanted to make sure that the Jews never had a temple on their sacred site in Jerusalem by founding a 'miniature Rome' on the site of the Jew's holy city. Aelia Capitolina was founded in 130 CE as a Roman colony.[13] This was not an attempt to appeal to Hellenised Jews with a new polis, but the founding of a new colony that would house foreign races and foreign religious rites that were deliberately Roman. The new city would accommodate a new population of Romans, and the new colony would be used to suppress the natives.[14]

Hadrian's 'solution' provoked its own uprising. As Benjamin Isaac noted, this is the only insurrection in Roman history to have been caused directly by the actions of a Roman emperor.[15] Instead of making the Jews contented allies, Roman policy sparked the formation of an underground movement that prepared itself for another armed conflict. Scholars have sometimes become bogged down in their discussion of the *casus belli*. Among the reasons given for the revolt was a supposed prohibition on circumcision, but this has turned out to be a red herring.[16]

There has also been much past discussion as to whether the foundation of Aelia Capitolina was a reaction to the revolt or its cause.[17] Dio Cassius 69.12–14 states that the outbreak of the war was due to the anger of the Jews at the dedication of a temple to Jupiter Capitolinus on the site of the Temple of Yahweh, but no archaeological evidence has been found to support such a notion. Yoram Tsafrir has pointed out that these arguments can easily be understood if we see Hadrian's announcement (and a few practical steps towards building) of a pagan Jerusalem as the cause of the revolt, and the actual building taking place after the suppression of the revolt.[18] A coin of Aelia Capitolina found in a hoard of Bar Kokhba denarii from the Judaean desert should confirm the early date without a doubt.[19]

The immediate causes of the war will, no doubt, continue to be debated, but once hostilities broke out in 132 CE the conflict assumed the character of a contest between cultures, ideologies and religions that gave the war an added dimension of totality and ferocity.[20] The aims for the Jews were very much the same as in the last two wars: regaining independence, the re-establishment of a sovereign Jewish state based on the tenets of Judaism and the practice of the Jewish religion, and getting the pagan Romans out of the country.[21]

Son of the Star

The revolt had one distinct advantage over its predecessor – it had a single, undisputed leader, and one who could direct intelligence operations. It is no coincidence that this is the only Jewish revolt named after its leader. This man was Shimon ben Kosiba, who is called Bar Kokhba, which in Hebrew or Aramaic means 'son of the star'.[22] The title has suggested to some a messianic dimension to his leadership.[23] In rabbinic sources, there is a variation: Bar (or Ben)

Koziba, which is similar but has a much different meaning: 'deceiver' or 'son of a liar'.[24] The literature of rabbinic Judaism is not very kind in its references to Bar Kokhba in spite of Rabbi Akiva's labelling him the messiah.[25] Bar Kokhba proclaimed himself prince (*nasi*) of Israel, a term with Old Testament echoes, but in reality he clearly saw himself as a military leader with a claim to absolute sovereignty, rather than as the ideal of a pious rabbi.[26]

In the end, we know very little about Bar Kokhba except that he was an excellent leader of men, military and otherwise, and had probably read the histories of the previous Jewish wars against the Greeks and the Romans. He may have started out as one of several guerrilla commanders, but he ended up as chief of them all. He is portrayed as a ruthless commander; indeed most of the orders given in the Bar Kokhba letters are connected with a threat of punishment.[27] Even before his letters were found in the Judaean desert there were legends of his harshness. One such legend says he tested the courage of his volunteers by ordering each of them to cut off one of their own fingers, which seems unlikely.[28]

It is perhaps ironic that Bar Kokhba is never mentioned in the epitome of Cassius Dio's account of the revolt. Ancient descriptions of native revolts always portray the leader as the central troublemaker and the cause of the revolt. In other words, Rome tended not to acknowledge native revolts as massive uprisings against Roman rule. Instead they were portrayed as an affront to the dignity of Rome caused by the insolence of an individual, and the end of the revolt coincided with the death or capture of that leader.[29] The Romans made famous the names of Jugurtha, Vercingetorix, Arminius, Boudicca, Civilis, Arminius and even the slave Spartacus, but they are silent on the subject of Bar Kokhba.[30]

The Jewish Underground

Only a strong, disciplined underground leader, who commanded the adherence of all conspiring factions and who could co-ordinate intelligence, would have a chance of success. Dio describes the forging of arms to 'battle standards' done clandestinely so that the Romans could not confiscate them or realise that the Jews were planning to revolt openly.[31] Dio also describes the construction of fortifications: Dio 69.14 (Xiphilinus) speaks of fifty strongholds (*phrouria*) and underground bunkers.[32] Such subterranean passages are well attested by archaeology. The insurgents' hiding places are among the most spectacular discoveries in recent times. Scores of subterranean complexes have been discovered in the foothills of southern Judaea, and some believe there are sites dated to the Bar Kokhba Revolt in lower Galilee.[33]

What the Jews Needed to Know – Strategic Intelligence

After the lessons of the Maccabean Revolt and the Great Jewish War of 66–73 CE, Bar Kokhba neither improvised his offensive nor unleashed it by a chance escalation. His campaign was thoroughly planned, prepared and timed. Letters from the documents hidden away in caves near the Dead Sea during the last stages of the war provide ample evidence that even the rebels' administration was planned so as to take over and function immediately on their victory, and to supplant the existing colonial apparatus.[34] It is perhaps ironic that the letters of the last commander-in-chief of an army of Israel should be found by Yigael Yadin, the first commander-in-chief during the Israeli War of Independence in 1948.[35]

Because of the size of the Roman forces, only a strong and disciplined underground movement, commanding the adherence of all conspiring factions, would have a chance of success.[36] Such an organisation would have to rely heavily on their intelligence apparatus, because surprise and speed would be of the utmost importance against the larger Roman force; their work would have to be done clandestinely so that the Romans could not detect their plans and rout out the rebels before the outbreak of the revolt. The fact that the Jews both planned and executed the revolt right under the noses of the Romans is not a compliment to the Roman intelligence establishment. The Romans were utterly deceived as to the true sentiments of the people of Judaea, and their warlike preparations. Roman intelligence had failed to gauge the scale of the coming insurrection.

Roman Intelligence

That the Romans were caught unawares by the outbreak is surprising because they were not without intelligence resources within the country.[37] The rabbinical sources mention Roman intelligence agents at work investigating the practices and opinions of the Jews both before and after the revolt. Military officers of all types are shown investigating Jewish activities. For example, a *quaestor* is recorded discovering the disciples of Rabbi Meir at secret prayer.[38] Another *quaestor* finds a Jew of Sepphoris examining a mezuzah, and extracts from him a bribe or fine of a thousand denarii.[39] Another passage describes a *speculator* and a *quaestor* handing a victim over for execution;[40] this *quaestor* is mentioned in another passage as interested in Jewish ritual.[41] Two *stratiotai* who visited the rabbinical school of Yavneh in Gamaliel's time were certainly acting for the authorities, as their remarks indicate.[42] In short, with the legions II Traiana, III Cyrenaica and X Fretensis serving in Judaea during the war of 132–135, all with *speculatores, frumentarii* and other military personnel known for their intelligence functions, the Romans should have had no trouble keeping an eye on subversive activities. The term *speculator* even found its way into contemporary Hebrew.[43] *Speculatores* are recorded as carrying out summary executions in the normal course of their duties.[44] Rabbi Simon of Timnah (*c*.80–120) reports the activities of *boleshot* (derived from the Hebrew word 'to spy'), who led military patrols and visited villages for fiscal purposes.[45] Specialist scouting units, in fact, were developed in the Roman army after the Bar Kokhba Revolt, which suggests that some lessons were learned too late.[46]

Jewish Intelligence

The Jews faced some formidable strategic and tactical problems. Their intelligence gathering probably made them aware that there were two legions stationed in the province with twelve thousand men and the same number of auxiliary troops; another five to seven legions with sizeable auxiliary units were stationed in the nearby provinces of Syria, Arabia and Egypt.[47] We do not know if they realised the Romans could call for reinforcements from a standing army of some 375,000 to 500,000 troops. These would have been daunting figures to anyone about to take on the Roman military apparatus. Even if Judaea could mobilise twelve per cent of its manpower, Bar Kokhba could produce perhaps sixty thousand men.[48] Not all Jews were actively organised in the underground, but those who were would have to be trained as guerrilla fighters.

Bar Kokhba had an advantage in geographical intelligence. As seen in the earlier chapters of this book, the traditional area of operation for the Jews had always been the Judaean desert. The Jews knew the area well, and had used it to their advantage in previous wars.[49] This time, however, the Romans had expelled large parts of the population from the Judaean mountains, and annexed their territory for the Tenth Legion stationed in Jerusalem. Since 70 CE, therefore, the Romans had deprived the Jews of their natural stronghold, the only part of the country that lent itself to long, drawn-out defence as well as to guerrilla action. Only there was the superiority of Roman arms outbalanced by lightly equipped insurgents. But these areas were under complete Roman control and considerably depleted of Jewish population. Galilee, the other natural stronghold with its large population, was cut off from the rest of the country by the anti-Jewish enclave in Samaria, and by the Legio VI Ferrata, which controlled the passages around the Carmel and through the Esdraelon valley, much of which served as its legionary territory. Outside allies might be tapped if Bar Kokhba could make diplomatic contact with them. Politically, Rome had to consider the possibility of a renewed war with the Parthians, since there was a strong, influential Jewish population there. In the reign of Hadrian, the Romans had also alienated the local population of Syria.[50]

Based on this political and military intelligence, or whatever segment of it he knew, Bar Kokhba had to plan a war that would surprise the Romans by keeping Jewish intentions secret. The surprise element can be inferred from the numismatic evidence. During his visit to Judaea in 130, Hadrian had the 'adventus Augusti Judaea' coin minted, which showed a personified Judaea, with her offspring, receiving the emperor joyously and peacefully. It seems unlikely that the Romans would have put such a coin into circulation had they known of the impending war.[51]

Tactical Intelligence – The Plan

The first phase of the war involved liberation of the Judaean piedmont, the destruction of the smaller garrisons, and the pinning down of the Roman legions in their bases. The second phase comprised organising the Jewish forces to repulse the Roman counteroffensive and gaining reinforcements from neighbouring provinces. The ultimate goal was the reconquest of the Judaean hills and the capture of Jerusalem. Bar Kokhba could then set up an administrative organisation for the country to repulse any attempts at Roman reconquest.

If these were indeed Bar Kokhba's plans, there is some doubt about the execution of all but the first one. According to some scholars, between the end of 131 and the summer of 132, Judaea was largely cleared of the Romans, Jerusalem was liberated and the new civil administration installed.[52] Others believe Jerusalem was never taken.[53] The large number of rebel coins minted are a significant organisational and technical achievement, and it suggests the existence of an effective administration and a large population in need of money. Whether there was a mint in Jerusalem is still an open question.[54] Since the rebels minted a considerable amount of money, it can only have been intended to serve the Jewish population over many more years than the three it actually did. This is clear testimony to both the size of the rebel economy and the faith of its constituents.[55]

Now You See Them, Now You Don't

The Jewish offence and defence were based on their ability to emerge from hiding places, strike against the Romans and then disappear once again. Dio describes the Jewish tactics:

They [the Jews] did not dare try conclusions with the Romans in the open field, but they occupied the advantageous positions in the country and strengthened them with mines and walls, in order that they might have places of refuge whenever they should be hard pressed, and might meet together unobserved underground; and they pierced these subterranean passages from above at intervals to let in air and light.[56]

Subterranean installations have been discovered in six localities ranging from the Judaean piedmont to the Galilee and the Judaean mountains south of Jerusalem.[57] Each of these complexes consisted of a series of underground caverns connected by narrow passages with more than one entrance and exit; each had a source of water nearby. All are dated to the Bar Kokhba period, and all were within striking distance of Roman installations or major highways, and near tactically useful high ground.[58] The rabbinic claim that there were tunnels to Jericho and Lydda are untrue.

Gichon interprets these tunnels as offensive installations.[59] He believes they served as clandestine staging areas during the initial surprise, and later as regular bases from which the Jews could confront the Romans on open ground with their hit-and-run tactics. The bitter experience of the war of 66–73 CE had taught the Jews the folly of letting themselves be shut up in one or more strongholds only to be overcome one by one, and isolated from one another, so that they could not offer mutual aid and co-operation.

Using these mobile tactics, it would be the Romans who became surrounded and were attacked simultaneously from flank or rear when venturing in between the Jewish subterranean positions. Often they did not realise either where their attackers were coming from, nor where they were disappearing to. Much of the fighting in the war should be understood in this context. The Jewish battle plan was based on the full use of the defensive qualities of the desert. Their superb use of advance intelligence kept the Jews informed about the Roman positions, while the use of counterintelligence kept their own positions a secret.

The Jews were not confined only to the mountains. Gichon credits the Jews with the destruction of the Legio XXII Deiotariana, which may have marched from Egypt through Gaza and then disappeared. The disappearance of this legion from the Roman order of battle has always been a mystery.[60] Mildenberg points out that, if the Jews had indeed intercepted the entire legion on its march from Egypt to Judaea and destroyed it, the legion's paymaster must have escaped with its money chest because none of the Bar Kokhba coins is counterstruck over coins from their legionary paymaster.[61] Still, legionary commanders had

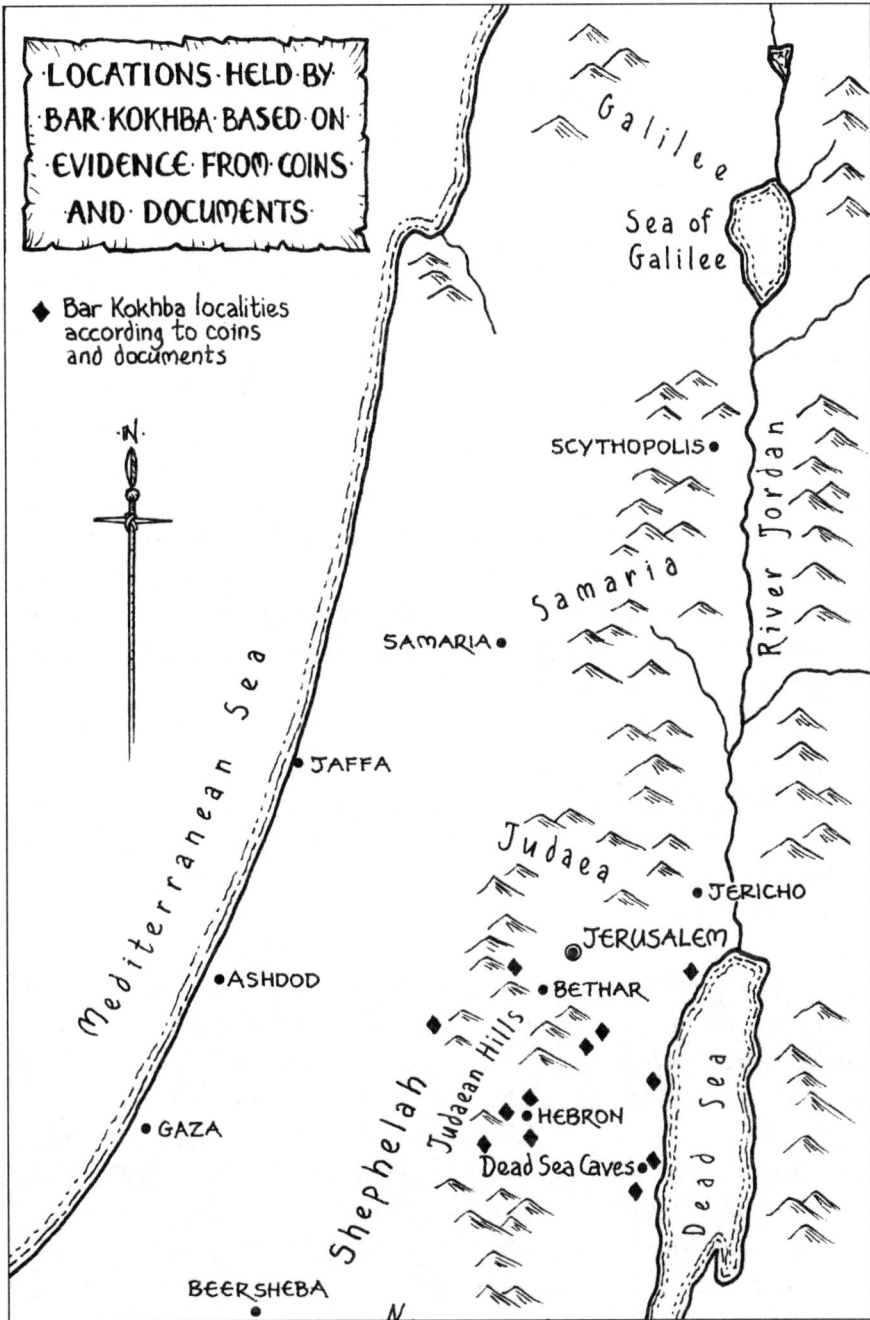

Map 8 *Locations held by Bar Kokhba based on evidence from coins and documents*

to beware of the possibility that large enemy numbers remained hidden in this terrain, and could launch a surprise attack and encircle Roman contingents. In a similar manner, Publius Marcellus, governor of Syria, had to bring the Legio III Gallica to the aid of Tinneius Rufus, governor of Judaea in Galilee, when the Jews made good use of the many treacherous defiles there.[62]

Scholars still do not agree on the geographical scope of the war, even though the coins and the documents from the Dead Sea caves seem to concur as to where Bar Kokhba operated. All the coin hoard discoveries are from the Judaean heartland, as are all the locations mentioned in the papyri; one of the Bar Kokhba hoards or the Dead Sea papyri came from the coastal plain, Jerusalem or sites in Samaria and Galilee. This has caused some scholars to draw a map of Bar Kokhba's territory that does not include anything to the north of Jerusalem, in the Negev desert or on the coast.[63] The hide-outs and subterranean strong-points found in the western foothills on the eastern edge of the coastal plain (the Shephelah) occur along a line more or less parallel with the coast, suggesting this was the first line of Jewish defence.[64] Werner Eck, on the other hand, rejected the idea that hostilities occurred only in Judaea. His argument makes no distinction between territories directly held and occupied for a long time by the rebels (where rebel coins were used and sometimes lost) and those territories outside Judaea where Bar Kokhba never exercised direct control but where battles did occur. He cites the erection of a triumphal arch for Hadrian in Galilee near Scythopolis as possibly marking the site of a major battle. The involvement of the governors of Arabia and Syria makes it very likely that the revolt spread beyond the limits of Judaea proper.[65]

One of Bar Kokhba's main problems was a shortage of manpower. Severely outnumbered, the Jews relied on intelligence as a force multiplier to even the odds. They were so outclassed in military proficiency for fighting set battles or siege warfare that they could not let the war devolve on those tactics. Bar Kokhba started with amateurs and forged them into a professional fighting force that used irregular tactics. This required arduous military training, and his army had to operate under severe discipline. Much like Judas Maccabeus, Bar Kokhba tried to augment his forces with Jewish volunteers from outside. Cassius Dio says: 'All Judaea had been stirred up, and the Jews everywhere were showing signs of disturbance, were gathering together and giving evidence of great hostility to the Romans, partly by secret and partly by overt acts.'[66] Bar Kokhba was especially seeking men with military experience for the important staff and training assignments. Gichon believed the name lists found in the

Qumran caves were the rolls of the Bar Kokhba fighters. The Greek script and Greek names belonged to foreign reinforcements.[67]

The Romans Strike Back

The Roman response was not very swift, as was the case in the Jewish Revolt of 66. The sources usually interpret the Roman reaction as cavalier indifference.[68] The Roman counteroffensive began in spring 133, led by the emperor Hadrian himself. As his second-in-command he had his best general, Julius Severus, former governor of Britain.[69] We do not have a complete list of the Roman forces, but they included troops from nine to twelve legions, and auxiliaries from as far away as England.[70]

Hadrian recaptured Galilee by a two-pronged attack launched from Acre. This site was an excellent base. Troops, equipment and supplies could be brought in by sea or from Gerasa in Trans-jordan, where the Syrian legions were concentrated.[71] Hadrian's troops proceeded south in a pincer movement along the Jordan valley and the coastal plain. He built roads into small regions of mountainous terrain and sliced them off from the rest of the country. He thus isolated and then slowly reduced these areas. The Romans established base camps in the Jordan valley on commanding ground with good all-around visibility. From there they pushed out into advance camps and sealed off each wadi. They surrounded the Jewish positions with a belt of fieldworks so as to 'exhaust and exterminate' them by depriving them of food and shutting them up. The pattern was repeated all the way down to Jericho and farther south.[72]

The Romans had a large intelligence problem of their own: how to find the Jews. There would be no open pitched battle in this war. There was guerrilla activity on the part of the Jews, and the systematic isolation and reduction of mountain strongholds by the Romans.[73] The Romans even hired experts to devise tactics that would allow them to operate in this kind of terrain and to locate the enemy. Apollodorus of Damascus wrote his *Poliorketika*, a tactical and engineering treatise, as a result of the Bar Kokhba War.[74] Apollodorus was an outstanding military engineer of his day. Among his achievements was the bridge over the Danube in Dacia. Now, when in trouble, Hadrian requested his advice on how best to fight a people who did not shut themselves up in conventional fortifications but rather opted for the more flexible stratagem of occupying easily defensible natural features that could readily be evacuated and changed at a moment's notice. Apollodorus designed an armoured Observation Platform that would be telescoped upwards from behind cover for quick exten-

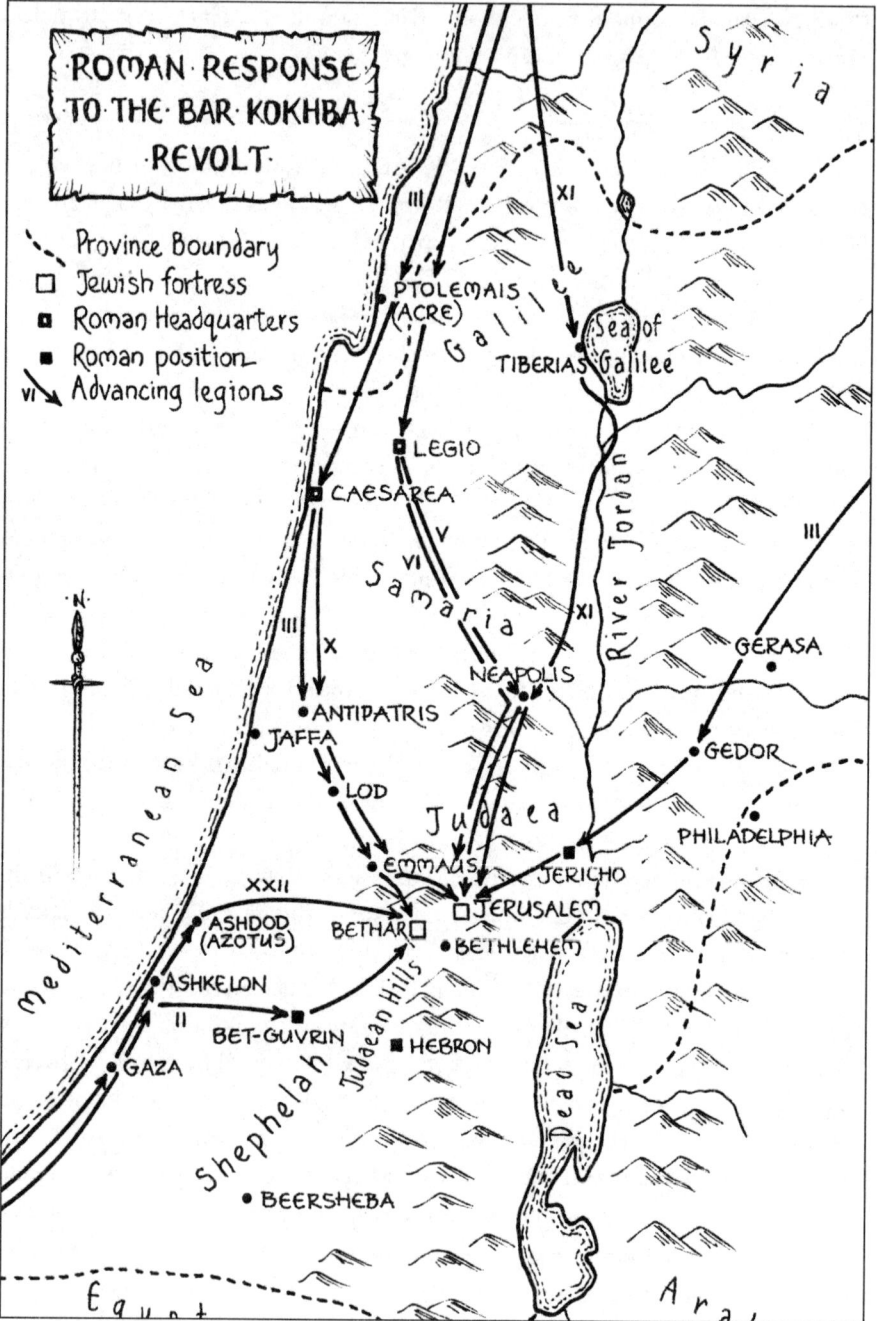

Map 9 Roman response to the Bar Kokhba Revolt

sion and quick hauling in. The broken terrain demanded many easy-to-assemble bridges constructed with a minimum of wood.[75]

Their adoption of hit-and-run tactics showed that the Jews had learned the lesson of the last war. By husbanding their forces and luring the Romans after them into unfavourable territory, they sustained their fight against the Roman counteroffensive. Once the decision to fight had been taken, this flexible in-depth defence was the only wise strategy against Roman imperial forces. As with any guerrilla war, the Jewish hope lay in drawing out the war long enough to induce other hostile forces, from within the empire or from without, to take up arms against Rome and to exhaust the Roman will to win this war at any cost. They did not have the modern option of waiting for world opinion to turn against the occupying force. Lacking our modern media, there was no 'world opinion', and the Romans were quite willing to commit genocide to win the war.

The Last Days

Extraordinary discoveries in the region of Nahal Hever, the documents from Wadi Murabba'at and the finds in Wadi ed-Daliya tell us a great deal about the last days of the Jewish refugees.[76] The Cave of Letters, in particular, contained a great variety of objects relating to the final stages of the Bar Kokhba Revolt, when fugitives occupied the caves. Excavators found the remains of food and cooking utensils, wrapped-up skeletons buried in the cave, and a great many things that were not used in cave dwelling but were obviously being taken along and protected in hopes of survival and return. A basket full of copper vessels was doubtless war booty taken from the Romans, and it is interesting that the human figures decorating the vessels had been wilfully obliterated in accordance with Mosaic law, which forbade any graven images. Cultic incense pans were found, as well as the prize of the 1960 season – the Bar Kokhba Letters.[77] A set of three magnificent glass plates had been carefully wrapped in palm fibres and bound with string. Someone had taken her best tableware with her. Also recovered were mirrors, coins, shoes, clothes, keys and small parts of documents that had been previously looted by local Bedouin.[78] The discovery of the Babatha archive alerted scholars to the possibility that Arabia was involved in the Bar Kokhba Revolt; Babatha was a woman from Arabia who had fled to Judaea.[79] An archive from Mahhoza in the Cave of Letters in Nahal Hever has another example.[80] Since we know that the single legion stationed in Arabia, the III Cyrenaica, was actively engaged in the campaign, we can suggest that the governor of Arabia took part in the suppression of the revolt.[81]

In the end, these discoveries show that this conflict was not an intelligence war or a war of wits. Force, as in the war of 66, was the deciding factor. The problem of dwindling manpower and resources caught up with the Jews, once they realised they had no access to reinforcements. In summer 135, Bar Kokhba died defending Bethar, the scene of the rebellion's last stand.[82] Very few Jews survived the aftermath, although it was probably not as bad as described in the Midrash Rabbah (Lamentations 2:2–4). During the siege, Bethar sheltered an enormous population, which gave rise to exaggerated rabbinical accounts that Bethar had several hundred schools and that children bragged they could rise up against the Romans and stab them with their writing pens.

The location of Bethar still remains a mystery. Some rabbinic sources put it close to Samaritan territory. Eusebius locates it close to Jerusalem (making it unlikely that Jerusalem was uninvolved in the battle); other scholars have identified it with the modern Bittir.[83] The traditional date of the destruction is the ninth of Ab – the same day the Temple was destroyed by the Romans and the Babylonians.[84] Even the death of Bar Kokhba is shrouded in legend. According to Talmudic sources, after the fall of Bethar, he was found with a serpent around his neck.[85]

The Aftermath – The Romans

In assessing Rome's intelligence capabilities, we should ask how much of a threat Bar Kokhba's revolt was to Rome. Did the Romans underestimate it? Were the military measures taken adequate or did the Romans overreact? Those who believe that the threat to Roman power by the Jews has been greatly exaggerated should reconsider. More than half the legions at Hadrian's disposal had been thrown into the fray, coming from the far reaches of the empire. The emperor himself had camped in Trans-jordan to direct the campaign. Besides the two regular legions that took part in the war, seven more legions represented by *vexillationes* also took part.[86] Werner Eck gathered the inscriptional evidence to show that Hadrian sent his best generals against the insurgents.[87] Hadrian also awarded them the rare honour of the *ornamenta triumphalia*.[88]

The Judaean campaign of 132–135 was still remembered in Rome some thirty years later as a major event. The war left a lasting impact, and cost the Romans much. It was not merely a suppression of some local provincials. M. Cornelius Fronto, the foremost orator of his day, wrote a consolatory treatise, *De Bello Parthico*, to comfort his former pupil, the emperor Marcus Aurelius, for severe military losses in the Parthian War. In this treatise, Fronto reminded

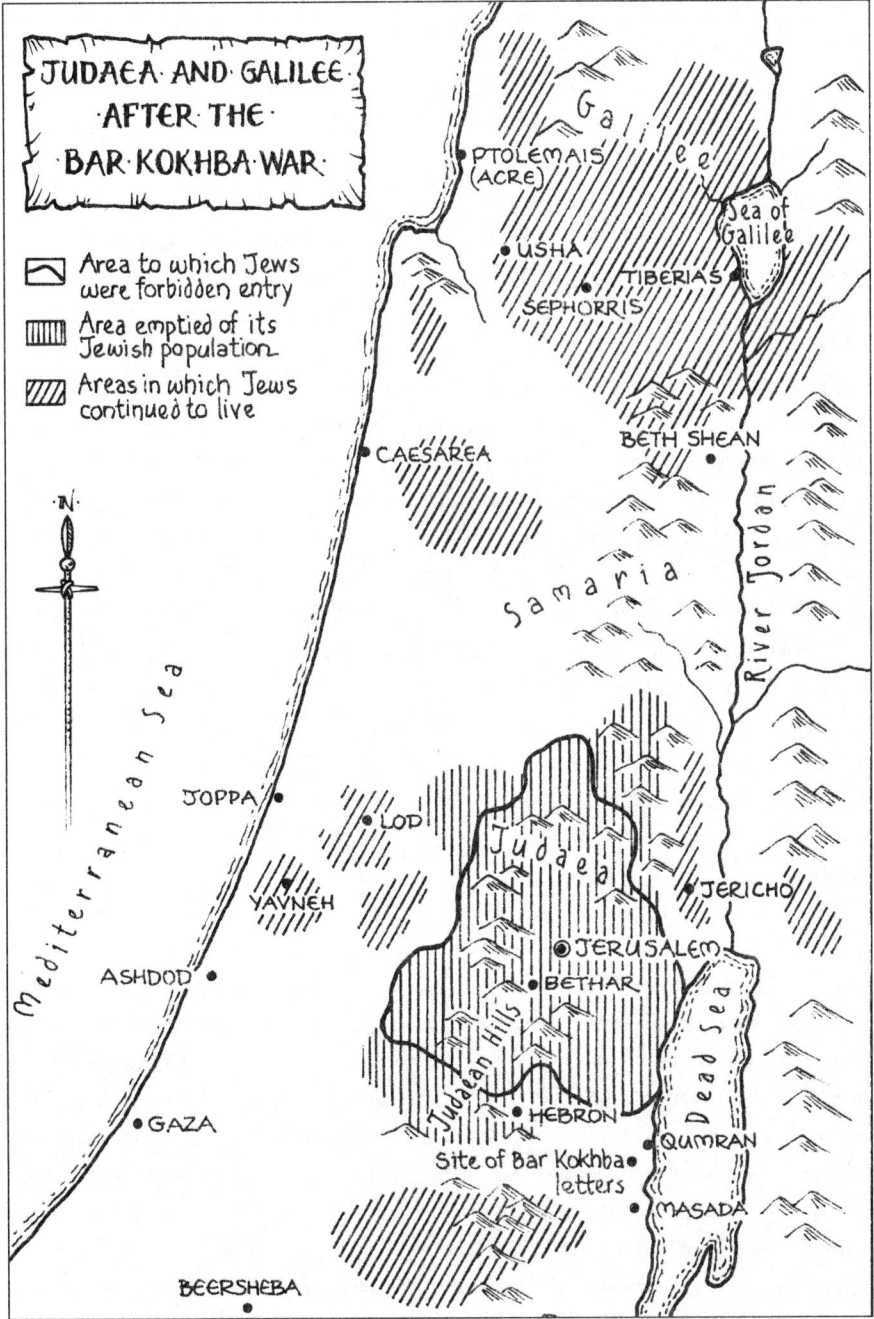

Map 10 *Judaea and Galilee after the Bar Kokhba War*

the emperor of Hadrian's previous misfortunes. He drew a direct comparison between the Roman casualties in the Bar Kokhba War and the continual frontier war in Britain; he also made an indirect comparison with the two earlier Parthian wars. In his Letter to Marcus Aurelius he presents the war against Bar Kokhba as if it were a military defeat and talks about the 'significant number of soldiers who were killed by the Jews'.[89] Hadrian's wish to let this 'Judaean mischief' fade into oblivion was impossible given Roman awareness of the facts. Pausanias 1.5.5 remembered Hadrian's operations against the Jews as a serious conflict. Dio Cassius tells us that the emperor, in view of the heavy Roman casualties, purposely omitted the usual salutation following a major victory when writing to the Senate: 'I and the legions are well.'[90] Dio refers to the revolt as a *polemos*, which he does not use when describing revolts in the diaspora. And it may be worth noting that most of the atrocities in this rebellion were civilian non-combatants, which suggests a total war against the Jews. Talmudic sources seem to capture Hadrian's mood. A midrash relates that Hadrian met a Jew who failed to salute him. The ruler ordered him killed. A second Jew, having witnessed this scene, hastened to greet Hadrian, who also killed the second Jew. When Hadrian's advisors asked why the second man was put to death, Hadrian replied: 'Don't tell me how to deal with my enemies.'[91] Both Dio and Fronto help to elucidate something unique in Roman numismatics: the omission of any allusion to this war in Roman coinage. For Hadrian, the empire's final defeat of the Jews was almost a Pyrrhic victory, best left unmentioned.[92]

The Aftermath – The Jews

Excavation of the caves at Nahal Hever has produced gruesome evidence about the final days of the last Bar Kokhba survivors. This site was without doubt a principal cave refuge of the Bar Kokhba troops in the area. Two Roman camps were placed directly above these caves at the edge of the canyon. In 1955, the cave was named the Cave of Horror because of the numerous skeletons found there, including those of infants and children. Coins found all date to the Bar Kokhba period, and have legends that read 'Freedom of Jerusalem' and the name 'Simeon'. About forty people took refuge in this cave. They met their death there not through violence, but because they ran out of food and water. All the Romans had to do was wait. The siege was long. Even when the Jews began to die, they buried their dead at the back of the cave. They chose to die rather than surrender. The cave is not very large, and there was no chance they could hide anything that would not be found by the Romans. They destroyed everything except a Greek scroll with the twelve minor prophets and some other important documents, which they buried between the rocks at the end of the chamber.[93] Further evidence from the Cave of Letters in Nahal Hever also provided evidence of makeshift burials, dead Bar Kokhba warriors and precious items stored for later retrieval.[94]

After the revolt, the Romans issued a number of decrees of religious persecution in Judaea, but their purpose did not seem to be the suppression of the Jewish religion as such. The decrees of persecution did not include demands to violate religious prohibitions such as idolatry or the consumption of prohibited foods.[95] The Romans wanted simply to suppress those elements of the religion that had led people to revolt. Anything that held a nationalistic purpose had to go, along with the autonomy of the Jewish people.[96]

Destruction on the Judaean side was even greater. Dio says fifty fortresses and 985 of the most important settlements were destroyed by the Romans.[97] Some 580,000 men were slaughtered in the many skirmishes and raids, and those who died of hunger, sickness and fire were innumerable. 'Thus nearly the whole of Judaea was made desolate, a result of which the people had been forewarned before the war, and many wolves and hyenas rushed howling into their cities.'[98]

Intelligence and Guerrilla Warfare

At least one question remains: how close had the Jews come to success in the Bar Kokhba Revolt? Bar Kokhba seems to have used the full tactical capabilities of peasant troops who knew the terrain, and he made use of ambush and the defensive virtues on the Judaean hills. At least he avoided the error of the last war and did not let it come down to defending a large town such as Jerusalem, populated by non-combatants and non-committed elements. He could bring the Roman forces to a standstill in the hill country and inflict heavy losses on them, but he failed to find a way to face them on the plains.[99]

How effective were their intelligence operations, their planned tactics and the execution of those plans? Guerrilla warfare places the colonial power in a difficult situation if its leaders have any reluctance about striking at villages and civilians who lend support to the insurgents. Such inhibitions were a severe limiting factor for the French in Algeria and the Americans in Vietnam. The Romans, on the other hand, had no such inhibitions. For them, there was little difference between combatants and civilians. They deemed the entire Judaean population hostile, and did not recoil from systematic extermination of villages. They treated Judaea as if it were a big fortified city, whose inhabitants, once captured, were

195

to be killed or enslaved. The type of warfare opted for by the Jews in the rebellion led to a situation in which the Romans could only prevail through a policy of extermination, even though that had not been their premeditated aim. In the end, however, the Romans were quite willing to use sheer force and brutality.

The intelligence that gave the guerrillas flexibility and mobility only served them well temporarily. The Jewish rebels emerged from their caves, and staged surprise attacks on the Romans, but as soon as the Romans came to know these caves and how they were used they developed countermeasures, such as sealing off their entrances and exits, throwing combustible material into them to force out those inside, and setting ambushes at cave outlets.[100] Once Roman intelligence learned how to detect Jewish insurgents, the caves became death traps for those who hid in them. The Jews tried to make this a war of attrition, but the Romans turned the tables by creating a siege around Judaea, and the Romans were experts in the art of siege warfare. Although the Jews were extremely clever and resourceful in their use of intelligence in both in the Great Jewish Revolt and the Bar Kokhba War, the Romans benefited from the same advantage in both wars – being able to move troops and to attain local superiority, whereas the Jews inevitably got tied down in an overall defensive posture.

Unlike in the Maccabean Revolt, the enemy no longer fought in the unwieldy Hellenistic hoplite phalanx. The Roman army had a structure that enabled it to split into smaller units and to spread over the area as required in counterguerrilla action or in fighting on hilly terrain. Roman military superiority was the product of superior organisation, not of superior technology, weaponry or intelligence. The Roman soldier was not necessarily a superior fighter to the religiously inspired Jew; the individual Jewish fighter may even have surpassed the Roman warrior in his courage or daring in battle. The Romans were successful because of their tactical organisation. Bar Kokhba had no such advantage. With little time at his disposal, he was unable to train his troops to the standard of tactical proficiency reached by the Romans, who were all professional soldiers. More importantly, time was lacking for the training of those junior commanders whose independent role and initiative were equally significant in small-unit action. We do not know what previous experience and knowledge Bar Kokhba had. It may have been enough to make him a reasonably good general, but that did not enable him to build a military system capable of ultimately defeating the Romans.[101]

Was Bar Kokhba misguided to think that he could get enough support from outside of Israel? There had been revolts in the diaspora before. Barely forty years had elapsed after the fall of Masada when the Roman Empire suffered an outbreak of Jewish revolts.[102] The communities in exile had militants among them who had survived the First Revolt, and occasionally the old spirit flamed into hostilities and the Jews suddenly started fighting for their spiritual and religious independence. In 115 CE in Cyrenaica, Jews under the leadership of a 'king' named Loukuas-Andreas fought against the local population so fiercely that eventually the Romans were compelled to intervene. Shortly thereafter the Jews of Egypt rose up, too. Cyprus followed, and so did Mesopotamia with a general revolt in 116 CE. The commander who finally crushed the revolt was Lucius Quietus, a romanised Moor who was later appointed governor of Palestine. In some Jewish sources there is a reference to the 'polemos of Quietus' – the war of Quietus.[103]

Bar Kokhba, however, never got any significant backing from outside Judaea, and he had no diplomatic contact with countries that might have otherwise come to his aid. The Jews 'pouring in', described by Dio, may have been equivalent to the volunteers coming into Iraq today from Syria, Saudi Arabia or Iran.[104] Not even the Galilean Jews were willing to join in Bar Kokhba's guerrilla war in spite of his initial successes. He was neither willing nor able to convince the Romans to reconcile themselves to the Jewish occupation of Judaea and to halt the war.

As Yehoshafat Harkabi has pointed out in his book, *The Bar Kokhba Syndrome*, the Jewish achievement on the tactical level became almost irrelevant when elevated to the strategic level. In war, the main thing is to win the last battle, not the first one. Clausewitz said that war is meant to achieve results. It is not supposed to be waged on impulse, to vent fury or to manifest grievances; it must be waged to reach a goal.[105] The goal of Bar Kokhba was to liberate his people from the Romans, but in the end the Jews lost half their population, they were banned from most of Judaea, Jerusalem was in ruins, and the losses to Jewish literature and learning are inestimable. By these standards, the war does not seem to have been such a good idea.[106]

The Jews have been criticised for starting the revolt, because: 'The Jewish army had no prospect of producing a force equal to a contest with the Roman army.'[107] One may ask, however, did they really need to? The point of the revolt was to expel the Romans and make a settlement that would allow a less-oppressive regime to rule over Judaea. The Jews could never expect to do this militarily, so they had to rely on guerrilla operations and superior intelligence gathering. The very fact that they were willing to take on the revolt makes a statement about the intolerable conditions under which they lived, and the price they were willing to pay to get out from under them. There was no military power in the Mediterranean world that could field a force as large as Rome's. This, however, did not stop revolts from occurring. It is also important to remember that the Jews under Bar Kokhba did not have the intelligence at their disposal that a modern commander might have today. It is easy to second guess their actions in hindsight. At the time, they thought revolt was their best alternative. The nation was united behind the leadership of that revolt, militarily as well as spiritually. Talmudic Judaism, however, did not have our sense of modern historiography. To the religious, the Jews were not just actors in world history, they were in the hands of God. Moreover, the modern world is not immune to such appeals. The modern Zionist movement of redemption made the revolt of Bar Kokhba a model for action. The slogan of the Ha-Shomer Watchmen's Society of the Second Aliyah period was: 'In blood and fire Judaea fell, in blood and fire Judaea shall rise.' This was not simple romanticism or an attachment to an epic heroic past, but a realistic view of how revolutions are made – through wars of liberation, whatever the odds.[108] The more serious the motivation for the revolt, the more intense it is and the less sense of probability it requires. That is not to say this was an emotional reaction or a spontaneous outburst, as Harkabi has charged. The preparations for the revolt went on for ten years prior to 132. Beyond the desire for liberty itself, the revolt was sparked by Hadrian's policies towards the Jews and the plan to turn Jerusalem into a city of idolatry – Aelia Capitolina.

The implications of these actions for the Jews of that period are clear. Some believe Rabbi Akiba joined forces with Bar Kokhba along with his entire camp to the extent of referring to him as king-messiah. These scholars believe this made the revolt distinct from the Great Revolt, because now they had the unity of the people under a joint spiritual and practical leadership, thanks to the personality of Rabbi Akiba.[109] Other scholars, however, point out that in the coin evidence and the papyri, Bar Kokhba only took the title of *nasi* (prince or ruler) and was simply a military leader.[110] Many of his followers believed in divine intervention; they were not called zealots because they were half-convinced. More than most commentators care to imagine, the ancient world was populated by people who were intensely religious and superstitious and who believed in signs, prophecies, soothsayers and miracles. It is precisely because the Jewish rebels were inspired by their faith that they fought so well and so effectively against the Romans. They believed they had nothing to lose, and were perfectly willing to die for their cause.

Harkabi admires the Roman killing machine, but the Romans were not invincible. The Battle of the Teutoburg Forest stopped Roman expansion in Germany in 9 CE and altered Roman foreign policy across the Rhine forever. Unlike the Germans, however, the Jews did not have endless numbers of warriors who could withdraw into the vast forests of the north when the Romans approached. Judaea was a small place with its back to the sea, and the Jews had nowhere to retreat. The Parthians could lure the Romans into the desert and count on the desert itself and the climate to weaken them, and then strike the Romans from a distance with long-range weapons. The Jews, unfortunately, were trapped in their mountain hide-outs. A talented leader like Spartacus could outmanoeuvre the Romans inside their own territory for years, but in the end the fate of the slaves was death in battle or mass crucifixion.

The Roman success was not without its cost. Historians such as Weber and Mommsen assigned the failure of Rome to subjugate Parthia to the Jewish revolts in North Africa and Cyprus during 114–117 CE, when Quietus was forced to recall his armies from the East. The Bar Kokhba Revolt may have added to Hadrian's resignation finally to give up all thought of conquering the East.[111]

The Jews chose to attack the Roman Empire when it was at the zenith of its power and organisation. They were located in a strategically important province that the Romans had no intention of giving away. There was no time when a negotiated solution might have been slipped in; that is, there was no interregnum such as that between the death of Nero and the accession of Vespasian in 69 CE. The Romans never let a challenge to their authority go unanswered: for example, in 70 CE they spent considerable time reducing Masada, a fortress that had no strategic importance whatsoever except that its destruction was an object lesson to people who might consider revolting. The Jews simply did not have sufficient time, space or manpower to resist the Roman occupation. They waged three of the most impressive anti-colonial wars in antiquity, and their use of intelligence was brilliant. The last two wars took a heavy toll on the Romans, but such wars are valuable only as a symbol of defiance, not as a model for success.

POSTSCRIPT TO PART II
Spying for Yahweh: Ancient Spies and Modern Historians

THERE IS NO DOUBT that the Holy Land has given birth to some of the most memorable spies in history and literature. Some of them are named, but the great majority of them are unknown to us, as happens with all good intelligence operatives who do their job well and do not have their covers blown. It does not take much imagination to figure out that any country that has seen as much warfare as Israel will have performed a great deal of intelligence gathering, analysis and dissemination, not to mention covert operations, assassination and terrorism.

The most difficult problem confronting any scholar writing about the ancient world is the limited, fortuitous and tendentious nature of the sources. The history of Israel is no different. In reconstructing Israel's intelligence history there are a great many uncertainties which we must fill in with hypotheses. Perhaps, ironically, this is a problem that sometimes plagues modern intelligence analysts. Neither historian nor analyst will ever have as much information as they might want or need. The one source at our disposal, the Bible, was not written as a history in our modern sense of the word, and therefore had another agenda entirely. There is virtually no agreed-on opinion in academic circles as to whether the Bible qualifies as history, its date of composition or the process it went through to reach its present form. I have tried to show that diversity of opinion, and yet, if we are honest, we need to admit that we will never have all the information we need to make even an informed guess about the historicity of the activities discussed in the text.

Mixed Results
Why do the Jews seem to have had so much success early in their history against Canaanites, Philistines and even Greeks, but then fared so poorly against the Romans? Surely part of the answer must be the nature of the people they were

fighting. When the Jews attacked desert Bedouin, single Canaanite cities or Greeks who were occupied with other wars, they had a chance of success. The rules changed when the Jews fought as inhabitants of an occupied territory, in a centralised Roman Empire, whose emperor had twenty-eight legions at his disposal. The Romans had the political will to commit genocide if it would keep them from losing a province.

Another reason for the great disparity in the results Israel experienced in its wars is the nature of the sources describing the battles. The Hebrew scriptures are filled with the early stories of great Jewish successes against what seem like insurmountable odds, but this is because Yahweh often fought their battles for them. The Hebrew Bible, as a literary creation, had an author who could control the outcome of battles with the stroke of a pen. This is not an unusual phenomenon. The famous *chanson de geste* 'The Song of Roland' describes a victory by Charlemagne in the Pyrenean mountains against the Saracens, and yet in the real battle in 778 the rearguard of Charlemagne's army was slaughtered in the Roncesvalles pass by Basques. In another famous epic, *The Iliad*, historians have been unable to verify whether the Trojan War ever happened, let alone prove that the Greeks were the victors. Great literature does not always reflect history. In sum, during the historical period of Jewish history we have a combination of Roman sources that are less than sympathetic to the Jewish cause, and a military situation in which the Jews could never prevail. Even a Jewish historian such as Josephus, who tried to give the Jewish people a fair hearing, chose to support the Roman point of view. The story of revolts against Rome inevitably become a story of unremitting Jewish losses.

The result of the battles shifts with the changing nature of the sources over a thousand years of Israelite history. From Polybius onwards, Graeco-Roman historiography as regards Judaea is suddenly characterised by an emphasis on rationality and power politics rather than the will of God. As Arnaldo Momigliano has pointed out, the revival of Jewish historical writing in the period 200 BCE to 100 CE is inseparable from Greek influence. As we pass into the Hellenistic and Roman worlds, we seem on much firmer ground when discussing military events, and we can make more definite statements about intelligence operations. The Hebrew Bible may have been written against an historical background, and may even contain allusions to historical events, but it is not, strictly speaking, history. 'Historical Israel is not the Israel of the Hebrew Bible. Rather, historical Israel produced biblical Israel.'[1] This problem alone forms an entire academic field of biblical studies. Scholars such as Baruch Halpern believe that the Israel of the pre-monarchic period is not significantly different from the picture painted in the biblical sources; others, especially the so-called 'minimalists', would totally disagree.

This does not mean that religious sources should be discounted entirely; Jewish religious life tells us about the literary aspects of their culture and about their social milieu. As a work of the exile or post-exilic period, the Dtr history can be seen as the collective memory of a people in exile trying to recast ancient traditions into a national history. The point was to create a history for a people who had previously had no written tradition of historiography.

The Jews in Arms

What can be said in summary about the way the Jews fought and the importance of intelligence operations in their military affairs? Part of the answer must be geographical. The centrality and the extraordinary smallness of Palestine is its defining feature. The major routes through the area have been followed century after century by both merchants and warriors.[2] The history of Palestine is very much conditioned by its position at a crossroads. It was, in theory, an independent state for less than ten per cent of its history and even much of that independence was illusory.[3] The Jews lived in a vast and menacing world in which the effective Jewish settlement was quite small. From Dan in the north to Beersheva in the south is little more than two hundred and forty kilometres as the crow flies. From Joppa to Jordan is no more than seventy-two kilometres.[4]

Unified action was not a strong point of Jewish history. Much of their torment came out of their own internal conflicts as much as from the stranglehold of foreign powers.[5] These two forces acted and reacted on each other. Imperial governments such as the Seleucids and the Romans used Jewish internal conflicts for their own purposes. The Palestinian communities in their desperation sought again and again the help of foreign authority to resolve their problems, only to find that they had solved nothing at all. The pattern has been true not merely for centuries but millennia. The pattern is demonstrably no different today.[6]

The nature of Jewish fighting changed as their organisation and centralisation changed. If we accept the biblical account as a conceptual model of the stages of Israelite development into a state, then Israel's wars can be roughly divided into three different types: tribal wars; wars during an independent monarchy with operations directed from a centralised capital; and guerrilla wars.

The Era of Tribal Wars In the tribal era of Israel's history, every able-bodied man was expected to fight. Subsistence agriculture was too labour-intensive

202

to allow for the maintenance of a regular army. Israel could not have supplied the manpower needed for such a force; and men were required in the fields and at home. Nor could it support such an army in the field of war. In pre-monarchichal Israel, there was just not enough centralisation of power to effect the necessary redistribution of production to this end. Recruitment was at the local level, as well as leadership and battle organisation.

We are not dealing here with a large number of fighters or fighting units. The Jews would not fight for strangers, and did not wander very far afield. There could not have been extensive and continuous control in the field, nor could tactics have been very complicated. Lengthy and costly campaigns were out of the question. This type of warfare did not have central command, centralised intelligence gathering and certainly the leadership was incapable of any grand strategy. Tactics were influenced by the familiarity of the fighters with the terrain, and wars tended to be defensive.[7] This is exactly the picture we get from the Book of Judges. The armies called up by Deborah, Barak and Gideon were for the defence of Israel against attacks by the Canaanite cities that were attempting to dislodge Israel from the hill country of Galilee or were repulsing an invasion of Midianites.[8] Wars of this period must have been relatively short-lived affairs. The battles themselves were probably not much more than skirmishes that lasted for a few hours at most. The supply problems were never acute, because these were local, defensive wars and the combatants were never far from local food supplies. Communication was easy for the same reason – the distances were small. Once in battle, units were informed by the use of runners and messengers, but exactly how well is not clear.

When confronted by an organised force, an irregular army such as described here was compelled to demoralise the enemy by the removal of their leader – the surprise causing panic – or by the inventive use of terrain and seasonal weather. As the Psalm says more poetically: 'Let them be turned back and confounded, who devise evil against me. Let them be like the chaff before the wind' (Psalms 35:4–5). This is precisely when soldiers discard the very things that would protect them – armour, weapons, shields. A back turned to the enemy is a vulnerable and exposed one. A well-aimed arrow could wound or kill; so could a sling stone, or the thrust of a javelin. Certainly Gideon's attack on the Midianite encampment is an example of this (Judges 7:19–22).

Wars During an Independent Monarchy The appearance of a monarchy in Israel presented an opportunity for centralised command, communications, control and intelligence. All of these elements were necessary on the field of battle whatever the sophistication level of the organisation. Those who step on to a battlefield must be told what to do and when to do it. Some element of control is required if the fighting is to be conducted with any degree of success. The need for control increased as the battle order and the supporting social system became more complicated. A standing army required a staff and administrative support as well as a command structure. Some of the burden of supporting such an army fell on the local population. We have no information on the structure of the Israelite army nor how the separate units of spearman, swordsmen, archers and slingers were organised or how they communicated. We do not even know exactly when the chariot was introduced (mid-ninth century, perhaps).

The battles Israel fought in the monarchic period remained a combination of surprise attacks and panic caused by the use of these tactics so that the confused enemy inflicted more damage on itself than did the Israelites. Small wars, skirmishes and surprise offensives relied entirely on intelligence gathering for their success. Jonathan's attack on the Philistines at Michmash (1 Samuel 14) is an example. It should not be assumed that the army of this period was well organised. There is often a tendency to read back into the past the concerns of the present. Creating a grand army to go along with the picture of a big Israel under David and Solomon may be an example of a logical fallacy.

Guerrilla Warfare Fought by an Occupied Israel With the destruction of the Temple and the loss of national independence, the Jews did not deal with military matters as a state until the rise of modern Israel. During the Roman occupation, the Jews went back to practising an essentially guerrilla-style warfare. They used quick, fierce raids and charges, and surprise if possible. Ambushes and attacks were designed to detach or corner a section of the enemy forces in order to gain numerical superiority in close hand-to-hand combat, or to bombard them with hand missiles.

The effort was always to exploit topographical advantages and to employ swiftness, mobility and particularly a certain stubbornness and boldness prominent among what Josephus called 'the peculiar characteristics of the nation' (*BJ* 6.17). One scholar has characterised this warfare as 'daring, violent attack, simultaneous charge and the refusal to retreat even while being defeated'.[9] The Israeli interest in guerrilla warfare is not simply historical. In the 1970s and 1980s there was wide interest in people's war of liberation, popular subversive wars and low-intensity conflict; and it is not surprising that the Israelis were in the forefront of the scholarship. Their concern with this issue far transcends the purely academic. They were occupied in a guerrilla war to gain their independence in

1948, and have been embroiled more recently in the process of putting down such wars, in the form of the *Intifada* and the current fight against Hezbollah.

The use of guerrilla tactics was dictated mainly by the historical experience of the Jews. Victories from the Hebrew Bible and the Books of the Maccabees showed the success that guerrilla warfare could bring. Jewish tactics were also dictated by their equipment: they remained dependent on swords and daggers – their mainstay throughout their history. They do not seem to have had long weapons in any significant quantity, nor did they use much body armour. They protected themselves with shields. Jewish archers are occasionally mentioned, but they do not seem to have played a major role in any of the battles. There is absolutely no sign of their having been organised into units – their numbers were probably too small and they were not an integral part of the Jewish defence strategy. Archery and combat with long weapons required development of skills that were not part of the repertoire of the revolutionaries-turned-army. Major changes in equipment and tactics would have been too costly. Moreover, the burden of less wieldy weapons or heavy armour would have cancelled out the Jews' great advantage of speed and manoeuvrability.[10] The Jews were specialists in the stone-throwing that seems to have been their immediate response to provocation during war. The defenders of Jerusalem certainly used stones, but they also threw anything at hand, especially when providing cover for a charge. This allowed the general population to join in assaults from atop roofs or walls and eventually the Temple Mount. Those with training in the sling could outrange a bow.[11] During the Siege of Jerusalem, the Jews' success in close combat and their use of projectiles served them well, but allowing the battle to devolve into a siege on the city in 66 CE was a big mistake.

Israel's forces, whenever they were deployed, usually featured smaller numbers and inferiority of armament and training compared to their enemies. More often than not, they used an indirect approach in order to avoid frontal assault by chariots in an open field, siege warfare or a direct attack by Greek or Roman heavy infantry. The Israelites resorted to tactics based on deception – feints, decoys, ambushes and diversionary manoeuvres. They used guile to attain surprise in overcoming the enemy. Echoes of this can be seen throughout the Bible.[12] Given the large numbers of battle stratagems mentioned in the Books of Joshua and Judges, one can only imagine what might have been contained in the 'Book of Wars of the Lord' and the 'Book of Jashar', both mentioned in the conquest cycle.[13] Also stratagems of ambush and feigned retreat from Palestine are mentioned in Graeco-Roman sources.[14]

The Jews and Intelligence Operations

Considering all the available evidence, can we say anything meaningful about intelligence as it was collected, analysed and disseminated in ancient Israel? We can certainly make an educated guess. Throughout their history in the Holy Land, the Jews were involved in warfare. To be victorious, armies were organised, men were trained and equipped, and intelligence had to be collected. Their pre-occupation with warfare and military matters should therefore seem natural. The Jews were a people under siege for much of their history. They had to develop techniques of warfare and intelligence gathering in order to survive. During the Roman period when sources were more plentiful and seemed more reliable, we can see that most of the descriptions depict the same types of operations.

Since political and military leadership in biblical times possessed the faculty of rational judgement, it may be assumed that ancient commanders displayed the usual talents, weaknesses and ambitions shared by their modern counter-parts. Certainly in the Hebrew scriptures there are no discernible scruples about spying, and no moral qualms are raised about the use of espionage. The level of sophistication shown by their leadership and their intelligence operations, however, suggests a much later date for the stories than is assumed by many historians. Nonetheless, there is no reason why an understanding of the use of intelligence was not a constant even in earlier times.[15]

Remarkably, spies were not always professional soldiers or intelligence offic-ers. They might have been men or women, high born or low, foreigner or Israel-ite, wives, lovers, prostitutes or civilians. The important factor was that they had access to information that someone else needed, and they were willing to trade it for love, money or religious ideology. This is similar to the situation of modern spies except that the motivating ideology has most recently been political. A spy may be a professional intelligence operative or a custodian at an American embassy who finds a scrap of paper a careless person forgot to shred.

The Israelites developed speed, strength and knowledge of the terrain in order to crush otherwise unbeatable enemies. The stratagem of feigned retreat was well known in ancient times and has been referred to as 'the oldest ruse in warfare'.[16] Sun Tzu also recognised the principle when he wrote: 'All warfare is based on deception. Therefore, when capable, feign incapacity; when active, inactivity. When near, make it appear that you are far away; when far away, that you are near. Offer the enemy a bait to lure him; feign disorder and strike him.'[17]

Darkness of night was also useful for laying ambushes, especially for irregular forces operating against a regular army; it would cover their advance and allow them to launch a surprise attack. The Book of Joshua describes well how advances were made at night in order to surprise the enemy at dawn. The ambush may seem like a minor action compared to major operations of entire armies, but it certainly was not considered so by its victims.[18]

If the Israelites ever decided to assault fortified places, they must have consciously decided to attack those places that seemed sufficiently weak to offer a chance of success. But even there, as besiegers, they needed to use various subtle ruses to take the towns by clever stratagems, not by force.[19] In the same way, diplomacy could work better than assault. The campaign and alliance with the Gibeonites is a fine example of the combined application of military action and diplomacy for the attainment of a political goal. The story of Joshua's actions at Ai and his superb handling of the divided forces during the second campaign suggest a sophisticated commander who handled the timely and exact execution of the intricate manoeuvres involved. These actions are not characteristic of wandering nomads. The Battle of Ai represented a superb example of the classic way a smaller force captured a fortified enclosure. It is a trap set in the open, and sprung by means of excellent pre-planning and timing. It is based on intelligence about the city itself, the likely behaviour of its inhabitants, and the local geography. It also required signalling and tactical manoeuvres. Thus even if we do not believe the Israelites took Ai in the thirteenth century, this was surely the way such a city could have been taken by an enemy.

Jewish Rebellion

The tradition of the successful use of stratagems may have actually misled the Jews. Rebellion against foreign occupation became entrenched, even respected, especially after 66 CE. Every Roman governor whose term is recorded in any detail clashed with the Jews so much so that the absence of such conflict required a comment from one well-informed observer. Tacitus wrote in his *Histories* 'under Tiberius all was quiet'.[20]

The Jewish attitude to foreign rule and the imposition of tribute made them seem irascible to the Romans, who viewed their behaviour as an insult to imperialists believing they should rule the world.[21] From the Maccabean Revolt onwards, Jews exhibited a kind of suicidal persistence that, according to some, always had a religious motivation.[22] The impression is confirmed by ancient writers such as Tacitus, Suetonius and Dio Cassius.[23] Martin Hengel believed that religion and politics were inseparably fused in ancient Judaism. Josephus cannot be truthful about this in his history. In an environment that was largely hostile to Judaism, he could not state openly that certain fundamental religious themes such as the idea of 'theocracy', 'zeal for the law' and the people's messianic expectation were the cause of the catastrophe in 66–70 CE.

The Jews understood themselves as the people chosen by God to reveal his ways and to be a 'light to the nations' (Isaiah 42:6). Many Jews believed therefore that they were destined for freedom from domination. The historical memory of the Maccabean period, and even Joshua's campaigns, helped to keep this hope burning in later years. God had vindicated the cause of those who fought for Yahweh, including that small band of Maccabean warriors who had defended the law and Temple against the foreign tyranny of the large Syrian Empire. Surely God would protect his people against any oppressors if they remained loyal to him in this way. Nonetheless, without divine intervention, the Jews lost.

Josephus viewed the Maccabean Revolt against Syrian domination as a righteous rebellion which had inaugurated a glorious period of independence for Israel. However, Josephus did not perceive the Maccabean Revolt as a justification for the later Jewish revolt against the Romans. On the contrary, he considered the latter revolt as an unwarranted attack by unlawful Jews against overlords who were basically sympathetic and tolerant. Other Jews, however, did see a parallel between the Maccabean Revolt and the Roman–Jewish War. The recollection of the revolt was part of a common heritage of first-century Jews. The people celebrated annual festivals in the Temple commemorating the great events that brought liberation.[24] As such, the Maccabean Revolt served as a model and source of inspiration for many Jews in their struggle to secure liberation from the Romans.

Writing Intelligence History
The problem in writing about intelligence operations in Israel is not, therefore, a lack of spies or intelligence operations, but it is in deciding which sources accurately portray history and which do not. Although the Hebrew scriptures are presented to us in historical terms, as we have seen, the material very often does not survive the litmus test of modern historical criticism. In any discussion of ancient events in the Holy Land, a clear distinction must be made between historical sources, on one hand, and literary/theological creations and the modern interpretations based on them on the other. Regardless of what one thinks of the reliability of religious sources as historical accounts, their concerns are clearly theological.

The main problem in writing the military history of the Holy Land, therefore, is methodological. Too often military historians have written about Israel's history while ignoring evidence brought to bear by literary critics, archaeologists and biblical scholars. Moses Finley, who wrote on the important question of slavery in antiquity, described a 'teleological fallacy', which consists in assuming the existence from the beginning of time of the writer's values and then examining an earlier thought and practice as if they were, or ought to have been, on the road to this realisation; as if [writers] in other periods were asking the questions and facing the same problems as those of the [modern] historian and his world.[25] This is exactly the fallacy into which too many military historians have fallen when describing warfare in the Hebrew scriptures. The common approach among military historians has been to take snippets of the past to prove some modern doctrine instead of examining the evidence in its own context. Many historians are quite willing just to ignore archaeological evidence. They take past literature and then use it in forced ways to answer questions that are imposed on, and often alien to, the literature itself. Even worse, they draw the evidence into an historical scheme that is more propagandist than historical. This is especially dangerous with biblical material that comes with its own *imprimatur* of holiness. Finley wrote about the habit of 'using the ancient world as a springboard for a larger [modern] polemic', and in no area is this danger more clearly seen than in biblical studies. When interpreting the past, what may be valid concerns and attitudes of the present may not have been the concern of ancient authors.

Why is there such a range of sophisticated intelligence techniques in accounts that supposedly describe nomadic peoples from the Bronze Age? Richard Gabriel has taken the text at face value, and portrayed the chosen people of the Exodus as equipped and familiar with weapons, led by experienced and tactically proficient commanders who were not Egyptian slaves but trained mercenaries. According to Gabriel, their tactical proficiency improved daily on their way to conquering the Land of Canaan.[26] This portrait of Joshua as the ancient George C. Patton is one way to explain the phenomenal success of Israelite armies. The study of Israel's origins, however, is much too complicated to fit into such a simple reductionist argument. Rather than analysing the complexity of ancient societies, some historians reduce a discussion to simple battlefield terms with which they are familiar. Even as conservative a scholar as J. Alberto Soggin has written that any history of Israel that attempts to reconstruct the pre-monarchic period simply by paraphrasing biblical texts and supplementing them, where possible, with alleged parallels from the ancient Near East (let alone modern military history) is using an inadequate method that results in a distorted picture of those events.[27]

A much more sophisticated approach would be to accept that the stories were written by an author, here called the Dtr historian, who lived during the later Iron Age when monarchy, sophisticated military operations, iron weapons and a familiarity with intelligence operations were *de rigueur*. The Gordian knot of biblical authorship cannot be unravelled in this study, but it stands to reason that the later one dates the authorship of the stories in Joshua, Judges and Kings, the stronger the argument gets for the existence and use of sophisticated espionage techniques. In other words, the more time the Israelites had to gain experience in wars, the more sophisticated their intelligence operations could have been.

A literal reading of the biblical texts should not be taken out of intellectual laziness or fear of reprisal from religious authorities. The reluctance of many scholars to break from the biblical route is because without the biblical account it is difficult to present with any confidence a 'story' of chronologically and causally related events. If the editors of the *Cambridge History of Judaism* admit that a history of Judaism is still not possible, how much more true is this of the history of Jewish spies.[28] Scholars abhor imprecision. As Marc Bloch has written: 'A scholar loves close dating. He finds it both an appeasement to his instinctive horror of the vague, and a great comfort to the conscience.' Bloch went on to warn against worshipping the idol of 'false precision'.[29]

The publishing boom that began in the 1980s of books on the history of Israel using the traditional approach is no doubt a reaction to the fall of the conquest model. The republication of Bright (1981) and Hermann (1981) and the translation of de Vaux (1978), Jagersma (1982) and Soggin (1984) disguise the reality that the similarity of these approaches and reconstructions is alarmingly sterile and does not represent the main direction in which historical research on Israel is headed.[30] To this publishing boom must be added the works of Richard Gabriel and Mordechai Gichon that dismiss or obscure serious methodological problems and consequently do nothing to encourage the exploration of alternative methods of approach. The complacency of some publishers and biblical historians stands in stark contrast to the debates in scholarly journals conducted by professional historians exploring different methodologies and alternative approaches.[31] The approach in many textbooks and traditional 'histories' creates a static view of the history of Israel, which is divorced from the historical process. These authors ignore the problems that scholars have faced over the last quarter of a century, which stem from new information and a changing intellectual climate. The extent to which textbook authors have clung persistently to the conquest model and ignored current scholarship has been eloquently argued by Jack Cargill.[32] Of course, one is entitled to adhere to any point of view and bolster it with any available evidence. What one is not allowed to do is ignore seventy-five years of research because it is inconvenient to one's theory, and then call the results 'history'.

The spy stories of the Bible may very well contain a core of truth, but that core is unrecoverable. What can be drawn from them are certain lessons about the nature of surprise, betrayal and intelligence failure. As with the lessons from Sun Tzu, the biblical examples can capture the essence of a principle. They are more important for the lessons they hold than as examples of actual history. Many of these episodes were probably written for their value as rousing good stories. Some of them carry familiar, even clichéd themes – woman as seducer or the spy who betrays a city. What these stories cannot be used for is dating battles or adding to the veracity of the Hebrew Bible. Some corroborating evidence may be found, but as with much of intelligence history its inherently secret nature will keep most of it shrouded in mystery for ever.

ABBREVIATIONS

AASOR	*Annual of the American Schools of Oriental Research*
ABD	*Anchor Bible Dictionary*
ADAJ	*Annual of the Department of Antiquities of Jordan*
AJT	*American Journal of Theology*
ANET	J. B. Pritchard (ed.), *Ancient Near Eastern Texts*
ANRW	*Aufstieg und Niedergang der Römischen Welt*
Ant.	Josephus, *Jewish Antiquities*, trans. by H. St J. Thackeray, Cambridge: Loeb Classical Library, 1961, 6 vols
AOAT	*Alter Orient and Altes Testament*
AUSS	Andrews University Seminary Studies
BA	*Biblical Archaeologist*
BAIAS	*Bulletin of the Anglo-Israel Archaeological Society*
BAR	*Biblical Archaeology Review*
BASOR	*Bulletin of the American Schools of Oriental Research*
BBR	*Bulletin for Biblical Research*
Berlin/Overman	Andrea M. Berlin and J. Andrew Overman, *The First Jewish Revolt. Archaeology, History and Ideology*, London and New York: Routledge, 2002.
BG	Caesar, *Bellum Gallicum*
Bib	*Biblica*
BJ	Josephus, *Bellum Judaicum*, trans. by H. St J. Thackeray, *The Jewish War*, Cambridge: Loeb Classical Library, 1956, 2 vols
BR	*Bible Review*
BRL	*Bulletin of the John Rylands Library,* Manchester University Press
BS	*Bibliotheca Sacra*

BWAT	*Beiträge zur Wissenschaft vom Alten Tesatament*
BZAW	*Beihefte zur Zeitschrift fur die Alttestamentliche Wissenschaft*
CAH	*Cambridge Ancient History*
CBQ	*Catholic Biblical Quarterly*
CHJ	*Cambridge History of Judaism*
CQ	*Classical Quarterly*
CQR	*Church Quarterly Review*
CTM	*Concordia Theological Monthly*
DJD	*Discoveries in the Judaean Desert*
EAEHL	Michael Avi-Yonah (ed.), *Encyclopedia of Archaeological Excavations in the Holy Land*, London: Oxford University Press (1975–8)
Eusebius, *HE*	Eusebius, *Historia Ecclesiastica*, trans. by Kirsopp Lake, *The Ecclesiastical History*, Cambridge: Loeb Classical Library, 1959, 2 vols
EvQ	*Evangelical Quarterly*
ExpTim	*Expository Times*
GRBS	*Greek, Roman and Byzantine Studies*
(H)	Hebrew, text written in
HDB	James Hastings (ed.), *Dictionary of the Bible*, New York: Scribner, 1963.
HJP	H. H. Ben-Sasson (ed.), *A History of the Jewish People*, I–III, Cambridge, MA; London: Weidenfeld & Nicolson, 1976
HSCP	*Harvard Studies in Classical Philology*
HSM	*Harvard Semitic Monographs*
HSS	*Harvard Semitic Studies*
HTR	*Harvard Theological Review*
HUCA	*Hebrew Union College Annual*
IDB	G. A. Buttrick (ed.), *Interpreter's Dictionary of the Bible*, Nashville: Abingdon, 1962
IEJ	*Israel Exploration Journal*
ILS	Hermann Dessau, *Inscriptiones Latinae Selectae*, Chicago: Ares Press, 1979, 3 vols in 5
INJ	*Israel Numismatic Journal*
JAAR	*Journal of the American Academy of Religion*
JAOS	*Journal of the American Oriental Society*
JBL	*Journal of Biblical Literature*

JES	*Journal of Ecumenical Studies*
JHS	*Journal of Hebraic Studies*
JJS	*Journal of Jewish Studies*
JMH	*Journal of Military History*
JNES	*Journal of Near Eastern Studies*
JPHD	Ernst Bammel and C. F. D. Moule (eds), *Jesus and the Politics of His Day*, Cambridge: Cambridge University Press, 1984
JPOS	*Journal of the Palestine Oriental Society*
JQ	*Jerusalem Quarterly*
JQR	*Jewish Quarterly Review*
JR	*Journal of Religion*
JRA	*Journal of Roman Archaeology*
JRS	*Journal of Roman Studies*
JSQ	*Jewish Studies Quarterly*
JSJ	*Journal for the Study of Judaism*
JSOT	*Journal for the Study of the Old Testament*
JSS	*Journal of Semitic Studies*
JTS	*Journal of Theological Studies*
LB	Yohanon Aharoni, *The Land of the Bible: A Historical Geography*, trans from the Hebrew and ed. by A. F. Rainey, Philadelphia: Westminster Press, 1979, 2nd edn
MHBT	J. Liver (ed.), *The Military History of the Land of Israel in Biblical Times*, Jerusalem: 1964 (H)
Moule Festschrift	Ernst Bammel (ed.), *The Trial of Jesus*, Studies in Biblical Theology, series II, no. 13, London: SCM, 1970
NEA	*Near Eastern Archaeology*
NEAEHL	Ephraim Stern (ed.), *The New Encyclopedia of Archaeological Excavations in the Holy Land*, New York: Simon & Schuster, 1993, 4 vols
NEB	*New English Bible*, Oxford Study Edition, 1976
NTS	*New Testament Studies*
NT	*Novum Testamentum*
OBO	*Orbis Biblicus et Orientalis*
PEQ	*Palestine Exploration Quarterly*
PJB	*Palastinajahrbuch. Deutsches Evangelische Institut für Altertumswissenschaft des Heiliges Landes zu Jerusalem [Berlin]*

RB	*Revue Biblique*
RE	A. Pauly, G. Wissowa et al. (eds), *Realencyclopaedie der Klassischen Altertumswissenschaft*, Stuttgart: J. B. Metzler, 1894–1963
REJ	*Revue des Etudes Juives*
REL	*Revue des Etudes Latines*
RES	*Revue des Etudes Semitiques*
RIHM	*Revue Internationale d'Histoire Militaire*
SBLMS	*Society of Biblical Literature Monograph Series*
SBLSBS	*Society of Biblical Literature Sources for Biblical Study*
SBLSP	*Society of Biblical Literature. Seminar Papers*
SBT	*Studies in Biblical Theology*
SCI	*Scripta Classica Israelica*
SHA	*Scriptores Historiae Augustae*
SHANE	*Studies in the History of the Ancient Near East*
SJOT	*Scandinavian Journal of the Old Testament*
SPAW	*Sitzungsberichte der Preussische Akademie der Wissenschaft*
TBB	*The Biblical Bulletin*
TS	*Theological Studies*
TvR	*Tijdschrift voor Rechtsgeschiedenis*, Leiden
VT	*Vetus Testamentum*
WTJ	*Westminster Theological Journal*
ZAW	*Zeitschrift für die Alttestamentliche Wissenschaft*
ZDPV	*Zeitschrift des Deutschens Palästina-Vereins*
ZNW	*Zeitschrift für Neutestamentliche Wissenschaft*
ZPE	*Zeitschrift für Papyrologie und Epigraphik*
ZTK	*Zeitschrift für Theologie und Kirche*

NOTES

ABBREVIATED REFERENCES ARE GIVEN in the footnotes. For full citations see the Bibliography (p. 271).

Preface (pp.13–20)

1   M. Gichon, 'The West Bank: The Geostrategic and Historical Aspects' in A. Shalev, *The West Bank: Line of Defense* (New York, 1985), pp. 178–9.

2   P. B. Kern, *Ancient Siege Warfare* (Bloomington, 1999), p. 39.

3   M. Van Creveld, *Technology and War. From 2000 BC to the Present* (New York, 1989).

4   Most handbooks on ancient warfare cover only the classical era, e.g. H. Delbrück, *Warfare in Antiquity* (Lincoln, NE, 1975), vol. I; D. Kagan, *On the Origins of War* (New York, 1995). See E. C. May, G. P. Stadler and J. F. Votaw, *Ancient and Medieval Warfare* (Wayne, NJ, 1984). O. Spaulding and H. Nickerson, *Ancient and Medieval Warfare* (New York, 1993) only covers the empires of Egypt, Assyria and Persia. R. A. Gabriel and D. W. Boose, jun., *The Great Battles of Antiquity* (Westport, CT, 1995) presents only the two Egyptian battles, of Kadesh and Megiddo, and the battles of Sargon.

5   On intelligence see A. Malamat, 'Conquest of Canaan', *RIHM* 42, 1 (1979), pp. 25–52, and D. G. Hansen, 'Intelligence, Deception and Military Operations in the Ancient Near East', *II International Conference on Intelligence and Military Operations*, US Army War College, Carlisle Barracks, PA, 11–15 May 1987. For a list of espionage events in Numbers, Deuteronomy, Joshua and Judges see F. Langlamet, 'Rahab et Les Espions', *RB* 78 (1971), pp. 321–54.

6   Eric Cline, *The Battles of Armageddon* (Ann Arbor, MI, 2000) and *Jerusalem Besieged* (Ann Arbor, MI, 2004) are a refreshing exception.

7   For a recent argument on the late composition of the Hebrew scriptures see I. Finkelstein and N. A. Silberman, *The Bible Unearthed* (New York, 2001); see also R. E. Friedman, *Who Wrote the Bible?* (New York, 1987).

8   For example, D. G. Hansen, 'Intelligence, Deception and Military Operations in the Ancient Near East', *II International Conference on Intelligence and Military Operations*, and T. C. Tatum, *The Evangelical Right and a Biblical Forecast of Military Operations in the Middle East* (Carlisle Barracks, PA, Apr. 1986).

9   R. A. Gabriel, *The Military History of Ancient Israel* (Westport, CT, 2003) rejects all evidence which would disagree with his fundamentalist reading of the biblical text. C. Herzog and M. Gichon refer to the alternative theories, but resort to studies before 1950 for the traditional view. Notes to Foreword, 1–4. See Sheldon's review in *Journal of Military History* 69, 1 (Jan. 2005), pp. 197–204.

10 W. F. Albright, 'The Israelite Conquest of Canaan in the Light of Archaeology', *BASOR* 74 (1939), pp. 11–23. For other adherents of the conquest model see J. A. Bright, *A History of Israel* (Philadelphia, 1959); G. E. Wright, 'Epic of Conquest', *BA* 3 (1940), pp. 25–40.

11 See P. W. Lapp, 'The Conquest of Palestine in the Light of Archaeology', *CTM* 38 (1967), pp. 495–548;

Y. Yadin, 'Is the Biblical Conquest of Canaan Historically Reliable?' *BAR* 8 (1982), pp. 16–23; A. Malamat, 'How Inferior Israelite Forces Conquered Fortified Canaanite Cities', *BAR* 8 (1982), pp. 24–35.

12 See H. Shanks, W. G. Dever, B. Halpern and P. Kyle McCarter, jun. (eds), *The Rise of Ancient Israel* (Washington, DC, 1992), p. 5 and *passim*; W. Dever, *What Did the Biblical Writers Know and When Did They Know It?* (Grand Rapids, MI, 2001).

13 For an example of the so-called 'Copenhagen School' of biblical minimalists see the work of N. P. Lemche, *Early Israel: Anthropological and Historical Studies on the Israelite Society Before the Monarchy* (Leiden, 1985); N. P. Lemche, *The Israelites in History and Tradition* (Louisville, Ky, 1998); N. P. Lemche, 'Is It Still Possible to Write a History of Ancient Israel?', *SJOT* 8 (1994), pp. 165–90; N. P. Lemche, *Prelude to Israel's Past* (Peabody, MA, 1998); N. P. Lemche, *Ancient Israel: A New History of Israelite Society* (Sheffield, 1988).

14 This is the view of a group of European biblical scholars who publish in the Sheffield Academic Press. See also P. R. Davies, *In Search of Ancient Israel* (Sheffield, 1992), and K. W. Whitelam, *The Invention of Ancient Israel: The Silencing of Palestinian History* (New York, 1996).

15 W. G. Dever, *Who Were the Early Israelites and Where Did They Come From?* (Grand Rapids, MI, 2003), p. ix, provides a less-than-sympathetic account of the Copenhagen School, literary critics and the 'minimalists'.

16 H. Shanks (ed.), *The Rise of Ancient Israel* (Washington, DC, 1992), p. 31.

17 N. J. E. Austin and N. B. Rankov, *Exploratio* (London and New York, 1995), p. 2.

18 See Malamat's comments on telescoping events into a unified narrative which covers a relatively brief time span: A. Malamat, 'Conquest of Canaan', *RIHM* 42, 1 (1979), p. 26.

19 A. Dulles, *The Craft of Intelligence* (New York, 1963), p. 9. See also R. D. Sawyer, *The Tao of Spycraft* (Boulder, CO, 1998), pp. 75 and 529, on the use of religious sources by the Chinese, and Sun Tzu's criticism of such techniques. R. M. Sheldon, *Intelligence Activities in Ancient Rome: Trust in the Gods, But Verify* (London, 2005), chap. 1; M. C. Lind, *Yahweh is a Warrior* (Scottsdale, PA, 1980), p. 141.

20 Assyrian inscriptions show the role of religious oracles in their military preparations. These 'oracles of assurance' named the personnel and the means by which the oracles were received. They urged the king to take action, with a promise of the presence and protection of the gods. For the Mari texts and the Assyrian material see M. Weippert, ' "Heiliger Krieg" in Israel und Assyrien', *ZAW* 84, 4 (1972), pp. 460–93, texts 2, 3, 6 and 11. See also J. Ackerman, 'Prophecy and Warfare in Early Israel: A Study of the Deborah and Barak Story', *BASOR* 220 (1975), p. 6.

21 A. Malamat, 'Conquest of Canaan', *RIHM* 42, 1 (1979), p. 38.

22 E. Cline, *Battles of Armageddon*, pp. 23–8, citing C. Breasted, *Pioneer to the Past: The Story of James Henry Breasted, Archaeologist* (New York, 1943), pp. 246–50.

23 R. E. Neustadt and E. May, *Thinking in Time* (New York, 1986), p. 233.

Introduction: Exodus and Entrance (pp. 21–37)

1 Num. 13:17–20. *The New English Bible* (New York, 1972). All quotations from the Hebrew Bible will be from this translation unless otherwise indicated.

2 See C. Herzog and M. Gichon, *Battles of the Bible* (London, 1997), p. 41.

3 Num. 13:20.

4 Num. 13:31.

5 Num. 14:36–8.

6 For an excellent summary of the views see T. L. Thompson, *Early History of the Israelite People. From the Written and Archaeological Sources* (Leiden, 1992), pp. 1–170; and S. V. Fritz, 'Conquest or Settlement. The Early Iron Age in Palestine', *BA* (June 1987), pp. 84–5.

7 R. E. Friedman, *Who Wrote the Bible?* (New York, 1987), who discussed the work of Julius Wellhausen. See also the comments of Finkelstein and Na'aman, *From Nomadism to Monarchy* (Jerusalem, 1994), pp. 9–17, and Finkelstein and Silberman, *The Bible Unearthed* (New York, 2001), pp. 10–14. On the

lengths to which scholars go to forge archaeological evidence for confirmation of biblical stories see N. A. Silberman and Y. Goren, 'Faking Biblical History', *Archaeology* (Sept.–Oct. 2003), pp. 20–9.

8   For those still claiming an external origin see A. J. Hauser, 'Israel's Conquest of Palestine: A Peasant's Rebellion?', *JSOT* 7 (1978), p. 14, who does not believe the Israelites rose from Canaanite peasants; J. M. Miller, 'The Israelite Occupation of Canaan' in J. H. Hayes and J. M. Miller (eds), *Israelite and Judean History* (London, 1977), p. 257, who believes the increase in highland settlements was caused by migration from the west; J. A. Soggin, *A History of Israel* (Philadelphia, 1984), p. 139, who asserts that Israel's self-perception of external origin is authoritative.

9   This has not stopped scholars from trying to salvage the story by changing the chronology on the 'high date' for the Exodus. J. Bimson, *Redating the Exodus and Conquest* (Sheffield, 1981), p. 223. See also the work of J. Currid, *Ancient Egypt and the Old Testament* (Grand Rapids, MI, 1997), and a very conservative survey of the evidence in J. K. Hoffmeier, *Israel in Egypt: The Evidence for the Authenticity of the Exodus Tradition* (New York, 1997). Contra see B. Halpern, 'Radical Exodus Re-Dating Fatally Flawed', *BAR* (Nov.–Dec. 1987), p. 56; B. Halpern, 'The Exodus from Egypt: Myth of Reality?' in H. Shanks et.al., *The Rise of Ancient Israel* (Washington, DC, 1992), pp. 87–113.

10 On dating the composition see N. Na'aman, 'The "Conquest of Canaan" in the Book of Joshua and in History' in Finkelstein and Na'aman, *From Nomadism to Monarchy* (Jerusalem, 1994), pp. 218–19.

11 D. B. Redford, 'An Egyptological Perspective on the Exodus Narrative' in A. F. Rainey (ed.), *Egypt, Israel and Sinai* (Tel Aviv, 1987), pp. 137–61.

12 W. F. Albright, *From the Stone Age to Christianity* (Baltimore, 1957); W. F. Albright, 'The Israelite Conquest of Canaan in the Light of Archaeology', *BASOR* 74 (1939), pp. 11–23; A. Malamat, 'Conquest of Canaan: Israelite Conduct of War According to Biblical Tradition', *Encyclopedia Judaica Year Book* 1975/76, pp. 166–82.

13 J. Bright, *A History of Israel* (Philadelphia, 1959), p. 117.

14 On how to tell Israelites from Canaanites see A. Kempinski, 'How Profoundly Canaanized Were the Early Israelites?', *ZDPV* 108 (1992), pp. 1–17; W. G. Dever, 'Archaeological Data on the Israelite Settlement', *BASOR* 284 (1991), pp. 70–90; V. Fritz, 'Israelites and Canaanites. You Can Tell Them Apart', *BAR* 28, 4 (July–Aug. 2002), pp. 28–63; V. Fritz, 'Conquest or Settlement? The Early Iron Age in Palestine', *BA* 50 (June 1987), pp. 84–100; I. Finkelstein, 'Searching for Israelite Origins', *BAR* 14, 5 (Sept.–Oct. 1988), pp. 34–42; V. Fritz, 'The Israelite Conquest', *BASOR* 241 (1980), pp. 61–73.

15 To the defenders of the theory should be added Manfred Weippert who published *The Settlement of the Israelite Tribes in Palestine* in 1971. He surveyed the archaeological evidence of the time, but essentially restated the theories of Alt and Noth. Weippert (p. 145) vigorously denied Gottwald's *Apiru*-Hebrew identification. See W. Dever, *Who Were the Early Israelites?*, pp. 130–1. For a rationalisation of the negative evidence regarding the conquest of Canaan see N. Glueck, *Rivers in the Desert* (New York, 1959), p. 114.

16 Y. Yadin, 'Is the Biblical Account of the Israelite Conquest of Canaan Historically Reliable?', *BAR* 8, 2 (Mar.–Apr. 1982) pp. 16–23. For a very critical account of how Yigael Yadin misused evidence to bolster traditional accounts see N. Ben-Yehuda, *Sacrificing Truth: Archaeology and the Myth of Masada* (Amherst, NY: 2002) the nationalistic agenda that underlay Yigael Yadin's excavations. On reconciling biblical evidence with the archaeological see A. Schoors, 'The Israelite Conquest: Textual Evidence in the Archaeological Argument' in E. Lipinski (ed.), *The Land of Israel: Cross-Roads of Civilizations* (Leuven, 1985), pp. 77–92.

17 P. W. Lapp, 'The Conquest of Palestine in the Light of Archaeology', *CTM* 38 (1968), p. 295.

18 For a critique of the conquest model see Finkelstein, *The Archaeology of Israelite Settlement* (Jerusalem, 1988), pp. 295–302.

19 W. G. Dever, 'Whatchamacallit. Why it's So Hard to Name Our Field', *BAR* 29, 4 (July–Aug. 2003), pp. 57–9. Dever preferred to call the field Syro-Palestinian archaeology. He has recently decided that Palestinian archaeology is not a useful term, and that biblical archaeology was a good name for a

dialogue between archaeologists and biblical scholars. See *BAR* 29, 5 (Sept.–Oct. 2003), p. 20.

20 W. G. Dever, *Who Were the Early Israelites?*, pp. 45–6.

21 For a chronology of the Late Bronze Age, the destruction levels and the ceramic evidence see A. Leonard, jun., 'Archaeological Sources for the History of Palestine: The Late Bronze Age', *BA* 52, 1 (Mar. 1989), pp. 4–55.

22 Ramses III celebrated a victory over the Sea Peoples in 1177. On the pillage of Megiddo by the Sea Peoples see H. Shanks, 'A Centrist at the Center of Controversy', *BAR* 28, 6 (Nov.–Dec. 2002), pp. 38–68. On the settlement of the sea people and other ethnic groups in the Late Bronze Age and Early Iron Age see B. Mazar, 'The Early Israelite Settlement in the Hill Country', *BASOR* 241 (winter 1981), pp. 75–85. N. K. Sandars, *The Sea Peoples. Warriors of the Ancient Mediterranean 1250–1150* (London, 1978); R. D. Barnett, 'The Sea Peoples', *CAH*, vol. II, pt 2, pp. 359–78.

23 See J. Strange, 'The Transition from the Bronze Age to the Iron Age in the Eastern Mediterranean and the Emergence of the Israelite State', *SJOT* 1 (1987), pp. 1–19.

24 See V. Fritz, 'Conquest or Settlement?', who concludes that the archaeological evidence supports neither conquest nor revolution. *BA* (June 1987), p. 97.

25 On the very complicated issue of the role of the Philistines, where they settled and under what circumstances see I. Singer, 'How Did the Philistines Enter Canaan. A Rejoinder', *BAR* 18, 6 (Nov. 1992), pp. 44–6, with bibliography which goes back to the traditional view of Alt and Noth that Ramses III tightened his control over Palestine, and settled the Philistines and the Sea Peoples and other captives in Egyptian strongholds along the coast of northern Palestine. For the opposite view see B. G. Wood, 'The Philistines Enter Canaan – Were They Egyptian Lackeys or Invading Conquerors?', *BAR* 16, 2 (Mar.–Apr. 1990), pp. 44–57, who follows Manfred Bietak and believes that the Egyptians were already defeated and the Philistines were conquerors in their own right. See also T. Dothan, 'The Philistines Reconsidered', *Biblical Archaeology Today* (Jerusalem, 1985), pp. 216–19.

26 Whether or not these settlers were Israelites is a hotly debated point. See N. Na'aman, 'The "Conquest of Canaan" in the Book of Joshua and in History' in I. Finkelstein and N. Na'aman, *From Nomadism to Monarchy* (Jerusalem, 1994), p. 223.

27 V. Fritz, 'Conquest or Settlement? The Early Iron Age in Palestine', *BA* (June 1987), p. 98; see also N. Na'aman, 'The "Conquest of Canaan" in the Book of Joshua and in History', p. 249: 'It is commonly accepted today that most of the conquest stories in the Book of Joshua are devoid of historical reality.'

28 A. Alt, *Essays on Old Testament History and Religion* (Oxford, 1966); M. Noth, *A History of Pentateuchal Traditions* (Englewood Cliffs, NJ, 1972); M. Noth, *The History of Israel* (New York, 1960). In 1944, Martin Noth argued that the books of Joshua through to 2 Kings were compiled by someone (or several persons of similar perspective) whom Noth named 'the Deuteronomistic historian'. See M. Noth, *The Deuteronomistic History* (Sheffield, 1981) and M. A. O'Brien, *The Deuteronomistic History Hypothesis: A Reassessment* (Göttingen, 1989).

29 Volkmar Fritz, who co-directed the excavations at Tel Masos near Beersheva, developed a distinctive version of the indigenous origins theory, sometimes called the 'symbiosis model' (although not by him). He believes the Canaanite and Israelite peoples had the same origins and continued to live alongside one another into Iron Age I. His theory has had considerable effect. See V. Fritz, 'Israelites and Canaanites. You *Can* Tell Them Apart', *BAR* 28, 4 (July–Aug. 2002), pp. 28–31, 63; V. Fritz, 'Conquest or Settlement? The Early Iron Age in Palestine', *BA* 50 (June 1987) pp. 84–100; V. Fritz, 'The Israelite Conquest in the Light of Recent Excavations at Khirbet el Meshash', *BASOR* 241 (1981), pp. 61–73; and W. G. Dever, *Who Were the Early Israelites?*, p. 146. See also A. Aharoni, 'Nothing Early and Nothing Late: Re-writing Israel's Conquest', *BA* 39 (1976), pp. 55–76.

30 W. G. Dever, *Who Were the Early Israelites and Where Did They Come From?* (Grand Rapids, MI, 2003), p. 52. See G. E. Mendenhall, 'The Hebrew Conquest of Palestine', *BA* 25 (1962), pp. 66–87.

31 W. G. Dever, *Who Were the Early Israelites?*, p. 52, citing texts from Mari.

32 G. E. Mendenhall, 'The Hebrew Conquest of Palestine', *BA* 25, 1 (1962), pp. 66–87.

33 Scholars such as M. Greenberg, *The Hab/piru* (New Haven, 1955) and E. F. Campbell, 'The Amarna Letters and the Amarna Period', *BA* 23, 1 (1960), pp. 2–22, have suggested that the word *apiru* and its alternative forms *hapiru* and *habiru* had a direct linguistic connection to the word *ibri (ivri;* 'Hebrew') and that therefore the *apiru* in the Egyptian sources were the early Israelites. I. Finkelstein and N. A. Silberman, *The Bible Unearthed*, pp. 102–3, 104, 239–40, 335–6, believe *apiru* is a socio-economic term not an ethnic one, as does Gottwald M. Weippert, *The Settlement of the Israelite Tribes in Palestine* (Naperville, IL, 1971), p. 145, vigorously denied Gottwald's identification; G. Mendenhall, 'The Hebrew Conquest of Palestine', p. 75, also sees the *apiru* as a social class, not an ethnic group. See H. Shanks et al., *Ancient Israel*, p. 43; W. G. Dever, *Who Were the Early Israelites?*, pp. 130–1. A. F. Rainey, in his review of John Bimson's *Redating the Exodus*, *IEJ* 30 (1980), wrote: 'The "*apiru*" outcasts and outlaws from the established society have nothing to do either linguistically or socially with the *ibrim* "Hebrews".'

34 G. Mendenhall, 'The Hebrew Conquest of Palestine', p. 75; I. Finkelstein and N. A. Silberman, *The Bible Unearthed*, p. 336.

35 N. K. Gottwald, *The Tribes of Yahweh* (New York, 1979); N. K. Gottwald, *The Bible and Liberation* (Maryknoll, NY, 1983); N. K. Gottwald, *The Hebrew Bible* (Philadelphia, 1985). N. K. Gottwald, 'Domain Assumptions and Societal Models in the Study of Pre-Monarchic Israel' in Carter and Meyers, *Community, Identity and Ideology* (Winona Lake, IN, 1996), pp. 170–81. On his work see P. K. McCarter, jun., 'A Major New Introduction to the Bible', *BR* (summer 1986), pp. 42–50, and W. Dever, *Who Were the Early Israelites?*, p. 54.

36 His theory was oddly rejected even by Mendenhall despite the affinity between the two theories. The two differed primarily over the definition of what constituted Yahwism. See G. Mendenhall, 'Ancient Israel's Hyphenated History' (Sheffield, 1983), pp. 91–103. For Gottwald's use of the sociological theories of Durkheim, Weber and Marx see G. A. Herion, 'The Impact of Modern and Social Science Assumptions on the Reconstruction of Israelite History' in C. E. Carter and C. L. Meyers (eds), *Community, Identity and Ideology. Social Science Approaches to the Hebrew Bible* (Winona Lake, IN, 1996), pp. 246–7.

37 Finkelstein and Na'aman, *From Nomadism to Monarchy*, pp. 10–11. William Dever tried to provide an archaeological context for the peasant revolt. He argued that the pottery and architecture of the new settlements in the highlands during Iron Age I resembled the ceramic and building traditions of the lowland inhabitants in the Late Bronze Age. He believed the Israelites emerged from the sedentary communities of Canaan. W. G. Dever, *Who Were the Early Israelites?*, pp. 101–28.

38 See the remarks of N. Gottwald, 'Israel's Emergence in Canaan', *BR* 55 (Oct. 1989), p. 26. For the debate over the characteristics of 'Israelite' settlement see W. G. Dever, 'Archaeological Data on the Israelite Settlement: A Review of Two Recent Works', *BASOR* 284 (Nov. 1991), pp. 77–90.

39 On the attempt of literary critics to remove the meta-narratives see K. Windshuttle, *The Killing of History: How Literary Critics and Social Theorists are Murdering Our Past* (Paddington, NSW, 1994). For a new historicist's analysis of the Book of Joshua see Lori L. Rowlett, *Joshua and the Rhetoric of Violence* (Sheffield, 1996).

40 W. G. Dever, *Who Were the Early Israelites?*, p. 137.

41 P. R. Davies, *Whose History? Whose Israel? Whose Bible?* JSOT Supplement Series 148 (Sheffield, 1992), pp. 104–22. For critics see the section on P. R. Davies work in W. G. Dever, *What Did the Biblical Writers Know and When Did They Know It?* (Grand Rapids, MI, 2001), pp. 28–30; and A. Rainey, 'The "House of David" and the House of the Deconstructionists', *BAR* 20, 6 (Nov.–Dec. 1994), p. 47, who calls Davies an 'amateur who can be safely ignored'.

42 Dever observed that the current population of Palestine was not present in the area until relatively modern times, thus making Whitelam's theory based not only on bad historical method but also on dishonest scholarship and inflammatory rhetoric. See also W. G. Dever, *What Did the Biblical Writers Know and When Did They Know It?*, pp. 34–7.

43 This study was almost diametrically opposed to his earlier work, N. P. Lemche, *Early Israel: Anthropological and Historical Studies on the Israelite Society Before the Monarchy* (Leiden, 1985). On N. P. Lemche see W. G. Dever, *What Did the Biblical Writers Know and When Did They Know It?*, pp. 37–40.

44 In 1997, the European revisionists published a collection of essays: L. L. Grabbe (ed.), *Can a 'History of Israel' be Written?* (Sheffield, 1997). Among the authors there are many scholars of biblical history and literature, but no archaeologists. What they call a 'needed dialogue' seems to remain a monologue according to W. G. Dever, *Who Were the Early Israelites?*, p. 142. On T. L. Thompson see W. G. Dever, *What Did the Biblical Writers Know and When Did They Know It?*, pp. 30–4.

45 Thompson lists the criticisms against him on the website: http://www.bibleinterp.com/articles/copenhagen.htm.

46 N. K. Gottwald, *The Politics of Ancient Israel* (Louisville, KY, 2001), p. 4.

47 J. S. Spong, *Born of a Woman* (San Francisco, 1992), p. 11.

48 J. S. Spong, *Rescuing the Bible from Fundamentalism* (San Francisco, 1991), p. 54.

49 I. Finkelstein and N. A. Silberman, *The Bible Unearthed*, p. 3.

50 M. Noth, *Überlieferungsgeschichtliche Studien* (Tübingen, 1943), esp. pp. 10ff. He then went on to analyse the sources and traditions which the Dtr historian used in *Das Buch-Josua* (Tübingen,1953), vol. 7, especially pp. 11–13. For a discussion of these theories of composition see L. L. Rowlett, *Joshua and the Rhetoric of Violence* (Sheffield, 1996), pp. 30–48.

51 See L. L. Rowlett, *Joshua and the Rhetoric of Violence*, p. 37, for the three major schools of thought on the dating and redaction of Dtr.

52 Among the scholars favouring a Josianic date, F. M. Cross, *Canaanite Myth and Hebrew Epic* (Cambridge, 1973), first put forth the idea of a Dtr historian as propaganda for Josiah; cf. R. D. Nelson, *The Double Redaction of the Deuteronomic History* (Sheffield, 1981); R. E. Friedman, *The Exile and Biblical Narrative* (Chico, CA, 1981); S. MacKenzie, *The Trouble with Kings* (Leiden: Brill, 1992).

53 Martin Noth was the first to suggest that the books of Deuteronomy, Joshua, Judges, 1 and 2 Samuel and 1 and 2 Kings comprised a single literary unit, and that the Dtr historian composed in the exilic period while using older sources and oral traditions.

54 I. Finkelstein and N. A. Silberman, *The Bible Unearthed*, p. 23.

55 I. Finkelstein and N. A. Silberman, *The Bible Unearthed* pp. 190, 238.

56 Finkelstein and Silberman believe there were two distinct Hebrew societies in the highlands of Canaan. Both were originally Canaanite, but a religious separation occurred that was reflected in the names of the two kingdoms: Israel and Judah. The diatribes against the Canaanites in the Bible are actually one group later trying to separate itself from the other. H. Shanks, *Rise of Ancient Israel*, p. 12; 'Israel's Emergence in Canaan. *BR* Interviews Norman Gottwald', *BR* (Oct. 1989), pp. 26–34; P. Trible, 'God's Ghostwriters' review of I. Finkelstein and N. A. Silberman, *The Bible Unearthed*, http://www.universityuus.org/books/feb02.htm.

57 B. Halpern, 'The Exodus from Egypt: Myth or Reality?' in H. Shanks, *The Rise of Ancient Israel* (Washington, DC, 1992), pp. 107–8.

58 I. Finkelstein and N. A. Silberman, *The Bible Unearthed*, p.70.

59 M. Sicker, *The Rise and Fall of the Ancient Israelite States* (Westport, CT, 2003), writes: 'Such contentious conclusions . . . will be ignored entirely in this study', p. 2; R. A. Gabriel, *The Military History of Ancient Israel*, who states as much in the introduction. The extent to which textbooks on western civilisation have clung to the conquest model and ignored much of current scholarship see J. Cargill, 'Ancient History in Western Civ Textbooks', *History Teacher* 34, 3 (May 2001), pp. 297–326.

60 Y. Zakovich, 'Humor and Theology or the Successful Failure of Israelite Intelligence: A Literary-Folkloric Approach to Joshua 2' in S. Niditch (ed.), *Text and Tradition* (Atlanta, GA, 1990), p.76.

61 A. Malamat, 'Conquest of Canaan: Israelite Conduct of War According to Biblical Tradition', *Encyclopedia Judaica Year Book*, 1975/76 (Jerusalem, 1976), p. 173.

Part I

Chapter 1 The Book of Joshua (pp.41–62)

1   For a traditional view see Y. Yadin, *Military and Archaeological Aspects of the Conquest of Canaan in the Book of Joshua* (New York, 1960).

2   N. Na'aman of Tel Aviv University called the saga of Joshua a 'fictive literary composition'. N. Na'aman, 'The "Conquest of Canaan" in the Book of Joshua and in History' in Finkelstein and Na'aman (eds), *From Nomadism to Monarchy* (Washington, DC, 1994), pp. 280–1.

3   See B. S. J. Isserlin, 'The Israelite Conquest of Canaan: A Comparative Review of the Arguments Applicable', *PEQ* 115 (1983), pp. 85–94, and J. M. Miller. 'Archaeology and the Israelite Conquest of Canaan: Some Methodological Observations', *PEQ* 109 (1977), pp. 87–93.

4   For a summary of problems about Israelite origins and identity see W. G. Dever, *Who Were the Early Israelites and Where Did They Come From?* (Grand Rapids, MI, 2003) with its excellent bibliography divided by topic.

5   G. E. Mendenhall, 'The Hebrew Conquest of Palestine', *BA* 25 (1962), pp. 66–87; N. K. Gottwald, *The Tribes of Yahweh* (New York, 1979), *passim*; M. L . Chaney, 'Ancient Palestine Peasant Movements and the Formation of Premonarchic Israel' in D. N. Freeman and D. F. Graf (eds), *Palestine in Transition: The Emergence of Ancient Israel* (Sheffield, 1983), pp. 39–90; J. A. Callaway, 'A New Perspective of the Hill Country Settlement of Canaan in Iron Age I' (London, 1985), pp. 31–49; N. Na'aman, 'The "Conquest of Canaan" in the Book of Joshua and in History' in Finkelstein and Na'aman (eds), *From Nomadism to Monarchy* (Washington, DC, 1994), p. 231 and n. 38.

6   C. H. J. de Geus, *The Tribes of Israel* (Assen/Amsterdam, 1976), pp. 164–81; B. Halpern, *The Emergence of Israel in Canaan* (Chico, CA, 1983), pp. 47–106; R. B. Coote and K. W. Whitelam, *The Emergence of Early Israel in Historical Perspective* (Sheffield, 1987), pp. 117–38, L. E. Stager, 'The Archaeology of the Family in Ancient Israel', *BASOR* 260 (1985), pp. 3–4.

7   V. Fritz, 'The Israelite "Conquest" in the Light of Recent Excavations at Khirbet el-Meshash', *BASOR* 241 (1981), pp. 61–73; V. Fritz, 'Conquest or Settlement? The Early Iron Age in Palestine', *BA* 50 (1987), pp. 84–100.

8   I. Finkelstein, *The Archaeology of the Israelite Settlement* (Jerusalem, 1988), pp. 336–51; I. Finkelstein, 'The Emergence of Early Israel', *JAOS* 110 (1990), pp. 682–5. Na'aman points out how close this is to Alt's classical model of peaceful infiltration and gradual sedentarisation and occupation of the land. N. Na'aman, 'The "Conquest of Canaan" in the Book of Joshua and in History', p. 232, n. 41.

9   T. R. Hobbs, *A Time for War*, p. 31.

10 See A. Malamat, 'Conquest of Canaan', *RIHM* 42 (1979), p. 25, who talks about 'generations of complex literary reworking'.

11 This is the argument of I. Finkelstein and N. A. Silberman, *The Bible Unearthed* (New York, 2001).

12 See A. O. Bellis, *Helpmates Harlots, and Heroes. Women's Stories in the Hebrew Bible* (Louisville, KY, 1994), pp. 112–114; N. P. Franklin, *The Stranger Within Their Gates*, Duke University PhD dissertation, 1990.

13 C. Herzog and M. Gichon, *Battles of the Bible* (London, 1997), p. 44.

14 In Num. 13 it was done on the initiative of Yahweh; in Deut. 1:22 the people ask Moses to send out the spies. See the comments of M. Ottosson, 'Rahab and the Spies' in H. Behrens et al., *DUMU-E$_2$-DUB-BA-A* (Philadelphia, 1989), p. 419. Moses sent out spies three other times, partly for diplomatic purposes: to the king of Edom (Num. 20:14), to Sihon the king of the Amorites (Num. 21:21), and spies into the villages of Jaazer (Num. 21:31).

15 This was the bridge that the Barak Brigade blew up in the Six Day War. The crossing point is still under Israeli control. Given the number of land mines that still remain in the area, Joshua's crossing was much easier that it would be today.

16 Josephus, *Ant.*, 5.1.2

17 The Targum on Josephus 2.1 has the noun translated *pundokita* = Gr. *pandokeutria* or *pandokissa* 'innkeeper'. M. A. Beek, 'Rahab in the Light of Jewish Exegesis', *Von Kanaan bis Kerala*, pp. 37–44. See Josephus, *Ant.* 3.276 and note, H. St J. Thackeray and Ralph Marcus translation in the Loeb edition. Josephus adds his own details to the story. He claims that they went undetected and surveyed the entire city unmolested. They observed where the ramparts were strong and where they offered a less secure protection to the inhabitants. They also examined the gates that would facilitate entrance for the army. Cf. *Ant.* 5.1,2.

18 C. Herzog and M. Gichon, *Battles of the Bible*, p. 45, but Thackeray thought this interpretation dubious; see his translation of Josephus, *Ant.* 3.276 note. On the meaning of *zonah* see H. Schulte, 'Beobachtungen zum Begriff der Zona im A. T.', *ZAW* 104 (1992), pp. 255–62. D. J. Wiseman, 'Rahab of Jericho', *The Tyndale House Bulletin* 14 (June 1964), pp. 8–11, compares *zonah* to the Akkadian *sabitu* and explains the various duties of Mesopotamian innkeepers that included notifying the palace of any stranger, especially one engaged in hostile activity. Cf. P. Bird, 'The Harlot as Heroine', *Semeia* 46 (1989), p. 120, on the meanings, attitudes and associations surrounding the use of such a word. Some commentators claim that the Israelites would not consort with prostitutes, and that Rahab was a hierodule, a ritual prostitute similar to those in Canaanite cities. See P. Bird, 'The Harlot as Heroine', p. 127, with earlier references; contra M. A. Beek, 'Rahab in the Light of Jewish Exegesis', p. 37, who sees no evidence for it. On the sexual connotations of the story see E. Assis, 'Animadversiones – The Choice to Serve God and Assist His People: Rahab and Yael', *Biblica* 85, 1 (2004), pp. 82–90.

19 Josh. 2:18 has her gathering her family to her own house when the Israelites attack. She also deals with the king of Jericho's representatives who are searching out the Israelite spies; there is no male intermediary (2:3). Finally, she enters into an agreement with the spies on her own (2:14). See S. Ackerman, 'Prostitutes and Delilah' in *Warrior, Dancer, Seductress, Queen. Women in Judges and Biblical Israel* (New York, 1998), p. 227.

20 F. A. Spina, 'Reversal of Fortune', *BR* 17, 4 (Aug. 2001), p. 26, on the various words in the Rahab story that have risqué overtones; also S. Ackerman, 'Prostitutes and Delilah' in *Warrior, Dancer, Seductress, Queen. Women in Judges and Biblical Israel* (New York, 1998), p. 231. The words of the king's emissaries also suggest possibilities. Whether these men 'came to you' (for sex) or 'came to your house' (for lodging) they are to be handed over. See Y. Zakovich, 'Humor and Theology or the Successful Failure of Israelite Intelligence' in S. Niditch, *Text and Tradition* (Atlanta, GA, 1990), p. 84.

21 See D. Merling, 'Rahab: The Woman Who Fulfilled the Word of YHWH', *Andrews University Seminary Studies* 41, 1 (spring 2003), pp. 31–44. C. Herzog and M. Gichon, *Battles of the Bible*, p. 45, point out that: 'Frederick the Great advised his heirs to have an innkeeper in their pay in every region of interest.' Cf. P. Bird, 'The Harlot as Heroine', p. 128.

22 Josh. 2:11. G. M. Tucker, 'The Rahab Saga (Joshua 2)' in *The Use of the Old Testament in the New and Other Essays* (Durham, NC, 1972), pp. 66–86, esp. p. 79. Tucker believes that the Rahab story is inserted to show that the conquest did not begin until the will of Yahweh had been determined, and had nothing to do with any real espionage. He also believes that the Rahab story once existed apart from the story of the destruction of Jericho now preserved in Joshua 6 (p. 83). On the combining of two sources see W. Moran, 'The Repose of Rahab's Israelite Guests', *Studi sull'Oriente e la Bibbia* (Genoa, 1967), pp. 273–84.

23 Josh. 2:18–20.

24 Y. Zakovich, 'Humor and Theology or the Successful Failure of Israelite Intelligence', p. 85.

25 See Y. Zakovich, 'Humor and Theology or the Successful Failure of Israelite Intelligence', p. 75, who believed some editors even tried to keep this story from inclusion in the Book of Joshua. See pp. 76–7, n. 1.

26 A. L. Laffey, *An Introduction to the Old Testament. A Feminist Perspective* (Philadelphia, 1988), p. 89. On the theme of a foreigner giving a credo and acknowledging Israel's God as the true God see F. M. Cross, 'A Response to Zakovich's "Successful Failure of Israelite Intelligence" ' in *Text and Tradition,*

p. 100. M. L. Newman saw Rahab as a representative of the *Habiru* outside Canaanite society, and the king of Jericho as the established authority. The story thus becomes anti-monarchical. M. L. Newman, 'Rahab and the Conquest' in J. T. Butler et al., *Understanding the Word. Essays in Honor of Bernhard W. Anderson* (Sheffield, 1985), p. 173.

27 Gary Rendsburg made much of Rahab's assistance in lowering the spies 'through the window', a phrase suggestive of aristocratic women in palaces. He suggests the author was elevating Rahab to a high level for her service to Israel. God has taken the lowly, the people of Israel, and elevated them to be partners in the covenant. See G. A. Rendsburg, 'Unlikely Heroes: Women as Israel', *BR* 19, 1 (Feb. 2003), pp. 20–1.

28 Rahab is mentioned three times in the New Testament: in Hebrews 11:31 as an example of faith; in James 2:25 as justified by her works; and in Matt. 1:5 as an ancestor of Jesus.

29 F. A. Spina, 'Reversal of Fortune', *BR* 17, 4 (Aug. 2001), pp. 25–6.

30 F. A. Spina, 'Reversal of Fortune', *BR* 17, 4 (Aug. 2001), p. 54.

31 J. Alberto Soggin, *Joshua. A Commentary* (Philadelphia, 1972), p. 86, found there is no trace of battle in the text in the common sense of the word. The command to encircle the city may represent a recollection of a siege. On the topography of the area see H. Rösel, 'Studien zur Topographie der Kriege in den Büchern Josua und Richter', *ZDPV* 92, 2 (1976), pp. 159–90 and the map on p. 189.

32 C. Herzog and M. Gichon, *Battles of the Bible*, p. 46, suggest that crossing the Jordan was facilitated by an earthquake. Such a natural occurrence like an earthquake would have easily been interpreted as a sign from God. When the earth quaked, the tribes got ready to move.

33 C. Herzog and M. Gichon, *Battles of the Bible*, p. 47.

34 C. Herzog and M. Gichon, *Battles of the Bible,* p. 48, cite the British misleading the Turkish and German foes at Romani, in Sinai, in 1916, and more recently the Syrians and Egyptians deceiving the Israelis before the October 1973 War by repeated mobilisation of their assault forces on Israel's borders.

35 A. Malamat, 'Conquest of Canaan', *RIHM* 42 (1979), pp. 41–2; C. Herzog and M. Gichon, *Battles of the Bible*, pp. 28–9.

36 See B. Wood, 'Did the Israelites Conquer Jericho? A New Look at the Archaeological Evidence', *BAR* 16, 2 (Mar.–Apr. 1990), p. 49, for a discussion of Garstang and Kenyon. Cf. D. Usshishkin, 'The Walls of Jericho', *BAIAS* 8 (1988/89), pp. 85–90. A summary of the archaeological evidence appears in G. Foerster, 'Jericho', *NEAEHL*, pp. 674–97.

37 Archaeologists have searched unsuccessfully for evidence of collapsed walls. The excavations of 1952–8 found no evidence that the city was occupied during the most likely period of the conquest. Two previous excavators who thought they had discovered evidence of a city destroyed by Joshua were off with their dates by several hundred years. On the Iron Age habitation at Jericho see K. M. Kenyon and T. A. Holland, *Excavations at Jericho* (London, 1984), vol. IV, fig. 215:1–2; 216:9; M. Weippert, 'Jericho in der Eisenzeit', *ZDPV* 92 (1976), pp. 105–48, published no pottery from Iron Age I; the report contained no unequivocal conclusion about the size of Jericho in LBII. See K. Kenyon, *Digging Up Jericho*, pp. 256–63; B. G. Wood, 'Did the Israelites Conquer Jericho?', *BAR* (Mar.–Apr. 1990), pp. 44–57, on the pottery sequences which, he claims, show a destruction level *c.*1400. This still does not identify the destroyers, and no one has produced evidence for Israelites there in 1400 BCE. Cf. P. Bienkowski, 'Jericho Was Destroyed in the Middle Bronze Age, Not the Late Bronze Age', *BAR* 16, 5 (Sept.–Oct. 1990), pp. 45–6, 69, who challenges Wood's pottery sequences. D. Ussishkin, 'The Walls of Jericho', *BAIAS* 8 (1988/89), pp. 85–90, summarises previous excavations and concludes: 'Late Bronze Age walls have not been identified there' (p. 90).

38 N. Na'aman, 'The "Conquest of Canaan" in the Book of Joshua and in History', p. 269.

39 I. Finkelstein and N. A. Silberman, *The Bible Unearthed*, p. 83

40 A. Rainey, *The Biblical Archaeologist Reader*, vol. 3, p. 92; T. H. Gaster, *Myth, Legend and Custom in the Old Testament* (New York, 1969), p. 412; T. H. Gaster, 'The Canaanite Epic of Keret', *JQR* 38 (1947), pp. 285–93; C. F. Pfeiffer, 'Epic Elements in Biblical History', *JHS* 1, 2 (1970), p. 11; J. C. L. Gibson,

Canaanite Myths and Legends (Edinburgh, 1977), 2nd edn, pp. 19–23; H. L. Ginzburg, 'The Legend of King Keret: A Canaanite Epic of the Bronze Age', *BASOR* Supplement 23 (ASOR, 1946); C. F. Pfeiffer, *Ras Shamra and the Bible* (Grand Rapids, MI, 1962), pp. 49–52.

41 For a discussion of the *Sitz im Leben* story see M. L. Newman, 'Rahab and the Conquest' in J. T. Butler et al., *Understanding the Word* (Sheffield, 1985), pp. 167–81, who observes that one point of the story is meant to portray the spies in more favourable light. He believes, however, that the story would have been useful as a 'security clearance' narrative only if it were true (p. 177).

42 On the battles of Joshua see R. Gabriel, *The Military History of Ancient Israel*, pp. 109–52; J. A. Soggin, *Joshua: A Commentary* (Philadelphia, 1972), pp. 88–105; N. Na'aman, 'The "Conquest of Canaan" in the Book of Joshua and in History', pp. 218–81; R. D. Nelson, *Joshua. A Commentary* (Louisville, 1997); C. Herzog and M. Gichon, *Battles of the Bible*, pp. 48–54; R. Gale, *Great Battles of Biblical History* (New York, 1970), pp. 17–24. For the topography of the site, and maps see H. Rösel, 'Studien zur Topographie der Kriege in den Büchern Josua und Richter', *ZDPV* 92, 1 (1976), pp. 10–46.

43 Archaeological excavations at Ai cast serious doubt on the historicity of this narrative. Excavations in 1933–4 demonstrated that there was a great walled city there in the Late Bronze Age, but it had been destroyed almost a millennium before the Israelites arrived. These results were confirmed by a recent American expedition, according to which there was only sparse settlement in the Iron Age, long after the conquest. Most likely the city was a ruin when the Israelites arrived, and remained so during most of the history of Israel, thus its name *ha'ai* (ruin). The scholars who believe in the conquest model reject the Ai/et-Tell equation. See J. M. Grintz, 'Ai which is Beside Beth-Aven. A Re-examination of the Identity of Ai', *Biblica* 42 (1961), pp. 201–16; D. J. Wiseman, 'Ai in Ruins', *Buried History* 7 (1971), pp. 4–6. D. Livingston's suggestion that Khirbet Nisya was the biblical Ai, in *Khirbet Nisya: 1979–2002. Excavation of the Site with Related Studies in Biblical Archaeology* (Associates for Biblical Research, 2002), was unconvincing and was adequately reviewed by A. Rainey, 'Bethel is still Beitin', *WTJ* 33 (1970/71), pp. 175–88. See J. Maxwell Miller, 'Archaeology and the Israelite Conquest of Canaan: Some Methodological Observations', *PEQ* (July–Dec. 1977), p. 89; J. Callaway, 'Ai: Problem Site for Biblical Archaeologists', *Archaeology and Biblical Interpretation* (Atlanta, 1987), pp. 87–99.

44 A. Malamat, "Conquest of Canaan', *RIHM* 42 (1979), p. 34, notes the risks of interferences of the spies in operational decisions which, in modern times, is prohibited to field agents since these decisions belong exclusively to the level of command.

45 Josh. 7:4. C. Herzog and M. Gichon, *Battles of the Bible*, p. 51.

46 D. G. Hansen, 'Intelligence, Deception and Military Operations in the Ancient Near East', *II International Conference on Intelligence and Military Operations*, p. 25. For a topographical account of the battle see Z. Zevit, 'Archaeological and Literary Stratigraphy in Joshua 7–8', *BASOR* 251 (summer 1983), pp. 23–35.

47 C. Herzog and M. Gichon, *Battles of the Bible*, p. 53.

48 On the use of sun telegraph in the Holy Land see C. Herzog and M. Gichon, *Battles of the Bible*, p.303, n. 7.

49 For a schematic plan of Ai's capture see A. Malamat, "Conquest of Canaan', *RIHM* 42 (1979), p. 45.

50 C. Herzog and M. Gichon, *Battles of the Bible*, p. 54.

51 J. A. Callaway, 'New Evidence on the Conquest of Ai', *JBL* 87, 3 (Sept. 1968), p. 312, says: 'Ai is simply an embarrassment to every view of the conquest that takes the biblical and archaeological evidence seriously.'

52 Challenges to the conquest model were already posed in the 1930s when Martin Noth dismissed the biblical account as an aetiological story. M. Noth, 'Bethel und Ai', *PJB* 31 (1935), pp. 7–29.

53 J. Marquet-Krause, 'La Deuxieme Campagne . . .', *Syria* 16 (1939), p. 17, and J. A. Callaway, 'New Evidence on the Conquest of Ai', *JBL* 87, 3 (Sept. 1968), p. 314.

54 See J. A. Callaway, 'A New Perspective on the Hill Country Settlement of Canaan in Iron Age I', p. 72. Compare this with the discussion by W. Dever, *Who Were the Early Israelites?*, pp. 47–8.

55 Two prominent spokesmen for this view are J. Bimson, *Redating the Exodus and Conquest* (Sheffield, 1978) and B. Wood, 'Did the Israelites Conquer Jericho? A New Look at the Archaeological Evidence', *BAR* (Mar.–Apr. 1990), pp. 44–59. Their solution was to lower the date of the Middle Bronze Age to the late fifteenth century and to place the Israelite Conquest then rather than at the end of the Late Bronze Age. This resolves the problem of Jericho, but not that of Ai. So they argue that archaeologists have misidentified the site of Ai. They believe el-Tell is not Ai, and that Ai has yet to be discovered. The biblical tradition clearly places Ai east of Bethel, which is normally identified with Beitin, and hence Bethel has been misidentified as well. Not surprisingly, their proposals have been dismissed by biblical scholars and archaeologists alike. Why was it called 'Ai' (ruin) unless it had been occupied and destroyed long before?

56 J. Bimson, *Redating the Exodus and Conquest* (Sheffield Press, 1978); B. Wood, 'Did the Israelites Conquer Jericho? A New Look at the Archaeological Evidence', *BAR* (Mar.–Apr. 1990), pp. 44–59. Followed recently by R. Gabriel, *The Military History of Ancient Israel* (Westport, CT, 2003); see the review of Gabriel in R. M. Sheldon, *JMH*, 69, 1 (Jan. 2005), pp. 197–204.

57 I. Finkelstein and N. A. Silberman, *The Bible Unearthed*, pp. 93, and pp. 288–9 on the Josianic conquests.

58 See N. Na'aman, 'The "Conquest of Canaan" in the Book of Joshua and in History', p. 251, who suggests it might be a literary reflection of the historical episode at Gibeah (Judg. 20:15–48). See also H. Rösel, 'Studien zur Topographie der Kriege den Buchern Josua und Richter', *ZDPV* 92 (1976), pp. 33–5; Z. Zevit, 'Archaeological and Literary Stratigraphy in Joshua 7–8', *BASOR* 251 (1983), pp. 28–33.

59 Gibeon is the present day el-Jib, eight kilometres northwest of Jerusalem.

60 J. B. Pritchard, *Gibeon: Where the Sun Stood Still* (Princeton, 1962), p. 136.

61 M. Gichon, 'Cestius Gallus' Campaign in Judaea', *PEQ* (1981), pp. 361–2; B. Bar-Kochba, 'Seron and Cestius Gallus at Beth Horon', *PEQ* 107 (1976), pp. 13–21.

62 C. Herzog and M. Gichon, *Battles of the Bible*, p. 57.

63 I. Finkelstein and N. A. Silberman, *The Bible Unearthed*, p. 82.

64 J. B. Pritchard, *Gibeon: Where the Sun Stood Still*, p. 136

65 J. H. Vriezen von Carel, 'Khirbet Kefire – Eine Oberflächenuntersuchung', *Sonderdruck aus ZDPV*, 91 (1975), pp. 135–58. Some pottery dated after 1200 BCE was found. Only further excavation of the site will reveal what village or city existed here after 1200 BCE.

66 N. Na'aman, 'The "Conquest of Canaan" in the Book of Joshua and in History', p. 253.

67 B. Halpern, 'Gibeon: Israelite Diplomacy in the Conquest Era', *CBQ* 37 (1975), pp. 303–16. N. Na'aman, *From Nomadism to Monarchy*, p. 254, claims that a treaty between Gibeon and the Israelites can hardly antedate the eleventh century when the settlement process reached the stage of regional unification. At that time there were no Amorite kingdoms to attack the Benjaminite–Gibeonite league.

68 I. Finkelstein and N. A. Silberman, *The Bible Unearthed*, p. 93. On the seventh century date and the *Sitz im Leben* of the poem see J. S. Holladay, jun., 'The Day(s) the Moon Stood Still', *JBL* 87, 2 (June 1968), pp. 166–78.

69 N. Na'aman, 'The "Conquest of Canaan" in the Book of Joshua and in History', p. 254; 2 Sam. 5:22–5 and 1 Chr. 14:13–16; and see the discussion in N. Na'aman, "The Conquest of Canaan", pp. 253–5.

70 N. Na'aman, 'The "Conquest of Canaan" in the Book of Joshua and in History', p. 256.

71 On Joshua's campaigns in the Jezreel valley see E. Cline, *Armageddon* (Ann Arbor, MI, 2004), p. 35, n. 2. The Waters of Merom is the spring of Wadi el-Mhamam, northeast of Tel Qarnei Hittin, the site of the Canaanite city of Marom/Merom. See N. Na'aman, *Borders and Districts in Biblical Historiography* (Jerusalem, 1986), p. 126. It is located on the main route leading to Hazor. On the topography of the area see H. Rösel, 'Studien zur Topographie . . . ', *ZDPV* 92, 2 (1976), pp. 159–90, for his map on p. 180.

72 A. Aharoni and A. Rainey identified the waters of Merom with Tell el-Khureibeh some three kilometres south of Marun er-Ras. Meron is mentioned in the campaign annals of Thutmose III (1504–1450 BCE) and Ramses II. Tiglath Pileser III (733/32) of Assyria also claimed to have taken Merom, which suggests the strategic nature of the place.

73 The chariot, introduced by the Hittites and the Hyksos in the eighteenth century BCE, was the ancient equivalent of the modern armoured fighting vehicle. C. Herzog and M. Gichon, *Battles of the Bible*, p. 58, compare its tactical employment to medieval cavalry, although the bowmen added firepower to its shock value. The earliest war chariots were the Sumerian four- and two-wheeled varieties from the first half of the third millennium BCE. See Y. Yadin, *Art of Warfare in Biblical Lands* (New York, 1963), vol. 1, pp. 36ff.; A. Salonen, *Notes on Wagons and Chariots in Ancient Mesopotamia* (Helsinki, 1950), pp. 1–8.

74 See similar uses of this stratagem in Frontinus 2.2.8 and Polyaenus 8.10.3: 'When the barbarians turned [toward the Romans], the sun was in their faces and they were blinded by its brilliance . . . and when they could no longer bear the rays of the sun, they raised their shields to their faces. Thus they exposed their bodies and were wounded, and were destroyed by the Romans. On the solar eclipse see B. Margalit, 'The Day the Sun Did Not Stand Still: A New Look at Joshua X 8–15', *VT* 42, 4 (1992), pp. 482–3. Both J. F. A. Sawyer, 'Joshua 10:12–14 and The Solar Eclipse of 30th September 1131 BC', *PEQ* 104 (July–Dec. 1972), pp. 139–46, and F. R. Stephenson, 'Astronomical Verification and Dating of Old Testament Passages Referring to Solar Eclipses', *PEQ* 107 (1975), pp. 107–20, cite the eclipse on 30 September 1131 BCE.

75 There is a parallel in the battle of Saul with the Philistines in 1 Sam. 14 where he forbids people to eat or drink until the battle is finished. In one case the day is prolonged by God and on the other the battle is prolonged by the people. See M. Weinfeld, 'Divine Intervention in War in Ancient Israel and in the Ancient Near East' (Jerusalem, 1983), pp. 146–7.

76 N. Na'aman, 'The "Conquest of Canaan" in the Book of Joshua and in History', p. 256, with references.

77 G. H. Jones, ' "Holy War" or "Yahweh War"?', *VT* 25, 3 (July 1975), pp. 651–8.

78 N. Na'aman, *From Nomadism to Monarchy*, p. 257.

79 I. Finkelstein and N. A. Silberman, *The Bible Unearthed*, p. 90. Josh. 11:10; Judg. 4:2, 23, 24. N. Na'aman, 'The "Conquest of Canaan" in the Book of Joshua and in History', p. 258.

80 I. Finkelstein and N. A. Silberman, *The Bible Unearthed*, p. 90.

81 N. Na'aman, 'The "Conquest of Canaan" in the Book of Joshua and in History', pp. 258–9.

82 I. Finkelstein and N. A. Silberman, *The Bible Unearthed*, p. 94.

83 J. Van Seters, 'Joshua's Campaign of Canaan and Near Eastern Historiography', *SJOT* 2 (1990), p. 1.

84 Debir was the only Canaanite city in Judah's hill country in the fourteenth and thirteenth centuries and was possibly conquered by the Kenizzites. Jerusalem was apparently captured by the Jebusites, who then settled there. Bethel was the only Canaanite city in the southernmost part of Ephraim conquered by one of the peoples that entered the Hill Country in early Iron Age I. See N. Na'aman, 'The "Conquest of Canaan" in the Book of Joshua and in History', p. 280.

85 N. Na'aman, 'The "Conquest of Canaan" in the Book of Joshua and in History', p. 259, who discusses Alt and Noth.

86 See J. Van Seters, 'Joshua's Campaign of Canaan and Near Eastern Historiography', *SJOT* 2 (1990), pp. 1–12.

87 J. Van Seters, 'Joshua's Campaign of Canaan', *SJOT* 2 (1990), p. 6, gives evidence for foreign monuments and texts in both kingdoms.

88 J. Van Seters, 'Joshua's Campaign of Canaan and Near Eastern Historiography', *SJOT* 2 (1990), pp. 1–12.

89 S. Wagner, 'Die Kundschaftergeschichten im Alten Testament', *ZAW* 76 (1964), pp. 255–69. Many believe that the Rahab story is not part of the earliest conquest account, but a later addition which fits

in rather awkwardly. See J. Van Seters, *SJOT* 2 (1990), p. 3.

90 This is a quite different interpretation from that of Newman who saw the legend as a 'security clearance' story for the family of Rahab. He believed that she and her family continued to reside in Jericho. M. L. Newman, 'Rahab and the Conquest' (Sheffield, 1985), p. 175.

91 Y. Kaufmann, *The Biblical Account of the Conquest of Canaan* (Jerusalem, 1984), p. 72. Kaufman argued that the text preceded the conquest and the establishment of the kingdom. It could be equally argued, however, that it was written long afterwards by people with no knowledge of the actual events.

92 On the lack of literary activity in the pre-monarchical period see N. Na'aman, 'The "Conquest of Canaan" in the Book of Joshua and in History', p. 230; contra A. Malamat, *The Proto-History of Israel: A Study in Method* (Winona Lake, IN, 1983), pp. 303–6.

93 J. Van Seters, 'Joshua's Campaign of Canaan and Near Eastern Historiography', *SJOT* 2 (1990), p. 1, on Noth's assessment of the literary growth of the Book of Joshua.

94 J. Van Seters, *SJOT* 2 (1990), p. 12.

95 N. Na'aman gives five examples where such borrowed material is used (N. Na'aman, 'The "Conquest of Canaan" in the Book of Joshua and in History', pp. 251–60).

96 J. Harris et al., *Joshua, Judges, Ruth* (Peabody, MA, 2000), p. 27.

97 M. C. Lind, *Yahweh is a Warrior* (Scottsdale, PA, 1980), p. 80.

98 A. Malamat, 'Conquest of Canaan', *RIHM* 42 (1979), p. 26; P. D. Miller, jun., *The Divine Warrior in Early Israel* (Cambridge, MA, 1973), pp. 156ff.

99 R. Gabriel, *The Military History of Ancient Israel* (Westport, CT, 2003), p. 112, claims that Joshua's army was well organised, with a high level of combat training, sophisticated battlefield manoeuvres and the ability to produce massive armament. He never considered the possibility that this description was the product of a later age rather than anachronism in the thirteenth century BCE.

100 Y. Yadin, *Warfare in Biblical Lands*. vol. 1, p. 110.

101 Num. 13: the twelve spies of Moses, which included Joshua; cf. Deut. 1:22ff. Moses sent spies to Jazer, a city in Trans-jordan (Num. 21:32). Joshua sent spies to Ai (Josh. 7:2ff.). The tribe of Dan sent five spies to locate a territory where they could move (Judg. 18:2ff.). All of these spies are charged simply with reconnoitring.

102 A. Malamat, 'Conquest of Canaan', *RIHM* 42 (1979), p. 40; A. Malamat, 'Conquest of Canaan: Israelite Conduct of War According to Biblical Tradition', *Encyclopedia Judaica Year Book*, 1975/76 (Jerusalem, 1976), pp. 49–51.

103 A. Malamat, 'Conquest of Canaan', *RIHM* 42 (1979), p. 40.

104 R. Gabriel, *The Military History of Ancient Israel*, p. 114, suggests that the Israelites coming out of Sinai outnumbered the Canaanites, but this is not generally accepted.

Chapter 2 The Book of Judges (pp.63–83)

1 On the Book of Judges see A. Malamat. 'The Period of the Judges', *World History of the Jewish People* (Jerusalem, 1971), pp. 135–6. B. G. Webb, *The Book of Judges: An Integrated Reading* (Sheffield, 1987).

2 C. Herzog and M. Gichon, *Battles of the Bible*, p. 63; A. Malamat, 'Charismatic Leadership in the Book of Judges', *History of Biblical Israel* (Leiden, 2001), p. 151.

3 For the nature of the office of Judge see A. Malamat, 'Charismatic Leadership in the Period of Judges' in *History of Biblical Israel* (Leiden, 2001), pp. 151–70.

4 It has been argued that the pervasiveness of the Israelites' religious zeal was an important factor in converting sizeable numbers of the Cis–Jordanian population without evident coercion into the Israelite tribal federation. See D. W. Dever, 'Ceramics, Ethnicity, and the Question of Israel's Origins', *BA* 58 (1995), pp. 200ff.

5 See Judg. 6:35, where the tribes are called up separately. Y. Yadin, *The Art of Warfare in Biblical Lands* (New York, 1963), vol. 2, p. 255.

6 Y. Yadin, *The Art of Warfare in Biblical Lands*, vol. 2, p. 254.

7 According to Judg. 1:26, the man went to Hittite country, built a city and named it Luz.
8 Y. Yadin, *The Art of Warfare in Biblical Lands*, vol. 2, pp. 254–5, comments that if the sword was double-edged this would suggest it was made of iron. This would also be the first mention in the Bible of an iron weapon in the possession of an Israelite soldier. J. Moyer, 'Weapons and Warfare in the Book of Judges' in T. Dowley (ed.), *Discovering the Bible* (Grand Rapids, MI, 1986), pp. 42–50; R. Gabriel, *The Military History of Ancient Israel* (Westport, CT, 2003), p. 156.
9 For the textual analysis of the biblical narrative and the interpretation of the final editors' purposes see H. D. Neef, 'Der Sieg Deboras und Baraks über Sisera', *ZAW* 101 (1989), pp. 28–49. On the relationship between the Song of Deborah and Judges 4 see B. Halpern, 'Sisera and Old Lace. The Case of Deborah and Yael' in *The First Historians* (San Francisco, 1988), pp. 76–103; B. Halpern, 'The Resourceful Israelite Historian: The Song of Deborah and Israelite Historiography', *HTR* 76, 4 (1983), pp. 379–401.
10 The same tale is told in a prose account placed immediately prior to the poetic version in the Book of Judg. 4:1–14. This was no doubt a later account which tried to fill in some of the details not given by the poem. See the comments of E. H. Cline, *The Battles of Armageddon* (Ann Arbor, MI, 2000), pp. 45–6.
11 For Deborah as Yahweh's representative see D. I. Block, 'Why Deborah's Different', *BR* (June 2001), p. 35. The assessment of woman as warrior has been generally negative because she is seen as usurping a male prerogative. See L. L. Bronner, 'Valorized or Vilified? The Women of Judges in Midrashic Sources' in A. Brenner (ed.), *The Feminist Companion to the Bible* (Sheffield, 1997), pp. 78–91. On the other hand, feminist scholars seem ambivalent towards this metaphor. Some find it a source of female empowerment while others reject the role because of its association with male martial values. See G. A. Yee, 'By the Hand of A Woman', p. 100.
12 Judges 4 has Barak as the hero of the Israelite–Canaanite battle, whereas in Judges 5 he is only Deborah's second-in-command. See S. Ackerman, 'Deborah, Women and War' in *Warrior, Dancer, Seductress, Queen. Women in Judges and Biblical Israel* (New York, 1999), p. 31; J. Shaw, 'Constructions of Woman in Readings of the Story of Deborah', pp. 123–4.
13 Traditionally 'woman of Lappidoth' was interpreted to mean that she was the wife of a man named Lappidoth. The new interpretation claims that Lappidoth is not a proper name, but a common noun meaning flames or torches. See A. Bronner, 'Valorized or Vilified?', pp. 78–9; M. Bal, *Death and Dissymmetry* (Chicago, 1988), p. 209; N. Aschkenasy, *Eve's Journey* (Philadelphia, 1986), p. 166. This is the occurrence of the word in Hebrew scriptures.
14 The problem is that there is a similar account in Joshua (11:1–15) which tells the story of Joshua successfully leading Israel against a Canaanite alliance led by Jabin, king of Hazor, who had a huge army (Josh. 11:4) and a vast arsenal of chariots. As in the Deborah–Barak version, this first battle took place near a water source, but this time the site was named – the Waters of Merom. Joshua captured and destroyed Hazor by fire, and he executed its king. Even if there were two kings named Jabin, how did Hazor, within a generation, regain enough of its former glory to have become a formidable adversary again? J. Harris et al., *Joshua, Judges, Ruth* (Peabody, MA, 2000), p. 176.
15 Sisera is not a semitic name and it is now widely held that he should not be identified with the Canaanites, but with the Sea Peoples such as the Philistines. See B. Lindars, 'Deborah's Song: Women in the Old Testament', *BRL* 65, 2 (spring 1983), p. 161.
16 G. A. Rendburg, 'Unlikely Heroes: Women as Israel', *BR* 19, 1 (Feb. 2003), p. 18.
17 G. A. Rendburg, 'Unlikely Heroes: Women as Israel', *BR* 19, 1 (Feb. 2003), p. 18. Feminists have written extensively on the violence perpetrated by women in Judges. Were they playing men's roles, or were they just strong women? Are other women the victims of their violence? See A. O. Bellis, *Helpmates Harlots, and Heroes*, pp. 115–19. G. A. Yee, 'By the Hand of A Woman', p. 100; D. N. Fewell and D. M. Gunn, 'Controlling Perspectives: Women, Men and the Authority of Violence in Judges 4 & 5', *JAAR* 58 (1991), pp. 389–411.

18 C. Herzog and M. Gichon, *Battles of the Bible,* p. 68. On the narrative structure, and the fact that Deborah is clearly the one in command, see D. F. Murray, 'Narrative Structure and Technique in the Deborah–Barak Story, Judges IV:4–22' in J. A. Emerton (ed.), *Studies in the Historical Books of the Old Testament* (Leiden, 1979), p. 173.

19 G. A. Yee, 'By the Hand of a Woman', p. 115, argues that Deborah shamed Barak, Yael shamed Sisera and then Barak. The effect is to underscore the normative maleness of the world in which these women move.

20 Judg. 4:8–9.

21 Judges 4 suggests a battle at the foot of Mount Tabor; the Song of Deborah says Ta'anach by Megiddo's waters. In verse 21 of the Song, the Canaanites are washed away by the waters of the wadi Kishon. C. Herzog and M. Gichon, *Battles of the Bible,* pp. 48–54, suggest two battles.

22 C. Herzog and M. Gichon, *Battles of the Bible,* p. 67, compare the number of Sisera's chariots with 924 chariots in the booty from the Battle of Megiddo under Thutmose III. Cf. Y. Yadin, *The Art of Warfare in Biblical Lands,* vol. 1, pp. 86ff., 206. Neither of them observes, however, that the Battle of Megiddo occurred three hundred years earlier, when the Canaanite coalition was larger and more prosperous. Another problem is that the chariots are called as 'chariots of iron', which is technological nonsense if it means chariots built of iron. See R. Gabriel, *The Military History of Israel,* p. 181. R. Drews, 'The Chariots of Iron of Joshua and Judges', *JSOT* 45 (1989), pp. 14–23, concludes that the enemies of Joshua and Deborah had either scythed chariots or chariots with iron-tyred wheels, and neither type was known before 700 BCE.

23 On possible locations for Kedesh see E. H. Cline, *The Battles of Armageddon,* pp. 48–9. He also comments that others tribes may have been too involved in economic and commercial activities with the Canaanites to go to war with them.

24 On chariots being inappropriate for warfare in the rugged highlands see C. Hauer, 'From Alt to Anthropology', *JSOT* 36 (1986), p. 9.

25 For the Israelite–Kenite understanding see F. C. Feuersham, 'Did a Treaty between the Israelites and the Kenites Exist', *BASOR* 175 (1964), pp. 51–4. On their identity see S. Ackerman, 'Deborah, Women and War', pp. 98–102.

26 On the Kenites as spies, and a comparison of their actions to those of the Bedouin, who betrayed the Egyptians to the Hittite king Muwatallis at the Battle of Kadesh, see B. Halpern, 'Sisera and Old Lace. The Case of Deborah and Jael', pp. 82–9.

27 See the comments of E. H. Cline, *The Battles of Armageddon,* p. 51, and Aharoni et al., *The Macmillan Bible Atlas* (New York, 1993), 3rd edn; the text to maps 61–2.

28 Jewish commentators have not missed the parallels between this and the story of the Moses' deliverance at the Red (Reed) Sea. See C. A. Brown, *No Longer Be Silent: First Century Jewish Portraits of Biblical Women* (Louisville, KY, 1992), pp. 39–92. See E. H. Cline, *The Battles of Armageddon,* pp. 54–5, for discussion of the battle's location, and the season in which the battle was fought.

29 Judg. 4:1–5:31. See B. Halpern, 'The Resourceful Israelite Historian: The Song of Deborah and Israelite Historiography', *HTR* 76, 4 (1983), p. 389; G. A. Rendsburg, 'Unlikely Heroes: Women as Israel', *BR* 19, 1 (Feb. 2003), pp. 16–23, 52–3. On similarities between the stories of Jael and Judith see B. Lindars, 'Deborah's Song: Women in the Old Testament', *BRL* 65 (1983), pp. 158–75; and M. Stocker, *Judith* (New Haven, 1998), pp. 13–15. There is a sexual allusion in the Hebrew text that Sisera was also unmanned. G. A. Yee, 'By the Hand of A Woman', p. 116. On the erotic overtones see also N. Aschkenasy, *Eve's Journey. Feminine Images in Hebraic Literary Tradition* (Philadelphia, 1986), pp. 170–1.

30 See comments by G. A. Yee, 'By the Hand of a Woman', p. 124. S. Ackerman, 'Deborah, Women and War', pp. 51–6, 90, argued that this image comes from Canaanite stories of the warrior goddess Anat. For a comparison of the same Canaanite tale, but with an opposite conclusion, see S. W. Hanselmann, 'Narrative Theory, Ideology, and Transformation in Judges 4' in M. Bal (ed.), *Anti-Covenant* (Sheffield,

1989), pp. 107–9.

31 Among those who have tried to date the battle see A. D. H. Mayes, 'The Historical Context of the Battle Against Sisera', *VT* 19, 3 (July 1969), pp. 353–60, who linked the battle to the destruction levels at Megiddo. Against this approach see E. Cline, *The Battles of Armageddon*, p. 58.

32 C. Herzog and M. Gichon, *Battles of the Bible*, pp. 64–71.

33 E. H. Cline, *The Battles of Armageddon*, p. 109, n. 15.

34 P. Lapp, 'Taanach by the Waters of Megiddo', *BA* 30 (1967), pp. 8–9; A. Malamat, 'The Period of the Judges' in B. Mazar (ed.), *The World History of the Jewish People* (Jerusalem, 1971), vol. 3, p. 136; I. Finkelstein, 'Notes on the Stratigraphy and Chronology of Iron Age Ta'anach', *Tel Aviv* 25 (1998), pp. 209–10, 215–16. (H)

35 The violent and fiery end of the city of Stratum VIIa at Megiddo is now dated to *c.*1140–1130 BCE, and has been suggested as a time period for Deborah and Sisera's battle. See I. Finkelstein, 'The Stratigraphy and Chronology of Megiddo and Beth-Shean in the Twelfth–Eleventh Centuries BCE', *Tel Aviv* 23 (1996), pp. 171–2 (H); D. Ussishkin, 'The Destruction of Megiddo at the End of the Late Bronze Age and Its Historical Significance', *Tel Aviv* 22 (1995), pp. 242, 246, 260; E. H. Cline, *The Battles of Armageddon*, p. 58.

36 See the comments of E. H. Cline, *The Battles of Armageddon*, pp. 60–1.

37 See G. A. Rendsburg, 'Unlikely Heroes: Women as Israel', *BR* 19, 1 (Feb. 2003), p. 18.

38 The phrase 'most blessed of women' is used elsewhere in the Bible only of Mary, mother of Jesus, and Judith in the Apocrypha, who also murdered an enemy. For Deborah as a liminal figure see G. A. Yee, 'By the Hand of A Woman: The Metaphor of the Woman Warrior in Judges 4', pp. 110–12.

39 For the myriad interpretations of the manner of death, the position of the body, and the erotic overtones of this scene see S. Niditch, 'Eroticism and Death in the Tale of Jael', pp. 305–15, and Y. Zakovitch, 'Sisseras Tod', *ZAW* 93 (1981), pp. 364–74. See also R. C. Rasmussen, 'Deborah the Woman Warrior' in M. Bal (ed.), *Anti-Covenant* (Sheffield, 1989), pp. 79–93. Even the rabbis found sexual allusions in Judg. 5:27. In several places the Talmud and the Midrash discuss the verse and declare that the literary repetition indicates she had sex with Sisera seven times. See L. L. Bronner, 'Valorized or Vilified', p. 89 and n. 2 for the rabbinical references.

40 On the parallels between Rahab and Yael see E. Assis, 'Animadversiones – The Choice to Serve God and Assist His People: Rahab and Yael', *Biblica* 85, 1 (2004), pp. 82–90. See G. A. Rendsburg, 'Unlikely Heroes: Women as Israel', *BR* 19, 1 (Feb. 2003), p. 20. On covert operations see G. A. Yee, 'By the Hand of a Woman', p. 114.

41 A. O. Bellis, *Helpmates, Harlots, and Heroes*, p. 117; G. A. Yee, 'By the Hand of A Woman', pp. 117–21.

42 E. Wavell, *Soldiers and Soldiering* (London, 1953), p. 134.

43 Besides the desire for plunder (2 Sam. 3:22), there were disputes over wells (Gen. 26:17–22) and pasturage rights (Gen. 13:5–7). See C. Herzog and M. Gichon, *Battles of the Bible*, p. 72.

44 On nomads see M. Gichon, 'The Origin of the Limes Palestinae and the Major Phases of its Development', *Bonner Jahrbucher*, Beiheft XIX (1967), pp. 175–93, and 'The Defense of the Negev in Military Retrospect', *Maarachot* (Apr. 1963), pp. 13–21 (H). For later periods see B. Isaac, 'Bandits in Judaea and Arabia', *HSCP* 88 (1984), pp. 171–203.

45 E. Wavell, *Soldiers and Soldiering* (London, 1953), p. 161.

46 Judg. 6:5, 7:12, 8:21 and the story of David and the Amelikites in 1 Sam 30:17 all suggest the large-scale use of camels for trade and military purposes at the end of Iron Age I. If accurate, this suggests the text was written at a much later date. Archaeological sites throughout the region have discovered only a small number of camel bones. See N. Na'aman, 'The "Conquest of Canaan" in the Book of Joshua and in History', p. 226, and my n. 38 above.

47 Judg. 6.35. In Judg. 8:10 the number of Midianites is given as 135,000, but this number seems exaggerated. Josephus' later account *Ant.*, 5.222 gives 138,000.

48 E. H. Cline, *The Battles of Armageddon*, p. 59 and n. 27.

49 See the comments of A. Malamat, 'The War of Gideon and Midian', *PEQ* 85 (1953), p. 62. Gideon is said to have had 32,000 men (Judg. 6:35, 7:3) versus 135,000 Bedouin (Judg. 8:10).

50 On the significance of the number 300 see S. Tolkowsky, 'Gideon's 300', *JPOS* 5 (1925), pp. 69–73.

51 A. Malamat, 'The War of Gideon and Midian', *PEQ* 85 (1953), p. 65.

52 Y. Yadin, *The Art of Warfare in Biblical Lands*, II, p. 257. See also the comments of A. Malamat, 'The War of Gideon and Midian', *PEQ* 85 (1953), p. 64; C. Herzog and M. Gichon, *Battles of the Bible*, p. 75; E. H. Cline, *The Battles of Armageddon*, pp. 62–3.

53 See A. P. Wavell, *Soldiers and Soldiering*, p. 162. There is pun here on the Hebrew words *yelek* ('he will go') and *yalloq* ('he will lap'). It has been compared to lapping the enemy's blood. See D. Daube, 'Gideon's Few', *JJS* 7 (1956), p. 156; C. Herzog and M. Gichon, *Battles of the Bible*, p. 75.

54 In Judg. 7:3 read 'Gilboa' instead of 'Gilead' and 'turn' instead of 'return'.

55 C. Herzog and M. Gichon, *Battles of the Bible*, p. 304 .

56 See M. Gichon, 'The Military Significance of Certain Aspects of the Limes Palestinae', *Roman Frontier Studies* (Tel Aviv, 1968), pp. 191–200.

57 Judg. 7:19. A. Malamat, 'The War of Gideon and Midian', *PEQ* 85 (1953), p. 64.

58 C. Herzog and M. Gichon, *Battles of the Bible*, p. 77.

59 Carl von Clausewitz, *On War*, ed. and trans. by Michael Howard and Peter Paret (Princeton, 1976), p. 275.

60 C. Herzog and M. Gichon, *Battles of the Bible*, pp. 78–9; R. Gale, *Great Battles of Biblical History* (New York, 1970), p. 34; A. Malamat, 'The War of Gideon and Midian', p. 62.

61 H. Gunkel, *The Folktale in the Old Testament* (Sheffield, 1987), p. 147.

62 T. Callahan, *Secret Origins of the Bible*, p. 99.

63 Judg. 6.36–40; T. Callahan, *Secret Origins of the Bible*, p. 200.

64 N. Na'aman, 'The "Conquest of Canaan" in the Book of Joshua and in History', p. 281.

65 R. Gabriel, *The Military History of Ancient Israel*, p. 176. See the critique of R. M. Sheldon, *Journal of Military History* 69, 1 (Jan. 2005), pp. 197–204.

66 For a description of the siege process see T. R. Hobbs, *A Time for War*, pp. 177–81.

67 Feminist scholars point to patriarchal bias in the text. J. B. Vickery even calls her 'a whore at heart'. J. V. Vickery, 'In Strange Ways: The Story of Samson', p. 69. Delilah's role is really unknown. There is no mention of marriage. Had he taken advantage of her? If so, she would not have been in a position to leave him. If she really does not love him, and she must stay with him for lack of alternatives, it might explain why she is so willing to betray him. See A. L. Laffey, *An Introduction to the Old Testament. A Feminist Perspective* (Philadelphia, 1988), p. 104. Samson had already divorced his wife, and may have been involved in her death. See A. O. Bellis, *Helpmates, Harlots, and Heroes*, p. 126; M. Cartledge-Hays, *To Love Delilah*, p. 43; S. Ackerman, 'Deborah, Women and War', pp. 231–3. On the act of betrayal as a social construction see B. Merideth, 'Desire and Danger: The Drama of Betrayal in Judges and Judith' in M. Bal (ed.), *Anti-Covenant* (Sheffield, 1989), p. 67.

68 Delilah is identified as from *nahal soreq*, 'The Valley of Sorek', far to the west. The connection with rushing water and fertility is noted by L. R. Klein, 'The Book of Judges: Paradigm and Deviation in Images of Women' in A. Brenner (ed.), *The Feminist Companion to the Bible* 4 (Sheffield, 1997), pp. 61–2. Klein also suggests that Delilah is a Philistine (p. 62, n. 1). If so, she may have simply aided her people by eliminating an outside threat.

69 The anachronism of using coined money betrays the later seventh or sixth century context of this story. Coined money does not appear until the late seventh century in Lydia.

70 See the comments of Mieke Bal, 'Delilah Decomposed', p. 51. In John Milton's *Samson Agonistes*, Delilah is Samson's wife, and thus divested of any justifiable reason for her treachery. See J. L. Crenshaw, *Samson: A Secret Betrayed*, p. 145.

71 A. J. Bledstein, 'Is Judges a Woman's Satire of Men Who Play God?' in A. Brenner (ed.), *The Feminist*

Companion to the Bible (Sheffield, 1997), p. 49, calls Samson a 'dodo' and 'an anti-hero, all brawn, little brain, aside from street smarts with riddles'. She suggests that the characters in Judges are primarily men with a tendency to get carried away with their own self-importance, and to behave as if they were gods. She concludes (p. 53) that the author of Judges was a woman who ridiculed Israelite men fancying themselves, instead of Yahweh, as deliverers of Israel. Consequently they made a mess of things. J. L. Crenshaw, *Samson, A Secret Betrayed*, p. 24, says Samson revealed his secret to a talkative lover because he could not endure 'her verbal assaults' any longer.

72 Delilah is the one who tells the truth from the beginning. She never pretends to love him, but is only interested in the source of his strength and how to bind him. Samson, on the other hand, lies consistently. Ironically, Delilah is portrayed as deceitful. A. L. Laffey, *An Introduction to the Old Testament. A Feminist Perspective* (Philadelphia, 1988), pp. 104–5.

73 The Samson story abounds in fire images. See R. Alter, 'Samson without Folklore', pp. 50–1.

74 For the view that Samson knew perfectly well this was no game see M. Bal, 'Delilah Decomposed', p. 52.

75 When she asks in Judg. 16:6 'and by what may you be bound to be afflicted', the last verb 'inna' has a range of meanings that includes affliction, torture, general miserable treatment and also rape. The Philistines do not simply want to kill Samson, but to torture him. Both Delilah and her lover tacitly understand this, as they play their game of 'psychological brinksmanship'. See R. Alter, 'Samson Without Folklore', p. 53.

76 See the parallels between the stories of Delilah and the Timnite wife (Judg. 14:5), where both women coax and nag, and use almost identical arguments about love in order to weaken Samson's resolve (S. Ackerman, 'Deborah, Women and War', pp. 232–3).

77 The visual image of the scene is revealing. Samson goes to sleep on Delilah's knees, although the Hebrew expression allows also for the translation 'between the knees'. For the image as a birthing metaphor see M. Bal, *Death and Dissymmetry. The Politics of Coherence in the Book of Judges* (Chicago, 1988), p. 225, and M. Bal, 'Delilah Decomposed', pp. 58–9.

78 There is actually a debate about who shaved Samson. Some say it is a barber whom Delilah summoned; others say it is Delilah herself. For both sides of the question see F. C. Fensham, 'The Shaving of Samson: A Note on Judges 16:19', *EvQ* 31 (1959), pp. 97–8, and J. M. Sasson, 'Who Cut Samson's Hair? (And Other Trifling Issues Raised by Judges 16)', *Prooftexts* 8 (1988), pp. 333–9. For haircutting as an act of castration see M. Bal, *Death and Dissymmetry*, pp. 225–6. Gouging out the eyes is also an orthodox Freudian image of castration. See R. Alter, 'Samson Without Folklore' in S. Niditch (ed.), *Text and Tradition: The Hebrew Bible and Folklore* (Atlanta, 1990), p. 52.

79 The theological argument would say that Yahweh delivered Samson into the hands of the Philistines to deceive them into thinking that Samson's strength was merely something magical–mechanical, to be manipulated at will by humans. In the end, Yahweh used Samson to destroy the Philistines. Only in his death does Samson make known God. B. G. Webb, *The Book of Judges: An Integrated Reading* (Sheffield, 1987), pp. 165–6. The Philistines appear later in the Book of Kings as the formidable enemy to the Jews.

80 That Delilah is hired by the Philistines, who seem to trust her, suggests she is either a Philistine or at least was not an Israelite. Whatever charges can be levelled against her, treason is not among them. A. L. Laffey, *An Introduction to the Old Testament. A Feminist Perspective*, p. 105.

81 On the folkloric background of the Samson story see R. Alter, 'Samson Without Folklore' in S. Niditch (ed.), *Text and Tradition* (Atlanta, 1990), pp. 47–56. D. E. Bynum, 'Samson as a Biblical *Pher Oreskos*' in S. Niditch (ed.), *Text and Tradition* (Atlanta, 1990), pp. 57–73, however, considered the stories not as epic or ballad or folktale, but as annalistic.

82 For discussion of Samson as solar deity see C. M. Layman (ed.), The *Interpreter's One-Volume Commentary on the Bible* (Nashville and New York, 1971), p. 147, and T. Callahan, *Secret Origins of the Bible* (Altadena, CA, 2002), pp. 208–21. D. E. Bynum, 'Samson as a Biblical *Pher Oreskos*' in S. Niditch

(ed.), *Text and Tradition*, p. 60, says of the Samson stories: 'Nothing in their narrative substance was an Israelite or Canaanite invention; it was all certainly much older than that.'

83   J. L. Crenshaw, *Samson. A Secret Betrayed, A Vow Ignored* (Atlanta, 1978), pp. 15–17, discussed the solar theory, only to reject it. He believed the origin was in 'saga'. For a Freudian approach to the story with Delilah as a mother substitute see M. Bal, *Death and Disymmetry*, pp. 200–3, and J. L. Crenshaw, 'The Samson Saga: Filial Devotion or Erotic Attachment?', *ZNW* 86, 4 (1971), pp. 470–504.

84   For an analysis of the parallel episodes in Joshua and Judges see N. Na'aman, 'The "Conquest of Canaan" in the Book of Joshua and in History' in Finkelstein and Na'aman (eds), *From Nomadism to Monarchy*, pp. 260–8.

85   On the size of these units see T. R. Hobbs, *A Time for War*, pp. 73–80. On the population for the hill country of Ephraim in the period of transition between Judges and the monarchy see L. E. Stager, 'The Archaeology of the Family in Ancient Israel', *BASOR* 260 (1985), pp. 1–16.

86   D. M. Gunn, 'Narrative Patterns and Oral Tradition in Judges and Samuel', *VT* 24, 3 (1974), p. 311, who argued that the stereotyped pattern was due the material coming from an oral tradition. This does not rule out, however, similar patterning in a written document taken from written sources. The 'oral' and 'literary' may have become fused.

88   Translated into English as *Holy War in Ancient Israel*, (ed.) Marva J. Dawn (Grand Rapids, MI, 1990). He restricted the concept to defensive wars in Judges. F. Stolz, *Jahwes und Israels Kriege. Kriegstheorien und Kriegserfahrungen im Glauben des alten Israel* (Zürich, 1972) covers the offensive aspect of holy war in Joshua. See also G. H. Jones, ' "Holy War" or "Yahwe War"?', *VT* 25 (1975), pp. 642–58; T. R. Hobbs, *A Time for War*, pp. 203–7.

89   P. C. Craigie, *The Problem of War in the Old Testament* (Grand Rapids, MI, 1978), p. 47.

90   See, for example, R. Smend, *Yahweh War and Tribal Confederation* (Eng trans.) (Nashville, 1970); G. H. Jones, ' "Holy War" or "Yahwe War"?', *VT* 25 (1975), pp. 642–58, who argues for stages in the development of the literary tradition of holy war; F. Stolz, *Yahwe und Israel's Krieg* (Zurich, 1972).

91   The image of the fighting god who came to his people's aid was widespread in the Ancient Near East, and not unique to Israel. See M. Weinfeld, 'Divine Intervention in War in Ancient Israel and in the Ancient Near East' in H. Tadmor and M. Weinfeld, *History, Historiography and Interpretation* (Jerusalem, 1983), pp. 121–47.

92   N. K. Gottwald, *The Tribes of Yahweh*, p. 140.

93   D. F. Murray, 'Narrative Structure and Technique in the Deborah–Barak Story, Judges IV.4–22', p. 184.

94   D. F. Murray, 'Narrative Structure', p. 187, comparing the Song of Deborah to other war poems of the period. There was a category of literary composition popular among the military aristocracy of chariot warriors, which arose in Western Asia in the seventeenth century; it continued to flourish for several centuries. See W. F. Albright, 'The Song of Deborah in Light of Archaeology', *BASOR* 62 (Apr. 1936), p.31. On the narrative structure of Judges see B. G. Webb, *The Book of Judges. An Integrated Reading*, and J. Cheryl Exum, 'Promise and Fulfillment: Narrative Art in Judges 13', *JBL* 99 (1980), pp. 3–29.

95   On stylistic and thematic parallels between the Samson and Gideon stories see B. G. Webb, *The Book of Judges*, pp. 164, 167, 175. On the late composition for the Samson stories see J. L. Crenshaw, *Samson, A Secret Betrayed*, p. 40.

96   J. L. Crenshaw, *Samson: A Secret Betrayed*, pp. 140–2.

97   An exception to this is evidence from Tel Dan. There seems to be a remarkable degree of similarity between the biblical narrative, other historical data and the archaeological finds for the tribe of Dan. See R. Frankel, 'Upper Galilee and the Late Bronze–Iron Age I Transition' in Finkelstein and Na'aman, *From Nomadism to Monarchy*, pp. 29–30.

98   See I. Singer, 'Egyptians, Canaanites and Philistines' in Finkelstein and Na'aman, *From Nomadism to Monarchy*, p. 318.

99   R. Drews, 'The "Chariots of Iron" of Joshua and Judges', *JSOT* 45 (Oct. 1989), pp. 15–23.

100 N. K. Gottwald, *The Tribes of Yahweh*, p. 124.

Chapter 3 The United Monarchy (pp.84–98)

1   On the Israelite monarchy as a socio-political system see I. Finkelstein, *The Emergence of the Monarchy in Israel: The Environmental and Socio-Economic Aspects* (Winona Lake, IN, 1966), pp. 377–403.

2   On the advantages of a more centralised, complex and stratified state with a superior military capacity see C. Hauer, jun., 'From Alt to Anthropology: The Rise of the Israelite State', *JSOT* 36 (1986), pp. 3–15; for a general discussion on the reconstitution of the army see T. R. Hobbs, *A Time for War* (Wilmington, DE, 1989), pp. 55–8. In Saul's first battle in defence of Jabesh–Gilead, which was being besieged by the Ammonites, one sees the usual tactics. The Israelites divide their forces into three groups, surprise the unsuspecting enemy with an attack during the first watch, and scattered the Ammonites (1 Sam. 11).

3   M. C. Lind, *Yahweh is a Warrior* (Scottsdale, PA, 1980), p. 114.

4   Even the existence of David was debated until the Tel Dan Stele, found in 1993, mentioned the 'House of David'. See H. Shanks, ' "David" Found at Dan', *BAR* 20, 2 (Mar.–Apr. 1994), pp. 26–39; for a translation of the text see S. L. McKenzie, *King David. A Biography* (Oxford, 2000), p. 12. The discovery of the Tel Dan Stele caused the announcement of the discovery of the same expression 'The House of David' on another inscription called the Mesha stele or Moabite stone, which exists now only in a reconstruction and a squeeze taken from the original stone; both are now in the Louvre. S. L. McKenzie, *King David*, p. 13. J. Andrew Dearman (ed.,) *Studies in the Mesha Inscription and Moab* (Atlanta, 1989). A. Lemaire, ' "House of David" Restored in Moabite Inscription', *BAR* 20, 3 (May–June 1994). Egyptologist Kenneth Kitchen suggested another appearance of David's name on the Shoshenq inscription. The text, damaged and difficult to read, is on a relief of the Pharaoh Shoshenq (Shishak in 1 Kings 14:25–7). On its discovery see E. H. Cline, *The Battles of Armageddon* (Ann Arbor, MI, 2000), pp. 75–82; H. Shanks, 'Has David Been Found in Egypt?' *BAR* 25, 1 (Jan.–Feb. 1999). On the missing tenth century see H. Shanks, 'Where is the Tenth Century?', *BAR* 24, 2 (Mar.–Apr. 1998), pp. 56–61. For the negative evidence see M. Steiner, 'It's Not There: Archaeology Proves Negative', *BAR* (July–Aug., 1998), pp. 26–33, 62–3.

5   See, most recently, B. Halpern, *David's Secret Demons. Messiah, Murderer, Traitor*, King (Grand Rapids, MI, 2001); C. M. Layman (ed.), *The Interpreter's One-Volume Commentary on the Bible* (Nashville, 1971), p. 156, demonstrates the complexity of Samuel and Kings. The stories about David do not present 'a consistent chronological pattern'. There are doublet accounts, and numerous contradictory accounts.

6   The stories that portray David as a shepherd boy with no military training and experience contrast markedly with the 'man of war' who had such great success on the battlefield. Before his confrontation with Goliath, he was so unaccustomed to a soldier's armour that, when he wore it for the first time, he could not move (1 Sam. 17:38–9). See S. L. McKenzie, *King David. A Biography*, p. 59. It has been suggested that population growth in the central highlands caused many people to become mercenaries. See L. E. Stager, 'Archaeology of the Family in Ancient Israel', *BASOR* 260 (1985), pp. 1–29.

7   On David's likely involvement in a plot to usurp the kingship see S. L. McKenzie, *King David. A Biography*, p. 88, and N. P. Lemche, 'David's Rise', *JSOT* 10 (1978), pp. 2–25.

8   On David as a *habiru* mercenary see N. P. Lemche, 'David's Rise', *JSOT* 10 (1978), pp. 12–13.

9   2 Sam. 21–30. The claim that David only attacked enemies of Israel is probably not true. Since he had to prove his loyalty to Achish in order to gain a fiefdom, he would probably have had to attack the Israelite settlements at some point. See N. P. Lemche, 'David's Rise', *JSOT* 10 (1978), pp. 10–11.

10 I. Finkelstein, *The Emergence of the Monarchy in Israel* (Winowa Lake, IN, 1996), pp. 378–9, on the reasons for the clash between Israel and the Philistines.

11 For the Philistine threat on the creation of the Israelite state see C. Hauer, 'From Alt to Anthropology', *JSOT* 36 (1986), p. 5; I. Finkelstein, 'The Emergence of the Monarchy in Israel', *JSOT* 44 (1989), p. 44.

12 T. R. Hobbs, *A Time for War*, p. 55.

13 1 Sam. 13:5.

14 Michmash is located in the hill country around Bethel about eleven kilometres north of Jerusalem.

A deep gorge – the wadi Suweinit – cuts through the terrain. Michmash is situated on the cliff on the north side of the wadi, and the town of Geba is on the southern cliff.

15 R. Gabriel, *The Military History of Ancient Israel* (Westport, CT, 2003), p. 207.

16 R. Gabriel, *The Military History of Ancient Israel*, p. 209, comments on this absurd claim. Without weapons, there could have been no army and battle. Moreover, after two centuries of Philistine occupation of Palestine, a black market in weapons could surely have been set up in spite of the Philistine ban.

17 On deities coming to the aid of armies in Israel and elsewhere see M. Weinfeld, 'Divine Intervention in War in Ancient Israel and in the Ancient Near East', pp. 121–47.

18 Josh. 9; 1 Sam. 14; under David: 2 Sam. 6; 1 Macc. 7; and the ambush of the force under Cestius Gallus see chap. 6.

19 Among the professional soldiers, there was the honour guard of David's *gibborim* mentioned in 2 Sam. 23. There was also a royal guard or bodyguard – the Cherethites and Pelethites. This royal guard was made up of Philistines. These are mentioned in 2 Sam. 15:18–22 along with a contingent of Gittites – Philistines from the city of Gath – who were among David's most loyal troops. They had been with him since his days as a mercenary. On his strategic base at Succoth, east of Jordan, see Y. Yadin, *The Art of Warfare in Biblical Lands*, vol. 2, pp. 271–2.

20 According to tradition, Saul created the first nucleus of a standing army with three thousand men whom he chose to serve with him permanently (C. Herzog and M. Gichon, *Battles of the Bible*, p. 87).

21 Solomon employed such a system for his army, but limited the conscription to Israel (1 Kings 9:22). Judah was exempted. S. L. McKenzie, *King David. A Biography*, pp. 143–4. On the size of his army see A. Van Selms, 'The Armed Forces of Israel under Saul and David', *Studies in the Book of Samuel* (Praetoria, 1960), pp. 55–66.

22 2 Sam. 3:27. This also avenged the death of his brother Asahel, whom Abner had killed. See R. G. Branch, 'David and Joab. United by Ambition', *BR* (Aug. 2003), p. 19.

23 S. L. McKenzie, *King David. A Biography*, pp. 111–27, on David as assassin.

24 In stark contrast to David's efficient intelligence gathering when detecting enemies outside Israel see 2 Sam. 5:17; 10:7–17 and C. E. Hauer, jun., 'Jerusalem, the Stronghold and Rephraim', *CBQ* 32 (1970), pp. 571–8.

25 2 Sam. 15:32–7; 17:5–22.

26 2 Sam. 18:14–16.

27 2 Sam. 18:33. Another similar situation arises with Sheba's revolt. David had Amasa executed. He had done so with Nabal, Saul, Abner, Ishbaal, Amnon and Absalom. David is always conveniently somewhere else when killing took place, but he is always the main beneficiary of the assassinations (S. L. McKenzie, *King David. A Biography*, pp. 169–71).

28 1 Sam. 30:8. M. C. Lind, *Yahweh is a Warrior*, p. 141, believes that David's reliance on prophetic and priestly oracles in warfare meant that there was some attempt to keep warfare in line with the ancient concepts rooted in the exodus and Sinai.

29 1 Sam. 30:11–15.

30 1 Sam. 30:16.

31 D. G. Hansen, 'Intelligence, Deception and Military Operations in the Ancient Near East', *II International Conference on Intelligence and Military Operations*, p. 34.

32 The biblical text is ambiguous. The present order of the text places David's encounters with the Philistines in the valley of Rephaim after his capture of Jerusalem. But the introduction to the account of the two battles presents at least one of them as an immediate Philistine reaction to the anointing of David at Hebron. See N. L. Tidwell, 'The Philistine Incursions into the Valley of Rephaim (2 Sam. 5:17ff.)', p. 190; C. E. Hauer, jun., 'Jerusalem, the Stronghold and Rephaim', *CBQ* 32, 3 (July 1970), pp. 576–8.

33 The enigma of the meaning of 'Rephaim' and the evidence from Ras Shamra is discussed by J. Gray,

'Rephaim', *PEQ* (July–Oct. 1949), pp. 127–39. C. E. Hauer, jun., 'Jerusalem, the Stronghold and Rephaim', *CBQ* 32 (1970), pp. 576–8, observes that Jerusalem was a recently captured city during the Philistine invasion. The loyalty of David's new Jebusite subjects was yet unproven, and the nature of the military forces at David's immediate disposal argued against a stand in Jerusalem. His militia had not yet been trained to defend a walled city. More was likely to be gained by a pitched battle than by a walled siege. Instead he retreated to the redoubt of Abdullam when he heard the Philistines were on the move.

34 N. L. Tidwell, 'The Philistine Incursions into the Valley of Rephaim', p. 195.

35 There is much debate over whether David held Jerusalem at this time. Some authors see the possibility of the Philistines marching either towards Hebron or Jerusalem, and David's position as having to defend both. R. Gabriel, *The Military History of Ancient Israel*, p. 243; C. E. Hauer, 'Jerusalem, The Stronghold and Rephaim', *CBQ* 32 (1970), pp. 576ff.; N. L. Tidwell, 'The Philistine Incursions into the Valley of Rephaim', p. 190.

36 B. Mazar, 'The Military Elite of King David', *VT* 13 (1963), p. 315, suggested that David's stronghold was closer to Jerusalem than Abdullam, perhaps a fortified camp near Bethlehem. Hauer suggested that this fits better with the second campaign, and that David may have spared his army extra marching by using a less-distant field base for his second counterattack. See C. E. Hauer, 'Jerusalem, the Stronghold and Rephaim', *CBQ* 32 (1970), p. 578.

37 The description in 1 Chr. 14:14–15 tells nothing of *asherahs* but suggests the sound came from the wind in the 'baca' bushes. The word 'baca' occurs rarely in the Bible; it is found in 2 Sam. 5:23, 24 and 1 Chr. 14:14, 15, where it identifies the valley in which David fought the Philistines. The word 'baca' could also describe a bush, probably a balsam bush, but translated in the AV as a mulberry tree and *NEB* as aspen. In 2 Samuel and 1 Chronicles the valley of Baca is a valley full of balsam bushes near the valley of Rephaim. This is to the southwest of Jerusalem and forms an approach route to the city.

38 It is difficult to talk about geographical intelligence since we do not know where the battle took place. David attacked Philistines encamped in the valley of Rephaim from Baca (2 Sam. 5:23, 24; 1 Chr. 14:14, 15). The text says Bachaim, but we do not know whether this is a town or a region, though it seems to be near Jerusalem. B. Mazar, 'Making a Capital' in A. Malamat (ed.), 'The Age of the Monarchies: Political History', vol. 4, 1, of B. Mazar (ed.), *World History of the Jewish People*, p. 78, suggests the battle was fought at Beth Horon. The mention of asherahs is puzzling because we do not know what this word refers to. It can mean groves or shrines to the goddess Astarte. It might be wooden pedestals that served as cult objects at a shrine. It might be a row of trees associated with a shrine to Astarte.

39 See C. E. Hauer, jun., 'Jerusalem. The Stronghold and Rephaim', *CBQ* 32 (1970), p. 573, n. 10; and N. L. Tidwell, 'The Philistine Incursion into the Valley of Rephaim' (2 Sam. v.17ff.), *Studies in the Historical Books of the Old Testament* (Leiden, 1979), p. 190.

40 Some believe it is a composite of several traditions and hence it narrates several different episodes. See N. L. Tidwell, 'The Philistine Incursion into the Valley of Rephaim', citing J. Flanagan, *A Study of the Traditions Pertaining to the Foundation of Monarchy* (Diss: University of Nôtre Dame, 1971), p. 47.

41 For discussion of this convention in discussing battles see A. F. Campbell, *The Ark Narrative. A Form-Critical and Traditio-Historical Study (1 Sam. 4–6; 2 Sam. 6)* (Missoula, 1975); J. Ploger, *Literarkritische, Formgeschichtliche und Stilkritische Untersuchungen zum Deuteronomium* (Bonn, 1967), pp. 16–19; N. L. Tidwell, 'The Philistine Incursion into the Valley of Rephaim', pp. 193–4.

42 The Ugaritic Rephaim texts show that 'Rephaim' may be a semi-divine caste of warriors. One of their tasks, mentioned in Ugaritic sources, was the visitation and inspection of plantations and threshing floors at harvest time. See F. Willesen, 'The Philistine Corps of the Scimitar from Gath', *JSS* 3 (1958), pp. 327–35; A. Caquot, 'Les Rephaims Ougaritiques', *Syria* 37 (1960), pp. 75–93; N. L. Tidwell, 'The Philistine Incursion into the Valley of Rephaim', p. 204; J. Gray, 'The Rephaim', *PEQ* 81 (1948/49), pp. 133, 136–7, who observes that in the narratives about David all the encounters with the Philistines

'seem to be limited to border skirmishes and plundering raids'.

43 On the literary or theological features which possibly influenced the placement in the text of the two Rephaim battles stories see H. W. Herzberg, *I and II Samuel; A Commentary* (London, 1964), p. 272, for similarity of content; R. A. Carlson, *David the Chosen King* (Stockholm, 1964), pp. 58ff., for associative words; and A. F. Campbell, *The Ark Narrative* (Missoula, 1975), p. 69, for common oracular element; N. L. Tidwell, 'The Philistine Incursion into the Valley of Rephaim', p. 193, n. 12.

44 2 Sam. 10–11; 1 Chr. 19:6–7.

45 Y. Yadin, *The Art of War in Biblical Lands*, vol 2, p. 274.

46 For example see Tel Qasile, outside Tel Aviv, which was destroyed by fire (I. Finkelstein and N. A. Silberman, *The Bible Unearthed*, New York: Free Press, 2001, pp. 134–5).

47 I. Finkelstein and N. A. Silberman, *The Bible Unearthed*, pp. 134–40.

48 T. L. Thompson, *Early History of the Israelite People*; N. P. Lemche, *Prelude to Israel's Past*; and P. R. Davies, *In Search of 'Ancient Israel'*. On the lack of archaeological evidence see M. Steiner, 'It's Not There: Archaeology Proves a Negative', *BAR* (July–Aug. 1998), pp. 26–33, 62–3. For a summary of the archaeology of Jerusalem see H. Geva, 'Jerusalem' in *NEAEHL*, pp. 698–757.

49 J. Sasson, 'On Choosing Models for Recreating Israelite Pre-Monarchic History', *JSOT* 21 (1981), p. 16.

50 Kathleen Kenyon excavated the southeastern hill in the oldest inhabited part of Jerusalem (called the 'City of David') between 1961 and 1967; Benjamin Mazar excavated south of the Temple Mount in the area known as Ophel from 1968 to 1978; Nahman Avigad excavated in the Jewish Quarter of the Old City from 1969 to 1983; and Yigal Shiloh excavated the City of David from 1978 to 1985. Teams of archaeologists are now working on these reports in Jerusalem, Manchester (England) and Leiden (The Netherlands). See M. Steiner, 'It's Not There. Archaeology Proves A Negative', *BAR* (July–Aug. 1998), p. 26; H. Shanks, 'Where is the Tenth Century?', *BAR* (Mar.–Apr. 1998), pp. 56–61.

51 See S. L. McKenzie, *King David*, p. 13. J. Andrew Dearman (ed.), *Studies in the Mesha Inscription and Moab* (Atlanta, 1989). A. Lemaire, ' "House of David" Restored in Moabite Inscription', *BAR* 20, 3 (May–June 1994), and n. 4 above.

52 See especially the investigations of the Bronze and Iron Age remains in the 1970s and 1980s by Yigal Shiloh of Hebrew University. H. Shanks, 'Yigal Shiloh – Last Thoughts', *BAR* 14, 2 (Mar.–Apr. 1988), pp. 14–27; H. Shanks, 'Yigal Shiloh – Last Thoughts, Pt. 2', *BAR* 14, 3 (May–June 1988), pp. 38–46. M. Steiner, 'It's Not There. Archaeology Proves a Negative', *BAR* (July–Aug. 1997), p. 27, believed that no traces of a town, let alone a city, have been found. There is no trace of an encircling wall, no gate, no houses, nor a single piece of architecture. Others like Nadav Na'aman believe this was the result of building and rebuilding.

53 See I. Finkelstein and N. A. Silberman, *The Bible Unearthed*, pp. 133–4; 230.

54 I. Finkelstein and N. A. Silberman, *The Bible Unearthed*, p. 133.

55 I. Finkelstein and N. A. Silberman, *The Bible Unearthed*, p. 134.

56 In the battle near Gibeon between David's and Ishbosheth's troops in 2 Sam. 2:30, 31 there were twenty killed on David's side, and 360 killed and on Ishbosheth's side, most of them fleeing. If ten per cent of a section is killed, the rest tend to be demoralised and not able to maintain themselves in open field. These statistics suggest an army of about three thousand warriors on the side of Abner and Ishbosheth. Also, if the entire army of David was housed in the town of Mahanaim in 2 Sam. 19:3, and we consider the size of an average Palestinian town as less than four hectares, then two thousand would have been a big force. See A. Van Selms, 'The Armed Forces of Israel under Saul and David' in *Studies in the Books of Samuel* (Praetoria, 1960), pp. 63–4.

57 The biblical text is lacking in details of the actual battle. This has not prevented the imagination of Richard Gabriel from filling in the details (*The Military History of Ancient Israel*, pp. 217–20).

58 R. Gabriel, *The Military History of Ancient Israel*, p. 238.

59 I. Finkelstein and N. A. Silberman, *The Bible Unearthed*, pp. 142–5.

60 I. Finkelstein and N. A. Silberman, *The Bible Unearthed*, pp. 285–9.

Chapter 4 The Maccabean Revolt (pp.99–111)

1   The story of Antiochus and the Maccabean Revolt is in 1 and 2 Maccabees (both thought to have been redacted about 100 BCE) and in Josephus, *Ant.* Antiochus' persecutions are echoed in the Book of Daniel. Maccabee was the nickname of Judas, the third son of Mattathias. It comes from the Syriac word *maqqaba* (hammer). For a full discussion see E. Schürer, *A History of the Jewish People in the Time of Jesus Christ* (New York, 1910), vol. 1, p. 212. The name was eventually extended to all the descendants of Mattathias, and even to all who took part in the rebellion. It was also given to the martyrs mentioned in 2 Macc. 6:18. The Third Book of Maccabees has no connection with the Maccabee period. The Fourth Book mentions the Maccabean martyrs. On the sources, their date, provenance and characteristics see B. Bar-Kochva, *Judas Maccabaeus* (Cambridge, 1989), pp. 151–93, and J. Goldstein, *1 Maccabees. Translation and Commentary* (Garden City, NY, 1976). For all the sources on the period see E. Schurer, *History of the Jewish People in the Age of Jesus Christ 175 BC–AD 135,* rev. by G. Vermes, F. Millar, M. Black (Edinburgh, 1973), 2 vols.

2   1 Macc. 1:41 reports a decree of Antiochus IV in which he made 'all in his kingdom one people', stipulating 'that each should give up his customs'. The decree is not mentioned in Daniel 11, 2 Maccabees or Josephus, and may probably have affected only Judaea if it occurred at all. See J. Jagersma, *The History of Israel from Alexander the Great to Bar Kochba* (Philadelphia, 1986), p. 50; contra J. G. Bunge, 'Die Sogenannte Religionsverfolgung Antiochus IV Epiphanes und Die Griechischen Städte', *JSJ* 10 (1979), pp. 155–65. On the degree of Hellenisation see M. Hengel, *Judaism and Hellenism* (Philadelphia, 1974), 2 vols, and F. Millar's comments on that work in 'The Background to the Maccabaean Revolution: Reflections on Martin Hengel's "Judaism and Hellenism" ' in *JJS* 29 (1978), pp. 1–21.

3   There are three reports of temple plundering by or on the orders of Antiochus IV. The first is at 1 Macc. 1:20–4 (169 BCE); 2 Macc 5:15ff. mentions a plundering in which Antiochus IV took part. Josephus, *Ant.* 12.248–50 also mentions a plundering under Antiochus IV. On the question of whether the Temple was actually plundered more than once see J. Jagersma, *The History of Israel,* p. 49.

4   C. Herzog and M. Gichon, *Battles of the Bible* (London, 1997), p. 265.

5   2 Maccabees was written by an unknown Greek-speaking Jew. It is supposedly an abridgement of an earlier work by a certain Jason of Cyrene with a variety of sources added to it. The work was probably composed in Greek in the first century BCE. Most suggest a date of 78–73 BCE. 2 Maccabees is not considered canonical in the Jewish faith, and no copy of the text has been found at Qumran. Roman Catholicism and Eastern Orthodoxy list it as part of the Apocrypha, but it is not considered doctrinally valid in the Protestant tradition, which rejects both First and Second Maccabees.

6   G. W. Bowersock, *Martyrdom and Rome* (Cambridge, 1995), p. 12.

7   Nebuchadrezzar is the same as Nebuchadnezzar, king of Babylon. The first spelling is nearer to the original name as it is found on the cuneiform monuments, namely Nabu-kudurri-usur, 'Nebo, defender of the landmark'. On the Jewish military forces see J. L. Wallach, 'The Wars of the Maccabees', *RIHM* 42 (1979), p. 60, who states that the Jews had performed military service during this period in Egypt and Persia.

8   That this indicates conflict between the rich upper class in Jerusalem and the peasant population in the country is argued in H. Jagersma, *History of Israel,* p. 205. The leaders of the revolt were from the lowly priestly class, and they opposed the rich and powerful priestly families in Jerusalem, who were allied to the rich Hellenising aristocracy.

9   The name is given in 1 Macc. 2:1–5; the exact site of ancient Modi'in is disputed. Some say it is the Arab village el-Midya (Mediyah) near a site many locals identify as the tombs of the Maccabees. Others point to a hill on the edge of the modern town of Modi'in known as the Tetora hill, where huge rectangular stones dating back to the Hasmonean period have been found at the base of a ruined Crusader watchtower.

10   1 Macc. 2:15. Josephus, *Ant.*, 12.268 does not mention which animals were to be sacrificed. Pig sacrifice

was not practised by the Syrians, and Greeks did not often offer pigs to Zeus as a sacrifice. Bickerman points out that the only aim in compelling the Jews to make this sacrifice was to attack their dietary laws. See E. Bickerman, *God of the Maccabees* (Leiden, 1979), p. 88; see also H. Jagersma, *The History of Israel*, pp. 52–3, who argues for the limited nature of the persecution to Hellenists in Jerusalem.

11 1 Macc. 2:15ff.; Josephus, *Ant.* 12.271ff. B. Bar-Kochva, *Judas Maccabaeus*, p. 196 (following Avi Yonah, 1964, p. 57) claims that the nature of the place made it an ideal base for guerrilla forces. C. Herzog and M. Gichon, *Battles of the Bible*, p. 268. The description of 2 Macc. 8:1ff. that Mattathias gathered six thousand men seems exaggerated. Cf. E. Schürer, vol. 1, p. 209.

12 H. Jagersma, p. 58, believes the social and economic factors largely determined the character and course of the war; E. Bickerman, *The God of the Maccabees*, pp. 90ff., stresses the religious motives. The primary sources – Daniel and 1 and 2 Maccabees – place most emphasis on the religious aspects because this was what was important to them and later generations. 2 Macc. 5:24–7:41 tells of the faithful who were martyred because they would not violate the law.

13 E. Bickerman, *The God of the Maccabees* (Leiden, 1979), p. 90ff. Cf. M. Hengel, *The Zealots*, p. 152, who discusses Phinehas the Zealot as the model for the Maccabees, pp. 171ff.

14 1 Macc. 2:31–2; Josephus, *Ant.,* 12.272.

15 1 Macc. 2:33–8; Josephus, *Ant.,* 12.274. The Hasidaeans (Greek) or Hasidim ('pious' in Hebrew) are mentioned first in 1 Macc. 2:42, when they joined the Maccabees shortly after the beginning of the revolt. In 1 Macc 7:13 they are those who wanted to collaborate with the newly nominated high priest Alcimus. In 2 Macc. 14:6 they are further described as a group of those 'who offered themselves willingly for the law'. These sources suggest the Hasidim took part in the rebellion for a short time and their aim was to live a religious life according to the Torah without interference. See P. Davies, 'Hasidim in the Maccabaean Period', *JJS* 28 (1977), pp. 127–40, who rejects the more important role assigned to them by M. Hengel, *Judaism and Hellenism*, pp. 175ff., and G. W. Bowersock, *Martyrdom and Rome* (Cambridge, 1995), pp. 9–13, who rejects the idea of Jewish martyrdom.

16 1 Macc 2:41; Josephus, *Ant.* 12.276. Notice that Josephus omits any reference to the Hasidim. M. Hengel, *The Zealots*, saw a connection between 1 Maccabees and the concept of holy war. On the concept of holy war see M. Weippert, 'Heiliger Krieg', *ZAW* 84, 4 (1972), pp. 460–93, and F. Stolz, *Jahwes und Israels Krieg* (Zürich, 1972).

17 1 Macc. 2:49; Josephus, *Ant.,* 12.279. See J. A. Goldstein, *I Maccabees*, pp. 13ff.

18 We do not know why Judas took over the leadership role instead of the oldest son of Mattathias. Judas was made military commander with Simon as adviser. Mattathias was buried in the family tomb at Modi'in amid great lamentations (1 Macc. 2:49–70).

19 C. Herzog and M. Gichon, *Battles of the Bible*, p. 268.

20 C. Herzog and M. Gichon, *Battles of the Bible*, p. 268. On the constitution of the Seleucid army and its tactics see J. L. Wallach, 'The Wars of the Maccabees', *RIHM* 42 (1979), pp. 57–60, and on the constitution of the Jewish forces, pp. 60–2.

21 See 1 Macc. 6:6: 'The strength of the Jews had grown by the capture of arms, equipment and spoils from the Syrian armies they had defeated' (*NEB* translation).

22 Mao Tse-tung, *On Guerrilla Warfare*, 6. Quoted in C. Herzog and M. Gichon, *Battles of the Bible*, p. 269.

23 For identification of Apollonius see B. Bar-Kochva, *Judas Maccabaeus*, pp. 202–4.

24 The description of the clash with Apollonius is not very good. B. Bar-Kochva, *Judas Maccabaeus*, p. 200, observes that it is inferior to the descriptions of the other battles. He does not give the rank and function of the enemy commander, the number of soldiers he had, or the composition of the army or the route that he took. The sources used by the author were not eyewitness accounts. In the absence of any real detail, he borrows phrases often taken from the story of David and Goliath. The battle is not discussed in 2 Maccabees. The account of the battle in Josephus, *Ant.* 12.287 is a prose version of the flowery account in 1 Maccabees.

25 C. Herzog and M. Gichon cite two thousand as the number of Syrians and six hundred as the number of Jews with no primary source for these numbers. They cite only Avisar's book *The Wars of Judah the Maccabee* (Tel Aviv, 1965) (H) with no page number. There are no numbers given in either Josephus or 1 and 2 Maccabees.

26 C. Herzog and M. Gichon, *Battles of the Bible*, p. 272. Avi-Yonah, Michael, *Essays and Studies in the Lore of the Holy Land*, Tel-Aviv: M. Nyuman, 1964 (H), p. 59, suggests the Lebonah Ascent, half-way between Shechem and Jerusalem, with its steep winding ascent was good for an ambush. B. Bar-Kochva, *Judas Maccabaeus*, p. 205, points out that how historians choose to locate the battle site depends on their determination of the purpose of the expedition undertaken by the Seleucid force. If one believes that the intent was to capture rebels in the Gophna Hills, the confrontation could then be located in any number of places along the road from Shechem to the Gophna area.

27 C. Herzog and M. Gichon, *Battles of the Bible*, p. 272.

28 On slaying the commander as 'a quick shot through the brain' see J. L. Wallach, 'The Wars of the Maccabees, *RIHM* 42 (1979), p. 69.

29 1 Macc. 3:12; Josephus, *Ant.* 12.7.1. Commentators have all noted the parallel to 1 Sam. 17:51, 54 and 21:10, 11. See B. Bar-Kochva, *Judas Maccabaeus*, p. 206.

30 Josephus, *Ant.*, 12.287; C. Herzog and M. Gichon, *Battles of the Bible*, pp. 272–3.

31 The battle against Seron, like that with Apollonius, is described only in 1 Macc. 3:13–26. Josephus' version of the battle in *Ant.* 12.288–92 is a paraphrase. Scholars reject Seron's rank as given in Josephus, who does not mention the surprise assault at all. See the account in B. Bar-Kochva, *Judas Maccabaeus*, pp. 207–18, esp. p. 208.

32 1 Macc. 3:13–26. See also B. Bar-Kochva, 'Seron and Cestius Gallus at Beth Horon', *PEQ* 107 (1976), pp. 13ff.; C. Herzog and M. Gichon, *Battles of the Bible*, p. 274.

33 C. Herzog and M. Gichon, *Battles of the Bible*, p. 274, note that this was the route taken by the British Ninetieth Division under General Allenby when he advanced on Jerusalem against the Turks in 1917. This was also the route chosen by the Israeli forces to advance on Jerusalem in 1967 Six Day War in order to take the Old City from the north.

34 1 Maccabees exaggerates both the enemy numbers and Seron's status in the royal army. The account never gives us the number of Maccabean fighters, but a small force was necessary if an ambush was Judas' intent. See B. Bar-Kochva, *Judas Maccabaeus* p. 207.

35 See B. Bar-Kokhba, *Judas Maccabaeus*, p. 216.

36 According to 2 Macc. 8:1, 16, 22, Judas had six thousand regulars, but this seem exaggerated. The force was probably bigger than Seron's, but an attack from ambush is generally conducted with a small force. See B. Bar-Kochva, *Judas Maccabaeus*, p. 213.

37 1 Macc. 3:23–4; Josephus, *Ant.*, 12.292.

38 The description of the campaign is given in 1 Macc. 3:38–4.25 and 2 Macc. 8:8–29, 34–6. There are major disagreements in the two accounts on important points such as the hierarchy and staffing of the Seleucid command, the size of the contending armies and the tactical division of the Jewish forces. See the discussion of B. Bar-Kochva, *Judas Maccabaeus*, pp. 219–74.

39 H. Jagersma, *The History of Israel*, p. 60; 1 Macc. 3:31; J. A. Goldstein, *I Maccabees*, p. 252. There seems to have been less interest in Judaea than sources such as 1 Maccabees and Josephus would suggest. See also J. L. Wallach, 'The Wars of the Maccabees', *RIHM* 42 (1979), p. 62.

40 1 Macc. 3:31–4; Josephus, *Ant.*, 12.297.

41 1 Macc. 3:38; 2 Macc. 8:9 cites twenty thousand but the number derives from a garble in the text. Josephus, *Ant.* 12.298 gives forty thousand foot soldiers and seven thousand horse. All these estimates are inflated. Bar-Kochva suggests ten thousand for the actual size of the force. On the identities of these generals see Ralph Marcus in his translation with commentary of Josephus, *Ant.* (Cambridge, 1986), vol. 7, pp.154–5, and B. Bar-Kochva, *Judas Maccabaeus*, pp. 239–40.

42 Emmaus is identified with the Arab village of Imwas destroyed in the Six Day War. It was situated on

the road from Jaffa to Jerusalem near the Latrun monastery. On the identification of the site see B. Bar-Kochva, *Judas Maccabaeus*, pp. 242–3, and on the location of the Seleucid camp see p. 245.

43 Josephus, *JA* 12.305; 1 Macc. 4:1; C. Herzog and M. Gichon, *Battles of the Bible*, p. 279. There is a great disparity between 1 Maccabees and 2 Maccabees as to the size of the Seleucid force. 2 Macc. 8:21–2 reports a six thousand-man Jewish force divided into four fifteen hundred-man units. On the wording of the divisions (thousands, hundreds, tens, etc.) see Exod. 18, 21, 25; Deut. 1:15. B. Bar-Kochva, *Judas Maccabaeus*, rejects the idea that a night attack on the Jewish camp was planned. He points out that if one plans a long, hard night march in which the element of surprise is vital, the numbers ascribed to Gorgias' task force seems quite inflated.

44 2 Macc. 8:12. B. Bar-Kochva, *Judas Maccabaeus*, p. 261, believes that Judas would not have learned that Gorgias was on the way to the Jewish camp and reached the region south of Emmaus on the same night if he had not had an efficient warning system, 'possibly signal fires, or fast riders'. A contemporary source, 1 Enoch 90:14, believed that an angel revealed Gorgias' plan to Judas.

45 Josephus, *Ant.*, 12.306ff.

46 This is the location suggested by C. Herzog and M. Gichon, *Battles of the Bible*, p. 279.

47 1 Macc. 4:19–22; 2 Macc. 8; Josephus, *Ant.*, 12.310–312.

48 On the location see S. Wibbing, 'Zur Topographie Einzelner Schlachten des Judas Makkabäus', *ZDPV* 78 (1962), pp. 159ff. The descriptions of Lysias' two expeditions at Beth Zur (1 Macc. 4:26–35 and 1 Macc. 6:28–54) are similar enough for scholars to suggest that they are doublets. B. Bar-Kochva, *Judas Maccabaeus*, p. 275, rejects this interpretation. The 2 Maccabees version of the Battle of Beth Zur has many characteristics of that source – exaggerated size of the enemy army, of enemy casualties, and divine intervention which decides the battle. For the dating of the battle see the discussion in B. Bar-Kochva, *Judas Maccabaeus*, pp. 276–83.

49 These events are in a different order in 1 Maccabees and 2 Maccabees. I discuss them here in the generally accepted order. For this chronological problem see J. Jagersma, *The History of Israel*, p. 173 n. 13; P. Schäfer, 'The Hellenistic and Maccabaean Periods' in J. Hayes and J. Maxwell Miller, *Israelite and Judaean History* (Philadelphia, 1997), pp. 566–8.

50 Josephus, *Ant.*, 12.313 and 1 Macc. 4:28 gave these figures; 2 Maccabees gives eighty thousand, a vastly inflated number, and the author even adds eighty elephants. B. Bar-Kochva, *Judas Maccabaeus*, p. 284, believes both sets of figures are wrong.

51 1 Macc. 4:29. Beth Zur was a natural fortress at the head of the road from the coastal plain, which follows the vale of Elah (a name derived from the ilex trees with which it abounded). The road turns south at the valley of the Zur, then rises steeply to the fortress.

52 The site of Beth Zur itself has been identified with Khirbet el Tabeiqa. See B. Bar-Kochva, *Judas Maccabaeus*, p. 285, where he discusses whether Judas camped in Beth Zur or nearby.

53 Josephus, *Ant.*, 12.301. 1 Maccabees has commanders of thousands, commanders of hundreds, fifties, tens. etc. C. Herzog and M. Gichon, *Battles of the Bible*, p. 284, see the division of the four groups as three thousand, one thousand, one thousand and five thousand, but with no note to suggest their source.

54 On the defeat at Beth Zur see 1 Macc. 4:28ff.; 2 Macc. 11:1; Josephus, *Ant.*, 12.314–315. Some parts of 2 Macc. 11 give the impression that circumstances forces Lysias and the Maccabees to negotiate, and that Lysias was compelled to return to Antioch by affairs of state, i.e. the serious illness of Antiochus IV.

55 1 Macc. 4:52. See 2 Macc. 1:10–2:18, which contains a letter about the purification of the Temple addressed to the Jews living in the diaspora. According to 1 Macc. 4:59, 2 Macc. 10:5–8 and Josephus, *Ant.*, 12.319–325, the feast of Hanukah was initiated by Judas and his followers, which is a break from tradition since it was made on the basis of human decision; before this, every feast was established on the basis of divine instruction given in Hebrew scripture.

56 Antiochus IV died in 164 BCE. 1 Macc. 6:55. See Polybius, *The Histories*, Book 21.9 and D. Mendels, 'A Note on the Tradition of Antiochus IV's Death', *IEJ* 31 (1981), pp. 53–6. His son Antiochus V (164–162 BCE) gave the Judaeans full religious freedom. See 2 Macc. 11:23–6; J. Jagersma, *The*

History of Israel, p. 61. Events after Beth Zur were also affected by Roman intervention. See 2 Macc. 11:34–8; T. Fischer, 'Zu Den Beziehungen Zwischen Rom und Den Juden Im 2 Jahrhundert v. Chr.', *ZAW* 86 (1974), pp. 90–3; T. Fischer, 'Rom und Die Hasmonäer. Ein Überblick Zu Den Politischen Beziehungen 164–37 v. Chr', *Gymnasium* 88 (1981), pp. 139–50.

57 On Lysias' second expedition and the Battle of Beth Zechariah see 1 Macc. 6:28–47; Josephus, *BJ* 1.41–6; Josephus, *Ant.* 13.362–81 is a paraphrase of 1 Maccabees. B. Bar-Kochva, *Judas Maccabaeus*, pp. 291–6 with commentary.

58 Josephus, *Ant.* 12.381. Judas was later killed at Laisa, near Jerusalem, in 161 BCE, in a battle against the general Bacchides, who had been sent by Demetrius I to restore order in Judaea. See 1 Macc. 9:11–20; 2 Macc. 10–15.

59 See J. L. Wallach, 'The Wars of the Maccabees', *RIHM* 42 (1979), pp. 70–2.

60 J. L. Wallach, 'The Wars of the Maccabees', *RIHM* 42 (1979), p. 56.

61 See the account in 1 Macc. 8, which gives the conditions of the treaty with Rome. See also Josephus, *Ant.,* 12.402–12, 417ff.; Diodorus 60.2, and T. Fisher, *Seleukiden und Makkabaër* (Bochum, 1980), pp. 105ff. On the political situation in Palestine after Judas' death and the alliance with Rome see H. Jagersma, *A History of Israel*, pp. 64–5; J. L. Wallach, 'The Wars of the Maccabees', *RIHM* 42 (1979), pp. 76–9; T. Fischer, 'Hasmonaeans and Seleucids: Aspects of War and Policy in the Second and First Centuries BCE', pp. 8–9.

62 J. A. Goldstein, *1 Maccabees*, p. 14.

63 D. J. Harrington, *The Maccabaean Revolt* (Wilmington, DE, 1988), p. 90.

64 D. J. Harrington, *The Maccabaean Revolt* (Wilmington, DE, 1988), p. 92.

Chapter 5 Judith's Disinformation Campaign (pp.112–16)

1 All quotations are from *The New English Bible. Oxford Study Edition* (New York, 1972). For a discussion of Judith as an icon of western culture see M. Stocker, *Judith. Sexual Warrior* (New Haven, 1998).

2 C. A. Moore, *Judith* (Garden City, NY, 1985), pp. 129–30. The story has a perspective that may reflect Judas' defeat of Nicanor, and subsequent failures of the Maccabean movement. For correlations between the Maccabean history and the story of Judith see D. J. Harrington, *The Maccabean Revolt. Anatomy of a Biblical Revolution* (Wilmington, DE, 1988), p. 114. Harrington sees a parallel in Judith ('Jewish woman') and Judas Maccabeus ('Jewish man').

3 See Judith 9:10, 13:15, 16:6.

4 The Apocrypha are writings found only in the Greek Septuagint. The book of Judith dates to the second century BCE near the time of the Maccabean Revolt. Originally written in Hebrew, it was translated into Greek, and by the time the Jewish canon was formed the Hebrew original might not have been extant. The Book of Judith is part of the Roman Catholic and Eastern Orthodox canon, but is considered apocryphal by Jews and Protestants, partly because it is full of historical inaccuracies. The Jewish canon included only Hebrew works, all dated before the Persian period 538–332 BCE. For theories on why the story of Judith was excluded see C. A. Moore, 'Judith: The Case of the Pious Killer', *BR* 6, 1 (Feb. 1990), pp. 26–36. On the story's historicity or lack thereof see S. C. White, 'Esther Not Judith. Why One Made it and the Other Didn't', *BR* 18, 1 (Feb. 2003), pp. 22–31, 45; A. Lacocque, *The Feminine Unconventional* (Minneapolis, 1990), pp. 31–2; and C. A. Moore, *Judith* (Garden City, NY, 1985), pp. 38–49.

5 A. O. Bellis, *Helpmates, Harlots, and Heroes.* (Louisville, KY, 1994), p. 219.

6 For parallels between the stories see S. A. White, 'In the Steps of Jael and Deborah: Judith as Heroine' in J. C. Vander Kam, *No One Spoke Ill of Her* (Atlanta, 1992), pp. 5–16; N. Aschkenasy, *Eve's Journey. Feminine Images in Hebraic Literary Tradition* (Philadelphia, 1986), p. 171; B. Lindars, 'Deborah's Song: Women in the Old Testament', *BRL* 65 (1983), pp. 158–75. For a comparison of Judith's story with Samson and Delilah see B. Merideth, 'Desire and Danger: The Drama of Betrayal in Judges and Judith' in M. Bal (ed.), *Anti-Covenant* (Sheffield, 1989), pp. 63–78; and for the suggestion that Judith *is*

actually Jael see E. J. Bruns, 'Judith of Jael', *CBQ* 16 (1954), pp. 12–14.

7   Many believe the name 'Bethulia' is simply a fictitious town. It is clearly distinguished from Jerusalem in Judith 4:6, 11, 14; 9:1; 11:14, 19; 15:8. For those who believe Bethulia existed, the location remains in dispute. Sanur, Mithiliyeh or Misiliyeh, Tell Kheibar and Beit-Ilfa, Haraiq el-Mallah, Khirbet Sheikh Shibel, el-Barid and Shechem have all been proposed. The city was supposed to be situated on a mountain, overlooking the plain of Jezreel, or Esdrelon, and it controlled narrow passes.

8   Some translations of this passage (Judith 11:21) are omitted where they say: 'The Lord gave her also a special beauty . . . in all men's eyes.' Some churchmen considered it less than proper that God had deliberately conferred sexual allure on her, i.e. had a *femme fatale* save Israel. See A. Lacocque, *The Feminine Unconventional*, p. 38.

9   See the comments of C. A. Moore, *Judith,* p. 204.

10 See C. A. Moore, *Judith,* p. 218, n. 2 with references.

11 In the first part of her prayer in Judith 9:2–4, Judith shows a strong concern for the sexual violation of women. She certainly believed that Holofernes might have raped her had she not been willing to sleep with him. By killing him, she saves her own honour and protects the women of Israel.

12 Display of the enemy's head has a long history in the Bible. On Goliath's head, 1 Sam. 17:54; Saul's at Beth Shean in 1 Sam. 31:9–10; the heads of Ahab's relatives in 2 Kings 10:7–8; John the Baptist's in Matt. 14:8. The incident is also reminiscent of 1 Macc. 7:47 and 2 Macc. 15:35, where Judas' men cut off Nicanor's head and right hand and displayed them outside Jerusalem. See D. J. Harrington, *The Maccabean Revolt*, p. 118.

13 On Judith as representative of the community see A.-J. Levine, 'Sacrifice and Salvation: Otherness and Domestication in the Book of Judith' in J. C. Vander Kam, 'No One Spoke Ill of Her' in *Essays on Judith* (Atlanta, 1992), pp. 17–30. On Judith as warrior see S. Ackerman, 'Deborah, Women and War' in *Warrior, Dancer, Seductress, Queen* (New York, 1999), p. 51.

14 M. Stocker, *Judith,* p. 5.

15 On a parallel between Judith beheading Holofernes with a subsequent celebration in Bethulia, and Judas Maccabee beheading Nicanor and the celebration in Jerusalem (1 Macc. 7:47; 2 Macc. 15:30–5) see A. Lacocque, *The Feminine Unconventional*, p. 39, n. 12; on the suggestion of castration see A.-J. Levine, 'Sacrifice and Salvation', p. 376, n. 23.

16 For alternating of masculinity and femininity see A. Lacocque, *The Feminine Unconventional*, p. 38; P. Montley, 'Judith in the Fine Arts: The Appeal of the Archetypal Androgyne', *Anima* 4 (1978), p. 40. See also S. Ackerman, 'Awake! Awake! Utter a Song! Deborah, Women and War' in *Warrior, Dancer, Seductress, Queen*, pp. 27–8.

17 J. Haswell, *The Tangled Web: The Art of Tactical and Strategic Deception* (Wendover, 1985), pp. 19–20, also notes elements of centralised control, flexibility and co-ordination more appropriate to much larger and more complex covert operations.

Postscript Part I: Spies in the Old Testament (pp.117–25)

1   R. de Vaux, *The Early History of Israel* (Philadelphia, 1978), p. 475. See also the comments of G. Mendenhall, 'The Hebrew Conquest of Palestine', *BA* 25, 1 (Feb. 1962), p. 66.

2   W. F. Albright, 'Archaeology and the Date of the Hebrew Conquest of Palestine', *BASOR* 58 (1935), pp. 10–18; W. F. Albright, 'The Israelite Conquest of Canaan in the Light of Archaeology', *BASOR* 74 (1939), pp. 11–23. G. W. Wright, *Biblical Archaeology* (Philadelphia, 1962); J. Bright, *Early Israel in Recent History Writing. A Study in Method* (London, 1956); J. Bright, *A History of Israel* (London, 1981), 3rd edn.

3   A. Malamat, 'Conquest of Canaan: Israelite Conduct of War According to Biblical Tradition' in *History of Biblical Israel. Major Problems and Minor Issues* (Leiden, 2001), p. 71.

4   R. Gabriel, *The Military History of Ancient Israel* (Westport, CT, 2003), Foreword, p. xv.

5   For a complete and recent discussion of the composition debate see L. L. Rowlett, *Joshua and the*

Rhetoric of Violence. A New Historicist Analysis (Sheffield, 1996), pp. 30–48.

6   H. Shanks, 'Israel's Emergence in Canaan', *BAR* (Oct. 1989), p. 26, quoting N. Gottwald, *The Tribes of Yahweh*. On the use of models see G. E. Mendenhall, 'The Hebrew Conquest of Palestine' in C. E. Carter and C. E. Meyers (eds), *Community, Identity and Ideology. Social Science Approaches to the Hebrew Bible* (Winona Lake, IN, 1996), pp. 152–3.

7   N. Gottwald, *The Tribes of Yahweh*, p. 27. See also R. M. Hals, 'Legend: A Case of Study in Old Testament Form–Critical Study', *CBQ* 34 (1972), pp. 166–76.

8   L. L. Rowlett, *Joshua and the Rhetoric of Violence*, p. 11.

9   L. L. Rowlett, *Joshua and the Rhetoric of Violence*, p. 11.

10 For a good discussion of the dating debate see R. N. Whybray, *The Making of the Pentateuch. A Methodological Study* (Sheffield, 1987).

11 N. P. Lemche, *Prelude to Israel's Past*, pp. 222–3.

12 N. P. Lemche, *Prelude to Israel's Past*, p. 223, and N. P. Lemche, *Ancient Israel: A New History of Israelite Society* (Sheffield, 1988), pp. 155–6.

13 J. Van Seters, *In Search of History* (New Haven, 1983), pp. 8–54 on early Greek historiography, pp. 55–99 on Mesopotamian historiography. Cf. N. P. Lemche, *Prelude to Israel's Past*, p. 224.

14 See A. Van der Lingen, *Les Guerres de Yahvé* (Paris, 1990). He believed that there was a similarity between the terminology of Yahweh war and that of the 'post-exilic prophets'.

15 L. L. Rowling, *Joshua and the Rhetoric of Violence*, p. 70. On 'holy war' see G. Von Rad, *Holy War in Ancient Israel* (Grand Rapids, MI, 1990). On 'Yahweh War' see R. Smend, *Yahwe War;* cf. M. C. Lind, *Yahweh is a Warrior*, p. 27; G. H. Jones, ' "Holy War" or "Yahwe War"?', *VT* 25 (1975), pp. 642–58; F. Stolz, *Jahwes und Israels Kriege* (Zürich, 1972).

16 S. M. Kang, *Divine War in the Old Testament and in the Ancient Near East* (Berlin, 1989).

17 E. Hobsbawm and T. Ranger, *The Invention of Tradition* (Cambridge, 1983), p. 1.

18 E. Hobsbawm and T. Ranger, *The Invention of Tradition*, p. 4; J. Van Seters, 'Tradition and Social Change in Ancient Israel' in *Perspectives in Religious Studies* 7 (1980), pp. 96–113.

19 John Bright's suggestion in *A History of Israel* (London, 1981), p. 119, that if the Jews had wanted to make up stories about themselves they would not have portrayed themselves as coming from such humble origins does not hold water. Numerous foundation stories from Africa and Mexico show the same pattern. They play an important social and political role in dealing with group identity, claims to land, right to rule etc. of particular communities or groups. See the discussion in K.W. Whitelam, 'Israel's Traditions of Origin', pp. 23–7.

20 A. Malamat, 'Conquest of Canaan: Israelite Conduct of War According to Biblical Tradition' in *History of Biblical Israel. Major Problems and Minor Issues* (Leiden, 2001), p. 46.

21 See especially R. A. Gabriel, *The Military History of Ancient Israel*.

22 S. W. Baron, 'The Ancient and Medieval Periods: Review of the History', p. 23.

23 Quoted by Salo Baron, 'The Ancient and Medieval Periods: Review of the History', p. 23.

24 One need only look at the way most college textbooks cling to the conquest model to see this idea at work. Jack Cargill has studied this phenomenon; see Jack Cargill, 'Ancient History in Western Civ Textbooks', *History Teacher* 34, 3 (May 2001), pp. 297–326.

25 For a detailed discussion of these problems see R. B. Coote and K. W. Whitelam, *The Emergence of Early Israel in Historical Perspective* (Sheffield, 1987).

Part II

Chapter 6 The Jews Against Rome

1   An earlier version of this chapter was published as 'Taking on Goliath: Low-Intensity Conflict in the Great Jewish War', *Small Wars and Insurgencies* 5, 1 (spring 1994), pp. 1–28.

2   On the details of Judaea becoming a province see M. Sicker, *Between Rome and Jerusalem* (Westport, CT, 2001), pp. 115–20.

3   Acts 5:37. The two sons of Judas were crucified by the Roman procurator Tiberius Alexander (46–48 CE), *c*.45 CE. See Josephus, *Ant.* 20.102.

4   J. J. Price, *Jerusalem Under Siege, The Collapse of the Jewish State 66–70 CE.* (Leiden, 1992), p. 2. On Josephus' interpretation of who caused the war see M. Goodman, 'The Origins of the Great Revolt: A Conflict of Status Criteria' in A. Kasher et al., *Greece and Rome in Eretz Israel* (Jerusalem, 1990), pp. 39–53, who observed that the Jewish leaders in the war were both ineffective and redundant. For a general discussion of problems between the Romans and Palestinian Jews see S. Stern, 'Dissonance and Misunderstanding in Jewish–Roman Relations' in M. Goodman, *Jews in a Graeco-Roman World* (Oxford, 2002), pp. 241–78. On economic problems in Judaea see M. Goodman, 'The First Jewish Revolt: Social Conflict and the Problem of Debt', *JJS* 33, 1, 2 (1982), pp. 417–27; J. McLaren, *Turbulent Times? Josephus and Scholarship on Judaea in the First Century* (Sheffield, 1998), chap. 4, on the turmoil in first-century Judaea, and how it is portrayed in contemporary scholarship.

5   P. A. Brunt, 'Social Conflicts in Roman Judaea' in *Roman Imperial Themes* (Oxford, 1990), p. 287, believed that religious fanaticism, messianic delusions and a desire for freedom from foreign rule played a much larger part in the revolt than economic considerations. Martin Goodman has suggested that Jewish discontent was so pervasive because the sources expressing it, e.g. Josephus and Philo, have survived. It is possible that many other provincials felt as oppressed as the Jews did, but their objections do not survive in the extant literature. See 'Current Scholarship on the First Revolt' in A. M. Berlin and J. A. Overmann (eds), *The First Jewish Revolt*, p. 21. On the themes of Roman administration and Jewish dissatisfaction see M. Goodman, *The Ruling Class of Judaea* (Cambridge, 1987). On hostility between the Jews and surrounding Greek cities, which made the revolt inevitable, see U. Rappaport, 'Jewish-Pagan Relations and the Revolt Against Rome in 66–70 CE', *Jerusalem Cathedra* 2 (1981), pp. 81–95.

6   The period's documents in Hebrew and Aramaic suggest that not every participant saw the uprising as a 'nationalistic' act. See A. M. Berlin and J. A. Overmann (eds), *The First Jewish Revolt, The First Jewish Revolt*, p. 10. This study reveals that for each region there was a separate reaction to revolt. Cf. S. Freyne, 'The Revolt from a Regional Perspective', A. M. Berlin and J. A. Overmann (eds), *The First Jewish Revolt*, pp. 43–56. Morton Smith points out that Josephus, *Ant.* 18.6–10, is probably a false claim that the prohibition of accepting any king but God was a motive common to all these parties; in fact, several of their leaders had royal pretensions. See M. Smith, 'The Trouble Makers.' *CHJ*, vol. 2, p. 509.

7   M. Oppenheimer, *The Urban Guerrilla* (Chicago, 1969), p. 92; C. Leiden and K. M. Schmitt, *Revolution in the Modern World* (Englewood Cliffs, NJ, 1968), p. 76; R. A. Horsley, 'The Sicarii: Ancient Jewish Terrorists', *JR* 59 (1979), p. 446. Opinion is divided over the extent to which the Jews were marginalised in the early Roman imperial period. See L. H. Feldman, *Jew and Gentile in the Ancient World* (Princeton, 1993); P. Schafer, *Judaeophobia: Attitudes Towards the Jewish in the Ancient World* (Cambridge, 1997); Z. Yavetz, *Judenfeindschaft in Der Antike* (Munich, 1997); E. S. Gruen, 'Roman Perspective on the Jews in the Age of the Great Revolt' in A. M. Berlin and J. A. Overman (eds), *The First Jewish Revolt*, pp. 27–42.

8   Archaeological evidence for the residences of Jerusalem's priestly and secular aristocracy shows some collaboration. See N. A. Silberman's comments on the impact of Roman imperial annexation, the breakdown of traditional patterns of farming, the growth of imperial cities and the increasing rift

between rich and poor ('The First Revolt and Its Afterlife' in A. M. Berlin and J. A. Overmann (eds), *The First Jewish Revolt*, pp. 248–9). See also M. Goodman, *The Ruling Class of Judaea*; E. Gabba, 'The Social, Economic, and Political History of Palestine 63 BCE–70 CE', *CHJ*, vol. 3, pp. 135–7.

9 It was certainly not only their religion that compelled the Jews to rebel against Rome. See Martin Goodman, 'Current Scholarship on the First Revolt' in A. M. Berlin and J. A. Overmann (eds), *The First Jewish Revolt*, p. 20. To suppose, however, that the Palestinian peasantry looted the estates of the rich because they were trying to restore a primitive 'egalitarian society', as per R. A. Horsley and J. S. Hanson, *Bandits, Prophets and Messiahs* (San Francisco, 1988), p. 166, has not been accepted by all. Morton Smith said simply that they looted because they wanted loot ('The Troublemakers', *CHJ*, p. 510). M. Hengel, *The Zealots*, p. xv, believes, on the other hand, that all Jewish revolts against Rome had an eschatological and messianic aspect. See the critique of T. L. Donaldson, 'Rural Bandits, City Mobs and the Zealots', *JSJ* 21, 1 (June 1990), pp. 19–40.

10 Josephus, *BJ* 2.308, complained that the Roman procurators responded to riots in Caesarea and Jerusalem by crucifying Jews, some of whom were so rich that they were Roman citizens of equestrian rank. If they lost Rome's support, their own power would crumble and so they capitalised on the current anti-Roman feeling after Florus raided the Temple and led the people in rebellion. See M. Goodman, 'The Origins of the Great Revolt: A Conflict of Status Criteria' in A. Kasher et al. (eds), *Greece and Rome in Eretz Israel*, (Yad Izhak Ben-Zvi, 1990), pp. 39–53. See also M. Goodman, *The Ruling Class of Judaea*; M. Goodman, 'Current Scholarship on the First Jewish Revolt' in A. M. Berlin and J. A. Overmann (eds), *The First Jewish Revolt*, pp. 15–24, where he updates his argument.

11 Josephus, *Ant.*, 18.8; M. Hengel, *The Zealots*, trans. by David Smith (Edinburgh, 1989), appendix, pp. 380–404, argued that Judas of Galilee's fourth philosophy was the single controlling idea behind all revolutionary movement from 6 to 66 CE. Against this interpretation see M. Smith, 'Zealots and Sicarii', *HTR* 64 (1971), pp. 12–13, and M. Smith, 'The Troublemakers', *CHJ*, vol. 2, pp. 543–4.

12 On differing accounts of who the Sicarii were see M. Hengel, *Die Zeloten* (Leiden, 1976); M. Smith, 'Zealots and Sicarii: Their Origins and Relations', *HTR* 64 (1971), pp. 1–19; and M. Smith, 'The Troublemakers', *CHJ*, vol. 2, p. 501, where he calls Hengel's book 'an outstanding work of creative theological imagination'.

13 Josephus, *BJ* 2.254, 425; 4.400, 516; 7.253, 254, 262, 275, 297, 311, 410, 412, 415, 437, 444; Josephus, *Ant.* 18.5–10; 20.204, 208, 210; S. Zeitlin, 'Zealots and Sicarii', *JBL* 82 (1962), p. 395. Josephus notes that they were also hired for private purposes. Even a Roman governor was a patron on occasion (*Ant.* 20.163–4).

14 R. A. Horsley, 'Menachem in Jerusalem: A Brief Messianic Episode Among the Sicarii – not "Zealot Messianism" ', *NT* 27, 4 (1985), p. 344.

15 M. Oppenheimer, *The Urban Guerrilla* (Chicago, 1969), p. 75.

16 S. D. Cohen, *From the Maccabees to the Mishnah* (Philadelphia, 1987), p. 165.

17 See W. R. Farmer, *Maccabees, Zealots and Josephus* (New York, 1956), *passim*, who tried to prove that the Zealots were simply the Maccabees' successors, and that their entire movement was determined by the Maccabees. For scholars who still believe in a group of revolutionaries with a united philosophy see M. Hengel, *The Zealots*, the updated English version of his *Die Zeloten. Untersuchungen Zur Jüdischen Freiheitsbewegung in Der Zeit Von Herodes I. bis 70 n. Chr* (Leiden, 1961).

18 M. Smith, 'Zealots and Sicarii: Their Origins and Relation', *HTR* 64 (1971), pp. 1–19; K. Lake and F. Jackson, 'Appendix A: The Zealots', *The Beginnings of Christianity* (New York, 1920–33), vol. 1, pt 1, pp. 421–5; S. Zeitlin, 'Zealots and Sicarii', *JBL* 81 (1962), pp. 395–8, who differed from Lake and declared that the Zealots were followers of Eleazar ben Simon; Lake believed that they were followers of John of Gischala; R. A. Horsley, 'The Sicarii: Ancient Jewish Terrorists', *JR* 59 (1979), pp. 435–58; R. A. Horsley, 'Menachem in Jerusalem', pp. 159–92; J. Price, *Jerusalem Under Siege*, p. 22.

19 Josephus, *BJ*, 2.651; 4.161, 162, 193, 196, 198, 199, 201, 209, 215, 216, 224, 284, 291, 298, 302, 305, 306, 310, 326, 340, 342, 346, 355, 378, 387, 388, 490, 514, 538, 544, 556, 558, 567, 568, 570,

574, 575, 577, 579; 5.3, 5, 7, 101, 104, 250, 359, 528; 6.92, 148; 7.268.

20 Morton Smith gave a very clear account of Josephus' precise portrayal in the *BJ* of the Zealot party's emergence in Jerusalem during the winter of AD 67/68 in 'Zealots and Sicarii: Their Origins and Relation', *HTR* 64 (1971), pp. 1–19.

21 E. J. Hobsbawm, *Primitive Rebels* (New York, 1969); R. A. Horsley and J. S. Hanson, *Bandits, Prophets and Messiahs* (Harrisburg, PA, 1999); T. L. Donaldson, 'Rural Bandits, City Mobs, and the Zealots', *JSJ* 21, 1 (June 1990), p. 27.

22 E. J. Hobsbawm, *Primitive Rebels* (New York, 1965), chap. 2; E. Hobsbawm, *Bandits* (New York, 1969), chap. 1–3, 6–7; B. Isaac, 'Bandits in Judaea and Arabia', *HSCP* 88 (1984), pp. 171–203.

23 R. A. Horsley, 'The Sicarii', p. 436; R. A. Horsley, 'Josephus and the Bandits', *JSJ* (autumn 1979), pp. 37–63. M. Smith, 'The Troublemakers', *CHJ*, vol. 2, p. 529.

24 S. D. Cohen, *From the Maccabees to the Mishnah,* pp. 165–6; S. Freyne, 'Bandits in Galilee', *The Social World of Formative Christianity and Judaism* (Philadelphia, 1988), p. 58, argued that the brigands in Galilee fit a different mould. They are the remains of a dying social class trying to regain its former position of wealth and status in Palestinian life after Herod's reign. He did not believe the Galilean rebels fit Horsley's definition of social bandits. R. A. Horsley, 'Josephus and the Bandits', *JSJ* 10 (1979), pp. 37–63; R. A. Horsley, 'Ancient Jewish Banditry and the Revolt against Rome', *CBQ* 43 (1981), pp. 409–32; R. A. Horsley, *Bandits, Prophets and Messiahs*, pp. 48–87.

25 See Josephus, *BJ* 2.4.3, for the attack on an entire Roman company engaged in conveying grain and arms to the troops that occupied Jerusalem. On bandit attacks on both Romans and wealthy Jews see *BJ* 2.13.6 (pp. 264–5). For bandits to operate on a large scale they need support from the outside: either from the community, or covert support of the powerful. See B. D. Shaw, 'Bandits in the Roman Empire', *Past and Present* 105 (1984), pp. 3–52.

26 Josephus, *BJ* 2.65; *Ant.* 17.285.

27 B. Isaac, 'Bandits in Judaea and Arabia', *HSCP* 88 (1984), p. 180. B. Isaac, 'Roman Colonies in Judaea: The Foundation of Aelia Capitolina', *Talanta* 12–13 (1980/81), pp. 31–54.

28 See *BJ* 2.253–279 on the outbreak of banditry. At least one bandit chieftain, Simon bar Giora, was transformed by events into a revolutionary leader.

29 T. L. Donaldson, 'Rural Bandits, City Mobs, and the Zealots', p. 30, and Horsley and Hanson, *Bandits, Prophets and Messiahs*, pp. 5–8, describe in more detail how they believe bandit groups transformed themselves from a pre-political movement of social protest to a revolutionary party with a conscious political strategy; i.e. to overthrow the ruling élite and bring them to justice, and to re-establish Israel as a communitarian and egalitarian theocracy.

30 One indication of this was the exclusion of Eleazar bar Simon from office in the new government, despite his leading role in the battle against Cestius Gallus. See Josephus, *BJ* 2.564 and T. L. Donaldson, 'Rural Bandits, City Mobs, and the Zealots', *JJS* 31 (1990), p. 31.

31 T. Rajak, *Josephus* (London, 1983), p. 85.

32 T. Rajak, *Josephus* (London, 1983), pp. 85–6.

33 M. Smith, 'Zealots and Sicarii', *HTR* 64 (1971), pp. 14–19; R. A. Horsley, 'The Sicarii', *JR* 59 (1979), p. 436. There are enough fragmentary indications, even in Josephus' account, to convince us that there was more in Zealot ideology and religious convictions than we can know; see T. Rajak, *Josephus*, p. 87, and M. Hengel, *The Zealots*, pp. 380–404, who believed there was a 'solidified will' on the part of members of the 'radical liberation movement', whose aim was an open 'people's war' with the Roman oppressors (p. 383).

34 J. Price, *Jerusalem Under Siege*, pp. 1–50.

35 Agrippa II (27–100 CE), son of Agrippa I, and like him originally named Marcus Julius Agrippa. Having grown up in the court of the emperor Claudius, on the death of his uncle Herod Agrippa inherited the oversight of the Temple in 48 CE. Claudius later invested him with the tetrarchy of Chalcis c.49/50. In 53 he was deprived of that kingdom by Claudius, who made him governor over the

tetrarchy of Philip and Lysanias (Acts 25:13; 26:2, 7). During the Jewish Revolt, Agrippa sent two
thousand men to support Vespasian, by which it appears that, though a Jew in religion, he was entirely
devoted to the Romans. He died in Rome in the third year of Trajan's reign.

36 Josephus, *BJ* 2. 433–48.

37 Josephus, *BJ* 2.449–56.

38 The Sicarii refused to raid far from Masada (Josephus, *BJ* 4.507), and even attacked local Jewish villages
near Ein Gedi (*BJ* 2. 508–11).

39 M. Gichon, 'Cestius Gallus's Campaign in Judaea', *PEQ* 113 (1981), p. 39.

40 M. Gichon, 'Cestius Gallus's Campaign in Judaea', *PEQ* 113 (1981), pp. 41–2, for the motivation
behind this delay.

41 He reported that the *legio* XII Fulminata was at full strength, six cohorts of auxiliary infantry and
four *alae* of cavalry. From the allies he got: two thousand more horse and three thousand foot-archers
of Antiochus, king of Commagene; four thousand men of Emesa, the majority being archers and some
cavalry; lastly, two thousand horsemen and some three thousand infantry from the army of Agrippa,
the Judaean. See M. Gichon, 'Cestius Gallus's Campaign in Judaea', *PEQ* 113 (1981), pp. 42–4, for the
disposition of Roman troops in the area.

42 M. Gichon, 'Cestius Gallus's Campaign in Judaea', *PEQ* 113 (1981), pp. 44–5.

43 M. Gichon, 'Cestius Gallus's Campaign in Judaea', *PEQ* 113 (1981), p. 45, citing Arrian, *Tactica* 17,
on bowmen; Vegetius, *Epitoma* 3.6, on *auxilia*.

44 With the exception of the small Temple guard, and the Idumaean border militia restricted to their
border estates.

45 M. Gichon, 'Cestius Gallus's Campaign in Judaea', *PEQ* 113 (1981), p. 50. The risks of penetrating
deeply into enemy territory with limited forces have been well understood since the days of the massacre
of Varus in the Teutoburgerwald. See also B. Bar-Kochva, 'Seron and Cestius Gallus at Beth Horon',
PEQ 108 (1976), pp. 18–21, on the route used by Cestius in the ascent.

46 This is same pass where Joshua defeated the Amorites (Josh. 10:10) and where Judas Maccabeus
vanquished a Seleucid army. The Philistines fought Saul here (1 Sam. 13); David also won a great
victory here over the Philistines (2 Sam. 5:25); Seron, the Seleucid commander was ambushed there in
166 CE (1 Macc. 3:24). The pass was used right up to the British conquest of Jerusalem in 1917 and the
Six Day War in 1967. B. Bar-Kochva, 'Seron and Cestius Gallus at Beth Horon', *PEQ* 108 (1976), pp.
18–21; Josephus, *BJ* 2.516. On the site of Gabao see M. Gichon, 'Cestius Gallus's Campaign in Judaea',
PEQ 113 (1981), p. 51, n. 53.

47 Josephus, *BJ* 2. 521.

48 Gichon observed that this was standard operating procedure in handbooks such as those of Vegetius,
the Anonymous Byzantine and Leo, but these were written centuries after this event. The Romans
were quite capable of being caught in this kind of carelessness. As an example see M. Gichon, 'Cestius
Gallus's Campaign in Judaea', *PEQ* 113 (1981), p. 60, on the slaughter in the Teutoburg Forest, and
R. M. Sheldon, *Intelligence Activities in Ancient Rome: Trust in the Gods, But Verify* (London, 2005),
chap. 10.

49 Josephus, *BJ* 2.518; M. Gichon, 'Cestius Gallus's Campaign in Judaea', *PEQ* 113 (1981), p. 53; B. Bar-
Kochva, 'Seron and Cestius Gallus at Beth Horon', *PEQ* 108 (1976), pp. 18–19.

50 See M. Gichon, 'Cestius Gallus's Campaign in Judaea', *PEQ* 113 (1981), p. 53, for a convincing
argument that this ambush was not staged along the public highway but on the shorter route along
the wadi Beth Khanina. The distance of eight or nine kilometres between Upper Beth Horon and the
neighborhood of Giv'on accords roughly with the length of the Roman marching line, and suggests that
the attack was launched simultaneously at Giv'on and Upper Beth Horon. See B. Bar-Kochva, 'Seron
and Cestius Gallus at Beth Horon', *PEQ* 108 (1976), pp. 18–19.

51 Josephus, *BJ* 2.519.

52 Logistic difficulties, B. Bar-Kochva, 'Seron and Cestius Gallus at Beth Horon', *PEQ* 108 (1976), p. 18.

53 Josephus, *BJ* 3.95. Gallus sent out foraging parties to collect grain in the surrounding villages; see Josephus, *BJ* 2.528.
54 Josephus, *BJ* 2.543–4.
55 Josephus, *BJ* 2.545.
56 M. Gichon, 'Cestius Gallus's Campaign in Judaea', *PEQ* 113 (1981), pp. 58–9. See also B. Bar-Kochva, 'Seron and Cestius Gallus at Beth Horon', *PEQ* 108 (1976), pp. 18–21.
57 Josephus, *BJ* 2.550–5.
58 According to Josephus, *BJ* 2.555, the Romans lost three hundred infantrymen, four hundred and eighty cavalry and most of their machines and heavy baggage.
59 Josephus, *Vita* 17; J. Price, *Jerusalem Under Siege*, p. 11.
60 The army of Vespasian consisted of three distinct legions: the Fifth, the Tenth and the Fifteenth. There were also twenty-three auxiliary cohorts, six *alae* of cavalry and the auxiliary troops of King Agrippa, King Antiochus of Commagene, Soemus of Emesa and Malchus of Arabia (Josephus, *BJ* 3.64–9; *Vita* 26–30).
61 Josephus, *BJ* 3.2.
62 R. A. Horsley, 'Power Vacuum and Power Struggle' in A. M. Berlin and J. A. Overmann (eds), *The First Jewish Revolt*, pp. 87–109, suggested that the priestly party tried to put down the revolt to mend fences with the Romans, and that Josephus was sent to Galilee to control affairs and restore order, not to fight alongside the revolutionaries. He believes that there was no unifying ideology or coherent anti-Roman revolt in Galilee. This contradicts the archaeological evidence summarised in the same volume by A. M. Berlin; see D. Avshalom-Gorni and N. Getzov, 'Phoenicians and Jews. A Ceramic Case Study' in A. M. Berlin and J. A. Overmann (eds), *The First Jewish Revolt*, pp. 74–83. On the lack of military training among the leaders see J. Price, *Jerusalem Under Siege*, pp. 60–2.
63 Price's hypothesis is that Jewish aristocratic leaders solved both their military and political problems by creating military units from armed rebel groups. They created a national army and diverted the energies of the rebel factions away from themselves (J. Price, *Jerusalem Under Siege*, p. 55).
64 On the ceramic evidence from Jotepata (Yodefat) see D. Avshalom-Gorni and N. Getzov, 'Phoenicians and Jews. A Ceramic Case Study' in A. M. Berlin and J. A. Overmann (eds), *The First Jewish Revolt*, pp. 74–83. On the excavation of the site and its documentation of certain aspects of Josephus' narrative see M. Aviam, 'Yodefat/Jotapata. The Archaeology of the First Battle' in A. M. Berlin and J. A. Overmann (eds), *The First Jewish Revolt*, pp. 121–33.
65 Josephus, *BJ* 3.177.
66 Josephus, *BJ* 3.186.
67 Josephus, *BJ* 3.192.
68 Josephus, *BJ* 3.222–4.
69 Josephus, *BJ* 3.272–3.
70 Josephus, *BJ* 3. 277–8.
71 Josephus, *BJ* 3.145–339, although the incident is thought to be apocryphal.
72 All Galilee and Gamala were conquered between 1 June and 1 December 67 (Josephus, *BJ* 3.132–4.115). On the role of Sepphoris see now E. M. Meyers, 'Sephoris: City of Peace' in A. M. Berlin and J. A. Overmann (eds), *The First Jewish Revolt*, pp. 110–20. On the siege and battle at Gamala, and the archaeological evidence, see D. Syon, 'Gamla. City of Refuge' in A. M. Berlin and J. A. Overmann (eds), *The First Jewish Revolt*, pp. 134–53.
73 Josephus, *BJ* 4.22–5.
74 Josephus, *BJ* 4. 62–9.
75 Josephus, *BJ* 4.54–61.
76 Josephus, *BJ* 4.115. See U. Rappaport, 'John of Gischala: From Galilee to Jerusalem', *Essays in Honor of Y. Yadin*, p. 483, who doubted the veracity of Josephus' story.
77 A long series in the Babylonian Talmud (*Gittin* 55b–59a) blamed the effort's disunity and the

destruction caused by the war on a lack of strong rabbinic leadership, lack of communal care for one another, and other social ills. See also A. J. Saldarini, 'Good from Evil' in A. M. Berlin and J. A. Overmann (eds), *The First Jewish Revolt*, p. 222.

78 Josephus, *BJ*, 4.503–8. See O. Michel, 'Simon bar Giora', *Fourth World Congress of Jewish Studies*, Papers I (Jerusalem, 1967), pp. 77–80; J. Price wrote that Simon's movement was distinguished from the other groups by violence against the Jewish upper classes (*Jerusalem Under Siege*, p. 59).

79 Josephus, *BJ* 4.377–88; J. Price, *Jerusalem Under Siege*, p. 95. The Romans learned, among other things, that the Jews could flee the city through secret routes (Josephus, *BJ* 5.493, 496, 497). Josephus also reports Romans deserting to the Jews and teaching them how to use captured Roman artillery (Josephus, *BJ* 5.269 and J. Price, *Jerusalem Under Siege,* p. 119).

80 Josephus, *BJ* 5.424–38; Tacitus, *Histories*, 5.12. The Talmudic version of the burning of the food supplies considers the revolutionary leaders destructive, the rabbinic leaders well intentioned but ineffective, and the loss of food as fatal to the city. See A. J. Saldarini, 'Good from Evil. The Rabbinic Response' in A. M. Berlin and J. A. Overmann (eds), *The First Jewish Revolt*, p. 232, who noted that one group the rabbis did not blame was the Romans, who barricaded the city and cut off food shipments.

81 S. Zeitlin, *The Rise and Fall of the Judaean State* (Philadelphia, 1978), vol. 3, p. 99. Titus set out from Caesarea with the three legions his father had used to ravage Judaea as well as with the Twelfth Legion, formerly commanded by Cestius Gallus. He was then joined by the Fifth and Tenth legions plus substantial contingents led by allied kings. On the Jewish side Simon had an army, exclusive of the Idumaeans, of ten thousand men commanded by fifty officers. The Idumaean contingent numbered five thousand. John, at the time of seizing the Temple, had an army of six thousand men, but he was now joined by the Zealots, under Eleazar, who numbered two thousand four hundred (Josephus, *BJ* 5.248ff.).

82 Josephus, *BJ* 5.81–4.

83 Josephus, *BJ* 5.109–19.

84 Josephus, *BJ* 5.302. The Roman infantry was almost always defeated in hand-to-hand combat, and was usually saved by the cavalry or archery units. See J. Price, *Jerusalem Under Siege*, p. 123.

85 Josephus, *BJ* 5.308–9.

86 Josephus, *BJ* 5.342. The Jewish defence was aided by the artillery captured in 66 from the Roman garrison at Antonia and from Cestius' routed forces. Once the fighting reached the Temple, the Jews had special towers like the Roman siege towers from which to carry out their bombardments. See J. Price, *Jerusalem Under Siege*, p. 124.

87 Josephus *BJ* 5.469.

88 Dio Cassius, 65.5.1. On Roman despondency see Josephus, *BJ* 5.472, 490; 6.9–14; J. Price, *Jerusalem Under Siege*, pp. 118–19.

89 Dio 66.4.5 mentions underground passages that led outside the city, which the Jews used to ambush Roman water carriers and detachments. They could also have been used to bring in food, but Titus blocked them. On underground passages, tunnels and escape routes see J. Price, *Jerusalem Under Siege*, pp. 141–2; on the report of cannibalism in the city see pp. 154–5.

90 Josephus, *BJ* 5.252–4.

91 Jeremiah 52.12ff. puts the burning of the Temple by Nebuchadrezzar's guard on the tenth of Ab while 2 Kings 25:8 gives the day as the seventh of Ab. Jewish tradition celebrates it on the ninth of Ab.

92 Josephus, *BJ* 6. 433–4; 7.154.

93 S. J. D. Cohen, 'Masada: Literary Tradition, Archaeological Remains, and the Credibility of Josephus', *JJS* 33 (1982), pp. 385–405; D. J. Ladouceur, 'Masada: A Consideration of the Literary Evidence', *GRBS* 21 (1980), pp. 245–60; L. H. Feldman, 'Masada: A Critique of Recent Scholarship' in J. Neusner, *Christianity, Judaism and Other Graeco-Roman Cults* (Leiden, 1975), pp. 218–48. The most trenchant critique is by N. Ben-Yehuda, The *Masada Myth: Collective Memory and Mythmaking in Israel* (Madison, 1995), and N. Ben-Yehuda, *Sacrificing Truth: Archaeology and the Myth of Masada* (Amherst, NY, 2002).

94 For the topography and an account of the siege see C. Hawkes, 'The Roman Siege of Masada', *Antiquity*

3 (1929), p. 200; Josephus, *BJ* 7.252–407; D. J. Ladouceur, 'Josephus and Masada' in *Josephus, Judaism and Christianity*, pp. 95–113, who challenged the belief that Josephus portrayed the Sicarii as heroic freedom fighters. On the exact location of the possible suicides see N. Ben-Yehuda, 'Where Masada's Defenders Fell. A Garbled Passage in Josephus Has Obscured the Location of the Mass Suicide', *BAR* 24, 6 (Nov.–Dec. 1998), pp. 34–9. For the identification of the bones as not those of the Jewish defenders see J. Zias, 'Whose Bones?', *BAR* 24, 6 (Nov.–Dec. 1998), pp. 40–5, 64–6. See also M. Smith, 'The Troublemakers', *CHJ*, vol. 2, p. 560, who refers to the eyewitness as: 'The Woman Who Escaped with her amazing gift for total recall of what Josephus wanted to say.'

95 N. A. Silberman, 'The First Revolt and Its Afterlife' in A. M. Berlin and J. A. Overmann (eds), *The First Jewish Revolt*, pp. 237–8.

96 See the comments by A. M. Berlin and J. A. Overmann (eds), *The First Jewish Revolt*, p. 6; J. Price, *Jerusalem Under Siege*, p. 72.

97 J. Price, *Jerusalem Under Siege*, p. 25.

98 J. Price, *Jerusalem Under Siege*, p. 75.

99 For example, S. G. F. Brandon, 'The Zealots: The Ancient Jewish Resistance against Rome' in M. Elliott-Bateman (ed.), *The Fourth Dimension of Warfare* (New York, 1970), pp. 1–18; M. Hengel, *The Zealots*, p. xv. M. Smith wrote that: 'The one "religious ideology" that determined the Jewish freedom movement is an hallucination of romantic historians,' *CHJ*, vol. 2, p. 566. See the corrective in J. Price, *Jerusalem Under Siege*, p. 31

100 B. Isaac, *The Limits of Empire*, pp. 21, 22, 28.

101 T. Rajak, *Josephus*, p. 107.

102 M. Gichon, 'Aspects of a Roman Army in War According to the Bellum Judaicum of Josephus', *BAR* 297 (1986), p. 287, suggested that Josephus, while apprenticing with the Essenes, studied military manuals such as the *Scroll of the War of the Sons of Light Against the Sons of Darkness*. He also suggests that Josephus had access to military training literature in Rome during his stay there three to four years prior to his command in Galilee (Josephus, *Vita* 2–3).

103 Babylonian Talmud, *Gittin* 55b–59a. The rabbis saw the effects of the war: a loss of sovereignty and their city, impoverishment, a devastation of lives and property, oppression, suffering and death.

104 Tacitus put the figure at six hundred thousand. See S. Zeitlin, *The Rise and Fall of the Judaean State* (Philadelphia, 1978), vol. 3, pp. 138–9, for population figures.

105 See R. M. Sheldon, *Intelligence Activities in Ancient Rome; Trust in the Gods, But Verify* (London, 2005), chap. 10 on Varus in the Teutoburg Forest. See also A. J. Saldarini, 'Good From Evil' in A. M. Berlin and J. A. Overmann (eds), *The First Jewish Revolt*, pp. 222, 227, 228.

106 M. Gichon, 'Aspects of a Roman Army in War', *BAR* 297 (1986), p. 303; J. Price, *Jerusalem Under Siege*, p. 11.

107 M. Gichon, 'Aspects of a Roman Army in War', *BAR* 297 (1986), p. 307.

108 M. Gichon, 'Aspects of a Roman Army in War', *BAR* 297 (1986), p. 299.

109 Josephus, *BJ* 5.124–5, H. St J. Thackeray's translation. It is very hard to know when exactly discipline deadens initiative. Josephus understood the drawbacks of 'iron-fisted routine and schematization'. M. Gichon, 'Aspects of a Roman Army in War', *BAR* 297 (1986), p. 301.

110 Josephus, *BJ* 5.79, trans. by M. Gichon, 'Aspects of a Roman Army in War', *BAR* 297 (1986), p. 301.

111 Josephus, *BJ* 3.228. H. St J. Thackeray translation.

112 Josephus, *BJ* 5.490.

113 M. Gichon, 'Aspects of a Roman Army in War', *BAR* 297 (1986), p. 302.

114 Josephus, *BJ* 7.416.

115 Y. Harkabi, *The Bar Kokhba Syndrome* (Chappaqua, NY, 1982), pp. 6–23.

116 Carl von Clausewitz, *On War*, 1.2–7 ed. and trans. by Michael Howard and Peter Paret (Princeton, 1976).

117 Daniel 12:1; *War of the Sons of Light Against the Sons of Darkness*, col. 1, lines 9–12. T. Rajak, 'Jewish

Millenarian Expectations' in A. M. Berlin and J. A. Overmann (eds), *The First Jewish Revolt*, pp. 180–3, warns against seeing messianic expectations behind leaders such as Simon bar Giora and John of Gischala. Apocalyptic beliefs or millenarianism may have existed in certain groups, but this thinking did not necessarily translate into revolutionary action.

118 M. Hengel, *The Zealots*, pp. 305–6, who cites religious sources on the expectation that Rome would be annihilated.

119 The term 'nationalism' would be an anachronism here. See the comments of R. A. Horsley, 'Power Vacuum and Power Struggle in 66–67 CE' in A. M. Berlin and J. A. Overmann (eds), *The First Jewish Revolt*, p. 87. For modern definitions see B. C. Shafer, *Nationalism: Myth and Reality* (New York, 1955), pp. 3–11, and *Faces of Nationalism: New Realities and Old Myths* (New York, 1972), pp. 3–22. Hans Kohn, however, has pointed out: 'Three essential traits of nationalism originated with the ancient Jews: the idea of the chosen people, the consciousness of national history, and national Messianism' in *The Idea of Nationalism* (New York, 1944), p. 36. For writers who attribute the revolt to a rather ill-defined sense of nationalism see D. Mendels, *The Rise and Fall of Jewish Nationalism* (New York, 1992), pp. 355–8.

120 Josephus, *BJ* 5.120–2.

121 Josephus, *Ant.* 2:165. See J. Price, *Jerusalem Under Siege*, p. 2.

122 Josephus, *BJ* 4.45–6.

123 M. Oppenheimer, *The Urban Guerrilla* (Chicago, 1969), p. 74.

124 G. Parker, 'The Worst-Kept Secret in Europe' in K. Neilson and B. J. C. McKercher (eds), *Go Spy The Land. Military Intelligence in History* (New York, 1992), p. 62.

125 SHA, *Hadrian* 15.13.

Chapter 7 The Jesus File (pp.154–79)

1 This chapter is a condensed version of an article originally published in *Small Wars and Insurgencies* 9, 2 (autumn 1998), pp. 1–37.

2 For a comprehensive study of Roman intelligence gathering see N. J. E. Austin and B. Rankov, *Exploratio* (New York, 1995) and R. M. Sheldon, *Intelligence Activities in Ancient Rome: Trust in the Gods, But Verify* (London: Frank Cass, 2005).

3 Josephus, *BJ* 2.169–77; Josephus, *Ant.* 18.55–62; Mark 15:17; Luke 13.1; and the commentary of J. Price, *Jerusalem Under Siege*, p. 6.

4 On the government of Pilate in Judea see J.-P. Lémonon, *Pilate et le Gouvernement de la Judée. Textes et Monuments* (Paris, 1981).

5 For a discussion with evidence see I. Wilson, *Jesus: The Evidence* (New York, 1984), pp. 51–65. W. D. Davies, 'Jesus: From the Jewish Point of View' in *CHJ* (Cambridge, 1984), vol. 3, p. 618, stated that: 'The Gospels often bear a polemical edge which often renders them of questionable historical value.'

6 R. Joseph Hoffman, *Jesus Outside the Gospels* (Buffalo, NY, 1984).

7 According to Luke 8:3 Antipas' steward, Chuza, was married to Joanna, one of Jesus' early converts.

8 See W. R. Herzog III, *Parables as Subversive Speech. Jesus as Pedagogue of the Oppressed* (Louisville, KY, 1994).

9 For a full explanation of who the Sicarii were see chap. 6. Cf. A. Ehrman, 'Judas Iscariot and Abba Saqqara', *JBL* 97 (1978), pp. 572–3; Y. Arbeitman, 'The Suffix of Iscariot', *JBL* 99 (1980), pp. 122–4.

10 The etymology is much debated, as is the idea that 'zealot' had anything other than a religious connotation before the war of 66 CE. See G. S. Sloyan, *Jesus on Trial* (Philadelphia, 1973), p. 39; B. Salomonsen, 'Some Remarks on the Zealots with Special Regard to the Term "Qannaim" in Rabbinic Literature', *NTS* 12 (1965/66), pp. 164–76.

11 *NEB* translation.

12 S. G. F. Brandon, *Jesus and the Zealots* (Manchester, 1967), pp. 283–321, for the concept of the Pacifist Christ; H. Maccoby, *The Mythmaker: Paul and the Invention of Christianity* (London, 1986); J. Carmichael, *The Death of Jesus* (New York, 1966), pp. 163–82; R. Eisler, *The Messiah Jesus and John*

the Baptist (New York, 1931), pp. 252–3; R. A. Horsley, *Sociology and the Jesus Movement* (New York, 1990), pp. 140–5; R. A. Horsley, *Jesus and the Spiral of Violence* (Minneapolis, 1993), pp. 318–26. For a diametrically opposed view see J. H. Yoder, *The Politics of Jesus* (Grand Rapids, MI, 1972).

13 For example, S. G. F. Brandon, *Jesus and the Zealots* (Manchester, 1967). For a history of the 'Jesus as revolutionary' theory from an author who rejects this interpretation and has his own 'theological agenda' see E. Bammel, 'The Revolutionary Theory from Reimarus to Brandon' in E. Bammel and C. F. D. Moule (eds), *JPHD* (Cambridge, 1984), pp. 11–68; M. Hengel, *Was Jesus a Revolutionist?*, pp. 3–7.

14 For further discussion see W. D. Davies, 'Jesus: From the Jewish Point of View' in *CHJ*, vol. 3, pp. 618–77.

15 Mark 11:1–11; Matt. 21:1–11; Luke 19:29–40; John 12:12–19. See also D. R. Catchpole, 'The "Triumphal" Entry' in *JPHD*, pp. 319–34. B. Kinman, *Jesus' Entry into Jerusalem in the Context of Lukan Theology and the Politics of His Day* (Leiden, 1995), p. 1, discusses the triumphal entry as a *parousia* or arrival of a distinguished person, a well-known tradition in the Greco–Roman world. Cf. M. Borg and J. D. Crossan, *The Last Week* (San Francisco, 2006), pp. 2–30.

16 B. A. Mastin, 'The Date of the Triumphal Entry', *NTS* 16 (1969/70), pp. 76–82.

17 Josephus, *BJ* 2.117.

18 Matt. 21:9; Luke 19:38.

19 B. Kinman, *Jesus' Entry into Jerusalem*, p. 4, believes Luke rewrote the context and content of the triumphal entry/Temple cleansing accounts to cause his audience to distance Jesus from the Jewish nationalists.

20 *NEB* translation (Oxford, 1976).

21 H. L. Ginsberg, *Encyclopedia Judaica*, vol. 11, p. 1407. See M. Hengel, *The Zealots*, pp. 275–81, with references on the messiah as the leader in an eschatological war.

22 For those who deny any connection between Jesus and a Davidic Messiah see E. Bammel, 'The Revolutionary Theory from Reimarus to Brandon', *JPHD*, p. 13, with references. On messianic pretenders in the Jewish freedom movement see M. Hengel, *The Zealots*, pp. 291–300, especially the 'son of David' phenomenon (pp. 298–300).

23 B. A. Mastin, 'The Date of the Triumphal Entry', *NTS* 16 (1969/70), p. 82. The Jesus Seminar agreed that the interpretation of this event as the arrival of the new messiah was a Christian fiction (Jesus Seminar, *The Acts of Jesus*, p. 413).

24 Matt. 26:6–13; Mark 14: 3–9; Luke 7:36–50; John 12:1–8. The significance is that this expensive oil, which was one of the components of the Temple incense, was poured on Jesus' head. According to the *Encyclopedia Judaica*: 'In the anointing of kings the whole head was covered with oil . . .' (vol. 3, p. 31). Mark's Gospel states that three hundred *denarii* of spikenard was used – the equivalent of around $10,000 today according to M. Baigent et al., *The Messianic Legacy* (London, 1986), p. 32; John specifies that the ritual was performed the day preceding Jesus' triumphal entry into Jerusalem; see also J. K. Elliott, 'The Anointing of Jesus', *ExpTim* 85 (1974), pp. 105–7; E. E. Platt, 'The Ministry of Mary of Bethany', *Theology Today* 34 (1977), pp. 29–39; M. de Jonge, 'The Use of the Word "Anointed" in the Time of Jesus', *NT* 8 (1966), pp. 132–48. The Jesus Seminar, *The Acts of Jesus*, pp. 135–6, was split on the historicity of the episode. They found the argument about the expense 'contrived' and believed the anointing was probably an act of courtesy.

25 Josephus relates two such incidents of public demonstrations. See *BJ* 2.8–13; *Ant.* 17:206–18; *Ant.* 18: 29–30; cf. B. Kinman, *Jesus' Entry into Jerusalem*, pp. 160–2.

26 A. N. Wilson, *Jesus. A Life* (NY, 1992), p. 177.

27 Mark 11:15–19; Matt. 21:12–17; Luke 19:45–4; John 2:13–22 (Jesus Seminar, *The Acts of Jesus*, pp. 130, 231, 338, 373). Had the event caused a small urban riot, the Temple police and the Roman garrison would have intervened. It is unthinkable that such an event was not brought up as a point of accusation in the trial proceedings against Jesus. Perhaps it was an act that, at most, disturbed peace momentarily, but nothing more. On why 'cleansing' is not a good term for what actually went on, and what the act symbolised, see W. D. Davies, 'Jesus: From the Jewish Point of View', *CHJ*, pp. 649–52;

cf. M. Borg and J. D. Crossan, *The Last Week*, pp. 75–83.

28 N. Q. Hamilton, 'Temple Cleansing and Temple Bank', *JBL* 83 (1964), pp. 365–72, who saw interference in the Temple's economic affairs without the authority of the Sanhedrin or the Roman authorities to be tantamount to acting as a 'king'. Cf. C. A. Evans, 'Jesus and the "Cave of Robbers": Toward a Jewish Context for the Temple Action', *BBR* 3 (1993), pp. 93–110.

29 P. Richardson, 'Why Turn the Tables? Jesus' protest in the Temple Precincts', *SBLSP* (1992), p. 523, noted that missing from Jesus' teachings are a radical critique of the Temple authorities; these were the product of later controversies and events.

30 Mark 11:18; Luke 19:47. The connection is less explicit in Matt. 21:12, but the incident is still placed in the context of the strife that lead up to Jesus' death.

31 Isaiah 56:7 'house of prayer'; Jeremiah 7:11 'den of robbers'. E. P. Sanders, *The Historical Figure of Jesus* (London, 1993), pp. 254–5, doubted the authenticity of the 'den of robbers' statement. He thinks it was an easy phrase for the evangelists to lift from Jeremiah to make Jesus appear politically innocuous to Greek-speaking gentile readers.

32 Mark 13:14–19; Matt. 24:15–21; Luke 21:5–7. The synoptic versions all foretold the destruction of the Temple; only the latest Gospel, John 2:19–20, mentions building it back up (i.e. purifying it).

33 Mark 14:58; Matt. 26:61.

34 Mark 15:29; Matt. 27:40.

35 Acts 6:14.

36 See C. A. Evans, 'Jesus' Actions in the Temple: Cleansing or Portent of Destruction?', *CBQ* 51 (1989), pp. 237–70.

37 Josephus, *BJ* 6.301.

38 Liberal students of the New Testament generally doubt the historicity of the event for exactly this reason; it would have been a major enterprise requiring force. J. Carmichael, *The Death of Jesus* (New York, 1982), p. 138.

39 J. Carmichael, *The Death of Jesus*, p. 140, who used the arguments of Eisler and Brandon (without much attribution). R. Eisler, *The Messiah Jesus and John the Baptist* (New York, 1931), pp. 457–60, and S. G. F. Brandon, *Jesus and the Zealots*. See M. Hengel, *Was Jesus a Revolutionist?* pp. 38–40.

40 E. P. Sanders, *The Historical Figure of Jesus*, p. 138.

41 Mark 14: 22–6; Matt. 26:26–30; Luke 22:14–20; John 13:1–20. M. Borg and J. D. Crossan, *The Last Week*, pp. 85–120; Jesus Seminar, *The Acts of Jesus*, pp. 137–8, 249–51, 347–8, 419–20.

42 Of course, this assumes that one accepts Judas Iscariot as a historical personage. Against this interpretation see J. S. Spong, *The Sins of Scripture* (San Francisco, 2005), chap. 23, 'The Role of Judas Iscariot in the Rise of Anti-Semitism'.

43 The word 'to betray' in Greek (*paradidomi)* means to 'hand over'. See B. W. Bacon, 'What did Judas Betray?', *Hibbert Journal* 19 (1920/21), pp. 476–93; J. V. Brownson, 'Neutralizing the Intimate Enemy: The Portrayal of Judas in the Fourth Gospel', *SBLSP* (1992), pp. 49–60.

44 The name 'Judas' is not given in Mark's version. Matt. 26:25 supplies the name. Luke 22:14–20 has Satan take possession of Judas. There is also the possibility that the entire story is unhistorical. See the comments of the Jesus Seminar, *The Acts of Jesus*, p. 346.

45 For bibliography see R. E. Brown, *The Death of the Messiah* (New York, 1994), vol. l, pp. 237–9.

46 Mark 14:43–52; Matt. 26:47–56; Luke 22:47–54a; John 18:1–12. M. Borg and J. D. Crossan, *The Last Week*, pp. 120–6.

47 W. Grundmann, 'The Decision of the Supreme Court to Put Jesus to Death (John 11:47–57) In Its Context: Tradition and Redaction in the Gospel of John', *JPHD*, p. 295.

48 Both S. G. F. Brandon, *Jesus and the Zealots*, p. 33, and R. Eisler, *The Messiah Jesus*, pp. 266ff., believed this. They cite Luke 22:36ff.: 'Whoever does not have a sword, let him sell his cloak and buy one.' Cf. Matt. 10:34: 'I have not come not to bring peace, but a sword' (*NEB* trans.).

49 According to Josephus, *BJ* 2.125, even the Essenes were allowed weapons to keep off bandits.

50 In Mark 14:47 and Luke 22:50 the ear is cut off. See G. W. Lampe, 'The Two Swords', *JPHD,* p. 343, and S. C. Hall, 'Swords of Offense', *Studia Evangelica,* vol. 1 (1959), pp. 499–502; Jesus Seminar, *The Five Gospels,* pp. 173–4.

51 There was a garrison at the Tower of Antonia during festivals. Josephus says: 'The usual crowd had assembled at Jerusalem for the Feast of Unleavened Bread, and the Roman cohort had taken up its position on the roof of the portico of the Temple; for a body of men invariably mounts guards at the feasts to prevent disorders from such a concourse of people,' *BJ* 2:244 (trans. by Robinson).

52 M. Baigent et al., *The Messianic Legacy* (London, 1986), p. 56.

53 Luke insisted elsewhere they only had two swords (Luke 22:38).

54 Mark 14:47; Luke says Jesus healed him (Luke 22:51).

55 Mark 15:27; Matt. 27:38. Note how Luke and John seemed to suppress the earlier tradition that Jesus was crucified with *lestai.* See Luke 23:32; John 19:18; E. J. Hobsbawm, *Bandits* (New York, 1981).

56 M. Baigent et al., *The Messianic Legacy,* p. 54.

57 Before the High Priest: Mark 14:53–4; Matt. 26:57–8; Luke 22:54; John 18:13–14, 15–18. Before the council: Mark 14:55–65; Matt. 26:59–68; Luke 22:66–71; John 18:19–24. On the sources see G. S. Sloyan, *Jesus on Trial* (Philadelphia, 1973). For a full discussion of the trial narratives and the subsequent problems see F. J. Matera, 'The Trial of Jesus: Problems and Proposals, *Interpretation* 45 (1991), pp. 5–16; R. Brown, *Death of the Messiah,* vol. I, pp. 315–27; R. Morgan, 'Nothing More Negative . . . . A Concluding Unscientific Postscript to Historical Jesus Research on the Trial of Jesus' in E. Bammel (ed.), *Moule Festschrift* (London, 1970), pp. 135–6; P. Winter, 'The Trial of Jesus and the Competence of the Sanhedrin', *NTS* 10 (1964), pp. 494–9; M. Borg and J. D. Crossan, *The Last Week,* pp. 126–35; Jesus Seminar, *The Acts of Jesus,* pp. 146–8, 254–5, 354–5, 430–1.

58 They differ about who took him there. We can discount Luke's claim (Luke 22:52) that the chief priests themselves went to fetch Jesus from the Garden of Gethsemane on the grounds of sheer improbability.

59 H. Lietzmann, 'Der Prozess Jesu' in *SPAW* 14 (1931), pp 313–22, argued that the Marcan account of the trial before the Sanhedrin is untrustworthy, inferential and anti-Jewish in tendency. He believed, however, that the Sanhedrin had the power of execution based on J. Juster, *Les Juifs Dans L'empire Romain* (Paris, 1914), 2 vols.; D. R. Catchpole, 'The Problem of the Historicity of the Sanhedrin Trial' in *Moule Festschrift,* pp. 47–65; see also P. Winter, 'The Trial of Jesus', pp. 494–9.

60 J. R. Sizoo, 'Did the Jews Kill Jesus?', *Interpretation* 1 (1947), pp. 201–6; S. Zeitlin, 'The Crucifixion of Jesus Re-examined', *JQR* 31 (1940/41), p. 358.

61 S. Zeitlin, 'The Trial of Jesus', *JQR* 53, 1 (1962), p. 78; E. Rivkin, 'Beth Din, Boulé, Sanhedrin: A Tragedy of Errors', *HUCA* 46 (1975), pp. 181–99, was one of the first articles published that recognised historical circumstances changed between the early first century CE and 200 CE and how the literary sources were related to particular historical circumstances.

62 J. Blinzler, 'The Jewish Punishment of Stoning in the New Testament Period', *Moule Festschrift,* pp. 147–61. On Jesus' possible attitude towards the law and his relationship to Judaism see W. D. Davies, 'Jesus From the Jewish Point of View', *CHJ,* pp. 627–31; P. Winter, *On the Trial of Jesus;* G. Vermes, *Jesus the Jew* (London, 1973).

63 Contra H. Merkel, 'The Opposition between Jesus and Judaism', *JPHD,* pp. 129–44; other authors who put Jesus in open conflict with the law are E. Käsemann, 'Das Problem des Historischen Jesus', *Zeitschrift für Theologie und Kirche* 51 (1954), pp. 125–53; G. Bornkamm, *Jesus of Nazareth* (New York, 1960), pp. 155–63. L. E. Keck, 'Bornkamm's Jesus of Nazareth Revisited', *JR* 49 (1969), pp. 1–17, argued that Bornkamm distorted 'Judaism' in order to make Jesus appear so unique and 'evangelical'.

64 See M. Smith, 'Jesus' Attitude Toward the Law', *Papers of the Fourth World Congress of Jewish Studies* (Jerusalem, 1965), pp. 241–4. For the opposing view see H. Merkel, 'The Opposition Between Jesus and Judaism', *JPHD,* pp. 129–44; S. Rosenblatt, 'The Crucifixion of Jesus from the Standpoint of Pharisaic Law', *JBL* 75 (1956), pp. 315–21.

65 R. A. Horsley, 'High Priests and the Politics of Roman Palestine. A Contextual Analysis of the Evidence

of Josephus', *JSJ* 17, 1 (June 1986), p. 39.

66 On the relationship between the Romans and the Jewish priesthood see R. A. Horsley, 'High Priests and the Politics of Roman Palestine', *JSJ* 17, 1 (June 1986), pp. 23–55.

67 E. P. Sanders, *The Historical Figure of Jesus*, p. 266.

68 J. C. O'Neill, 'The Charge of Blasphemy at Jesus' Trial before the Sanhedrin', *Moule Festschrift*, pp. 72–7; G. Schneider, 'The Political Charge Against Jesus (Luke 23:2)', *JPHD*, pp. 403–41.

69 See F. J. Matera, 'The Trial of Jesus', *Interpretation* 45 (1991), p. 5. 'Historically, Jesus stood trial only once, before Pilate. Persuaded by the chief priests that Jesus was a political threat, Pilate sentenced him to death for insurgency' (E. P. Sanders, *The Historical Figure of Jesus*, p. 269).

70 See, for example, Thucydides 1.22.

71 Mark 15:1–15; Matt. 27:1–2, 11–26; Luke 23:1–7, 13–25; John 18:28–19:16. E. Bammel (ed.), 'The Trial of Jesus', *Moule Festschrift*; S. G. F. Brandon, *The Trial and Death of Jesus* (London, 1970); R. J. Blinzler, *The Trial of Jesus of Nazareth* (Westminster, MD, 1959); A. P. Drucker, *The Trial of Jesus from the Jewish Sources* (New York, 1907); W. Horbury, 'The Trial of Jesus in Jewish Tradition', *Moule Festschrift*, pp.102–21; K. Kertelge (ed.), *Der Prozess Gegen Jesus* (Freiburg, 1989); Jesus Seminar, *The Acts of Jesus*, pp. 149–53, 256–8, 357–60, 431–2.

72 For bibliography on Jesus' trial before Pilate see R. Brown, *The Death of the Messiah*, vol. I, pp. 665–75. Some scholars believe that an official record of the trial of Jesus before Pilate was made and preserved. See G. W. H. Lampe, 'The Trial of Jesus in the *Acta Pilati*', *JPHD*, pp. 173–82; see also W. Horbury, 'The Trial of Jesus in Jewish Tradition', *Moule Festschrift*, pp. 103–21.

73 A. N. Sherwin-White, *Roman Society and Roman Law in the New Testament* (Oxford, 1963), and A. N. Sherwin-White, 'The Trial of Christ' in *Historicity and Chronology in the New Testament* (London, 1965), pp 97–116. He wrote this in response to Juster's work, on whom most of the treatments from Lietzmann to Winter (and later Catchpole) were based. T. A. Burkill's response – 'The Condemnation of Jesus: A Critique of Sherwin-White's Thesis', *NT* 12 (1970), pp. 321–42 – appears to misunderstand the thrust of his argument, i.e. that portrayals of the trial fit the Roman imperial context and practices.

74 See H. P. Kingdon, 'Had the Crucifixion a Political Significance?' *Hibbert Journal* 35 (1936/37), pp. 556–67. There is a charge of practising magic in John 18:28ff., where the priests tell Pilate: 'If this fellow were not a criminal (doer of evil) we should not have brought him before you' (*NEB* trans.). 'Doer of evil' is a common euphemism in Roman law codes for practising magic. See M. Smith, *Jesus the Magician* (San Francisco, 1978), p. 41.

75 R. Eisler, *The Messiah Jesus and John the Baptist* (New York, 1931), p. 459.

76 Mark 15:2–4; Matt. 27:1–14; Luke 23:3; John 18:3–37. See also J. C. O'Neill, 'The Silence of Jesus', *NTS* 15 (1968/69), pp. 153–67.

77 I have not mentioned the episode with Barabbas because there is no evidence to support the alleged custom of pardoning a criminal at Passover outside Mark 15:6, Matt. 27:15 and John 18:39. See C. B. Chavel, 'The Releasing of a Prisoner on the Eve of Passover in Ancient Jerusalem', *JBL* 60 (1941), pp. 273–8; R. Brown, *The Death of the Messiah*, pp. 793ff.; P. Winter, *On the Trial of Jesus* (Berlin, 1961), pp. 91–9; H. Maccoby, 'Jesus and Barbabbas', *NTS* 16 (1969/70), pp. 55–60; R. A. Horsley, 'The Death of Jesus' in B. Chilton and C. A. Evans, *Studying the Historical Jesus* (Leiden, 1994), p. 403. They have all thoroughly discussed this incident and attribute the story to an apologetic need to blame the Jews and exonerate the Romans as a mainspring behind the story. The evangelists manufactured the story that Pilate wished to release Jesus, but the Jewish crowd (to whom a custom of Passover reprieve gave the decision) refused.

78 E. P. Sanders, *The Historical Figure of Jesus*, p. 273.

79 Matt. 27:11–26; John 18:28–19:16.

80 A. Ehrhardt, 'Was Pilate a Christian?', *CQR* 137 (1944), pp. 157–67.

81 Ernst Renan in his *Vie de Jésus* [1863] (Paris, 1992), pp. 232–4, blamed the Jews for not merely the death of Jesus but also for all the subsequent eighteen hundred years of religious persecutions by the

Christian church. J. Blinzler, *The Trial of Jesus of Nazareth* (Westminster, MD, 1959), p. 42, argued that the Jews must bear responsibility for the death of Jesus. It was against such accusations that P. Winter's book *On the Trial of Jesus* made such an impact. On anti-semitic language and polemic in the Gospels see L. K. Johnson, 'The New Testament's Anti-Jewish Slander and the Conventions of Ancient Polemic', *JBL* 108, 3 (1989), pp. 419–41; H. Maccoby, 'Is the Political Jesus Dead?', *Encounter* 46 (1976), pp. 80–9, who wrote: 'To ignore the anti-Semitism of the Gospels may be ecumenically useful and conducive to good relations in academic life between Jews and Christians; what it is not, is objective' (p. 88). D. M. Crossan, 'Anti-Semitism in the Gospel', *TS* 26 (June 1965), p. 200; R. Reuther, 'Theological Anti-Semitism in the New Testament', *The Christian Century* 85, 7 (Feb. 1968), p. 191; S. Zeitlin, 'The Crucifixion, A Libelous Accusation Against the Jews', *JQR* 55, 1 (1964), pp. 1–22; John Shelby Spong, *The Sins of Scripture* (San Francisco, 2005), section 6, 'The Bible and Anti-Semitism'.

82 D. M. Crossan, 'Anti-Semitism in the Gospel', *TS* 26 (June 1965), p. 189.

83 J. S. McLaren, *Turbulent Times? Josephus and Scholarship on Judaea in the First Century CE* (Sheffield, 1998), p. 131.

84 Philo, *Embassy to Gaius*, 38.302.

85 B. C. McGing, 'Pontius Pilate and the Sources', *CBQ* 53 (1991), p. 416. On modern bias in interpreting the sources see D. R. Schwartz, 'Josephus and Philo on Pontius Pilate', *The Jerusalem Cathedra* 3 (1983), pp. 27–31.

86 Josephus, *Ant.* 18.88ff.

87 Josephus, *Ant.* 18.60ff.

88 H. W. Kuhn, 'Die Kreuzesstrafe Während der Frühen Kaiserzeit. Ihre Wirklichkeit und Wertung in der Umweit des Urchristentums', *ANRW* 2.25.1 (1982), pp. 706ff., claims such evidence produces 'very clear consequences for understanding the historical execution of Jesus . . . he was crucified by the Roman Prefect Pontius Pilate as a political rebel.' Cf. R. A. Horsley, 'The Death of Jesus' in B. Chilton and C. A. Evans, *Studying the Historical Jesus* (Leiden, 1994), p. 411. E. Bammel, 'Crucifixion as a Punishment in Palestine', *Moule Festschrift*, p. 165, wrote: 'An execution on the cross says less about the authority which called for it than about the kind of crime with which the victim was charged.'

89 Indeed, E. P. Sanders, *Jesus and Judaism* (Philadelphia,1985), p. 306, asked: 'Why did it take so long for the Romans to execute Jesus? Why were the disciples not rounded up and killed?' See J. C. O'Neill, 'The Silence of Jesus', *NTS* 15 (1968/69), pp. 153–67.

90 E. P. Sanders, *The Historical Figure of Jesus*, p. 274.

91 Josephus, *Ant.* 18:63–4.

92 Some scholars have rejected the historicity of the inscription, but realise that it would have been much too dangerous for the Gospel writers to make up such a charge if it were not real. They were themselves trying to keep themselves free of being the followers of a known seditionist. See M. Hengel, *Was Jesus a Revolutionist?*, p. 15, versus P. L. Maier, 'The Inscription of the Cross of Jesus of Nazareth', *Hermes* 124 (1996), pp. 58–75.

93 The *titulus* corresponds extremely closely to the practice documented in Cassius Dio 54.3.7; see Suetonius, *Caligula* 32.2; Suetonius, *Domitian* 10; Eusebius, *HE* 5.1.44. On its historicity see E. Bammel, 'The *Titulus*' in *JPHD*, pp. 353–64. The Gospels actually have four slightly different wordings. *Iesus Nazarenus Rex Iudaeorum* comes from John 19:19. Bultmann doubted the historicity of the inscription. Theories of Jesus as a revolutionary figure must accept the accuracy of the *titulus* as what was written over the cross and believe that it also represented what Jesus believed.

94 J. Marcus, 'The Jewish War and the *Sitz im Leben* of Mark', *JBL* 111, 3 (1992), pp. 441–62.

95 On crucifixion as a method of execution see J. H. Charlesworth, 'Jesus and Jehohanan: An Archaeological Note on Crucifixion', *ExpTim* 84 (1972/73), pp. 147–50, and W. B. Primrose, 'A Surgeon Looks at the Crucifixion', *Hibbert Journal* 47 (1949), pp. 382–8.

96 M. Hengel, *Was Jesus a Revolutionist?*, p. 9; S. G. F. Brandon, *The Fall of Jerusalem and the Christian Church* (London, 1957), chap. 11–12, pp. 185–243; S. G. F. Brandon, *Jesus and the Zealots* (New York,

1968), chap. 5–6, pp. 221–321.

97 Modern sceptical criticism of the trial narratives derives from, repeats or enlarges on an article written by the historian H. Lietzmann, 'Der Prozess Jesu', *SPAW* (1931), pp. 313ff. His thought was to discover which narrative was closest to a first-hand source. His solution was that Mark had the kernel of historical fact which was properly elaborated in Luke, while Matthew and John contained parallel versions, differently elaborated, of a tendentious account in which the blame for the death of Christ was transferred wrongly from the Roman governor to the Jewish Sanhedrin.

98 See H. Koester, 'Jesus the Victim', *JBL* 111, 1 (1992), pp. 3–15.

99 J. P. M. Sweet, *JPHD*, p. 6. The Romans sought 'to curb popular unrest by removing one man, not for what he had said and done in itself so much as for the effect it might have on the people'.

100 See M. Smith, *Jesus the Magician*, for a thorough discussion of how Jesus was seen in his own time, by his enemies, as a practitioner of magic.

101 W. D. Davies, points out that it is precarious to try to distinguish between a 'religious' and 'political' dispute in the context of Jesus' milieu ('Jesus: From the Jewish Point of View', *CHJ*, p. 674).

102 M. Smith, *Jesus the Magician*, p. 10. W. Horbury, 'Christ as a Brigand in Ancient Anti-Chrstian Polemic', *JPHD*, pp. 183–95, begins: 'The ancient world described Christ in language readily associated with criticism of government.'

103 For a list of the men who led revolts against Rome see n. 10.

104 Josephus, *BJ* 2.306, described the procurator Florus as one who crucified 'many of the moderates' and Jewish equestrians. One did not have to be an extremist to threaten the Romans.

105 H. Montefiore, 'Revolt in the Desert (Mark 4:30ff.)?', *NTS* 8, 2 (1962), pp. 135–41; cf. E. Bammel, 'The Feeding of the Multitude', *JPHD*, pp. 211–40.

106 S. G. F. Brandon, *Jesus and the Zealots,* pp. 345–9.

107 S. G. F. Brandon, *Jesus and the Zealots,* pp. 345–9.

108 See O. Cullmann, *The State in the New Testament* (New York, 1956), pp. 8–23. In a later work, *Jesus and the Revolutionaries* (New York, 1970) he tried to disengage from his original position and portray Jesus as an 'eschatological radical' but not of this world, who was arrested by mistake.

109 R. M. Sheldon, 'Spying in Mesopotamia: The World's Oldest Classified Documents', *Studies in Intelligence* 33, 1 (spring 1989), pp. 7–12, citing C. F. Jean, 'La Langue Des Letters De Mari', *RES* (1937), fasc. 3, 110:9ff.

110 This aspect of Jesus' career is covered most thoroughly by Morton Smith in his book, *Jesus the Magician* (New York, 1977), *passim.*

111 M. Smith, *Jesus the Magician* (New York, 1977), p. 24.

112 S. Zeitlin, 'The Crucifixion of Jesus Re-examined', *JQR* 31 (1940/41), pp. 327–69; but see W. D. Davies, 'Jesus: From the Jewish Point of View' in *CHJ*, who believed 'Jesus' conception of the kingdom of God cannot be made into a programme of military and political revolt', p. 625, following M. Hengel, *Was Jesus a Revolutionist?* (Philadelphia, 1971).

113 J. Neusner, *Judaism in the Beginning of Christianity* (Philadelphia, 1984), p. 30, states that after 6 CE when Judaea became part of the Roman province of Syria, the Sanhedrin lost the authority to impose capital punishment. It must, however, be said that other experts such as P. Winter, *The Trial of Jesus*, and H. Cohn, *The Trial and Death of Jesus* (New York, 1967), disagreed with Neusner. Cohn believed that the Sanhedrin tried to save Jesus from crucifixion by Romans. E. Mary Smallwood in *The Jews Under Roman Rule from Pompey to Diocletian* (Leiden, 1981) concluded that the Sanhedrin could pass a death sentence in religious cases, but of course that sentence would be carried out by stoning.

114 See D. Seeley, 'Was Jesus like a Philosopher? The Evidence of Martyrological and Wisdom Motifs in Q, Pre-Pauline Traditions and Mark', *SBLSP* 28 (1989), pp. 540–9; B. L. Mack, *A Myth of Innocence: Mark and Christian Origins* (Philadelphia, 1988), pp. 88–9, argued that the factors that led to Jesus' execution are unclear, and that the Marcan evangelist's linkage of Jesus to his public teachings to the story of his death is a narrative fiction.

115 M. Smith, *Jesus the Magician*, p. 23.

116 St Matthew's Gospel is dated sometime after 70 CE. See Jesus Seminar, *The Acts of Jesus*, p. 8.

117 The fall of Judah and its Temple was c.587 BCE. The Second Temple was rebuilt and dedicated in the sixth year of the Persian king Darius (561 BCE). The Second Temple fell to the Romans in 70 CE. The destruction of both temples is mourned by Jews on the ninth day of Ab every year.

118 R. A. Horsley, 'The Death of Jesus' in Chilton and Evans, *Studying the Historical Jesus* (Leiden, 1994), p. 399.

119 The Jews considered these followers as heretics who, in the name of Jesus, tried to abrogate the precepts of the Torah. See S. Zeitlin, 'The Crucifixion of Jesus Re-Examined', *JQR* 32 (1941/42), pp. 175–89, on the trials of Peter, Stephen and Paul.

120 Eusebius, *HE* 3.5.3, claimed that these Jewish Christians fled to Pella *en masse* because of a prophetic revelation. S. G. F. Brandon, *The Fall of Jerusalem and the Christian Church* (London, 1951), p. 167ff., believed the flight to Pella was unhistorical. Contra M. Hengel, *The Zealots*, p. 301.

121 On the portrait of Jesus and the Christians in later sources see E. Bammel, 'Jesus As a Political Agent In a Version of the Josippon' in *JPHD*, pp. 197–209.

122 P. Winter, *The Trial of Jesus*, maintained the view that the Gospel presentation of Jesus' conflict with the Sadducees, scribes and Pharisees was not objective, but dominated by anti-Jewish *tendenz*. According to Winter's thesis, Mark already shows how, from the beginning, Jesus met with a growing resistance and animosity on the part of the Jewish spiritual and political leaders of the day; arrest, cross-examination and surrender to Pilate seemed the inevitable consequence of what was, even at the beginning, determined and inexorable opposition.

123 On the low status of Judaean governors see M. Goodman, *The Ruling Class of Judaea* (Cambridge, 1987), pp. 7–9.

Chapter 8 The Bar Kokhba Revolt (pp.180–99)

1 On dating the war see B. Kanael, 'Notes on the Dates Used During the Bar Kokhba Revolt', *IEJ* 21 (1971), pp. 39–46.

2 See the discussion in B. Isaac, 'Cassius Dio and the Revolt of Bar Kokhba', *SCI* 7 (1983/84), p. 68; on the sources see M. Stern, *Greek and Latin Authors on Jews and Judaism* (Jerusalem, 1980), vol. 2, nos 332, 342, 343, 440, 511.

3 P. Schäfer (ed.), *The Bar Kokhba War Reconsidered* (Tübingen, 2003), p. 55. On the dubiousness of the date, reliability and purpose of the *SHA* see R. Syme, *Ammianus Marcellinus and the Historia Augusta* (Oxford, 1968); R. Syme, *Emperors and Biography: Studies in the Historia Augusta* (Oxford, 1971).

4 Re-evaluation of the evidence was made at a conference at Princeton University in November 2001. The proceedings have been published by P. Schäfer (ed.), *The Bar Kokhba War Reconsidered* (Tübingen, 2003); see also B. Isaac and A. Oppenheimer, 'The Revolt of Bar Kokhba: Ideology and Modern Scholarship', *JJS* 36 (1985), p. 33.

5 L. Mildenberg, *The Coinage of the Bar Kokhba War* (Aarau, 1984); L. Mildenberg, 'The Bar Kokhba War in Light of the Coins', p. 31. L. Mildenberg, 'Rebel Coinage in the Roman Empire' in A. Kasher et al., *Greece and Rome in Eretz Israel* (Jerusalem, 1990), p. 74, noted that the Bar Kokhba money is an even more classic example of rebel coinage than that issued during the Jewish war.

6 See M. Goodman, 'Trajan and the Origins of the Bar Kokhba War' in P. Schäfer, *The Bar Kokhba War Reconsidered*, p. 26. The numismatic evidence suggests that Nerva either altered the collection of the special Jewish tax, or abolished it. See D. C. Shotter, 'The Principate of Nerva; Some Observations on the Coin Evidence', *Historia* 32 (1983), pp. 218–23; M. Goodman, 'Nerva, the Fiscus Judaicus and Jewish Identity', *JRS* 79 (1989), pp. 40–4; L. Mildenberg, *The Coinage*, p. 92.

7 See S. Applebaum, 'Point of View on the Second Jewish Revolt', *SCI* 7 (1983/84), pp. 77–87, contra Glen W. Bowersock, 'A Roman Perspective on the Bar Kochba War'. J. S. McLaren, *Turbulent Times? Josephus and Scholarship on Judaea in the First Century CE* (Sheffield, 1998), p. 134, on the years after 66

CE and relations between the Romans and the Jews becoming increasingly tense.

8   M. Goodman, 'Trajan and the Origins of the Bar Kokhba War' in P. Schäfer, *The Bar Kokhba War Reconsidered*, p. 26. On the career of the elder Trajan see G. Alföldy, 'Traianus Pater' in J. Gonzalez (ed.), *Trajano: Emperador de Roma* (Roma, 2000).

9   Goodman believes that the Great Diaspora Revolt in Cyprus, Cyrene, Egypt and Mesopotamia under Trajan was caused by a Jewish reaction to Rome's refusal to permit rebuilding the Temple in Jerusalem. See M. Goodman, 'Diaspora Reactions to the Destruction of the Temple' in J. D. G. Dunn (ed.), *Jews and Christians* (Tübingen, 1992), pp. 27–8.

10   H. G. Pflaum examined the epigraphical evidence in 'Remarques Sur le Changement de Statut Administrative de la Province de Judée . . .' *IEJ* 19, 4 (1969), p. 232, and showed that the last three governors of Judaea were *consulares* and therefore Judaea must have been a consular province with two legions before 132 CE. See M. Goodman, 'Trajan and the Origins of the Bar Kokhba War' in P. Schäfer, *The Bar Kokhba War Reconsidered*, p. 27; M. Avi-Yonah, 'When Did Judea Become a Consular Province?', *IEJ* 23 (1973), pp. 209–13; D. L. Kennedy, 'Legio VI Ferrata; The Annexation and Early Garrison of Arabia', *HSCP* 84 (1980), p. 308.

11   There are both ancient narratives and papyrus evidence from Egypt. See A. R. Birley, *Hadrian: The Restless Emperor* (London, 1997).

12   M. Goodman, 'Trajan and the Origins of the Bar Kokhba War' in P. Schäfer, *The Bar Kokhba War Reconsidered*, p. 28.

13   On the foundation date of Aelia Capitolina see L. Mildenberg, *The Coinage*, p. 100.

14   On foreign nations and religious rites see Dio Cassius 69.12.2. On evidence of pagan cults established see N. Belayche, *Judaea–Palaestina: The Pagan Cults in Roman Palaestina* (second to fourth century) (Tübingen, 2001). On the suppression see M. Goodman, 'Trajan and the Origins of the Bar Kokhba War' in P. Schäfer, *The Bar Kokhba War Reconsidered*, p. 29. On Hadrian's policy of urban reconstruction see M. T. Boatwright, *Hadrian And the Cities of the Roman Empire* (Princeton, NJ, 2000); note, however, that Aelia Capitolina is unique in its attempt to repress rather than flatter the natives.

15   See B. Isaac, 'Cassius Dio and the Revolt of Bar Kokhba', *SCI* 7 (1983/84), pp. 68–9. S. Applebaum believed that the midrashic accounts of agrarian conditions between 70 and 132, and the Halakhic rulings connected with them, are genuine sources that should be seriously considered when assessing the condition of the Jews. They attest to harassment by the Roman government against Jewish practices. See S. Applebaum, 'Points of View on the Second Jewish Revolt', *SCI* 7 (1983/84), pp. 77–8. See also S. Safrai, 'The Relations Between the Roman Army and the Jews of Eretz Israel after the Destruction of the Second Temple', *Roman Frontier Studies* (Tel Aviv, 1967), p. 225; E. Schürer, *History of the Jewish People*, 1, 2 (Edinburgh, 1890), pp. 62–3. On persecution of Jews after the uprising see D. M. Herr, 'Persecution and Martyrdom in Hadrian's Day', *Scripta Hierosolymitana* (Jerusalem, 1972), pp. 85–125. Z. Safrai, *The Economy of Roman Palestine* (London, 1994), pp.3–8, 14–15. For discussion of the causes see B. Isaac and A. Oppenheimer, 'The Revolt of Bar Kokhba: Ideology and Modern Scholarship', *JJS* 36 (1985), pp. 33–60.

16   SHA, *Hadrian* 14.2: 'At this time also the Jews began a war because they were forbidden to mutilate their genitals.' Note that the word used is 'mutilation' not 'circumcision'. Some have tried to connect Hadrian's ban on castration to his ban on circumcision. See A. M. Rabello, 'The Edicts on Circumcision as a Factor in the Bar-Kokhva Revolt' in A. Oppenheimer and U. Rappaport (eds), *The Bar Kokva Revolt: A New Approach* (Jerusalem, 1984), pp. 33–46 (H), A. M. Rabello, 'The Ban on Circumcision as a Cause of Bar-Kokhba's Rebellion', *Israel Law Review* 29 (1995), pp.176–214. For a comprehensive discussion of the circumcision issue see A. Oppenheimer, 'The Ban on Circumcision as a Cause of the Revolt: A Reconsideration' in P. Schäfer (ed.), *The Bar Kokhba War Reconsidered*, pp. 55–69. Oppenheimer believes that the ban on circumcision belonged to the repressive legislation after the Bar Kokhba Revolt and could *not* have been one of its causes (p. 68). See also B. Isaac, 'Roman Religious Policy and the Bar Kokhba War', P. Schäfer (ed.), *The Bar Kokhba War Reconsidered*, pp. 37–54;

R. Abusch, 'Negotiating Difference: Genital Mutilation in Roman Slave Law and the History of the Bar Kokhba Revolt', P. Schäfer (ed.), *The Bar Kokhba War Reconsidered*, pp. 71–91. Contra G. A. Alon, *The Jews in Their Land in the Talmudic Age* (Jerusalem, 1984), vol. 2, p. 585; E. Mary Smallwood, 'The Legislation of Hadrian and Antoninius Pius Against Circumcision', *Latomus* 18 (1959), pp. 334–47, and the addendum in *Latomus* 20 (1961), pp. 93–6.

17 Y. Tsafrir, 'Numismatics and the Foundation of Aelia Capitolina' in P. Schäfer (ed.), *The Bar Kokhba War Reconsidered*, p. 36, argues that Hadrian did not intend to name the city 'Aelia Capitolina' until after the revolt was over.

18 Y. Tsafrir, 'Numismatics and the Foundation of Aelia Capitolina' in P. Schäfer (ed.), *The Bar Kokhba War Reconsidered*, p. 32. On revolts surrounding the foundation of other colonies see B. Isaac, 'Cassius Dio on the Revolt of Bar Kokhba', *SCI* 7 (1983/84), p 71. See also M. Avi-Yonah, 'The Development of the Roman Road System in Palestine', *IEJ Reader*, II, p. 1045. Eusebius, *HE* 4.6.1–4, dates the foundation to after the war. The *Chronicon Paschale* I.474 (7th century) also dates the foundation to after the war. See Y. Z. Eliav, 'The Urban Layout of Aelia Capitolina: A New View from the Perspective of the Temple Mount' in P. Schäfer (ed.), *The Bar Kokhba War Reconsidered*, pp. 55–69. G. W. Bowersock, 'A Roman Perspective on the Bar Kokhba War', *Approaches to Ancient Judaism*, vol. II (Chico, CA, 1980), pp. 131–41; H. Eschel, 'Aelia Capitolina: Jerusalem No More' in *BAR* 23, 6 (Nov.– Dec. 1997), pp. 46–8, 73, on the coin evidence which clearly associates the founding of Aelia with Hadrian's tour.

19 Y. Meshorer, *Jewish Coins of the Second Temple Period* (Tel Aviv, 1967), pp. 92–3.

20 For a full discussion of the causes of the revolt with relevant literature see L. Mildenberg, *The Coinage of the Bar Kokhba War* (Aarau, 1984), pp. 102–9; S. Applebaum, *Prolegomena to the Study of the Second Jewish Revolt (AD 132–135)* (*BAR* Supplement Series 7, 1976), pp. 5–9. The date of 132 CE has been established by numismatic evidence, and documentary discoveries at wadi Murabba'at. See L. Mildenberg, 'The Bar Kokhba War in the Light of the Coins', *INJ* 8 (1984/85), p. 29, and J. T. Milik, *DJD* II (Oxford, 1961), p. 125.

21 Judaea had the largest Roman forces of any province relative to its size (Z. Safrai, *Economy of Roman Palestine*, p. 341): two legions plus *auxilia* on 18,000 square kilometres. The effect of the army on the residents of Judaea could not be ignored. On the socio-economic influence of the Roman army on Palestine see Z. Safrai, *Economy of Roman Palestine*, pp. 345–9. There was also a problem of taxation: taxes were particularly high in Judaea because of the special tax levied on the Jews after 70 CE (Appian, *Syr.* 50).

22 L. Mildenberg, 'The Bar Kokhba War in the Light of the Coins and Document Finds 1947–1982', *INJ* 8 (1984/85), p. 27, gives evidence that the name Shimon appears on all copper and silver coins and that the documents found in the desert in 1950/51 and 1960/61 contain the correct pronunciation 'Kosiba'.

23 See Jerome, *Against Rufinus* 3.31, where he is described as carrying a lighted blade of straw in his mouth to give the impression that he was spewing forth flames. This is a direct reference to the Messiah in 4 Esra: 'I saw how he sent forth from his mouth as it were a stream of fire, and from his lips a flaming breath, and from his tongue he shot forth a storm of sparks.' Yigael Yadin trans. from *Bar Kokhba* (New York, 1971), p. 258.

24 On a negative equation Kosiba–Koziba (liar) see P. Schäfer, *Der Bar-Kokhba Aufstand.* (Tübingen, 1981), pp. 51–2; and B. Isaac and A. Oppenheimer, 'The Revolt of Bar Kokhba', *JJS* 36 (1985), p. 57. E. Mary Smallwood, *The Jews Under Roman Rule from Pompey to Diocletian* (Leiden, 1981), p. 439.

25 See P. Schäfer, 'Bar Kokhba and the Rabbis' in P. Schäfer, *The Bar Kokhba War Reconsidered*, pp. 1–22; A. Reinhartz, 'Rabbinic Perceptions of Simeon Bar Kosiba', *JSJ* 20, 2 (Dec. 1989), p. 194, shows that there was no single view or perception of Bar Kokhba among the rabbis, or even the population as a whole, during the revolt.

26 See P. Schäfer, 'Bar Kokhba and the Rabbis', p. 8. G. S. Aleksandrov, 'The Role of Aqiba in the Bar Kokhba Rebellion', *REJ* 132 (1973), pp. 65–77, esp. 73–4, argues that the Bar Kokhba Revolt did not have a messianic leader. L. Mildenberg, *The Coinage of the Bar Kokhba War*, p. 76, also believed that Bar

Kokhba did not consider himself the Messiah and Rabbi Akiva did not consider him the Messiah either.

27 This tone can just as easily be attributed to his desperate situation as his personality. See P. Schäfer, 'Bar Kokhba and the Rabbis', p. 9.

28 A. Haimi, 'From Bar Kokhba – Greetings', *New Outlook* 4, 8 (Oct.–Nov. 1981), p. 38.

29 B. Isaac, 'Cassius Dio on the Revolt of Bar Kokhba', *The Near East Under Roman Rule* (Leiden, 1998), pp. 211–19, and R. Syme, *Sallust* (Berkeley, 1964), pp. 150ff., on Jugurtha.

30 Christian and Jewish sources mention Bar Kokhba by name. Eusebius, *HE* 4.6.1; Eusebius, *Chronicon* (ed. Schoene, II), pp. 166–7; Babylonian Talmud, *Ta'anit* 29a. These sources also mention Tinnaeus Rufus as commander not Severus, while Dio mentions Severus but not Tinnaeus Rufus. The role of Severus in the Bar Kokhba Revolt has independent confirmation in *ILS* 1056. Christian and Talmudic sources, but not Cassius Dio, mention the final siege at Bethar. Isaac concludes that the Jewish Christian literature on one hand and the Cassius Dio account on the other derive from different but 'basically trustworthy sources'.

31 On secret preparations by other rebels see Caesar, *Bellum Gallicum* (*The Gallic Wars*), 7.1, on the Gauls in 52 BC, and Tacitus, *Annals* 3.40.3, 41.3 and 43.1, concealing their plans and keeping their arms production hidden in 21 CE. On the Germans under Arminius keeping their intentions secret see Dio 56.18.5–19, Velleius Paterculus 2.118 and on the intelligence failure in general see R. M. Sheldon, 'Slaughter in the Forest: German Insurgency and Roman Intelligence Mistakes', *Small Wars and Insurgencies* 12, 3 (autumn 2001),
pp. 1–38, and R. M. Sheldon, *Intelligence Activities in Ancient Rome: Trust in the Gods, But Verify* (London: Frank Cass, 2005), chap. 10. On the Batavians see Tacitus, *Histories* 4.13; for the Britons see Tacitus, *Annals* 14.31.

32 The authenticity of this figure is confirmed by the rabbinical sources *Mid. Lam. R* 2.5 (20). Cf. S. Yeivin, *The War of Bar Kokhba* (Jerusalem, 1946) (H).

33 For evidence in northern Judaea at Wadi ed-Dalieh see N. L. Lapp and G. W. E. Nickelsburg, jun., 'Discoveries in the Wadi ed-Daliyeh', *AASOR* 41 (1974), pp. 49ff.; in a cave at Ein el-Arub between Bethlehem and Hebron, Y. Tsafrir, 'A Cave of the Bar Kokhba Period near Ain Arrub', *Qadmoniot* 8 (1975), pp. 24–7 (H), and in a cave at Khirbet el-Aqd east of Emmaus. Cf. M. Gichon, 'Military Aspects of the Bar-Kokhba Revolt and the Subterranean Hideaways', *Cathedra* 26 (1982), pp. 30–42 (H), and E. Damati, 'Four Bar Kokhba Coins from Khirbet el-Aqd', *INJ* 4 (1980), pp. 27–9. Further sites have been found to the north and south of Beth Govin (Khirbet Tayyibet el-Ism). Some archaeologists and historians doubt that all these hide-outs are exclusively related to the Bar Kokhba Revolt. They cite the fact that caves and underground passages were used by bandits and terrorists in many periods. See B. Isaac, 'Bandits in Judaea and Arabia', *HSCP* 88 (1984), pp. 171–203; B. Isaac and A. Oppenheimer, 'The Revolt of Bar Kokhba: Ideology and Modern Scholarship', *JJS* 36 (1985), p. 43, and the list of articles by Israeli archaeologists on p. 44, n. 49. See also A. Kloner and B. Zissu, 'Hiding Complexes in Judaea: An Archaeological and Geographical Update on the Area of the Bar Kokhba Revolt' in P. Schäfer, *The Bar Kokhba War Reconsidered*, pp. 181–216. For a list of the sites see M. Gichon, 'The Bar Kochba War: A Colonial Uprising Against Imperial Rome', *RIHM* 42 (1979) p. 18, n. 15. The available evidence shows that the main fighting took place in Judaea: W. Eck, 'The Bar Kokhba Revolt: The Roman Point of View', *JRS* 89 (1999), pp. 76–8; A. Kloner and B. Zissu, 'Hiding Complexes in Judaea: An Archaeological and Geographical Update on the Area of the Bar Kokhba Revolt' in P. Schäfer, *The Bar Kokhba War Reconsidered*, p. 189.

34 See J. L. Teicher, 'Are the Bar Kokhba Documents Genuine?', *JJS* 4, 1 (1953), pp. 39–40, who challenged Solomon Zeitlin's assertion that the documents are medieval forgeries.

35 I. Eldad, 'In Praise of Bar Kokhba', *JQ* 30 (winter 1984), pp. 113–19.

36 Bar Kokhba is often described as authoritarian. See the Letters from Simon bar Kokhba discovered at the caves of Wadi Murabba'at and Nahal Hever in the 1960s by Yigael Yadin's team.

37 Certainly by the time of Hadrian, the *frumentarii* were intelligence agents both in Rome and in the

legions. See R. M. Sheldon, *Intelligence Activities in Ancient Rome; Trust in the Gods, But Verify*, chap. 12.

38 S. Applebaum, *Prolegomena*, p. 21 and n. 174 quoting Tosephta Betzah II, 13.

39 S. Applebaum, *Prolegomena*, p. 21.

40 S. Applebaum, *Prolegomena*, p. 21 quoting Mid. Lam R. II.

41 S. Applebaum, *Prolegomena*, p. 21, n. 177, quoting M. Bekh, V, 3.

42 S. Applebaum, *Prolegomena*, p. 21, n. 179, quoting Sif. Deut, para. 143, p. 344; Jer, BQ IV, 4a. On intelligence supervision of a Greek religious centre under Hadrian see *ILS* 9473 where a *frumentarius* is directing building at Delphi.

43 S. Applebaum, *Prolegomena*, p. 21.

44 Mark 6:27 where a *speculator* executes John the Baptist. See also R. M. Sheldon, *Intelligence Activities in Ancient Rome*, chap. 9, 'Roman Military Intelligence'.

45 They may have included discharged soldiers settled in Judaea. See S. Applebaum, *Prolegomena*, p. 21, citing Tosephta Betzah II, 6; Z. Safrai, *Roman Frontier Studies* (1967), p. 225.

46 See S. Applebaum, *Prolegomena*, p. 21.

47 For the disposition of troops in the region see J. F. Keppie, 'The Legionary Garrison of Judaea Under Hadrian', *Latomus* 32 (1973), pp. 859–64; G. W. Bowersock, 'The Annexation and Initial Garrison of Arabia', *ZPE* 5 (1970), pp. 37–47; S. Applebaum, *Prolegomena*, pp. 44–9.

48 M. Avi-Yonah, *The Jews of Palestine* (Oxford, 1976), pp. 18–19, who gives 1,300,000 as the Jewish population on the eve of the Bar Kokhba War.

49 See J. Patrich, 'Hideouts in the Judean Wilderness – Jewish Revolutionaries and Christian Ascetics Sought Shelter and Protection in Cliffside Caves', *BAR* 15, 5 (Sept.–Oct. 1989), pp. 32–42; A. Kloner and B. Zissu, 'Hiding Complexes in Judaea: An Archaeological and Geographical Update on the Area of the Bar Kokhba Revolt' in P. Schäfer, *The Bar Kokhba War Reconsidered*, pp. 181–216.

50 B. Isaac and I. Roll, 'Judaea in the Early Years of Hadrian's Reign' in B. Isaac, *Under Roman Rule. Selected Papers* (Leiden, 1998), pp. 182–97, for the disposition of the legions in the area.

51 See J. M. C. Toynbee, *The Hadrianic School* (Cambridge, 1934), pp. 199–221. Gichon observes that no official issue would bear the name of Judaea after the renaming of the province of Syria 'Palestina' on the Roman victory (M. Gichon, 'The Bar Kokhba War', *RIHM* 42 (1979), p. 86, n. 13).

52 On the two-year occupation of Jerusalem by Bar Kokhba's forces and the coin evidence see B. Kanael, 'Notes on the Dates Used During the Bar Kokhba Revolt', *IEJ* 21 (1971), p. 45. This is in contradiction to L. Mildenberg, 'The Bar Kokhba War in the Light of the Coins and Document Finds 1947–1982', *INJ* 8 (1984/85), p. 28, who believed that there was no mint at Jerusalem, and that Shimon ben Kosiba did not succeed in conquering Jerusalem or holding it. See also L. Mildenberg, 'Bar Kokhba in Jerusalem?' *Schweizer Münzblätter* 105 (1977), pp. 1–6.

53 Appian, *Syr.* 50. 252 and Christian authors lend support to the view that the city fell into Jewish hands and was later reconquered by Roman troops. See Eusebius, *Demonstratio Evangelica* 6.18.10; Eusebius, *HE* 4.5,2; 5.12. See Isaac and Oppenheimer, 'The Revolt of Bar Kokhba', *JJS* 36 (1985), p. 54, n. 95, on evidence from Wadi Murabba'at which they consider uncertain. See S. Applebaum, *Prolegomena*, p. 27, and M. Smallwood, *The Jews Under Roman Rule*, p. 446, for further patristic sources. On the coin evidence see J. Meyshan, 'The Legion which Reconquered Jerusalem in the War of Bar Kokhba, AD 132–5', *PEQ* 90 (1958), pp. 19–26.

54 The coin legend 'For the Freedom of Jerusalem' may just be a hope. It has also been interpreted as meaning Jerusalem had been captured, or even that the coins were minted in Jerusalem. See B. Isaac and A. Oppenheimer, p. 55, n. 98; S. Applebaum, *Prolegomena*; L. Mildenberg, *HSCP*, p. 323.

55 L. Mildenberg, *The Coinage of the Bar Kokhba* War, p. 85.

56 Dio 69.12.3. E. Cary translation. Loeb Classical Library edn.

57 B. Isaac and A. Oppenheimer, 'The Revolt of Bar Kokhba: Ideology and Modern Scholarship', *JJS* 36 (1985), p. 54.

58 M. Gichon, 'The Bar Kokhba War', *RIHM* 42 (1979), p. 88, n. 15. Many items of spoil and captured

Roman paraphernalia were found in the caves – an illustration of this point. See also A. Kloner, 'Underground Hiding Complexes from the Bar Kokhba War in the Judaean Shephelah', *BA* (Dec. 1983), pp. 210–21. See the references in St Jerome to underground crevices and deep caves, cited in Y. Yadin, *Bar Kokhba*, p. 23.

59 M. Gichon, 'The Bar Kokhba War', *RIHM* 42 (1979), p. 88.

60 W. Eck, 'The Bar Kokhba Revolt: The Roman Point of View', p. 81, believed that the XXII Deiotariana was a candidate for being the second legion stationed in Jerusalem and that it was destroyed during the revolt. Julius Africanus in Eusebius' *Chronicle* suggests a Roman unit was got rid of by a party of Pharisees who arranged for the soldiers to be given poisoned wine! M. Avi Yonah, *The Jews of Palestine* (Oxford, 1976), pp. 12–13, believes the story. See also S. Applebaum, *Prolegomena*, p. 26; M. Avi-Yonah, 'The Development of the Roman Road System in Palestine', *IEJ Reader*, II; G. W. Bowersock, 'A Roman Perspective on the Bar Kokhba War' in W. S. Green (ed.), *Approaches to Ancient Judaism*, pp. 132–4, disagreed. In 99 CE, the legion had been part of the garrison in Egypt, but it was probably rushed from here to Judaea in 131/2 and there totally annihilated. The legion, anxious to reach the Jewish heartland, and just having left a friendly coast, was negligent in reconnaissance and screening its column. This is not unusual for a Roman legion; see chap. 6 on the marching habits of Cestius Gallus. Menachem Mor, 'Two Legions – The Same Fate?' (The Disappearance of the Legion IX Hispana and XXII Deiotariana)', *ZPE* 62 (1986), p. 270, n. 40, with bibliography, believed that the Legio XXII was destroyed before the Bar Kokhba Revolt; cf. J. Schwartz, 'Ou a Passé La Legio XXII Deiotariana?', *ZPE* 76 (1989), pp. 101–2. L. J. F. Keppie, 'The History and Disappearance of the Legion XXII Deiotariana' in A. Kasher et al., *Greece and Rome in Eretz Israel* (Jerusalem, 1990), pp. 54–61, noted that the disappearance of a legion does not always have to have a military explanation.

61 L. Mildenberg, *The Coinage*, p. 87.

62 *Inscriptiones Graecae ad res Romanas Pertinentes Auctoritate et Impensis Academiae Inscriptionum et Litterarum Humaniorum Collectae et Editae* (Paris: Leroux, 1906–, 6 vols), III, pp. 174–5, cited by E. Schürer, *History of the Jewish People*, vol. 1, p. 549; Eusebius, *Chronicle Hadrian*, year 16; M. Gichon, 'The Bar Kochba War', *RIHM* 42 (1979), p. 90. Knowledge of the units brought to Judaea during the war is very much dependent on chance discoveries of inscriptions. See B. Isaac and A. Oppenheimer, 'The Revolt of Bar Kokhba', *JJS* 36 (1985), p. 56 and n. 101.

63 L. Mildenberg, 'The Bar Kokhba War in the Light of the Coins', *INJ* 8 (1984/85), p. 29; D. Barag, 'A Note on the Geographical Distribution of Bar-Kokhba Coins', *INJ* 4 (1980), pp. 30–3.

64 A. Kloner and B. Zissu, 'Hiding Complexes in Judaea: An Archaeological and Geographical Update on the Area of the Bar Kokhba Revolt' in P. Schäfer, *The Bar Kokhba War Reconsidered*, p. 181, who identified 125 sites. Kloner and Zissu believe the number of settlements inhabited during the Bar Kokhba Revolt (800–1,000) is consistent with Cassius Dio's report.

65 W. Eck, 'The Bar Kokhba Revolt: The Roman Point of View', *JRS* 89 (1999), p. 81, n. 41, on the coin evidence and p. 88 on the arch; W. Eck, 'Ein Spiegel der Macht. Lateinische Inschriften Römischer Zeit in Judaea/Syria Palaestine', *ZDPV* 117 (2001), pp. 47–63.

66 Dio Cassius 69.13.2 says: 'Many outside nations, too, were joining them through eagerness for gain, and the whole earth, one might almost say, was being stirred up over the matter' (trans. by E. Cary). Fifteen letters written by Bar Kokhba, or his scribes, to his officers in en-Gedi were found in 1960 by Yigael Yadin in the Cave of Letters at Nahal Hever. Eight letters are in Aramaic, three (or possibly five) are in Hebrew, and two are in Greek. The writer of one Greek letter, although a member of Bar Kokhba's army, was unable to write in the Semitic tongues. See G. Howard and J. C. Shelton, 'The Bar Kokhba Letters and Palestinian Greek', *IEJ* 23 (1973), pp. 101–12. For the report on the letters see Y. Yadin, 'Expedition D', *IEJ* 11 (1961), pp. 40–52; the Greek letters were published by B. Lifshitz, 'Papyrus Grecs Du Desert De Judea', *Aegyptus* 42 (1962), pp. 240–58. M. Mor, 'The Bar-Kokhba Revolt and Non-Jewish Participants', *JJS* 36, 2 (autumn 1985), pp. 200–9, rejects the evidence from the letters, but accepts Dio Cassius.

67 M. Gichon, 'The Bar Kokhba Revolt', *RIHM* 42 (1979), p. 92.

68 See Sallust, *Jugurthine War*, 5; Tacitus, *Annals* 4.23, on the revolts of Tacfarinas; Tacitus, *Annals* 4.73, on the Frisians; Tacitus, *Annals* 3.41, 44, on the Treveri and Aedui; Tacitus, *Histories* 4.12, on Civilis; and B. Isaac, 'Cassius Dio and the Revolt of Bar Kokhba', *SCI* 7 (1983/84), pp.74–5.

69 Dio Cassius 69.13.2. On the relationship of the two consular commanders Tineius Rufus and Julius Severus see S. Applebaum, 'Tineus Rufus and Julius Severus' in *Judaea in Hellenistic and Roman Times* (Leiden, 1988), pp. 120–3.

70 Altogether Hadrian had sixty to eighty thousand men fighting under his command in Judaea (M. Gichon, 'The Bar Kokhba Revolt', *RIHM* 42 (1979), p. 93).

71 Support for Bar Kokhba on the other side of the Jordan has been a topic of considerable interest lately. Werner Eck proposed that erasures on inscriptions from Gerasa show that the governor of Arabia T. Haterius Nepos may have suffered a local *damnatio memoriae* because of his strong efforts to repress the spread of the Jewish revolt into Arabia. The erasures were certainly not done by the Romans since Nepos had a brilliant career. Indeed, a recently published Sofartic text refers to the three years of the rebellion 'against the tyrant Nepos'. This shows that there was a real possibility that the Bar Kokhba Revolt spread into northern Trans-jordan. Another document shows the use of Hebrew as promoted by Bar Kokhba. These documents amply demonstrate that Jews living in Arabia and in the Province of Judaea belonged to a single Jewish society whose internal ties overrode provincial boundaries. These provincial boundaries were disregarded in their residences, marriages and property holdings. See *JRS* 4 (1991), pp. 336–44.

72 M. Gichon, 'The Bar Kokhba Revolt', *RIHM* 42 (1979), p. 95.

73 For similar tactics see Tacitus, *Annals*, 13, on Corbulo's Armenian campaign, and B. Levick, *Roman Colonies in Southern Asia Minor* (Oxford, 1967), chap. 4 and appendix 5, on the Homanadensian war in southern Asia Minor. See also B. Isaac, 'Cassius Dio and the Revolt of Bar Kokhba', *SCI* 7 (1983/84), p. 75, who noted that these were wars of conquest, not campaigns against insurgents.

74 There is controversy over which emperor received the advice, and what war was being discussed. See S. Applebaum 'For Whom Did Apollodorus Write the Poliorketika?' in S. Applebaum, *Judaea in Hellenistic and Roman Times* (Leiden, 1989), pp. 111–16.

75 M. Gichon, 'The Bar Kokhba Revolt', *RIHM* 42 (1979), p. 96.

76 See Y. Yadin, 'Expedition D' in *The Expedition to the Judaean Desert*, 1960, *IEJ* 11, 1 (1961), pp. 41–52. Y. Yadin, *IEJ* 12 (1962), 248ff. Cf. P. Benoit et al., *Discoveries in the Judaean Desert* II: *Les Grottes de Murabba'at* (Oxford, 1961), pp. 124ff.

77 A. Haimi, 'From Bar Kokhba – Greetings', *New Outlook* 4, 8 (Oct.–Nov. 1981), p. 42.

78 A. Haimi, 'From Bar Kokhba – Greetings', *New Outlook* 4, 8 (Oct.–Nov. 1981), p. 43. There was also evidence in the caves in the desert of occupation in the Chalcolithic period, the First Temple period, and the Christian and Byzantine periods. See J. Patrich, 'Hideouts in the Judean Wilderness', *BAR* 15, 5 (Sept.–Oct. 1989), pp. 32–42.

79 W. Eck, 'The Bar Kokhba Revolt: The Roman Point of View', *JRS* (1999), p. 84.

80 Salome Komaise discussed in H. M. Cotton and A Yardeni, *Aramaic, Hebrew and Greek Documentary Texts from Nahal Hever and Other Sites. Discoveries in the Judaean Desert* XXVII (Oxford, 1997), pp. 166ff.

81 W. Eck, 'The Bar Kokhba Revolt: The Roman Point of View', *JRS* (1999), p. 84, with the inscriptional evidence.

82 Babylonian Talmud, *Gittin* 57–58; Midrash Rabbah, *Lamentations* 2.2–4; Mishnah, *Ta'anit* 4.6.135. Bethar has not been excavated, but surface exploration has produced plans of the extant remains of the Roman siege works and the walls of the Roman camps near the site. See B. Isaac and A. Oppenheimer, 'The Revolt of Bar Kokhba', *JJS* 36 (1985), pp. 40, with the relevant bibliography in n. 30.

83 On the reliability of rabbinical sources see Z. Safrai, *The Economy of Roman Palestine* (London, 1994), pp. 14–15; S. Applebaum, *Prolegomena*, p. 52; E. Schürer, *History of the Jewish People*, vol. 1, p. 551.

84 Jer. 52:12ff. puts the burning of the Temple by Nebuchadrezzar's guard on the tenth of Ab; 2 Kings 25:8 gives the day as the seventh of Ab; Jewish tradition celebrates it on the ninth of Ab.

85 A. Haimi, 'From Bar Kokhba – Greetings', *New Outlook* 4, 8 (Oct.–Nov. 1981), p. 38.

86 W. Eck, 'The Bar Kokhba Revolt: The Roman Point of View', *JRS* (1999), p. 81.

87 W. Eck, 'The Bar Kokhba Revolt: The Roman Point of View', *JRS* (1999), p. 78.

88 W. Eck, 'The Bar Kokhba Revolt: The Roman Point of View', *JRS* (1999), pp. 82–3.

89 M. C. Fronto, *De Bello Parthico*, 2 on the losses on the Roman side; M. C. Fronto, *Letter to Marcus Aurelius* (trans. by C. R. Haines).

90 Dio 69.14.3.

91 I. Eldad, 'In Praise of Bar Kokhba', *JQ* 30 (winter 1984), p. 119.

92 L. Mildenberg, *The Coinage*, p. 97.

93 Y. Aharoni, 'Expedition B – The Cave of Horror', *IEJ* 11 (1962), pp. 186–99, compares the defenders to the martyrs on Masada.

94 R. A. Freund and Rami Arav, 'Return to the Cave of Letters. What Still Lies Buried?', *BAR* 27, 1 (Jan.–Feb. 2001), pp. 25–39.

95 M. D. Herr, 'Persecutions and Martyrdom in Hadrian's Days', *Scripta Hierosolimitana* 23 (1972), pp. 82–125; P. Schäfer, *Der Bar-Kokba Aufstand*, pp. 194–235, disagrees.

96 B. Isaac and A. Oppenheimer, 'The Revolt of Bar Kokhba', *JJS* 36 (1985), p. 59.

97 For discussion of the village figures see S. Applebaum, *Prolegomena*, pp. 34–5, who believed that the evidence from the archaeological surveys carried out in Judaea and Samaria confirmed the genuineness of Dio's report. Cf. A. Kloner, 'Underground Hiding Complexes from the Bar Kokhba War in the Judaean Shephelah', *BA* (Dec. 1983), pp. 210–21.

98 Dio 69.14.3.

99 S. Applebaum, 'Points of View', *SCI* 7 (1983/84), p. 86.

100 Y. Harkabi, *The Bar Kokhba Syndrome* (Chappaqua, NY, 1983), p. 33, n. 12; M. Smallwood, *The Jews Under Roman Rule*, p. 454; *DJD* II, pp. 37–48.

101 Y. Harkabi, *The Bar Kokhba Syndrome*, p. 34.

102 Y. Yadin, *Bar Kokhba*, p. 17.

103 Y. Yadin, *Bar Kokhba*, p. 18; E. Schürer, *A History of the Jewish People*, vol. I, rev. edn, p. 533, n. 88.

104 Why does Dio say the world joined hands with the rebels, as did many non-Jews, because of their lust for booty?

105 Carl von Clausewitz, *On War*, edited and trans. by Michael Howard and Peter Paret (Princeton, 1976), 1.11, 1.23, 8.6.

106 On the destruction of Jerusalem see Appian, *Syrian Wars* 8.50; Eusebius, *Demonstratio Evangelica* 6.13; See also Eusebius, *Chronicle*, Hadrian year 18 on the Jews being banned from Jerusalem. He also claimed that the Romans set up an idol of a pig in marble, which signified the subjugation of the Jews to Roman authority (Hadrian, Year 19).

107 Y. Harkabi, *The Bar Kokhba Syndrome*, pp. 34–5; M. Gichon, 'The Bar Kochba War', *RIHM* 42 (1979), p. 97.

108 I. Eldad, 'In Praise of Bar Kokhba', *JQ* 30 (winter 1984), p. 116.

109 I. Eldad, 'In Praise of Bar Kokhba', *JQ* 30 (winter 1984), p. 118.

110 L. Mildenberg, *The Coinage*, p. 91; Glen W. Bowersock, 'A Roman Perspective on the Bar Kochba War', insultingly calls him 'a would-be prince'. The coins and documents show him to have been a very real ruler albeit for a short time and over a limited territory.

111 I. Eldad, 'In Praise of Bar Kokhba', *JQ* 30 (winter 1984), p. 118.

Postscript Part II: Spying for Yahweh (pp.200–11)

1 B. Halpern, *The Emergence of Israel in Canaan* (Chico, CA, 1983), p. 239.

2 *CHJ*, vol. 1, p. 1.

3   *CHJ*, vol. 1, p. 2. C. Herzog and M. Gichon's statement that the Jews created a national commonwealth that lasted twelve hundred years is wishful thinking. See their *Battles of the Bible*, p. 29.

4   *CHJ*, vol. 1, p. 2.

5   *CHJ*, vol. 1, p. 2.

6   *CHJ*, vol. 1, p. 3.

7   T. R. Hobbs, *A Time for War. A Study of Warfare in the Old Testament* (Wilmington, DE, 1989), p. 72.

8   Judg. 4–5, 6–7.

9   J. Price, *Jerusalem Under Siege, The Collapse of the Jewish State 66–70 CE* (Leiden, 1992), p. 121.

10 J. Price, *Jerusalem Under Siege*, p. 121. Josephus points out the disadvantage of being lightly armed (*BJ* 2.512, 2.543, 3.15, 3.113). The advantages to being swift and mobile are pointed out in *BJ* 2.543, 3.207, 3.275.

11 J. Price, *Jerusalem Under Siege*, p. 122.

12 Prov. 24:6: 'By stratagems you shall wage war, and victory [comes] through much planning.' Prov. 20:18: 'Devices are established by plan; wage war by stratagems'. Prov. 11:14: 'For want of stratagems an army falls, but victory [comes] through much planning.' On the Hebrew vocabulary see A. Malamat, 'Conquest of Canaan', *RIHM* 42 (1979), p. 39.

13 Num. 21:14; Josh. 10:13.

14 See Polybius 5.70.6. Antiochus III used a stratagem which lured the Ptolemaic garrison down from the summit in 218 BCE. See Josephus, *BJ* 4.1.8. In 67 CE, one of Vespasian's generals, Placidus, enticed the Jewish defenders from a mountain top using the same ruse. See A. Malamat, 'Conquest of Canaan', *RIHM* 42 (1979), p. 46 and n. 38. See also Frontinus 2.5.8, 3.10 and Polyaenus 5.10.4.

15 J. W. Wallach, 'The Wars of the Maccabees', *RIHM* 42 (1979), p. 54.

16 D. G. Hansen, 'Intelligence, Deception and Military Operations in the Ancient Near East', p. 27, n. 55.

17 For night attacks see Ai, Josh. 8:3; Gibeon, Josh. 10:9; Abimelech's ambush against Shechem, Judg. 9:34; Saul's deployment against the Ammonites besieging Jabesh–Gilead, 1 Sam. 11:11; and possibly David's raid on the Amalekite camp, 1 Sam. 30:17. D. G. Hansen, 'Intelligence, Deception and Military Operations in the Ancient Near East', pp. 24–7; A. Malamat, 'Conquest of Canaan', *RIHM* 42 (1979), p 50.

18 Y. Yadin, *Warfare in Biblical Lands*, vol. 1, pp. 111–12.

19 On the lack of siege capability by the Israelites see P. B. Kern, *Ancient Siege Warfare* (Bloomington, IN, 1999), chap. 3. See also R. G. Bolling, 'Joshua, Book of', *Anchor Bible Dictionary*, III, pp. 1002–15.

20 Tacitus, Histories, 5.9.2. See J. Price, *Jerusalem Under Siege*, p. 6.

21 See J. S. McLaren, *Turbulent Times? Josephus and Scholarship on Judaea in the First Century CE* (Sheffield, 1998), p. 131.

22 M. Hengel, *The Zealots*, p. 384.

23 Tacitus, *Histories* 5.5, on the Jewish religion; Dio Cassius, 65.6.2ff., for the oracle that led to the Jewish War; Tacitus, *Histories* 5.13, and Suetonius, *Vespasian* 4, 5, on the prophecies of salvation shortly before the conquest of the Temple.

24 D. M. Rhoads, *Israel in Revolution 6–74 CE* (Philadelphia, 1976), pp. 22–3.

25 M. I. Finley, *Ancient Slavery and Modern Ideology* (Harmondsworth, 1982), p. 17.

26 R. A. Gabriel, *The Military History of Ancient Israel*, p. 60.

27 J. A. Soggin, *A History of Israel* (Philadelphia, 1984), pp. 32–3.

28 *CHJ*, vol. 1, p. vi: 'Much textual and exegetical work remains to be done before Judaism can be satisfactorily interpreted.'

29 M. Bloch, *The Historian's Craft* (Manchester, 1954), p. 183.

30 See the remarks of K. W. Whitelam, 'Recreating the History of Israel', *JSOT* 35 (1986), pp. 45–70.

31 K. W. Whitelam, 'Recreating the History of Israel', *JSOT* 35 (1986), pp. 45–6.

32 J. Cargill, 'Ancient History in Western Civ Textbooks', *History Teacher* 34, 3 (May 2001), pp. 297–326.

BIBLIOGRAPHY

History – General
Cargill, Jack, 'Ancient History in Western Civ Textbooks', *History Teacher* 34, 3 (May 2001), pp. 297–326.
Hobsbawm, Eric, *Bandits*, New York: Delaware Press; London: Weidenfeld & Nicolson, 1969.
    Primitive Rebels, New York: W. W. Norton, 1965.
    and T. Ranger, *The Invention of Tradition*, Cambridge: Cambridge University Press, 1983.

Military History – General
Austin, N. J. E., and N. B. Rankov, *Exploratio*, London and New York: Routledge, 1995.
Baron, Salo W., 'The Ancient and Medieval Periods: Review of the History' in S. W. Baron and George S. Wise (eds), *Violence and Defense in the Jewish Experience*: Papers prepared for a seminar on violence and defence in Jewish history and contemporary life, Tel Aviv University, 18 August–4 September 1974, Philadelphia: Jewish Publication Society of America, 1977.
Clausewitz, Carl Von, *On War*, ed. and trans. by Michael Howard and Peter Paret, Princeton: Princeton University Press, 1976.
Delbrück, Hans, *Warfare in Antiquity*, trans. by W. J. Renfroe, jun., Lincoln, NE: University of Nebraska Press, 1975, 3 vols.
Gabriel, Richard A., and W. Boose, jun., *The Great Battles of Antiquity*, Westport, CT: Praeger, 1995.
Gichon, Mordechai, 'The West Bank: The Geostrategic and Historical Aspects' in A. Shalev, *The West Bank: Line of Defense*, New York: Praeger, 1985, pp. 178–201.
Hansen, D. G., 'Intelligence, Deception and Military Operations in the Ancient Near East', *II International Conference on Intelligence and Military Operations*, US Army War College, Carlisle Barracks, PA, 11–15 May 1987.
Haswell, Jock, *The Tangled Web: The Art of Tactical and Strategic Deception*, Wendover: J. Goodchild, 1985.
Kagan, Donald, *On the Origins of War*, New York: Doubleday, 1995.
Kohn, Hans, *The Idea of Nationalism*, New York: Macmillan, 1944.
Leiden, C., and K. M. Schmitt, *Revolution in the Modern World*, Englewood Cliffs, NJ: Prentice Hall Inc., 1968.
May, E. C., E. C. Stadler and J. F. Votaw, *Ancient and Medieval Warfare*, Wayne, NJ: Avery Publishing Group Inc., 1984.
Neilson, K., and B. J. C. McKercher (eds), *Go Spy The Land. Military Intelligence in History*, New York: Praeger, 1992.
Neustadt, R. E., and E. May, *Thinking in Time*, NY: Free Press, 1986.
Oppenheimer, M., *The Urban Guerrilla*, Chicago: Quadrangle Books, 1969.
Shafer, B. C., *Nationalism: Myth and Reality*, New York: Harcourt Brace, 1955.
Sheldon, Rose Mary, 'Spying in Mesopotamia: The World's Oldest Classified Documents', *Studies in Intelligence* 33/1 (spring 1989), pp. 7–12.
Spaulding, O., and H. Nickerson, *Ancient and Medieval Warfare*, New York: Barnes & Noble Books, 1993.

Tatum, T. C., *The Evangelical Right and a Biblical Forecast of Military Operations in the Middle East*, US Army War College, Carlisle Barracks, PA, April 1986.

Van Creveld, Martin, *Technology and War. From 2,000 BC to the Present*, New York: Free Press, 1989.

Wavell, A. P., 'Night Attacks – Ancient and Modern' in *Soldiers and Soldiering*, London: Jonathan Cape, 1953, pp. 159–174.

Whaley, Barton, *Stratagem: Deception and Surprise in War*, Cambridge, MA: Centre for International Studies, Massachusetts Institute of Technology, 1969.

Near Eastern History, Biblical Studies, History of Israel

Aharoni, Y., M. Avi-Yonah, A. Rainey and Z. Safrai, *The Macmillan Bible Atlas*, New York: Macmillan, 1993, 3rd edn.

Albright, William F., *From the Stone Age to Christianity*, Baltimore: Johns Hopkins University Press, 1957.
  'The Israelite Conquest of Canaan in the Light of Archaeology', *BASOR* 74 (1939), pp. 11–23.

Alt, Albrecht, *Essays on Old Testament History and Religion*, Garden City, NY: Doubleday, 1968.
  The Formation of the Israelite State in Palestine. Essays in Old Testament History and Religion, Oxford: Blackwell, 1966.

Amiran, David, 'A Revised Earthquake Catalogue of Palestine', *IEJ* 1, 4 (1961), pp. 223–46.

Aschkenasy, Nehama, *Eve's Journey. Feminine Images in Hebraic Literary Tradition*, Philadelphia: University of Pennsylvania Press, 1986.

Bal, Mieke (ed.), *Anti-Covenant: Counter-Reading Women's Lives in the Hebrew Bible*, *JSOT* Supplement 8, Sheffield: Almond Press, 1989.
  Lethal Love. Feminist Literary Readings of Biblical Love Stories, Bloomington, IN: Indiana University Press, 1987.

Bellis, Alice Ogden, *Helpmates, Harlots, and Heroes. Women's Stories in the Hebrew Bible*, Louisville, KY: Westminster/John Knox Press, 1994.

Ben-Sasson, H. H. (ed.), *A History of the Jewish People*, I–III, Cambridge, MA; London: Weidenfeld & Nicolson: 1976

Bimson, John, *Redating the Exodus and Conquest*, Sheffield: JSOT Press, 1978.

Brenner, Athalya, *The Israelite Woman: Social Role and Literary Type in Biblical Narrative*, Sheffield: JSOT Press, 1985.

Brenner, Athalya (ed.), *The Feminist Companion to the Bible*, Sheffield: JSOT Press, 1997.

Bright, John, *A History of Israel*, Philadelphia: Westminster Press, 1981.
  Early Israel in Recent History Writing. A Study in Method, London: SCM Press, 1956.

Brown, C. A., *No Longer Be Silent: First Century Jewish Portraits of Biblical Women*, Louisville, KY: Westminster/John Knox Press, 1992.

Buttrick, G. A. (ed.), *Interpreter's Dictionary of the Bible*, Nashville: Abingdon, 1962.

Callahan, T., *Secret Origins of the Bible*, Altadena, CA: Millennium Press, 2002.

Campbell, A. F., *The Ark Narrative*, Missoula, MT: Scholars' Press, 1975.

Campbell, Edward F., jun., and D. N. Freedman (eds), *The Biblical Archaeologist Reader,* Sheffield: Almond Press in association with American Schools of Oriental Research, 1983.

Coote, R. B., and M. P. Coote, *Power, Politics, and the Making of the Bible: An Introduction*, Minneapolis: Fortress Press, 1990.

Cotton, Hannah, and A. Yardeni, *Discoveries in the Judaean Desert XXVII: Documents from Nahal Hever and Other Sites with an Appendix Containing Alleged Qumran Texts (The Seiyâl Collection II)*, Oxford: Clarendon Press, 1997.

Crim, Keith (ed.), *The Interpreter's Dictionary of the Bible*, Nashville: Abingdon Press, 1976.

Cross, Frank M., *Canaanite Myth and Hebrew Epic*, Cambridge: Harvard University Press, 1973.

Davies, P. R., *In Search of 'Ancient Israel'*, *JSOT* Supplement Series 148, Sheffield: Sheffield Academic Press, 1992.

Davies, W. D., and Louis Finkelstein (eds), *The Cambridge History of Judaism*, Cambridge: Cambridge University Press, 1984.

Dever, William G., 'Whatchamacallit. Why It Is So Hard to Name Our Field', *BAR* 29, 4 (July–Aug. 2003), pp. 40–9, 82–3.

What Did the Biblical Writers Know and When Did They Know It?, Grand Rapids, MI; Cambridge, UK: Eerdmans, 2001.

Douglas, J. D., N. Hillyer, F. F. Bruce (eds), *The Illustrated Bible Dictionary*, Wheaton, IL: Tyndale House, 1980.

Dowley, T. (ed.), *Discovering the Bible*, Grand Rapids, MI: Eerdmans, 1986.

Fewell, Danna Nolan, 'Feminist Reading of the Hebrew Bible: Affirmation, Resistance and Transformation', *JSOT* 39 (1987), pp. 77–87.

Finkelstein, Israel, and N. A. Silberman, *The Bible Unearthed*, New York: Free Press, 2001.

Finley, M. I., *Ancient Slavery and Modern Ideology*, Harmondsworth: Penguin, 1982.

Friedman, Richard E., *The Exile and Biblical Narrative; The Formulation of the Deuteronomic and Priestly Works*, Chico, CA: Scholars Press, 1981.

Who Wrote the Bible?, San Francisco: HarperCollins, 1997.

Gibson, J. C. L., *Canaanite Myths and Legends*, Edinburgh: T. & T. Clark, 1974, 2nd edn.

Ginzburg, H. L., 'The Legend of King Keret: A Canaanite Epic of the Bronze Age', *BASOR* Supplementary Studies 2–3, American Schools of Oriental Research, 1946.

Gunkel, Hermann, *The Folktale in the Old Testament*, Sheffield: Almond Press, 1987.

Halpern, Baruch, *The First Historians. The Hebrew Bible and History*, San Francisco: Harper & Row, 1988.

Hastings, James (ed.), *Dictionary of the Bible*, New York: Scribner, 1963.

Hauer, Chris, jun., 'Anthropology in Historiography', *JSOT* 39 (1987), pp. 15–21.

Laffey, A. L., *An Introduction to the Old Testament. A Feminist Perspective*, Philadelphia: Fortress Press, 1988.

Layman, C. M. (ed.), The *Interpreter's One-Volume Commentary on the Bible*, Nashville: Abingdon Press, 1971.

Lemche, Niels Peter, 'Is It Still Possible to Write a History of Ancient Israel?' *SJOT* 8 (1994), pp. 165–90.

Mendenhall, George, 'Ancient Israel's Hyphenated History' in D. N. Freeman and D. F. Graf (eds), *Palestine in Transition,* Sheffield: Almond Press, ASOR, 1983.

Miller, J. Maxwell, 'In Defense of Writing a History of Israel', *JSOT* 39 (1987), pp. 53–7.

Na'aman, Nadav, *Borders and Districts in Biblical Historiography,* Jerusalem: Simor, 1986.

Nelson, Richard D., *The Double Redaction of the Deuteronomic History*, Sheffield: JSOT Press, 1981.

Netanyahu, Benzion, et al. (eds), *The World History of the Jewish People,* Tel-Aviv: Jewish History Publications, 1964–, 8 vols.

Niditch, Susan (ed.), *Text and Tradition: The Hebrew Bible and Folklore*, Atlanta, GA: Scholars Press, 1990.

Polybius, *The Histories*, trans. by W. R. Paton, Cambridge: Loeb Classical Library, 1960, 6 vols.

Pfeiffer, Charles F., 'Epic Elements in Biblical History', *Journal of Hebraic Studies* 1, 2 (1970), 1–15.

Ras Shamra and the Bible, Grand Rapids, MI: Baker Book House, 1962.

Sicker, Martin, *The Rise and Fall of the Ancient Israelite States*, Westport, CT: Praeger, 2003.

Silberman, Neil Asher, and Y. Goren, 'Faking Biblical History', *Archaeology* (Sept.–Oct. 2003), pp. 20–9.

Spong, John Shelby, *Born of a Woman*, San Francisco: Harper, 1992.

Rescuing the Bible from Fundamentalism, San Francisco: Harper, 1991.

The Sins of Scripture, San Francisco: Harper, 2005.

Thompson, T. L., *Early History of the Israelite People*, Leiden: Brill, 1992.

Van Seters, J., *In Search of History: Historiography in the Ancient World and the Origins of Biblical History*, New Haven: Yale University Press, 1983.

Vaux, Roland de, *The Early History of Israel*, Philadelphia: Westminster Press, 1978.

Wellhausen, Julius, *Prolegomena to the History of Ancient Israel*, Gloucester, MA: Peter Smith, 1973.

Whitelam, Keith W., 'Recreating the History of Israel', *JSOT* 35 (1986), pp. 45–70.

Whybray, R.N., *The Making of the Pentateuch; A Methodological Study*, Sheffield: JSOT, 1987.

Zevit, Ziony, *The Religions of Ancient Israel. A Synthesis of Parallactic Approaches*, London and New York: Continuum, 2001.

Biblical Warfare and the Conquest

Ackerman, James S., 'Prophecy and Warfare in Early Israel: A Study of the Deborah and Barak Story', *BASOR* 220 (1975), pp. 5–13.

Cline, Eric H., *Jerusalem Besieged*, Ann Arbor, MI: University of Michigan Press, 2004.

— *The Battles of Armageddon. Megiddo and the Jezreel Valley from the Bronze Age to the Nuclear Age*, Ann Arbor, MI: University of Michigan Press, 2000.

Craigie, P. C., *The Problem of War in the Old Testament*, Grand Rapids: Eerdmans, 1978.

Drews, R., 'The "Chariots of Iron" of Joshua and Judges', *JSOT* 45 (Oct. 1989), pp. 15–23.

Fredriksson, H., *Jahwe Als Krieger*, Lund: C. W. K. Gleerup, 1945.

Gabriel, Richard A., *The Military History of Ancient Israel*, Westport, CT: Praeger, 2003.

Gale, Richard Nelson, *Great Battles of Biblical History*, London: Hutchinson, 1968.

Goodman, Martin, and A. J. Holladay, 'Religious Scruples in Ancient Warfare', *CQ* 36 (1986), pp. 151–71.

Grintz, J. M., 'Ai Which Is Beside Beth-Aven. A Re-examination of the Identity of Ai', *Biblica* 42 (1961), pp. 201–16.

Hansen, D. G., 'Intelligence, Deception and Military Operations in the Ancient Near East', *II International Conference on Intelligence and Military Operations*, US Army War College, Carlisle Barracks, PA, 11–15 May 1987.

Hauer, Chris, jun., 'From Alt to Anthropology. The Rise of the Israelite State', *JSOT* 36 (1986), pp. 3–15.

Herzog, Chaim, and Mordechai Gichon, *Battles of the Bible*, London: Greenhill Books, 1997.

Hobbs, T. R., *A Time for War. A Study of Warfare in the Old Testament*, Wilmington, DE: Michael Glazier, 1989.

Jones, G. H., ' "Holy War" or "Yahwe War"?', *VT* 25 (1975), pp. 642–58.

Kang, Sa-M, *Divine War in the Old Testament and in the Ancient Near East*, *BZAW* 177, Berlin and New York: W. de Gruyter, 1989.

Kaufmann, Yehezkel, *The Biblical Account of the Conquest of Canaan*, Jerusalem: The Magnes Press, The Hebrew University, 1985, 2nd edn.

Kern, P. B., *Ancient Siege Warfare*, Bloomington, IN: University of Indiana Press, 1999.

Lind, Millard C., *Yahweh is a Warrior. The Theology of Warfare in Ancient Israel*, Scottsdale, PA: Herald Press, 1980.

McCarthy, Dennis J., 'Some Holy War Vocabulary in Joshua 2', *CBQ* 33 (1971), pp. 228–30.

Malamat, Abraham, 'Conquest of Canaan', *RIHM* 42, Tel Aviv: Edition de la Commission Israelienne d'Histoire Militaire, 1979; reprinted in *History of Biblical Israel. Major Problems and Minor Issues*, Leiden: Brill, 2001, pp. 25–52, 68–96.

— 'Conquest of Canaan: Israelite Conduct of War According to Biblical Tradition', *Encyclopedia Judaica Year Book*, 1975/76 (Jerusalem, 1976), pp. 25–52.

— 'How Inferior Israelite Forces Conquered Fortified Canaanite Cities', *BAR* 8 (1982), pp. 24–35.

— *The Proto-History of Israel: A Study in Method*, Winona Lake, IN: 1983.

Miller, J. Maxwell, 'Archaeology and the Israelite Conquest of Canaan: Some Methodological Observations', *PEQ* (July–Dec. 1977), pp. 86–93.

Miller, P. D., *The Divine Warrior in Early Israel*, Cambridge, MA: Harvard University Press, 1973.

Rösel, Hartmut, 'Studien zur Topographie der Kriege in den Büchern Josua und Richter', *ZDPV* 92, 1 (1976), pp. 10–46; and *ZDPV* 92, 2 (1976), pp. 159–90.

Rosenthal, Monroe, and Mozeson, Isaac, *Wars of the Jews: A Military History from Biblical to Modern Times*, New York: Hippocrene Books, 1990.

Salonen, A., *Notes on Wagons and Chariots in Ancient Mesopotamia*, Helsinki: *Studia Orientalia Edidit Societas Orientalis Fennica*, vol. 14, no. 2, 1950.

Schwally, F., *Semitische Kriegsaltertumer I: Der Heilige Krieg im Alten Israel*, Leipzig: Dieterich, 1901.

Smend, R., *Yahweh War and Tribal Confederation*, Nashville: Abingdon Press, 1970, trans. by Max Gray Rogers from the 2nd edn of R. Smend, *Jahwekrieg und Stämmebund*, Göttingen: Vandenhoeck & Ruprecht, 1963.

Stolz, Fritz, *Jahwes und Israels Kriege. Kriegstheorien und Kriegserfahrungen im Glauben des Alten Israel*,

Zürich: Zwingli Verlag, 1972.

Van der Lingen, A., *Les Guerres de Yahvé: L'implication de YHWH Dans Les Guerres d'Israël Selon Les Livres Historiques de l'Ancien Testament*, Paris: Cerf, 1990.

Von Rad, Gerhard, *Holy War in Ancient Israel*, trans. and ed. by Marva J. Dawn, Grand Rapids, MI: Eerdmans, 1990. Translation of *Der Heilige Krieg im Alten Israel*, Göttingen: Vandenhoeck & Ruprecht, 1969.

Weimar, P., 'Die Jahwekriegerzälungen in Exodus 14, Josua 10, Richter 4 und 1 Samuel 7', *Biblica* 57 (1976), pp. 38–73.

Weinfeld, M., 'Divine Intervention in War in Ancient Israel and in the Ancient Near East' in H. Tadmor and M. Weinfeld (eds), *History and Historiography and Interpretation: Studies in Biblical and Cuneiform Literatures*, Jerusalem: Magnes Press, 1983, pp. 121–47.

Weippert, M., ' "Heiliger Krieg" in Israel und Assyrien: Kritische Anmerkungen zu Gerhard von Rads Konzept des "Heilige Krieg" im Alten Israel', *ZAW* 84, 4 (1972), pp. 460–93.

Wright, G. E., 'Epic of Conquest', *BA* 3 (1940), pp. 25–40.

Yadin, Yigael, *The Art of Warfare in Biblical Lands. In the Light of Archaeological Study*, New York: McGraw Hill; London: Weidenfeld & Nicolson, 1963.

Younger, K. Lawson, *Ancient Conquest Accounts: A Study in Ancient Near Eastern and Biblical History*, JSOT Supplement Series 98, Sheffield: Sheffield Academic Press, 1990.

Israelites, Canaanites and the History of Early Israel

Aharoni, A., 'Nothing Early and Nothing Late: Re-writing Israel's conquest', *BA* 39 (1976), pp. 55–76.

Albright, W. F., 'The Israelite Conquest of Canaan in the Light of Archaeology', *BASOR* 74 (1939), pp. 11–23.

Callaway, Joseph A., 'A New Perspective on the Hill Country Settlement of Canaan in Iron Age I', pp. 31–49, in J. N. Tubb (ed.), *Palestine in the Bronze and Iron Ages: Papers in Honour of Olga Tufnell*, Institute of Archaeology Occasional Publications 11, London: Institute of Archaeology, 1985, pp. 31–49.

Campbell, Edward F., jun., 'The Amarna Letters and the Amarna Period', *BA* 23, 1 (1960), pp. 2–22.

Davies, Philip R., *In Search of 'Ancient Israel'*, JSOT Supplement Series 148, Sheffield: Sheffield Academic Press, 1992.

Dever, William G., 'Archaeological Data on the Israelite Settlement: A Review of Two Recent Books', *BASOR* 284 (1991), pp. 77–90.

'Ceramics, Ethnicity and the Question of Israel's Origin', *BA* 58 (1995), pp. 200–12.

'Cultural Continuity, Ethnicity in the Archaeological Record and the Question of Israelite Origin', *Eretz Israel* 24 (1993), pp. 22–33.

'How to Tell a Canaanite from an Israelite' in H. Shanks et al., *The Rise of Ancient Israel*, Washington, DC: Biblical Archaeological Society, 1992, pp. 26–60.

What Did the Biblical Writers Know and When Did They Know It?: What Archaeology Can Tell Us About the Reality of Ancient Israel, Grand Rapids, MI: Eerdmans, 2001.

Who Were the Early Israelites and Where Did They Come From? Grand Rapids, MI: Eerdmans, 2003.

'Will the Real Israel Please Stand Up? Archaeology and Israelite Historiography. Part I', *BASOR* 297 (1995), pp. 261–80.

Finkelstein, Israel, 'Ethnicity and Origin of the Iron Age I Settlers in the Highlands of Canaan: Can the Real Israel Stand Up?' *BA* 59 (1996), pp. 198–212.

'Searching for Israelite Origins', *BAR* 14, 5 (Sept.–Oct. 1988), pp. 34–42.

The Archaeology of Israelite Settlement, Jerusalem: Israel Exploration Society, 1988.

'The Emergence of Early Israel. Anthropology, Environment and Archaeology', *JAOS* 110 (1990), pp. 682–5.

'The Great Transformation. The Conquest of the Highland Frontiers and the Rise of the Territorial States' in T. E. Levy (ed.), *The Archaeology of Society in the Holy Land*, New York: Facts on File, 1995, pp. 349–65.

and Nadav Na'aman, *From Nomadism to Monarchy. Archaeological and Historical Aspects of Early Israel*, Jerusalem: Yad Izhak Ben-Zvi; Washington, DC: Biblical Archaeology Society, 1994.

Freeman, David Noel, and David F. Graf (eds), *Palestine in Transition*, Sheffield: Almond Press, ASOR, 1983.

Fritz, Volkmar, 'Conquest or Settlement? The Early Iron Age in Palestine', *BA* 50 (June 1987), pp. 84–100.

'Israelites and Canaanites. You Can Tell Them Apart', *BAR* 28, 4 (July–Aug. 2002), pp. 28–63.

'The Israelite "Conquest" in the Light of Recent Excavations at Khirbet el-Meshash', *BASOR* 241 (1981), pp. 61–73.

Geus, C. H. J. de, *The Tribes of Israel*, Assen/Amsterdam: Van Gorcum, 1976.

Glueck, Nelson, *Rivers in the Desert,* Philadelphia: Jewish Publication Society of America; London: Weidenfeld & Nicolson, 1959.

Gottwald, Norman K., 'Domain Assumptions and Societal Models in the Study of Pre-Monarchic Israel' in Charles E. Carter and Carol L. Meyers (eds), *Community, Identity and Ideology. Social Science Approaches to the Hebrew Bible*, Winona Lake, IN: Eisenbrauns, 1996, pp. 170–81.

'Israel's Emergence in Canaan', *BR* 55 (Oct. 1989), pp. 26–34.

The Hebrew Bible – A Socio-literary Introduction, Philadelphia: Fortress Press, 1985.

The Politics of Ancient Israel, Louisville, KY: Westminster/John Knox Press, 2001.

The Tribes of Yahweh: A Sociology of the Religion of Liberated Israel 1250–1050 BC, Maryknoll, NY: Orbis Books, 1979.

Gottwald, Norman K. (ed), The *Bible and Liberation: Political and Social Hermeneutics*, Maryknoll, NY: Orbis Books, 1983.

Greenberg, Moshe, *The Hab/piru*, New Haven: American Oriental Society, 1955.

Halpern, Baruch, *The Emergence of Israel in Canaan*, Chico, CA: Scholars Press, 1983.

Hauser, A. J., 'Israel's Conquest of Palestine: A Peasant's Rebellion?' *JSOT* 7 (1978), pp. 2–19.

Hayes, A., and J. Maxwell Miller (eds), *Israelite and Judaean History*, Philadelphia: Westminster Press, 1977.

Herion, Gary A., 'The Impact of Modern and Social Science Assumptions on the Reconstruction of Israelite History' in Charles E. Carter and Carol L. Meyers (eds), *Community, Identity and Ideology. Social Science Approaches to the Hebrew Bible*, Winona Lake, IN: Eisenbrauns, 1996, pp. 230–57.

Kempinski, A., 'How Profoundly Canaanized Were the Early Israelites?', *ZDPV* 108 (1992), pp. 1–17.

Lapp. Paul, 'The Conquest of Palestine in the Light of Archaeology', *CTM* 38 (1968), pp. 495–548.

Prelude to Israel's Past, Peabody, MA: Hendrickson, 1998.

Lemche, Niels Peter, *Ancient Israel: A New History of the Israelite Society*, Sheffield: Sheffield Academic Press, 1988.

Early Israel: Anthropological and Historical Studies on the Israelite Society Before the Monarchy, Leiden: Brill, 1985.

The Canaanites and Their Land: the Tradition of the Canaanites, Sheffield: JSOT Press, 1991.

The Israelites in History and Tradition, Louisville, KY: Westminster/John Knox Press, 1998.

Leonard, A., jun., 'Archaeological Sources for the History of Palestine: The Late Bronze Age', *BA* 52, 1 (Mar. 1989), pp. 4–55.

McCarter, P. Kyle, jun., 'A Major New Introduction to the Bible. Norman Gottwald's Sociological–Literary Perspective', *Bible Review* 11, 2 (summer 1986), pp. 42–50.

Mendenhall, George, 'The Hebrew Conquest of Palestine', *Biblical Archaeologist* 25 (1962), pp. 66–87.

Reprinted in *Community, Identity and Ideology. Social Science Approaches to the Hebrew Bible*, Winona Lake, IN: Eisenbrauns, 1996, pp. 152–69.

Miller, J. M., 'The Israelite Occupation of Canaan' in H. Hayes and J. Maxwell Miller (eds), *Israelite and Judaean History*, Philadelphia: Westminster Press, 1977, pp. 213–79.

Na'aman, Nadav, 'The "Conquest of Canaan" in the Book of Joshua and in History' in I. Finkelstein and N. Na'aman, *From Nomadism to Monarchy*, Jerusalem: Yad Izhak Ben-Zvi; Washington, DC: Biblical Archaeology Society, 1994, pp. 218–30.

Sasson, Jack, 'On Choosing Models for Recreating Israelite Pre-Monarchic History', *JSOT* 21 (1981), pp. 3–24.

Schoors, A., 'The Israelite Conquest: Textual Evidence in the Archaeological Argument' in E. Lipinski (ed.),

The Land of Israel: Cross-Roads of Civilization, Leuven: Uitgeverij Peeters, 1985, pp. 77–92.

Shanks, Hershel, 'A "Centrist" at the Center of Controversy. *BAR* Interviews Israel Finkelstein', *BAR* 28, 6 (Nov.–Dec. 2002), pp. 38–49, 64–6.

'Israel's Emergence in Canaan – *BR* Interviews Norman Gottwald', *Bible Review* 5, 5 (Oct. 1989), pp. 26–34.

and W. G. Dever, B. Halpern, P. K. McCarter, jun. (eds), *The Rise of Ancient Israel*. Symposium at the Smithsonian Institution, 26 October 1991, Washington, DC: Biblical Archaeological Society, 1992.

Singer, Itamar, 'Egyptians, Canaanites and Philistines in the Period of the Emergence of Israel' in I. Finkelstein and N. Na'aman, *From Nomadism to Monarchy*, Jerusalem: Yad Izhak Ben-Zvi; Washington, DC: Biblical Archaeology Society, 1994, pp. 282–338.

Soggin, J. A., *A History of Israel*, Philadelphia: Westminster, 1984.

Stager, Lawrence E., 'The Archaeology of the Family in Ancient Israel', *BASOR* 260 (autumn 1985), pp. 1–35.

Thompson, Thomas L., *The Early History of the Israelite People*, Leiden: Brill, 1994.

'The Origin Tradition of Ancient Israel' in *Perspectives in Religious Studies* 7 (1980), pp. 96–113.

Whitelam, Keith W., 'Israel's Traditions of Origin: Reclaiming the Land', *JSOT* 44 (June 1989), pp. 19–42.

'Recreating the History of Israel', *JSOT* 35 (1986), pp. 45–70.

'The Identity of Early Israel: The Realignment and Transformation of Late Bronze–Iron Age Palestine', *JSOT* 63 (1994), pp. 57–87.

Yadin, Yigael, 'Is the Biblical Conquest of Canaan Historically Reliable?' *BAR* 8 (1982), pp. 16–23.

Yeivin, Shmuel, *The Israelite Conquest of Canaan*, Istanbul: Nederlands Historisch-Archaeologisch Instituut in Het Nabije Oosten, 1971.

Zertal, Adam, 'Israel Enters Canaan – Following the Pottery Trail', *BAR* (Sept.–Oct. 1991), pp. 28–49.

Old Testament – General

Bellis, Alice Ogden, *Helpmates, Harlots, Heroes. Women's Stories in the Hebrew Bible*, Louisville, KY: Westminster/John Knox Press, 1994.

Bird, Phyllis, 'Images of Women in the Old Testament' in R. R. Reuther (ed.), *Religion and Sexism*, New York: Simon & Schuster, 1974.

Brown, C. A., *No Longer Be Silent: First Century Jewish Portraits of Biblical Women*, Louisville, KY: Westminster/John Knox Press, 1992.

Camp, Claudia V., and Carole R. Fontaine (ed.), 'Women, War, and Metaphor: Language and Society in the Study of the Hebrew Bible', *Semeia* 61 (1993).

Currid, J., *Ancient Egypt and the Old Testament*, Grand Rapids, MI: Baker Books, 1997.

Day, Peggy L. (ed.), *Gender and Difference in Ancient Israel*, Minneapolis: Fortress Press, 1989.

Emerton, J. A. (ed.), *Studies in the Historical Books of the Old Testament*, *VT* Supplement 30, Leiden: Brill, 1979.

Frank, H. T., and W. L. Reed (eds), *Translating and Understanding the Old Testament. Essays in Honor of Herbert G. May*, Nashville: Abingdon Press, 1970.

Gaster, Theodore Herzl, *Myth, Legend, and Custom in the Old Testament; A Comparative Study with Chapters from Sir James G. Frazer's Folklore in the Old Testament*, New York: Harper & Row, 1969.

Goitein, S. D., 'Women as Creators of Biblical Genres', *Prooftexts* 8 (1988), pp. 1–33.

Halpern, Baruch, 'Radical Exodus Re-Dating Fatally Flawed', *BAR* (Nov.–Dec. 1987), pp. 56–61.

'The Exodus from Egypt: Myth of Reality?' in H. Shanks et al., *The Rise of Ancient Israel*, Washington, DC: Biblical Archaeological Society, 1992, pp. 87–113.

Hoffmeier, J. K., *Israel in Egypt: The Evidence for the Authenticity of the Exodus Tradition*, New York: Oxford University Press, 1997.

Myers, C. L., and M. O'Connor (eds), *The Word of the Lord Shall Go Forth: Essays in Honor of David Noel Freedman*, Winona Lake: Eisenbrauns, 1983.

Na'aman, N., *Borders and Districts in Biblical Historiography: Seven Studies in Biblical Geographical Lists*, Jerusalem Biblical Studies 4, Jerusalem: Simor, 1986.

Noth, Martin, *A History of Pentateuchal Traditions*, trans. with an introduction by Bernhard W. Anderson,

Englewood Cliffs, NJ: Prentice Hall, 1972.

The Deuteronomistic History, Sheffield: JSOT Press, 1981.

The History of Israel, New York: Harper, 1960.

Überlieferungsgeschichtliche Studien, Halle: Niemeyer, 1943.

O'Brien, M. A., *The Deuteronomistic History Hypothesis: A Reassessment*, Göttingen: Vandenhoeck & Ruprecht, 1989.

Rainey, Anson F. (ed.), *Egypt, Israel and Sinai*, Tel Aviv: Tel Aviv University, 1987.

Redford, Donald B., 'An Egyptological Perspective on the Exodus Narrative' in A. F. Rainey (ed.), *Egypt, Israel and Sinai*, Tel Aviv: Tel Aviv University, 1987, pp. 137–61.

Stern, Ephraim, 'Pagan Yahwism: The Folk Religion of Ancient Israel', *BAR* 27, 3 (May–June 2001), pp. 21–9.

Van Seters, J., 'Tradition and Social Change in Ancient Israel' in *Perspectives in Religious Studies* 7 (1980), pp. 96–113.

Weippert, Manfred, *The Settlement of the Israelite Tribes in Palestine*, trans. from the German by James D. Martin, London: SCM Press, 1971.

Whitelam, K. W., *The Invention of Ancient Israel: The Silencing of Palestinian History*, New York: Routledge, 1996.

Book of Joshua

Albright, William F., 'Archaeology and the Date of the Hebrew Conquest of Palestine', *BASOR* 58 (1935), pp. 10–18.

Assis, Elie, 'Animadversiones – The Choice to Serve God and Assist His People: Rahab and Yael', *Biblica* 85, 1 (2004), pp. 82–90.

Beek, M. A., 'Rahab in the Light of Jewish Exegesis' in W. C. Delsman et al., *Von Kanaan bis Kerala*, Festschrift für Prof. Mag, Dr J. P. M. van der Ploeg O. P. zur Vollendung des Siebzigsten Lebensjahres am 4 Juli 1979, Neukirken-Vluyn: Neukirchener Verlag, 1982, pp. 37–44.

Bienkowski, Piotr, 'Jericho Was Destroyed in the Middle Bronze Age, Not the Late Bronze Age', *BAR* 16, 5 (Sept.–Oct. 1990), pp. 45–6, 69.

Bird, Phyllis, 'The Harlot as Heroine; Narrative Art and Social Presupposition in Three Old Testament Texts', *Semeia* 46 (1989), pp. 119–39.

Boling, Robert G., and Wright G. Ernest, *Joshua: A New Translation with Notes and Commentary*, Anchor Bible Dictionary, vol. 6, Garden City, NY: Doubleday, 1982.

Callaway, Joseph A., 'Ai: Problem Site for Biblical Archaeologists', *Archaeology and Biblical Interpretation*, Atlanta, 1987, pp. 87–99.

'New Evidence on the Conquest of Ai', *JBL* 87, 3 (Sept. 1968), pp. 312–20.

Cross, Frank Moore, 'A Response to Zakovich's "Successful Failure of Israelite Intelligence" ' in S. Niditch (ed.), *Text and Traditions: The Hebrew Bible and Folklore*, Atlanta, GA: Scholars Press, 1990. pp. 99–104.

Foerster, G., 'Jericho', *NEAEHL*, pp. 674–97.

Franklin, N. P., *The Stranger Within Their Gates*, Duke University PhD dissertation, 1990.

Gray, J., *Joshua, Judges, and Ruth*, Grand Rapids, MI: Eerdmans, 1967.

Grintz, J. M, 'Ai which is Beside Beth-Aven. A Re-examination of the Identity of Ai', *Biblica* 42 (1961), pp. 201–16.

Halpern, Baruch, 'Gibeon: Israelite Diplomacy in the Conquest Era', *CBQ* 37 (1975), pp. 303–16.

Harris, J. Gordon, Cheryl A. Brown, Michael S. Moore, *Joshua, Judges, Ruth*, Peabody, MA: Hendrickson; Carlisle, Cumbria: Paternoster Press, 2000.

Holladay, John S., jun., 'The Day(s) the Moon Stood Still', *JBL* 87, 2 (June 1968), pp. 166–78.

Isserlin, B. S. J., 'The Israelite Conquest of Canaan: A Comparative Review of the Arguments Applicable', *PEQ* 115 (1983), pp. 85–94.

Kearney, P. J., 'The Role of the Gibeonites in the Deuteronomic History', *CBQ* 35 (1973), pp. 1–19.

Kenyon, Kathleen M., and T. A. Holland, *Excavations at Jericho*, London: British School of Archaeology in Jerusalem, 1960–1983, 5 vols.

Langlamet, F., 'Josué II – Rahab et Les Espions', *RB* 78 (1971), pp. 321–54.

Lipschitz, O., 'Pre-Israelite Residues in the Conquest Stories' in A. Rofé and Y. Zakovich (eds), *Isac Leo Seeligmann Volume: Essays on the Bible and the Ancient World*, vol. I, Jerusalem: E. Rubinshtain, 1983, pp. 100–110, with earlier literature (H).

Livingston, D., *Khirbet Nisya: 1979–2002. Excavation of the Site with Related Studies in Biblical Archaeology*, Akron, PA: Associates for Biblical Research, 2002.

McCarthy, D.J., 'The Theology of Leadership in Joshua 1–9', *Bib* 52 (1971), pp. 165–75.

Margalit, Baruch, 'The Day the Sun Did Not Stand Still: A New Look at Joshua X 8–15', *VT* 42, 4 (1992), pp. 466–91.

Marquet-Krause, J., 'La Deuxieme Campagne de Fouilles á Ay, (1934) Rapport Sommaire', *Syria* 16, 4 (1935), pp. 325–45.

Miller, J. Maxwell, 'Archaeology and the Israelite Conquest of Canaan: Some Methodological Observations', *PEQ* 109 (1977), pp. 87–93.

and Gene M. Tucker, *The Book of Joshua*, Cambridge: Cambridge University Press, 1974.

Moran, W., 'The Repose of Rahab's Israelite Guests' in G. Rinaldi (ed.), *Studi Sull'Oriente e La Bibbia*, Genoa: G. Buccellati, 1967, pp. 273–84.

Nelson, R. D., *Joshua: A Commentary*, Louisville, KY: Westminster/John Knox Press, 1997.

'Josiah in the Book of Joshua', *JBL* 100 (1981), pp. 531–40.

Newman, Murray L., 'Rahab and the Conquest' in J. T. Butler, E. W. Conrad and B. C. Ollenburger (eds), *Understanding the Word. Essays in Honor of Bernhard W. Anderson*, *JSOT* Supplement Series 37, Sheffield: JSOT Press, 1985, pp. 167–81.

Noth, Martin, 'Bethel und Ai', *PJB* 31 (1935), pp. 7–29.

Das Buch-Josua, Tübingen: Mohr Siebeck, 1953.

Ottosson, Magnus, 'Rahab and the Spies' in H. Behrens et al. (eds), *DUMU-E2 DUB-BA-A Studies in Honor of A. Sjoberg*, Philadelphia: Occasional Papers of the Samuel Noah Kramer Fund, 1989, pp. 419–27.

Pritchard, James B., 'Gibeon', *NEAEHL*, vol. 2, pp. 511–14.

Gibeon Where the Sun Stood Still. The Discovery of the Biblical City, Princeton: Princeton University Press, 1962.

Rainey, A., 'Bethel is still Beitin', *Westminster Theological Journal* 33 (1970/71), pp. 175–88.

Rösel, H., Studien zur Topographie der Kriege in den Büchern Josua und Richter', *ZDPV* 91 (1975), pp. 159–90; 92 (1976), pp. 10–46.

Rowlett, Lori L., 'Disney's Pocahontas and Joshua's Rahab in Postcolonial Perspective' in George Aichele, *Culture, Entertainment and the Bible*, *JSOT* Supplement 309, Sheffield: Sheffield Academic Press, 2000, pp. 66–75.

Joshua and the Rhetoric of Violence. A New Historicist Analysis, Sheffield: Sheffield Academic Press, 1996.

Sawyer, John F. A., 'Joshua 10:12–14 And The Solar Eclipse of 30th September 1131 BC.', *PEQ* 104 (July–Dec. 1972), pp. 139–46.

Schulte, H., 'Beobachtungen zum Begriff der Zona im A.T.', *ZAW* 104 (1992), pp. 255–62.

Soggin, J. Alberto, *Joshua. A Commentary*, trans. by R. A. Wilson, London: SCM Press, 1972.

Spina, F. A., 'Reversal of Fortune', *BR* 17, 4 (Aug. 2001), pp. 24–30, 53–4.

Stephenson, F. R., 'Astronomical Verification and Dating of Old Testament Passages Referring to Solar Eclipses', *PEQ* 107 (1975), pp. 107–20.

Tucker, G. M., 'The Rahab Saga (Joshua 2): Some Form Critical and Traditio-Historical Observations' in James M. Efird (ed.), *The Use of the Old Testament in the New and Other Essays. Studies in Honor of William Franklin Stinespring*, Durham, NC: Duke University Press, 1972, pp. 66–86.

Ussishkin, D., 'The Walls of Jericho', *BAIAS* 8 (1988/89), pp. 85–90.

Van Seters, J., 'Joshua's Campaign of Canaan and Near Eastern Historiography', *SJOT* 2 (1990), pp. 1–12, and in V. Philips Long, *Israel's Past in Present Research. Essays on Ancient Israel Historiography*, Winona Lake, IN: Eisenbrauns, 1999, pp. 170–80.

Vriezen von Carel, J. H., 'Khirbet Kefire – Eine Oberflächenuntersuchung', *Sonderdruck aus ZDPV* 91 (1975), pp. 135–58.

Wagner, Siegfried, 'Die Kundschaftergeschichten im Alten Testament', *ZAW* 76 (1964), pp. 255–69.

Weippert, Manfred, 'Jericho in der Eisenzeit', *ZDPV* 92 (1976), pp. 105–48.

Wiseman, D. J., 'Ai in Ruins', *Buried History* 7 (1971), pp. 4–6.

'Rahab of Jericho', *The Tyndale House Bulletin* 14 (June 1964), pp. 8–11.

Wood, Bryant, 'Dating Jericho's Destruction: Bienkowski is Wrong on All Counts', *BAR* 16, 5 (Sept.–Oct. 1990), pp. 45, 47–9, 68.

'Did the Israelites Conquer Jericho?', *BAR* (Mar.–April, 1990), pp. 44–57.

Yadin, Yigael, *Military and Archaeological Aspects of the Conquest of Canaan in the Book of Joshua*, Jerusalem: Jewish Education Committee Press, 1963.

Zakovich, Yair, 'Humor and Theology or the Successful Failure of Israelite Intelligence: A Literary–Folkloric Approach in Joshua 2' in S. Niditch (ed.), *Text and Traditions: The Hebrew Bible and Folklore*, Atlanta, GA: Scholars Press, 1990, pp. 75–104.

Zevit, Ziony, 'Archaeological and Literary Stratigraphy in Joshua 7–8', *BASOR* 251 (1983), pp. 28–33.

Book of Judges

Ackerman, Susan, *Warrior, Dancer, Seductress, Queen*, New York: Doubleday, 1998.

Albright, W. F., 'Midianite Donkey Caravans' in H. T. Frank and W. L. Reed (eds), *Translating and Understanding the Old Testament. Essays in Honor of Herbert G. May*, Nashville: Abingdon Press, 1970, pp. 198–205.

'The Song of Deborah in Light of Archaeology', *BASOR* 62 (Apr. 1936), pp. 26–31.

Alter, Robert, 'Samson Without Folklore' in S. Niditch (ed.), *Text and Tradition: The Hebrew Bible and Folklore*, Atlanta: Scholars Press: 1990, pp. 47–56.

Bal, Mieke, 'Delilah Decomposed' in *Lethal Love. Feminist Literary Readings of Biblical Love Stories*, Bloomington, IN: Indiana University Press, 1987, pp. 37–67.

Murder and Difference: Gender, Genre and Scholarship on Sisera's Death, Bloomington, IN: Indiana University Press, 1988.

Bird, Phyllis A., 'The Harlot as Heroine. Narrative Art and Social Presupposition in Three Old Testament Texts', *Semeia* 46 (1989), pp. 119–40.

Bledstein, Adrien Janis, 'Is Judges a Woman's Satire of Men Who Play God?' in A. Brenner (ed.), *Judges: A Feminist Companion to the Bible*, Sheffield: Sheffield Academic Press, 1997, pp. 34–54.

Block, Daniel I., 'Why Deborah's Different', *BR* 17, 3 (June 2001), pp. 34–40, 49.

Brenner, Athalya (ed.), *Judges: A Feminist Companion to the Bible*, The Feminist Companion to the Bible 4, Sheffield: Sheffield Academic Press, 1993.

Bronner, L. L., 'Valorized or Vilified? The Women of Judges in Midrashic Sources' in A. Brenner (ed.), *Judges: A Feminist Companion to the Bible*, Sheffield: Sheffield Academic Press, 1993, pp. 72–95.

Bynum, David E., 'Samson as a Biblical *pher oreskos*' in S. Niditch (ed.), *Text and Tradition. The Hebrew Bible and Folklore*, Atlanta, GA: Scholars Press, 1990, pp. 57–73.

Cartledge-Hays, Mary, *To Love Delilah*, San Diego, CA: Lura Media, 1990.

Craigie, P.C., 'The Song of Deborah and the Epic of Tukulti-Ninurta', *JBL* 88, 2 (Sept. 1969), pp. 253–65.

Crenshaw, J. L., *Samson: A Secret Betrayed, A Vow Ignored*, Atlanta: John Knox Press, 1978.

'The Samson Saga: Filial Devotion or Erotic Attachment?' *ZAW* 86 (1974), pp. 470–504.

Daube, David, 'Gideon's Few', *JJS* 7 (1956), pp. 155–61.

Engberg, Robert M., 'Historical Analysis of Archaeological Evidence: Megiddo and the Song of Deborah', *BASOR* 78 (Apr. 1940), pp. 4–9.

Exum, J. Cheryl, 'Promise and Fulfillment: Narrative Art in Judges 13', *JBL* 99 (1980), pp. 3–29.

Fensham, F. C., 'The Shaving of Samson: A Note on Judges 16:19', *EvQ* 31 (1959), pp. 97–8.

Feuersham, F. C., 'Did a Treaty between the Israelites and the Kenites Exist', *BASOR* 175 (1964), pp. 51–4.

Fewell, Danna Nolan, and David Miller Gunn, 'Controlling Perspectives: Women, Men and the Authority of Violence in Judges 4 & 5', *JAAR* 58 (1991), pp. 389–411.

Finkelstein, Israel, 'The Stratigraphy and Chronology of Megiddo and Beth-Shean in the Twelfth–Eleventh Centuries BCE', *Tel Aviv* 23 (1996), pp. 171–2 (H).

Gunn, D. M., 'Narrative Patterns and Oral Tradition in Judges and Samuel', *VT* 24, 3 (1974), pp. 286–317.

Hackett, J. A., 'In the Days of Jael: Reclaiming the History of Women in Ancient Israel' in C. W. Atkinson, C. H. Buchanan and M. R. Miles (eds), *Immaculate and Powerful: The Female in Sacred Image and Social Reality*, Boston: Beacon, 1985, pp. 15–38.

Halpern, Baruch, 'Sisera and Old Lace. The Case of Deborah and Yael' in *The First Historians. The Hebrew Bible and History*, San Francisco: Harper & Row, 1988, pp. 76–103.

'The Resourceful Israelite Historian: The Song of Deborah and Israelite Historiography', *HTR* 76, 4 (1983), pp. 379–401.

Hanselmann, S. W., 'Narrative Theory, Ideology, and Transformation in Judges 4' in M. Bal (ed.), *Anti-Covenant: Counter-Reading Women's Lives in the Hebrew Bible*, *JSOT* Supplement 8, Sheffield: Almond Press, 1989, pp. 95–112.

Klein, Lillian R., 'The Books of Judges. Paradigm and Deviation in Images of Women' in A. Brenner (ed.), *Judges: A Feminist Companion to the Bible*, Sheffield: Sheffield Academic Press, 1993, pp. 55–71.

Lapp, Paul, 'Taanach by the Waters of Megiddo', *BA* 30, 1 (Feb. 1967), pp.2–32.

Lindars, Barnabas, 'Deborah's Song: Women in the Old Testament', *BRL* 65, 2 (1983), pp. 158–75.

Malamat, Abraham, 'Charismatic Leadership in the Period of Judges' in *History of Biblical Israel. Major Problems and Minor Issues*, Leiden: Brill, 2001, pp. 151–70.

'The Period of the Judges' in B. Mazar (ed.), *The World History of the Jewish People*, New Brunswick, NJ: Rutgers University Press, 1971, vol. 3, pp. 129–63.

Mayes, A. D. H., 'The Historical Context of the Battle Against Sisera', *VT* 19, 3 (July 1969), pp. 353–60.

Merideth, Betsy, 'Desire and Danger: The Drama of Betrayal in Judges and Judith' in M. Bal (ed.), *Anti-Covenant: Counter-Reading Women's Lives in the Hebrew Bible*, *JSOT* Supplement 8, Sheffield: Almond Press, 1989, pp. 63–78.

Murray, D. F., 'Narrative Structure and Technique in the Deborah–Barak Story (Judges IV 4–22)' in J. A. Emerton (ed.), *Studies in the Historical Books of the Old Testament*, *VT* Supplement 30, Leiden: Brill, 1979, pp. 155–89.

Neef, H. D., 'Der Sieg Deboras und Baraks über Sisera', *ZAW* 101 (1989), pp. 28–49.

Niditch, Susan, 'Eroticism and Death in the Tale of Jael' in Peggy L. Day (ed.), *Gender and Difference in Ancient Israel*, Minneapolis: Fortress Press, 1989, pp. 43–57.

Rasmussen, R. C., 'Deborah the Woman Warrior' in M. Bal (ed.), *Anti-Covenant: Counter-Reading Women's Lives in the Hebrew Bible*, *JSOT* Supplement 8, Sheffield: Almond Press, 1989, pp. 79–93.

Sasson, Jack M., 'Who Cut Samson's Hair? (And Other Trifling Issues Raised by Judges 16)', *Prooftexts* 8 (1988), pp. 333–9.

Shaw, Jane, 'Constructions of Woman in Readings of the Story of Deborah' in Mieke Bal (ed.), *Anti-Covenant. Counter-Reading Women's Lives in the Hebrew Bible*, Sheffield: Almond Press, 1989, pp. 113–32.

Tolkowsky, S., 'Gideon's 300', *JPOS* 5 (1925), pp. 69–73.

Ussishkin, David, 'The Destruction of Megiddo at the End of the Late Bronze Age and Its Historical Significance', *Tel Aviv* 22 (1995), pp. 240–67.

Vickery, John B., 'In Strange Ways: The Story of Samson' in B. O. Long (ed.), *Images of God and Man: Old Testament Short Stories in Literary Focus*, Sheffield: Almond Press, 1981, pp. 58–73.

Webb, B. G., *The Book of Judges: An Integrated Reading*, *JSOT* Supplement 46, Sheffield: JSOT Press, 1987.

Yee, Gale A., 'By the Hand of A Woman: The Metaphor of the Woman Warrior in Judges 4', *Semeia* 61 (1993), pp. 99–132.

Zakovitch, Yair, 'Sisseras Tod', *ZAW* 93 (1981), pp. 364–74.

United Monarchy

Blenkinsopp, Joseph, 'The Quest for the Historical Saul' in J. W. Flanaghan and A. Weisbrod (eds), *No Famine in the Land: Studies in Honor of John L. McKenzie*, Missoula: Scholars Press, 1975.

Branch, Robin Gallaher, 'David and Joab; United by Ambition', *BR* (Aug. 2003), pp.14–23, 62.

Cahill, Jane M., 'David's Jerusalem: Fiction or Reality?' Part II. 'It is There: The Archaeological Evidence Proves It', *BAR* 24, 2 (1998), pp. 34–41, 63.

'Jerusalem at the Time of the United Monarchy. The Archaeological Evidence' in Andrew G. Vaughn and
Ann E. Killebrew (eds), *Jerusalem in Bible and Archaeology: The First Temple Period*, Atlanta: Society
of Biblical Literature, pp. 13–80.

and David Taraler, 'Excavations Directed by Yigal Shiloh at the City of David, 1978–1985' in Hillel
Geva (ed.), *Ancient Jerusalem Revealed*, rev. and expanded edn: Israel Exploration Society, 2000,
pp. 31–45.

Caquot, A., 'Les Rephaims Ougaritiques', *Syria* 37 (1960), pp. 75–93.

Carlson, Rolf August, *David, The Chosen King: A Tradition-historical Approach to the Second Book of Samuel*,
Stockholm: Almqvist & Wiksell, 1964.

Cryer, F. H., 'On the Recently Discovered "House of David" Inscription', *JSOT* 8 (1994), pp. 3–19.

Dearman, J. Andrew, 'Historical Reconstruction of the Mesha Inscription' in J. A. Dearman (ed.), *Studies in
the Mesha Inscription and Moab*, Atlanta: Scholars Press, 1989, pp. 155–210.

Dearman, J. Andrew (ed.), *Studies in the Mesha Inscription and Moab*, Atlanta, GA: Scholars Press, 1989.

Finkelstein, Israel, *The Emergence of the Monarchy in Israel: The Environmental and Socio-Economic Aspects*,
Winona Lake, IN: Eisenbrauns, 1996.

Flanagan, J., *A Study of the Traditions Pertaining to the Foundation of Monarchy*, PhD dissertation, University
of Nôtre Dame, 1971.

Franken, Hendricus J., 'Jerusalem in the Bronze Age 200–1000 BC' in Kamil J. Asali (ed.), *Jerusalem in
History*, New York: Olive Branch Press, 2000, pp. 11–41.

Geva, H., 'Jerusalem' in *NEAEHL*, pp. 698–757.

Gray, Rev. John, 'The Rephaim', *PEQ* (July–Oct. 1949), pp. 127–39.

Halpern, Baruch, *David's Secret Demons. Messiah, Murderer, Traitor, King*, Grand Rapids, MI: Eerdmans,
2001.

'The Stela from Dan: Epigraphic and Historical Considerations', *BASOR* 296 (1994), pp. 63–80.

Hauer, Chris E., jun., 'Jerusalem, the Stronghold and Rephaim', *CBQ* 32, 3 (July 1970), pp. 576ff.

Lemaire, André, ' "House of David" Restored in Moabite Inscription', *BAR* 20, 3 (May–June 1994), pp. 30–7.

Lemche, Niels Peter, 'David's Rise', *JSOT* 10 (1978), pp. 2–25.

McKenzie, Steven L., *King David: A Biography*, New York: Oxford University Press, 2000.

The Trouble with Kings, *VT* Supplement 42, Leiden: Brill, 1992.

Malamat, Abraham, 'The Struggle Against the Philistines' in H. H. Ben-Sasson (ed.), *A History of the Jewish
People*, Cambridge, MA; London: Weidenfeld & Nicolson, 1976, pp. 80–7.

Mazar, Benjamin, 'Making a Capital' in A. Malamat (ed.), 'The Age of the Monarchies: Political History',
vol. 4, 1 of Netanyahu, Benzion, et al. (eds), *The World History of the Jewish People*, pp. 78–80.

'The Military Élite of King David', *VT* 13 (1963), pp. 312–20.

Na'aman, Nadav, 'Cow Town or Royal Capital? Evidence from Iron Age Jerusalem', *BAR* 23, 4 (1997),
pp. 43–47, 67.

'David's Jerusalem: Fiction or Reality? Part III It is There: Ancient Texts Prove It', *BAR* 24, 2 (1998),
pp. 42–4.

Rainey, Anson F., 'The House of David and the House of the Deconstructionists', *BAR* 20, 6 (1994), p. 47.

Schniedewind, William M., 'David's Jerusalem: The Lessons of Historical Geography', *BAR* 24, 6 (1998),
p. 12.

Shanks, Hershel, ' "David" Found at Dan', *BAR* 20, 2 (1994), pp. 26–39.

'Has David Been Found in Egypt?' *BAR* 25, 1 (Jan.–Feb. 1999), pp. 34–5.

'Where is the Tenth Century?' *BAR* 24, 2 (Mar.–Apr. 1998), pp. 56–61.

Silberman, Neil A., 'Archaeology, Ideology, and the Search for David and Solomon' in Andrew G. Vaughn
and Ann E. Killibrew (eds), *Jerusalem in Bible and Archaeology: The First Temple Period*, Atlanta:
Society of Biblical Literature, pp. 395–405.

Steiner, Margreet, 'David's Jerusalem: Fiction or Reality? Part I: It's Not There. Archaeology Proves a
Negative', *BAR* 24, 4 (1998), pp. 62–3.

Tidwell, N. L., 'The Philistine Incursions into the Valley of Rephaim' in J. A. Emerton (ed.), *Studies in the
Historical Books of the Old Testament*, *VT* Supplement 30, Leiden: Brill, 1979.

Van Selms, A., 'The Armed Forces of Israel Under Saul and David', *Studies in the Book of Samuel*, Papers read at the third meeting of Die Alt-testamentliese Werkgemeenskap in SudAfrika held at Stellenbosch, 26–28 January 1960, Pretoria: 1960, pp. 55–66.

Whitelam, Keith W., 'Recreating the History of Israel', *JSOT* 35 (1986), pp. 45–70.

Willesen, F., 'The Philistine Corps of the Scimitar from Gath', *JSS* 3 (1958), pp. 327–35.

Maccabean Revolt

ANCIENT TEXTS

Goldstein, Jonathan A., *1 Maccabees. Translation and Commentary*, Garden City, New York: Doubleday, 1976.

2 Maccabees. Translation and Commentary, Garden City, NY: Doubleday, 1983.

Josephus, Flavius, *Jewish Antiquities*, trans. by H. St J. Thackeray, Cambridge: Loeb Classical Library, 1961, 6 vols.

The Jewish War, trans. by H. St J. Thackeray. Cambridge: Loeb Classical Library, 1956, 2 vols.

MODERN SOURCES

Abel, F. M., 'Topographie des Campagnes Machabéenes', *RB* 32 (1923), pp. 495–521.

Avi Yonah, M,. 'The War of the Sons of Light and the Sons of Darkness and Maccabean Warfare', *IEJ* 2, 1 (1952), pp.1–5.

Bar-Kochva, Bezalel, *Judas Maccabaeus. The Jewish Struggle Against the Seleucids*, Cambridge: Cambridge University Press, 1989.

'Seron and Cestius Gallus at Beth Horon', *PEQ* 107 (1976), pp. 13–21.

The Seleucid Army, Organization, and Tactics in the Great Campaigns, Cambridge: Cambridge University Press, 1976.

Bickerman, Elias, *The God of the Maccabees. Studies on the Meaning and Origin of the Maccabean Revolt*, trans. by Horst R. Moehring, Leiden: Brill, 1979.

Bowersock, Glen W., *Martyrdom and Rome*, Cambridge: Cambridge University Press, 1995.

Collins, John J., *Daniel, First Maccabees, Second Maccabees* (Old Testament Message 16), Wilmington, DE: Michael Glazier, 1981.

Davies, P., 'Hasidim in the Maccabean Period', *JJS* 28 (1977), pp. 127–40.

Doran, R., *Temple Propaganda: The Purpose and Character of 2 Maccabees*, Washington, DC: Catholic Biblical Association of America, 1981.

Eddy, Samuel Kennedy, *The King is Dead. Studies in the Near Eastern Resistance to Hellenism 334–31 BC*, Lincoln: University of Nebraska Press, 1961.

Fischer, Thomas, 'Rom und Die Hasmonäer. Ein Überblick zu Den Politischen Beziehungen 164–37 v. Chr', *Gymnasium* 88 (1981), pp. 139–50.

Seleukiden und Makkabäer. Beiträge zur Seleukidengeschichte und zu den Politischen Ereignissen in Judaa Wahrend der 1 Halfte des 2 Jahrhunderts v. Chr., Bochum: In Kommission beim Studienverlag N. Brockmeyer, 1980.

Harrington, Daniel J., *The Maccabean Revolt. Anatomy of a Biblical Revolution*, Wilmington, DE: Michael Glazier, 1988.

Hengel, Martin, *Judaism and Hellenism. Studies in their Encounter in Palestine during the Early Hellenistic Period*, Philadelphia: Fortress Press, 1974, 2 vols.

The Zealots: Investigations into the Jewish Freedom Movement in the Period from Herod I until 70 AD, trans. by David Smith, Edinburgh: T. & T. Clark, 1989.

Jones, Bruce W., 'Antiochus Epiphanes and the Persecution of the Jews' in Carl D. Evans, William W. Hallo and John B. White (eds), *Scripture in Context: Essays on Comparative Method*, Pittsburgh, PA: The Pickwick Press, 1980, pp. 263–90.

McEleney, Neil J., '1–2 Maccabees' in Raymond E. Brown, Joseph A. Fitzmyer and Roland E. Murphy (eds), *The New Jerome Biblical Commentary*, with a foreword by Carlo Maria Cardinal Martini, Englewood Cliffs, NJ: Prentice-Hall, 1990, pp. 421–41.

Mendels, D., 'A Note on the Tradition of Antiochus IV's Death', *IEJ* 31 (1981), pp. 53–6.

Millar, F., 'The Background of the Maccabaean Revolution: Reflections on Martin Hengel's "Judaism and Hellenism" ', *JJS* 29 (1978), pp. 1–21.

Sievers, Joseph, *The Hasmoneans and Their Supporters: From Mattathias to the Death of John Hyrcanus I*, Atlanta: Scholars Press, 1990.

Tcherikover, V. A., *Hellenistic Civilization and the Jews*, trans. by S. Applebaum, New York: Atheneum, 1970.

Wallach, J. L., 'The War of the Maccabees', *RIHM* 42 (1979), pp. 53–81.

Wibbing, S., 'Zur Topographie Einzelner Schlachten des Judas Makkabäus', *ZDPV* 78 (1962), pp. 159–70.

Book of Judith

Bal, Mieke, 'Head Hunting: "Judith" on the Cutting Edge of Knowledge', *JSOT* 63 (1994), pp. 3–34.

Brenner, Athalya, *A Feminist Companion to Esther, Judith and Susanna*, The Feminist Companion to the Bible 7, Sheffield: Sheffield Academic Press, 1995.

Bruns, Edgar J., 'Judith or Jael', *CBQ* 16 (1954), pp. 12–14.

Coote, M. P., 'Comment on Narrative Structures in the Book of Judith', *Colloquies* 11 (1975), pp. 21–22.

Craghan, J. F., 'Esther, Judith and Ruth: Paradigms for Human Liberation', *TBB* 12 (1982), pp. 11–19.
    Esther, Judith, Tobit, Jonah, Ruth, Wilmington, DE: Michael Glazier, 1982.

Craven, Toni, *Artistry and Faith in the Book of Judith*, Atlanta: Scholars Press, 1983.
    'Tradition and Convention in the Book of Judith', *Semeia* 28 (1983), pp. 49–61.

Enslin, Morton A., and Solomon Zeitlin, *The Book of Judith*, Jewish Apochyphal Literature 8, Leiden: Brill, 1972.

Lacocque, André, *The Feminine Unconventional*, Minneapolis: Fortress Press, 1990.

Levine, Amy-Jill, 'Sacrifice and Salvation: Otherness and Domestication in the Book of Judith' in Alice Bach (ed.), *Women in the Hebrew Bible. A Reader*, New York: Routledge, 1999, pp. 367–76.

Montley, P., 'Judith in the Fine Arts: The Appeal of the Archetypal Androgyne', *Anime* 4 (1978), pp. 37–42.

Moore, Carey A., *Judith*, Anchor Bible edn vol. 40, Garden City, NY: Doubleday, 1985.
    'Judith: The Case of the Pious Killer', *BR* (Feb. 1990), pp. 26–36.

Niditch, S., *Underdogs and Tricksters*, San Francisco: Harper & Row, 1987.

Skehan, Patrick W., 'The Hand of Judith', *CBQ* 25 (1963), pp. 94–110.

Stocker, Margarita, *Judith. Sexual Warrior. Women and Power in Western Culture*, New Haven: Yale University Press, 1998.

Vander Kam, James C. (ed.), *No One Spoke Ill of Her: Essays on Judith*, Atlanta: Scholars Press, 1992.

White Crawford, Sidnie Ann, 'Esther not Judith. Why One Made It and the Other Didn't', *BR* 18, 1 (Feb. 2003), pp. 22–31, 45.

White, Sidnie Ann, 'In the Steps of Jael and Deborah: Judith as Heroine' in J. Vander Kam (ed.), *No One Spoke Ill of Her: Essays on Judith*, Atlanta: Scholars Press, 1992.

Yee, Gale A., 'By the Hand of a Woman: The Metaphor of the Woman Warrior in Judith', *Semeia* 61 (1993), pp. 99–132.

Jews and Romans – General

ANCIENT SOURCES

Arrian, Flavius, *Tactica* in *Scripta Minora et Fragmenta*, ed. by A. G. Roos, Leipzig: Teubner, 1968.

Cassius Dio, *Dio's Roman History*, trans. by E. Cary, Cambridge: Loeb Classical Library, 1954, 9 vols.

Josephus, Flavius, *Jewish Antiquities*, trans. by H. St J. Thackeray, Cambridge: Loeb Classical Library, 1961, 6 vols.
    Life of Josephus, trans. and commentary by Steve Mason, Leiden: Brill, 2003.
    The Jewish War, trans. by H. St J. Thackeray, Cambridge: Loeb Classical Library, 1956, 2 vols.

Scriptores Historiae Augustae, trans. by David Magie, Cambridge: Loeb Classical Library, 1960, 3 vols.

Tacitus, *The Histories*, trans. by Clifford H. Moore, Cambridge: Loeb Classical Library, 1962, 2 vols.

Vegetius, *Epitome of Military Science*, trans. with notes and introduction by N. P. Milner, 2nd edn, Liverpool [England]: Liverpool University Press, 1996.

BIBLIOGRAPHY

Modern Sources

Alon, Gedalia, *The Jews in Their Land in the Talmudic Age (70–640 CE)*, trans. from the 1961 Hebrew edn by Gershon Levi, Cambridge: Harvard University Press, 1989.

Applebaum, Shimon, *Judaea in Hellenistic and Roman Times. Historical and Archaeological Essays*, Leiden: Brill, 1989.

Brauer, George C., *Judaea Weeping; The Jewish Struggle Against Rome from Pompey to Masada 63 BC to AD 73*, New York: Thomas Y. Crowell, 1970.

Cohen, Shaye J. D., *From the Maccabees to the Mishnah*, Philadelphia: Westminster Press, 1987.

Edwards, D., 'Religion, Power and Power Politics: Jewish Defeats by the Romans in Iconography and Josephus' in J. A. Overman and R. S. MacLennan (eds), *Diaspora Jews and Judaism*, South Florida Studies in the History of Judaism 41, Atlanta: Scholars Press, 1992.

Feldman, *Jew and Gentile in the Ancient World*, Princeton: Princeton University Press, 1993.

Gabba, Emilio, 'The Social, Economic, and Political History of Palestine 63 BCE–70 CE', *CHJ*, vol. 3, pp. 94–167.

Gichon, Mordechai, 'The Defense of the Negev in Military Retrospect', *Maarachot* (Apr. 1963), pp. 13–21 (H). 'The Origin of the *Limes Palestinae* and the Major Phases of Its Development', *Bonner Jahrbucher*, Beiheft XIX (1967), pp. 175–93.

Goodman, Martin, 'Nerva, the Fiscus Judaicus and Jewish Identity', *JRS* 79 (1989), pp. 40–4. *State and Society in Roman Galilee, 132–212*, Totowa, NJ: Rowman & Allanheld, 1983.

Gruen, Erich S., 'Hellenism and Persecution: Antiochus IV and the Jews' in Peter Green (ed.), *Hellenistic History and Culture*, Berkeley: University of California Press, 1993, pp. 238–74.

Horsley, Richard A., and J. S. Hanson, *Bandits, Prophets and Messiahs*, Minneapolis: Winston Press, 1985.

Isaac, Benjamin, 'Bandits in Judaea and Arabia', *HSCP* (1984), pp. 171–203; reprinted in B. Isaac, *The Near East Under Roman Rule*, pp. 122–51.
The Limits of Empire; The Roman Army in the East, Oxford: Clarendon Press, 1990.
The Near East Under Roman Rule. Selected Papers, Leiden: Brill, 1998.
'The Roman Army in Jerusalem and its Vicinity' in C. Unz (ed.), *Studien zu Militärgrenzen Roms III*, 13th Limes Congress, Stuttgart, 1983, pp. 635–40.

Jagersma, Henk, *A History of Israel from Alexander the Great to Bar Kochba*, Philadelphia: Fortress Press, 1986.

Kennedy, D. L., 'Legio VI Ferrata: The Annexation and Early Garrison of Arabia', *HSCP* 84 (1980), pp. 283–308.

McLaren, J. S., *Power and Politics in Palestine: The Jews and the Governing of Their Land 100 BC–AD 70*, Sheffield: JSOT Press, 1991.
Turbulent Times? Josephus and Scholarship on Judaea in the First Century CE, Sheffield: Sheffield Academic Press, 1998.

Mendels, D., *The Rise and Fall of Jewish Nationalism*, New York: Doubleday, 1992.

Rea, J. R., 'The Legio II Traiana in Judaea', *ZPE* 38 (1980), pp. 220–1.

Roll, Israel, 'The Roman Road System in Judaea', *The Jerusalem Cathedra* 3 (1983), pp. 136–61.

Roth, Jonathan, *The Logistics of the Roman Army at War (264 BC–AD 235)*, Leiden: Brill, 1999.

Safrai, Ze'ev, *The Economy of Roman Palestine*, London and New York: Routledge, 1994.

Schäfer, P., *Judaeophobia: Attitudes Towards the Jewish in the Ancient World*, Cambridge: Harvard University Press, 1997.

Schürer, Emil, *A History of the Jewish People in the Age of Jesus Christ (175 BC–AD 135)*, trans. by T. A. Burkill, rev. and ed. by Geza Vermes and Fergus Millar, Edinburgh: T. & T. Clark, 2 vols.

Smallwood, E. Mary, *The Jews Under Roman Rule from Pompey to Diocletian*, Leiden: Brill, 1981.

Smith, Morton, 'The Troublemakers', *Cambridge History of Judaism*, New York: Cambridge University Press, 1984, 3 vols.

Speidel, M. P., 'Arabia's First Garrison', *ADAJ* 16, pp. 111–12.

Vermes, Geza, and Jacob Neussner (eds), *Essays in Honour of Yigael Yadin*, Totowa, NJ: Allanheld, Osmun, 1983.

Yavetz, Zvi, *Judenfeindschaft in der Antike*, Munich: C. H. Beck, 1997.

Great Jewish War

Adan-Bayewitz, D., and M. Aviam, 'Iotapata, Josephus, and the Siege of 67: Preliminary Report on the 1992–1994 Seasons', *JRA* 10 (1997), pp. 131–65.

Applebaum, Shimon, 'For Whom Did Apollodorus Write the Poliorketika?' in S. Applebaum, *Judaea in Hellenistic and Roman Times Historical and Archaeological Essays*, Leiden: Brill, 1989.

'The Zealots. The Case for Revaluation', *JRS* 61 (1971), pp. 155–70.

Aviam, Mordechai, 'Yodephat/Jotopata: The Archaeology of the First Battle' in Berlin/ Overman (eds), *The First Jewish Revolt*, London and New York: Routledge, 2002, pp. 121–33.

Berlin, Andrea M., and J. Andrew Overman, *The First Jewish Revolt. Archaeology, History and Ideology*, London and New York: Routledge, 2002.

Bar, Doron, 'Aelia Capitolina and the Location of the Camp of the Tenth Legion', *PEQ* 130, 1, pp. 8–19.

Bar-Kochva, Bezalel, 'Seron and Cestius Gallus at Beth Horon', *PEQ* 107 (1976), pp. 13–21.

Borg, Marcus, 'The Currency of the Term Zealot', *JTS* 22 (1971), pp. 504–12.

Brandon, F. J. F., 'The Zealots: The Ancient Jewish Resistance Against Rome' in Michael Elliott (ed.), *The Fourth Dimension of Warfare*, New York: Praeger, 1970, pp. 1–18.

Brandon, S. G. F., *Jesus and the Zealots*, Manchester: Manchester University Press, 1967.

Brunt, P. A., 'Josephus on Social Conflicts in Roman Judaea', *Klio* 59 (1977), pp. 149–53.

Cohen, S. J. D., *Josephus in Galilee and Rome*, Leiden: Brill, 1979.

'Literary Tradition, Archaeological Remains, and the Credibility of Josephus', *Essays in Honour of Y. Yadin*, Totowa, NJ: Barnes & Noble, 1983, pp. 385–405.

Donaldson, T., 'Rural Bandits, City Mobs and the Zealots', *JJS* 31 (1990), pp. 18–36.

Eshel, Hanan, 'Documents of the First Jewish Revolt from the Judaean Desert' in Berlin/Overman, *The First Jewish Revolt*, London and New York: Routledge, 2002, pp. 157–63.

Farmer, William Ruben, *Maccabees, Zealots and Josephus. An Inquiry into Jewish Nationalism in the Graeco-Roman Period*, New York: Columbia University Press, 1956.

Freyne, Sean, 'Bandits in Galilee. A Contribution to the Study of Social Conditions in First-century Palestine' in J. Neusner et al. *The Social World of Formative Christianity and Judaism. Essays in Tribute to Howard Clark Kee*, Philadelphia: Fortress Press, 1988.

'The Revolt from a Regional Perspective' in Berlin/Overman, *The First Jewish Revolt*, London and New York: Routledge, 2002, pp. 43–56.

Furneaux, Rupert, *The Roman Siege of Jerusalem*, New York: David McKay, 1972.

Gabba, Emilio, 'La Rivolta Giudaica del 66 CE', *Congresso Internazionale di Studi Vespasianei* (1981), pp. 153–73.

Gichon, Mordechai, 'Aspect of a Roman Army in War According to the Bellum Judaicum of Josephus', *BAR* 297 (1986), pp. 287–310.

'Cestius Gallus' Campaign in Judaea', *PEQ* 113 (1981), pp. 39–62.

Goodman, Martin, 'Current Scholarship on the First Revolt' in Berlin/Overman, *The First Jewish Revolt*, London and New York: Routledge, 2002, pp. 15–24.

Jews in the Graeco-Roman World, New York: Oxford University Press, 1998.

'The First Jewish Revolt: Social Conflict and the Problem of Debt', *JJS* 33, 1–2 (1982), *Essays in Honour of Y. Yadin*, pp. 417–27.

'The Origins of the Great Revolt: A Conflict of Status Criteria' in A. Kasher, U. Rappaport and G. Fuks (eds), *Greece and Rome in Eretz Israel*, Yad Izhak Ben-Zvi: Israel Exploration Society, 1990, pp. 39–53.

The Ruling Class of Judaea, Cambridge: Cambridge University Press, 1987.

Hengel, Martin, *Die Zeloten, Untersuchungen zur Jüdischen Freiheitsbewegung in der Zeit von Herodes I bis 70 n. Chr*, Leiden: Brill, 1976. Second edn trans. by David Smith as *The Zealots. Investigations into the Jewish Freedom Movement in the Period from Herod I until 70 AD*, Edinburgh: T & T Clark, 1989.

Hoenig, S., 'The Sicarii in Masada', *Traditio* 11 (1970), pp. 5ff.

Horsley, Richard A., 'Ancient Jewish Banditry and the Revolt against Rome, AD 66–70', *CBQ* 43 (1981), pp. 409–32.

'Josephus and the Bandits', *JSJ* 10 (1979), pp. 37–63.

'Menachem in Jerusalem: A Brief Messianic Episode Among the Sicarii – not Zealot Messianism', *Novum Testamentum* 27, 4 (1985), pp. 159–92.

'Power Vacuum and Power Struggle in 66–67 CE' in Berlin/Overman, *The First Jewish Revolt*, London and New York: Routledge, 2002, pp. 87–109.

'The Sicarii: Ancient Jewish Terrorists', *JR* 59 (1979), pp. 435–58.

'The Zealots, Their Origin, Relationships, and Importance in the Jewish Revolt', *Novum Testamentum* 28, 2 (1986), pp. 159–92.

and J. Hanson, *Bandits, Prophets and Messiahs. Popular Movements at the Time of Jesus*, New York: Winston Press, 1985.

Jossa, G., 'Josephus' Action in Galilee during the Jewish War' in F. Parente and J. Sievers (eds), *Josephus and the History of the Greco-Roman Period*, Leiden: Brill, 1974, pp. 150–9.

Kadman, Leo, *The Coins of the Jewish War of 66–73*, Tel Aviv: Schocken, 1960.

Kleinfeller, Art, 'Sicarius' in *RE* (1922–7) series 2, cols 2185–6.

McLaren, J., *Turbulent Times? Josephus and Scholarship on Judaea in the First Century*, Sheffield: Sheffield Academic Press, 1998.

Michel, O., 'Simon Bar Giora', *Fourth World Congress of Jewish Studies*, Jerusalem, 1967, pp. 77–80.

Overman, J. Andrew, 'The First Revolt and Flavian Politics' in Berlin/Overman, *The First Jewish Revolt*, London and New York: Routledge, 2002, pp. 213–20.

Price, Jonathan J., *Jerusalem Under Siege, The Collapse of the Jewish State 66–70 CE*, Leiden: Brill, 1992.

Rajak, Tessa, *Josephus*, London: Duckworth, 1983.

Rapoport, David C., 'Terror and the Messiah: An Ancient Experience and Some Modern Parallels' in Michael Elliott (ed.), *The Fourth Dimension of Warfare*, New York: Praeger, 1970, pp. 13–42.

Rappaport, Uriel, 'Jewish–Pagan Relations in the Revolt against Rome in 66–70 CE', *Jerusalem Cathedra* 2 (1983), pp. 81–95.

'John of Gischala. From Galilee to Jerusalem', *Essays in Honor of Y. Yadin* 479–493, *JJS* 33 1, 2 (1982), pp. 479–93.

Rhoads, D., *Israel in Revolution 6 –74 CE. A Political History Based on the Writings of Josephus*, Philadelphia: Fortress Press, 1976.

Schwartz, S., 'Josephus in Galilee: Rural Patronage and Social Breakdown' in F. Parente and J. Sievers (eds), *Josephus and the History of the Greco–Roman Period,* Leiden: Brill, 1994, pp. 290–306.

Shaw, B. D., 'Bandits in the Roman Empire', *Past and Present* 105 (1984), pp. 3–52.

Silberman, Neil A., 'The First Revolt and Its Afterlife' in Berlin/Overman, *The First Jewish Revolt*, London and New York: Routledge, 2002, pp. 237–52.

Smith, Morton, 'Zealots and Sicarii: Their Origins and Relations', *HTR* 64 (1971), pp. 1–19.

Stern, Menachem, 'Sicarii and Zealots' in Michael Avi-Yonah, *Society and Religion in the Second Temple Period*, Jerusalem: Jewish History Publications, 1977, pp. 263–301.

Syon, Danny, 'Gamla: City of Refuge' in Berlin/Overman, *The First Jewish Revolt*, London and New York: Routledge, 2002, pp. 134–53.

'Gamla – Portrait of a Rebellion', *BAR* 18, 1 (Jan.–Feb. 1992), pp. 21–37.

Yadin, Yigael, *The Scroll of the War of the Sons of Light Against the Sons of Darkness*, ed. with an introduction, emendations and a commentary, Jerusalem: The Bialik Institute, 1955.

Zeitlin, Solomon, *The Rise and Fall of the Judaean State*, Philadelphia: Jewish Publication Society of America, 1976.

'Zealots and Sicarii', *JBL* 81, 4 (Dec. 1962), pp. 395–8.

Masada

Ben-Yehuda, Nachman, 'Questioning Masada: Where Masada's Defenders Fell', *BAR* 24, 6 (Nov.–Dec. 1998), pp. 33–45, 64–6.

Sacrificing Truth: Archaeology and the Myth of Masada, Amherst, NY: Humanity Books, 2002.

'Where Masada's Defenders Fell. A Garbled Passage in Josephus Has Obscured the Location of the Mass Suicide', *BAR* 24, 6 (Nov.–Dec. 1998), pp. 34–9.

Campbell, Duncan, 'Dating the Siege of Masada', *ZPE* (1988), pp. 156–8.

Cohen, S. J. D., 'Masada. Literary Tradition, Archaeological Remains, and the Credibility of Josephus' in G. Vermes and J. Neusner (eds), *Essays in Honour of Y. Yadin*, Totowa, NJ: Allanheld, Osmus & Co., 1983, pp. 385–405.

Feldman, L. H., 'Masada: A Critique of Recent Scholarship' in J. Neusner, *Christianity, Judaism and Other Graeco-Roman Cults*, Leiden: Brill, 1975.

Gruen, Erich S., 'Roman Perspective on the Jews in the Age of the Great Revolt' in Berlin/Overman, *The First Jewish Revolt*, London and New York: Routledge, 2002, pp. 27–42.

Hawkes, Christopher, 'The Roman Siege of Masada', *Antiquity* 3 (1929), pp. 195–213.

Hoenig, S. B., 'The Sicarii in Masada; Glory or Infamy?' *Tradition* 11 (1970), pp. 5–30.

Ladouceur, David J., 'Josephus and Masada' in L. H. Feldman and G. Hata (eds), *Josephus, Judaism and Christianity*, Detroit: Wayne State University Press, 1987, pp. 95–113.

'Masada: A Consideration of the Literary Evidence', *GRBS* 21 (1980), pp. 245–60.

Magness, Jodi, 'Masada – Arms and the Man', *BAR* 18, 4 (July–Aug. 1992), pp. 58–67.

Netzer, Ehud, 'The Last Days and Hours at Masada', *BAR* 17 (1991), pp. 20–32.

Newell, R. Raymond, 'The Forms and Historical Value of Josephus' Suicide Acts' in L. H. Feldman and G. Hata (eds), *Josephus, the Bible and History*, Detroit: Wayne State University, 1989.

Richmond, Ian, 'The Roman Siege Works at Masada, Israel', *JRS* 52 (1962), pp. 142–55.

Roth, J., 'The Length of the Siege at Masada', *Scripta Classica Israelica* 14 (1995), pp. 87–110.

Yadin, Yigael, *Masada: Herod's Fortress and the Zealots Last Stand*, New York: Random House; London: Weidenfeld & Nicolson, 1966.

Zias, Joseph, 'Whose Bones? Were They Really Jewish Defenders? Did Yadin Deliberately Obfuscate', *BAR* 24, 6 (Nov./Dec. 1998), pp. 41–5, 64–6.

Jesus

Aland, Kurt, et al. (eds), *The Greek New Testament*, New York: American Bible Society, 1966.

Funk, R. W., et al, *The Five Gospels*, New York: Macmillan, 1993.

Suetonius, *Lives of the Caesars*, trans. by J. C. Rolfe, Cambridge: Loeb Classical Library, 1960, 2 vols.

MODERN SOURCES

Aicher, G., *Der Prozess Jesu*, Kanonistische Studien und Texte 3, Bonn: Schroeder, 1929.

Allen, J. E., 'Why Pilate?' in E. Bammel (ed.), *The Trial of Jesus* (Moule Festschrift), pp. 78–83.

Arbeitman, Y., 'The Suffix Iscariot', *JBL* 99 (1980), pp. 122–24.

Bammel, Ernst, 'Crucifixion as a Punishment in Palestine' in E. Bammel, *The Trial of Jesus* (Moule Festschrift), pp. 162–5, and *Kleine Schriften* I, pp. 76–8.

'Jesus as a Political Agent in a Version of the Josippon', *JPHD*, pp. 197–209.

'The Feeding of the Multitude', *JPHD*, pp. 211–40.

'The Revolutionary Theory from Reimarus to Brandon', *JPHD*, pp. 11–68.

'The *titulus*', *JPHD*, pp. 353–64.

'The Trial Before Pilate', *JPHD*, pp. 415–51.

Bammel, Ernst (ed.), *The Trial of Jesus* (Moule Festschrift), Studies in Biblical Theology, series II, no. 13, London: SCM, 1970.

and C. F. D. Moule (eds), *Jesus and the Politics of His Day*, Cambridge: Cambridge University Press, 1984.

Berkey, R. F, and S. A. Edwards (eds), *Christological Perspectives*, New York: Pilgrim's Press, 1982.

Borg, Marcus, and John Dominic Crossan, *The Last Week*, San Francisco: Harper, 2006.

Brandon, S. G. F., *Jesus and the Zealots*, Manchester: Manchester University Press, 1967.

The Fall of Jerusalem and the Christian Church. A Study of the Effects of the Jewish Overthrow of AD 70 on Christianity, London: SPCK, 1951, 2nd edition 1957.

The Trial and Death of Jesus, London: SCM, 1970.

'The Zealots: The Jewish Resistance Against Rome AD 6–73', *History Today* 15 (1965), pp. 632ff.

Brown, Raymond E., *The Death of the Messiah*, New York: Doubleday, 1994, 2 vols.

Brownson, James V., 'Neutralizing the Intimate Enemy: The Portrayal of Judas in the Fourth Gospel', *SBL 1992 Seminar Paper*, pp. 49–60.

Burkill, T. A., 'The Condemnation of Jesus: A Critique of Sherwin White's Thesis', *NT* 12 (1970), pp. 321–42.

Carmichael, J., *The Death of Jesus*, New York: Horizon Press, 1982.

Catchpole, David R., 'The Problem of the Historicity of the Sanhedrin Trial', *Moule Festschrift,* pp. 47–65.
　The Trial of Jesus. A Study in the Gospels and Jewish Historiography from 1770 to the Present Day, Leiden: Brill, 1971.

　'The "Triumphal" Entry', *JPHD*, pp. 319–34.

Charlesworth, J. H., 'Jesus and Jehohanan, An Archaeological Note on Crucifixion', *Exp Tim* 84 (1972–73), pp. 147–50.

Chavel, C. B., 'The Releasing of a Prisoner on the Eve of Passover in Ancient Jerusalem', *JBL* 60 (1941), pp. 273–8.

Cohn, Haim, *The Trial and Death of Jesus*, New York: Harper & Row, 1967.

Collins, J. J., 'The Archaeology of the Crucifixion', *CBQ* 1 (1939), pp. 154–9.

Crossan, Dominic M., 'Anti-Semitism in the Gospel', *Theological Studies* 26 (June 1965), pp. 189–214.

Crossan, J. D., *Jesus: A Revolutionary Biography*, San Francisco: Harper & Row, 1994.
　The Historical Jesus: The Life of a Mediterranean Jewish Peasant, New York: Harper & Row, 1994.

Cullmann, Oscar, *Jesus and the Revolutionaries*, New York: Harper & Row, 1970.

Davies, W. D., 'Jesus: From the Jewish Point of View', *CHJ*, Cambridge: Cambridge University Press, 1984– vol. 3, pp. 618–77.

Edwards, G. R., *Jesus and the Politics of Violence*, New York: Harper & Row, 1972.

Ehrhardt, A., 'Was Pilate a Christian?', *CQR* 137 (1944), pp. 157–67.

Eisler, Robert, *The Messiah Jesus and John the Baptist,* English edn by A. H. Krappe, New York: The Dial Press, 1931. Originally published as *Iesous Basileus ou Basileusas*, 2 vols.

Evans, C. A., 'Jesus and the "Cave of Robbers": Toward a Jewish Context for the Temple Action', *BBR* 3 (1993), pp. 93–110.
　'Jesus' Actions in the Temple: Cleansing or Portent of Destruction?', *CBQ* 51 (1989), pp. 237–70.

Feldman, L. H., 'The Testimonium Flavianum: The State of the Question' in R. F. Berkey and S. A. Edwards (eds), *Christological Perspectives*, New York, 1982, pp. 179–99.

Flusser, D., 'The Crucified One and the Jews', *Immanuel* 7 (1977), pp. 25–37.

Freyne, Sean, *Galilee. From Alexander the Great to Hadrian*, University of Notre Dame Press, 1980.

Garnsey, Peter, 'The Criminal Jurisdiction of Governors', *JRS* 58 (1968), pp. 51–9.

Gordis, Robert (ed.), 'The Trial of Jesus in the Light of History: A Symposium', *Judaism* 20 (1971), pp. 37–42.

Grant, Frederick Clinton, 'On the Trial of Jesus (P. Winter): A Review Article', *Journal of Religion* 44 (1964), pp. 230–7.

Grundmann, W., 'The Decision of the Supreme Court to Put Jesus to Death (John: 11: 47–57) . . .', *JPHD*, pp. 295–318.

Haas, N., 'Anthropological Observations on the Skeletal Remains from Giv'at ha-Mivtar', *IEJ* 20 (1970), pp. 38–59.

Hall, S. G., 'Swords of Offense', *Studia Evangelica* 1, TU 73 (1959), pp. 499–505.

Hamilton, N. Q., 'Temple Cleansing and Temple Bank', *JBL* 83 (1964), pp. 365–72.

Hein, K., 'Judas Iscariot: Key to the Last Supper Narratives?', *NTS* 17 (1970–71), pp. 227–32.

Hengel, Martin, *Die Zeloten,* Leiden: Brill, 1961; *The Zealots*, Edinburgh: T. & T. Clark, 1989.
　Was Jesus a Revolutionist?, Philadelphia: Fortress Press, 1971.

Herzog III, William R., *Parables as Subversive Speech. Jesus as Pedagogue of the Oppressed*, Louisville, KY: Westminster/John Knox Press, 1994.

Hobsbawm, Eric, *Bandits*, New York: Delaware Press; London: Weidenfeld & Nicolson, 1969.

Hoffman, R. Joseph, *Jesus Outside the Gospels,* Buffalo, NY: Prometheus Books, 1984.

Horbury, W., 'Christ as a Brigand in Ancient Anti-Christian Polemic', *JPHD*, pp.183–95.

'The Trial of Jesus in Jewish Tradition' in *Moule Festschrift*, pp. 102–21.

Horsley, R. A., *Jesus and the Spiral of Violence. Popular Resistance in Roman Palestine*, New York: Harper & Row, 1987.

'Popular Messianic Movements Around the Time of Jesus', *Catholic Biblical Quarterly* 46 (1984), pp. 471–95.

Sociology and the Jesus Movement, New York: Crossroad, 1989.

Jean, C. F., 'La Langue des Letters de Mari', *RES* 1937, fasc. 3, 110:9ff.

Jensen, Ellis E., 'The First Century Controversy Over Jesus as a Revolutionary Figure', *JBL* 60 (1941), pp. 261–72.

Jeremiahs, Joachim, 'The Problem of the Historical Jesus' in Ernst Käsemann, *Essays on New Testament Themes*, SBT 41, London: SCM, 1964, pp. 15–47.

Jesus Seminar, *The Acts of Jesus: The Search for the Authentic Deeds of Jesus*, ed. by Robert W. Funk and the Jesus Seminar, San Francisco: Harper, 1998.

Johnson, L. T., 'The New Testament's Anti-Jewish Slander and the Convention of Ancient Polemic', *JBL* 108 (1989), pp. 419–41.

Jonge, M. de, 'The Use of the Word "Anointed" in the Time of Jesus', *NT* 8 (1966), pp. 132–48.

Keck, L. E., 'Bornkamm's Jesus of Nazareth Revisited', *JR* 49 (1969), pp. 1–17.

Kertelge, K. (ed.), *Der Prozess Gegen Jesus: Historische Rückfrage und Theologische Deutung*, Freiburg im Breisgau: Herder, 1989.

Kingdon, H. P., 'Had the Crucifixion a Political Significance?' *Hibbert Journal* 35 (1936–37), pp. 556–67.

Kinman, Brent, *Jesus' Entry into Jerusalem in the Context of Lukan Theology and the Politics of His Day*, Leiden: Brill, 1995.

Klausner, Joseph, *Jesus of Nazareth*, New York: Macmillan, 1925.

Koester, H., 'Jesus the Victim', *JBL* 111/1 (1992), pp. 3–15.

Kraeling, C., 'The Episode of the Roman Standards at Jerusalem', *HTR* 35 (1942), pp. 263–81.

Kuhn, H. W., 'Die Kreuzesstrafe Während der Frühen Kaiserzeit. Ihre Wirklichkeit und Wertung in der Umweit des Urchristentums', *ANRW* 2.25.1 (1982), pp. 658–751.

Lampe, G. W. H., 'The Trial of Jesus in the *Acta Pilati*', *JPHD*, pp. 173–82.

'The Two Swords (Luke 22:35–38)', *JPHD*, pp. 335–51.

Langdon, S., 'The Release of the Prisoner at the Passover', *Exp. Tim* 29 (1918), pp. 328–30.

Lémonon, Jean Pierre, *Pilate et le Gouvernement de la Judée*, Paris: J. Gabalda, 1981.

Lietzmann, H., 'Der Prozess Jesu', *SPAW* 14 (1931), pp 313–22.

Maccoby, Hyam, 'Is the Political Jesus Dead?', *Encounter* 46 (1976), pp. 80–9.

'Jesus and Barabbas', *NTS* 16 (1969–70), pp. 55–60.

Judas Iscariot and the Myth of Jewish Evil, New York: Free Press; London: Peter Halban, 1992.

Revolution in Judaea, Jesus and the Jewish Resistance, New York: Taplinger, 1980.

The Mythmaker: Paul and the Invention of Christianity, London: Weidenfeld & Nicholson, 1986.

McGing, Brian C., 'Pontius Pilate and the Sources', *CBQ* 53 (1991), pp. 416–39.

Mack, Burton L., *A Myth of Innocence: Mark and Christian Origins*, Philadelphia: Fortress Press, 1988.

MacRuer, J. C., *The Trial of Jesus*, London: Blandford, 1965.

Maier, John P., 'Jesus in Josephus: A Modest Proposal', *CBQ* 52 (1990), pp. 76–103.

Maier, Paul L., 'Sejanus, Pilate, and the Date of the Crucifixion', *Church History* 37 (1968), pp. 2–13.

'The Inscription on the Cross of Jesus of Nazareth', *Hermes* 124 (1996), pp. 58–75.

'Who Killed Jesus', *Christianity Today* 34 (1990), pp. 16–19.

'Who Was Responsible for the Trial and Death of Jesus', *Christianity Today* 18 (12 April 1974), pp. 806–9.

Mantel, Hugo, *Studies in the History of the Sanhedrin*, Cambridge: Harvard University Press, 1961.

Marcus, J., 'The Jewish War and the *Sitz im Leben* of Mark', *JBL* 111/3 (1992), pp. 441–62.

Mastin, B.A., 'The Date of the Triumphal Entry', *NTS* 16 (1969), pp. 76–82.

Matera, F. J., 'The Trial of Jesus: Problems and Proposals', *Interpretation* 45 (1991), pp. 5–16.

Meier, J. P., *A Marginal Jew: Rethinking the History of Jesus*, New York: Doubleday, 1991.

'Jesus in Josephus: A Modest Proposal', *CBQ* 52 (1990), pp. 76–103.

Meier, P. L., 'The Inscription of the Cross of Jesus of Nazareth', *Hermes* 124 (1996), pp. 58–75.

Merkel, H., 'The Opposition Between Jesus and Judaism', *JPHD*, pp. 129–44.

Millar, Fergus, 'Reflections on the Trial of Jesus' in P. R. Davies and R. T. White (eds), *A Tribute to Geza Vermes, JSOT* Supplement Series 100, Sheffield: Sheffield Academic Press, 1990, pp. 355–81.

Møller-Christiansen, V., 'Skeletal Remains from Giv'at ha-Mivtar', *Israel Exploration Journal* 26 (1976), pp. 35–8.

Montefiore, H. W., 'Revolt in the Desert (Mark vi.30ff)?', *NTS* 8 (1961–62), pp. 135–41.

Morgan, R., 'Nothing More Negative . . .: A Concluding Unscientific Postscript to Historical Jesus Research on the Trial of Jesus' in E. Bammel (ed.), *The Trial of Jesus* (Moule Festschrift), pp. 135–65.

Neusner, Jacob, *Judaism in the Beginning of Christianity*, Philadelphia: Fortress Press, 1984.

O'Neill, J. C., 'The Charge of Blasphemy at Jesus' Trial Before the Sanhedrin' in E. Bammel (ed.), *The Trial of Jesus* (Moule Festschrift), pp. 72–7.

'The Silence of Jesus', *NTS* 15 (1968/69), pp. 153–67.

Platt, E. E., 'The Ministry of Mary of Bethany', *Theology Today* 34 (1977), pp. 29–39.

Powell, F. J., 'The Plot to Kill Jesus from Three Different Perspectives: Point of View in Matthew', *SBLSP*, 1990, pp. 603–13.

Primrose, W. B., 'A Surgeon Looks at the Crucifixion', *Hibbert Journal* 47 (1949), pp. 382–8.

Renan, Ernst, *Vie de Jésus*, Paris: Arlea, 1992.

Reuther, Rosemary, 'Theological Anti-Semitism in the New Testament', *The Christian Century* 85, 7 (Feb. 1968), pp. 191–6.

Richardson, Peter, 'Why Turn the Tables? Jesus' Protest in the Temple Precincts', *SBLSP* (1992), pp. 507–23.

Rivkin, E., 'Beth Din, Boulé, Sanhedrin: A Tragedy of Errors', *HUCA* 46 (1975), pp. 181–99.

Rosenblattt, S., 'The Crucifixion of Jesus from the Standpoint of Pharisaic Law', *JBL* 75 (1956), pp. 315–21.

Salomonsen, B., 'Some Remarks on the Zealots with Special Regard to the Term "Qannaim" in Rabbinic Literature', *NTS* 12 (1965/66), pp. 164–76.

Sanders, E. P., *Jesus and Judaism*, Philadelphia: Fortress Press, 1985.

The Historical Figure of Jesus, London: Allen Lane, 1993.

Schneider, Gerhard, 'The Political Charge Against Jesus (Luke 23:2)', *JPHD*, pp. 403–14.

Schonfield, Hugh Joseph, *The Jesus Party*, New York: Macmillan, 1974.

Schwartz, R., 'Josephus and Philo on Pontius Pilate', *The Jerusalem Cathedra* 3 (1983), pp. 27–31.

Schwartz, Seth, *Josephus and Judaean Politics*, Leiden: Brill, 1990.

Seeley, D., 'Was Jesus like a Philosopher? The Evidence of Martyrological and Wisdom Motifs in Q, Pre-Pauline Traditions and Mark', *SBLSP* 28 (1989), pp. 540–9.

Sherwin-White, A.N., *Roman Society and Roman Law in the New Testament*, Oxford: Clarendon Press, 1963.

'The Trial of Christ' in *History and Chronology in the New Testament*, Oxford: Clarendon Press, 1963.

Sizoo, R., 'Did the Jews Kill Jesus?', *Interpretation* 1 (1947), pp. 201–6.

Sloyan, G., *Jesus on Trial*, Philadelphia: Fortress Press, 1973.

Smallwood, E. Mary, 'High Priests and Politics in Roman Palestine', *JTS* 13 (1962), pp. 14–34.

'Some Notes on the Jews under Tiberius', *Latomus* 15 (1956), pp. 314–29.

'The Date of the Dismissal of Pontius Pilate from Judaea', *JJS* 5 (1954), pp. 12–21.

The Jews Under Roman Rule from Pompey to Diocletian, Leiden: Brill, 1981.

Smith, Morton, 'Jesus' Attitude Toward the Law', *Papers of the Fourth World Congress of Jewish Studies*, Jerusalem, 1967, pp. 241–4.

Jesus The Magician, New York: Harper & Row, 1977.

Sweet, J. P. M., 'The Zealots and Jesus', *JPHD*, pp. 1–9.

Torrey, C. C., 'Studies in Aramaic of the First Century AD', *ZAW* 65 (1953), pp. 228–47

'The Name Iscariot', *HTR* 36 (1943), pp. 51–62.

Tzaferis, V., 'Crucifixion – The Archaeological Evidence', *BAR* 11, 1 (Jan.–Feb. 1985), pp. 44–53.

Vermes, Geza, *Jesus the Jew*, London: Collins, 1973.

Wells, G. A., *Did Jesus Exist?*, London: Pemberton, 1975.

The Historical Evidence for Jesus, New York: Prometheus Books, 1982.

Wilson, A. N., *Jesus: A Life*, New York: Norton, 1992.

Wilson, Ian, *Jesus: The Evidence*, New York: Harper & Row, 1984.

Wilson, William R., *The Execution of Jesus: A Judicial, Literary and Historical Investigation*, New York: Scribner, 1970.

Winter, Paul, *On the Trial of Jesus*, Berlin: De Gruyter, 1974, 2nd edn.

'The Trial of Jesus and the Competence of the Sanhedrin', *NTS* 10 (1963/64), pp. 494–9.

'The Trial of Jesus as a Rebel Against Rome', *JQR* 16 (1968), pp. 31–7.

Witherington, Ben, *The Jesus Quest. The Third Search for the Jew of Nazareth*, Downers Grove, IL: InterVarsity Press, 1995.

Yamauchi, E. M., 'Historical Notes on the Trial and Crucifixion of Jesus Christ', *Christianity Today* 15 (1970/71), pp. 634–9.

Yoder, J. H., *The Politics of Jesus*, Grand Rapids, MI: Eerdmans, 1972.

Zeitlin, Solomon, 'The Crucifixion of Jesus Re-Examined', *JQR* 31 (1940/41), pp. 327–69.

'The Crucifixion of Jesus Re-Examined', *JQR* 32 (1941/42), pp. 175–89, 279–301.

'The Dates of the Birth and Crucifixion of Jesus: II. The Crucifixion, A Libelous Accusation Against the Jews', *JQR* 55 (1964), pp. 1–22.

'The Hoax of the "Slavonic Josephus" ', *JQR* 39 (1948/49), pp. 171–80.

'The Trial of Jesus', *JQR* 53 (1962), pp. 77–88.

Who Crucified Jesus, New York and London: Harper Bros, 1947.

Bar Kokhba War

ANCIENT WORKS

Appian, *Appian's Roman History*, trans. by Horace White, Cambridge: Loeb Classical Library, 1958, 4 vols.

Cassius Dio, *Dio's Roman History*, trans. by E. Cary, Cambridge: Loeb Classical Library, 1954, 9 vols.

Eusebius, Bishop of Caesarea, *c.*260–*c.*340. Demonstration of the Gospel, *Dimostrazione Evangelica, Introduzione, Traduzione e Note di Paolo Carrara*, Milan: Paoline, 2000.

Chronicon in *Eusebius Werke*, Herausgegeben im Auftrage der Kirchenväter-Commission der Königl, Preußischen Akademie der Wissenschaften, Leipzig: J. C. Hinrichs, 1902.

Historica Ecclesiastica, trans. by Kirsopp Lake, *The Ecclesiastical History*, Cambridge: Loeb Classical Library, 1959, 2 vols.

Fronto, Marcus Cornelius, *The Correspondence of Marcus Cornelius Fronto with Marcus Aurelius, T. Antoninus, Lucius Verus, Antoninus Pius and Various Friends*, trans. and ed. by C. R. Haines, Cambridge, MA: Harvard University Press, 1962, 2 vols.

Scriptores Historiae Augustae, trans. by David Magie, Cambridge: Loeb Classical Library, 1960, 3 vols.

Talmud, Hebrew–English edition of the *Babylonian Talmud*, trans. into English with notes and glossary under I. Epstein (ed.), introduction by the editor, New York, NY: Traditional Press, 1979–1983, 30 vols.

MODERN WORKS

Abusch, R., 'Negotiating Difference: Genital Mutilation in Roman Slave Law and the History of the Bar Kokhba Revolt' in P. Schäfer (ed.), *The Bar Kokhba War Reconsidered*, Tübingen: Mohr Siebeck, 2003, pp. 71–91.

Aharoni, Yohanan, 'Expedition B – The Cave of Horror', *IEJ* 11 (1962), pp. 186–99.

Aleksandrov, G. S., 'The Role of Aqiba in the Bar Kokhba Rebellion', *REJ* 132 (1973), pp. 65–77.

Alföldy, Geza, 'Traianus Pater' in J. Gonzalez (ed.), *Trajano: Emperador de Roma*, Roma: Bretschneider, 2000.

Alon, Gedaliah A., *The Jews in Their Land in the Talmudic Age*, Jerusalem: Magnes Press, The Hebrew University, 1984.

Applebaum, Shimon, 'Points of View on the Second Jewish Revolt', *SCI* 7 (1983/84), pp. 77–87.

Prologomena to the Study of the Second Jewish Revolt (AD 132–135), BAR Supplement Series 7, 1976.

'The Burial Place of Rabbi "Aqiva" ', *Proceedings of the Seventh World Congress of Jewish Studies in Jerusalem in 1977*, Jerusalem: 1981, pp. 37–47.

'The Jewish Revolt in Cyrene in 115–117 and the Subsequent Re-Colonization', *JJS* 2 (1951), pp. 177–81.

'The Second Jewish Revolt (AD 131–35), *PEQ* 116 (1984), pp. 35–7.

'Tineus Rufus and Julius Severus' in *Judaea in Hellenistic and Roman Times. Historical and Archaeological Essays*, Leiden: Brill, 1988, pp. 120–3.

'For Whom Did Apollodorus Write the Poliorketika?' in S. Applebaum: *Judaea in Hellenistic and Roman Times. Historical and Archaeological Essays*, Leiden: Brill, 1989, pp. 111–16.

Bar, Doron, 'Aelia Capitolina and the Location of the Camp of the Tenth Legion', *PEQ* 130 (Jan.–June 1998), pp. 8–19.

Barag, Daniel, 'The Two Mints of the Bar Kokhba War' in D. Barag (ed.), 'Studies in Memory of Leo Mildenberg', *INJ* 14 (2002), pp. 153–6.

Belayche, Nicole, *Judaea–Palaestina: The Pagan Cults in Roman Palaestina* (second to fourth century), Tübingen: Mohr-Siebeck, 2001.

Benoit, Pierre, et al., *Discoveries in the Judaean Desert* II: *Les Grottes de Murabba'at*, Oxford: Clarendon Press, 1961, 2 vols.

Birley, A. R., *Hadrian: The Restless Emperor*, London and New York: Routledge, 1997.

Boatwright, Mary T., *Hadrian and the Cities of the Roman Empire*, Princeton, NJ: Princeton University Press, 2000.

Bowersock, Glen W., 'A Roman Perspective on the Bar Kochba War' in William S. Green (ed.), *Approaches to Ancient Judaism,* Chico, CA: Scholars Press, 1980, vol. 2, pp. 131–41.

'The Babatha Papyri, Masada, and Rome', review article on Naphtali Lewis (ed.), *Judean Desert Studies: The Documents from the Bar Kokhba Period in the Cave of Letters. Greek Papyri*, and Hannah M. Cotton and Joseph Geiger (eds), 'Masada II, The Yigael Yadin Excavations 1963–1965: Final Reports. The Latin and Greek Documents', *Journal of Roman Archaeology* 4 (1991), pp. 336–44.

'The Annexation and Initial Garrison of Arabia', *ZPE* 5 (1970), pp. 37–47.

'The Tel Shalem Arch and P. Nahal Hever/Seiyal 8' in P. Schäfer (ed.), *The Bar Kokhba War Reconsidered*, Tübingen: Mohr Siebeck, 2003, pp. 171–80.

Cordier, P., 'Les Romains et La Circoncision', *REL* 160 (2001), pp. 337–55.

Cotton, Hannah M., 'The Bar Kokhba Revolt and the Documents from the Judaean Desert: Nabataean Participation in the Revolt (P. Yadin 52)' in P. Schäfer (ed.), *The Bar Kokhba War Reconsidered*, Tübingen: Mohr Siebeck, 2003, pp. 133–52.

and Ada Yardeni, *Aramaic, Hebrew and Greek Documentary Texts from Nahal Hever and Other Sites*, Oxford: Clarendon Press, 1997.

Damati, E., 'Four Bar Kokhba Coins from Khirbet el-Aqd', *INJ* 4 (1980), pp. 27–9.

Eck, Werner, 'Ein Spiegel der Macht. Lateinische Inschriften Römischer Zeit in Judaea/Syria Palaestine', *ZDPV* 117 (2001), pp. 47–63.

'Hadrian, the Bar Kokhba Revolt, and the Epigraphic Transmission' in P. Schäfer (ed.), *The Bar Kokhba War Reconsidered*, Tübingen: Mohr Siebeck, 2003, pp. 153–70.

'The Bar Kokhba Revolt: The Roman Point of View', *JRS* 89 (1999), pp. 76–89.

and Gideon Foerster, 'Ein Triumphbogen für Hadrian im Tal von Beth Shean bei Tel Shalem', *JRA* 12 (1999), pp. 294–313.

Eldad, Israel, 'In Praise of Bar Kokhba', *JQ* 32 (summer 1984), p. 113.

Eliav, Yaron Z., 'Hadrian's Actions in the Jerusalem Temple Mount According to Cassius Dio and Xiphilinus', *JSQ* 4 (1997) pp. 125–44.

'The Urban Layout of Aelia Capitolina: A New View from the Perspective of the Temple Mount' in P. Schäfer (ed.), *The Bar Kokhba War Reconsidered*, Tübingen: Mohr Siebeck, 2003, pp. 241–75.

Eshel, Hanan, 'Aelia Capitolina: Jerusalem No More', *BAR* 23, 6 (Nov.–Dec. 1997), pp. 46–8, 73.

Finkelstein, Louis, 'Rabbi Akiba, Rabbi Ishmael, and the Bar Kokhba Rebellion' in J. Neusner (ed.), *Approaches to Ancient Judaism*, vol. 1, Atlanta: Scholars Press, 1990, pp. 1–10.

Freund, Richard A., and Rami Aran, 'Return to the Cave of Letters. What Still Lies Buried?' *BAR* 27, 1 (Jan.–Feb. 2001), pp. 24–9.

Fuks, A., 'Aspects of the Jewish Revolt in AD 115–117', *JRS* 51 (1961), pp. 98–104.

Gichon, Mordechai, 'New Insight into the Bar Kokhba War and a Reappraisal of Dio Cassius 69.12–13, *JQR* 77 (1986), pp. 15–43.

'The Bar Kochba War: A Colonial Uprising Against Imperial Rome', *RIHM* 42 (1979), pp. 82–97.

Golan, D., 'Hadrian's Decision to Supplant Jerusalem by Aelia Capitolina', *Historia* 35 (1986), pp. 226–39.

Goodman, Martin, 'Diaspora Reactions to the Destruction of the Temple' in J. D. G. Dunn (ed.), *Jews and Christians,* Tübingen: Mohr-Siebeck, 1992, pp. 27–38.

'Nerva, The Fiscus Judaicus and Jewish Identity', *JRS* 79 (1989), pp. 40–4.

'Trajan and the Origins of the Bar Kokhba War' in P. Schäfer (ed.), *The Bar Kokhba War Reconsidered,* Tübingen: Mohr Siebeck, 2003, pp. 23–9.

Haimi, Avinoam, 'From Bar Kokhba – Greetings', *New Outlook* 4, 8 (Oct.–Nov. 1981), pp. 37–44.

Harkabi, Yehoshafat, *The Bar Kochba Syndrome,* Chappaqua, NY: Rossel Books, 1983.

Harris, Rendel, 'Hadrian's Decree of Expulsion of the Jews from Jerusalem', *HTR* 19 (1926), pp. 199–206.

Herr, M. D., 'Persecutions and Martyrdom in Hadrian's Days', *Scripta Hierosolymitana* 23 (1972), pp. 85–125.

Holum, Kenneth, 'Hadrian's Imperial Tour', *BAR* 23, 6 (1997), pp. 5–51, 76.

Howard, G., and J. C. Shelton, 'The Bar Kokhba Letters and Palestinian Greek', *IEJ* 23 (1973), pp. 101–12.

Isaac, Benjamin, 'Cassius Dio on the Revolt of Bar Kokhba', *SCI* 7 (1983–84), pp. 68–76. Reprinted with postscript in B. Isaac, *The Near East Under Roman Rule,* Leiden: Brill, 1998, pp. 211–19.

'Judaea After AD 70', *JJS* 35 (1984), pp. 44–50.

'Roman Colonies in Judaea: The Foundation of Aelia Capitolina', *Talanta* (1980/81), pp. 12–13, 31–54. Reprinted in *Near East Under Roman Rule,* Leiden: Brill, 1998, pp. 87–108.

'Roman Religious Policy and the Bar Kokhba War' in P. Schäfer (ed.), *The Bar Kokhba War Reconsidered,* Tübingen: Mohr Siebeck, 2003, pp. 37–54.

'The Babatha Archive' in *The Near East Under Roman Rule,* Leiden: Brill, 1998, pp. 159–81.

The Near East Under Roman Rule, Selected Papers, Leiden: Brill, 1998.

and A. Oppenheimer, 'The Revolt of Bar Kokhba: Ideology and Modern Scholarship, *JJS* 36 (1985), pp. 33–60. Reprinted in *The Near East Under Roman Rule,* pp. 220–256.

and I. Roll, 'Judaea in the Early Years of Hadrian's Reign', *Latomus* 388 (1979), pp. 54–66. Reprinted in *The Near East Under Roman Rule,* Leiden: Brill, 1998, p. 182.

Kanael, B., 'Notes on the Dates Used During the Bar Kokhba Revolt', *IEJ* 21 (1971), pp. 39–46.

Keppie, Lawrence J. F., 'The History and Disappearance of the Legion XXII Deiotariana' in A. Kasher, U. Rappaport and G. Fuks (eds), *Greece and Rome in Eretz Israel, Collected Essays,* Jerusalem: Yad Izhak Ben Zvi, 1990, pp. 54–61 (republished as L. J. F. Keppie, *Legions and Veterans, Roman Army Papers 1971–2000,* Stuttgart: Franz Steiner Verlag, 2000, pp. 225–32, 322).

'The Legionary Garrison of Judaea under Hadrian', *Latomus* 33 (1973), pp. 859–64.

Kloner, Amos, 'Lead Weights of Bar Kokhba's Administration', *IEJ* 40 (1990), pp. 58–67.

'Name of Ancient Israel's Last President Discovered on Lead Weight', *BAR* (July–Aug. 1988), pp. 12–17.

'The Subterranean Hideaways of the Judaean Foothills and the Bar-Kokhba Revolt', *The Jerusalem Cathedra* 3 (1983), pp. 83–96.

'Underground Hiding Complexes from the Bar Kokhba War in the Judaean Shephelah', *BA* (Dec. 1983), pp. 210–21.

and Boaz Zissu, 'Hiding Complexes in Judaea: An Archaeological and Geographical Update on the Area of the Bar Kokhba Revolt' in P. Schäfer (ed.), *The Bar Kokhba War Reconsidered,* Tübingen: Mohr Siebeck, 2003, pp. 181–216.

Lapp, N. L., and G. W. E. Nickelsburg, jun., 'Discoveries in the Wadi ed-Daliyeh', *AASOR* 41 (1974), pp. 49ff.

Levick, Barbara, *Roman Colonies in Southern Asia Minor,* Oxford: Clarendon Press, 1967.

Lewis, Naphtali, *Desert Studies: The Documents from the Bar Kokhba Period in the Cave of Letters, Greek Papyri,* Jerusalem: Israel Exploration Society, 1989.

Lifshitz, B., 'Papyrus Grecs du Desert de Judea', *Aegyptus* 42 (1962), pp. 240–58.

Mantel, H., 'The Causes of the Bar Kokhba Revolt', *JQR* 58 (1968), pp. 224–42.

Margalit, S., 'Aelia Capitolina', *Judaica* 45 (1989), pp. 45–56.

Marks, Richard Gordon, *The Image of Bar Kokhba in Traditional Jewish Literature: False Messiah and National Hero*, University Park, PA: Pennsylvania State University, 1994.

Meshorer, Yaacov, *Jewish Coins of the Second Temple Period*, Tel Aviv: Am Hassefer, 1967.

The Coinage of Aelia Capitolina, Jerusalem: Israel Museum, 1989.

Meyshan, J., 'The Legion Which Reconquered Jerusalem in the War of Bar Kokhba, AD 132–5', *PEQ* (1958), pp. 19–26 (republished as J. Meyshan, *Essays in Jewish Numismatics*, Jerusalem: Israel Numismatic Society, 1960, pp. 143–50).

Mildenberg, L., 'Bar Kokhba in Jerusalem?', *Schweizer Münzblätter* 105 (1977), pp. 1–6.

'Rebel Coinage in the Roman Empire' in A. Kasher, U. Rappaport and G. Fuks (eds), *Greece and Rome in Eretz Israel*, Jerusalem: Yad Izhak Ben-Zvi, Israel Exploration, 1990, pp. 62–74.

'The Bar Kokhba War in the Light of the Coins and Document Finds 1947–1982', *INJ* 8 (1984/85), pp. 27–32.

The Coinage of the Bar Kokhba War, Aarau: Verlag Sauerländer, 1984.

Mor, Menachem, 'The Bar Kokhba Revolt and Non-Jewish Participants', *JJS* 36 (1985), pp. 200–9.

'The Roman Army in Eretz–Israel in the Years AD 70–132' in P. Freeman and D. Kennedy (eds), *The Defense of the Roman and Byzantine East. II Proceedings of a Colloquium held at the University of Sheffield in April 1986*, Oxford: BAR International Series 297, 1 (1986), pp. 575–602.

'The Roman Legions and the Bar Kokhba Revolt 132–135 AD' in H. Vetters and M. Kandler (eds), *Akten des 14th Internationalen Limeskongresses, 1986*, Vienna: Verlag der Österreichischen Akademie der Wissenschaften, 1990, pp. 163–78.

'Two Legions – The Same Fate? The Disappearance of the Legion IX Hispana and XXII Deiotariana', *ZPE* 62 (1986), pp. 267–78.

Netzer, E., 'Jewish Rebels Dig Strategic Tunnel System', *BAR* 14, 4 (1988), pp. 18–33.

Oppenheimer, Aharon, 'The Ban on Circumcision as a Cause of the Revolt: A Reconsideration' in P. Schäfer (ed.), *The Bar Kokhba War Reconsidered*, Tübingen: Mohr Siebeck, 2003, pp. 55–69.

and Uri Rappaport (eds), *The Bar Kokva Revolt: A New Approach*, Jerusalem: Yad Yitshak Ben-Tsevi, 1984 (H).

Patrich, Joseph, 'Hideouts in the Judean Wilderness – Jewish Revolutionaries and Christian Ascetics South Shelter and Protection in Cliffside Caves', *BAR* 15, 5 (Sept.–Oct. 1989), pp. 32–42.

Pflaum, H. G., 'Remarques Sur le Changement de Statut Administrative de La Province de Judée a Propos D'une Inscription Récément Découverte a Sidé de Pamphylie', *IEJ* 19, 4 (1969), pp 225–33.

Rabello, A. M., 'The Edicts on Circumcision as a Factor in the Bar-Kokhva Revolt' in A. Oppenheimer and U. Rappaport (eds), *The Bar Kokva Revolt: A New Approach*, Jerusalem: Yad Yitshak Ben-Tsevi, 1984, pp. 33–46 (H).

Raffaeli, Shmuel, 'Jewish Coinage and the Date of the Bar Kokhba Revolt', *JPOS* 3 (1923), pp. 123–96.

Rappaport, Uriel, 'John of Gischala in Galilee', *The Jerusalem Cathedra* 3 (1981), pp. 46–57.

Reinhartz, Adele, 'Rabbinical Perceptions of Simeon Bar Kosiba', *JSJ* 20 (1985), pp. 171–94.

Rokeah, D., 'Comments on the Revolt of Bar Kokhba', *Tarbiz* 35 (1965/66), pp. 122–31 (H).

Safrai, S., 'The Relations between the Roman Army and the Jews of Eretz Israel after the Destruction of the Second Temple' in S. Applebaum (ed.), *Roman Frontier Studies 1967*; proceedings of the seventh international congress held at Tel Aviv, Tel-Aviv: Students' Organization of Tel Aviv University, 1971, pp. 224–9.

Schäfer, Peter, 'Bar Kokhba and the Rabbis' in P. Schäfer (ed.), *The Bar Kokhba War Reconsidered*, Tübingen: Mohr Siebeck, 2003, pp. 1–22.

Der Bar-Kokhba Aufstand. Studien zum Zweiten Jüdischen Krieg gegen Rom, Tübingen: Mohr Siebeck, 1981.

'Hadrian's Policy in Judaea and the Bar Kokhba Revolt. A Reassessment' in P. R. Davies and R. T. White (eds), *A Tribute to Geza Vermes. Essays on Jewish and Christian Literature and History*, Sheffield: JSOT Press, 1990, pp. 281–303.

Judeophobia: Attitudes Toward the Jews in the Ancient World, Cambridge: Harvard University Press, 1997.

'Rabbi Aqiva und Bar Kockba' in *Approaches to Ancient Judaism 11*, Chico, CA: Scholars Press, 1980, pp. 113–30.

'Rabbi Aqiva and Bar Kokhba' in P. Schäfer, *Studien Zur Geschichte und Theologie des Rabbinischen Judentums*, Leiden: E. L. Brill, 1978, pp. 65–121.

'Rabbi Akiva and Bar Kokhba' in William Scott Green (ed.), *Approaches to Ancient Judaism*, Ann Arbor, MI: Scholars Press, 1980, vol. 2, pp. 121–4.

'The Bar Kokhba Revolt and Circumcision – Historical Evidence and Modern Apologetics' in A. Oppenheimer (ed.), *Judische Geschichte in Hellenistisch-römischer Zeit*, Munich: Oldenbourg, 1999, pp. 119–32.

'The Causes of the Bar Kokhba Revolt' in Jakob Petuchowski and Ezra Fleischer (eds), *Studies in Aggadah, Targum and Jewish Liturgy in Memory of Joseph Heinemann,* Jerusalem: Magnes Press, 1981, pp. 74–94.

Schäfer, Peter (ed.), *The Bar Kokhba War Reconsidered*, Tübingen: Mohr Siebeck, 2003.

Schwartz, Jacques, 'Ou a Passé La Legio XXII Deiotariana?', *ZPE* 76 (1989), pp. 101–2.

Schürer, E., *The History of the Jewish People in the Age of Jesus Christ (175 BC–AD 135)*, A New English Version rev. and ed. by Geza Vermes and F. Millar, Edinburgh: T. & T. Clark, 1973, pp. 514–57.

Shahar, Yuval, 'The Undergound Hideouts in Galilee and Their Historical Meaning' in P. Schäfer (ed.), *The Bar Kokhba War Reconsidered*, Tübingen: Mohr Siebeck, 2003, pp. 217–40.

Shotter, D. C., 'The Principate of Nerva; Some Observations on the Coin Evidence', *Historia* 32 (1983), pp. 218–23.

Smallwood, E. Mary, 'The Legislation of Hadrian and Antononius Pius Against Circumcision', *Latomus* 18 (1959), pp. 334–47.

'Addendum, The Legislation of Hadrian and Antoninus Pius Against Circumcision', *Latomus* 20 (1961), pp. 93–6.

Stern, M., *Greek and Latin Authors on Jews and Judaism*, Jerusalem: Israel Academy of Sciences and Humanities, 1980.

Syme, Ronald, *Ammianus Marcellinus and the Historia Augusta*, Oxford: Clarendon Press, 1968.

Emperors and Biography: Studies in the Historia Augusta, Oxford: Clarendon Press, 1971.

Sallust, Berkeley: University of California Press, 1964.

Teicher, J. L., 'Are the Bar Kokhba Documents Genuine?', *JJS* 5, 1 (1954), pp. 39–40.

Toynbee, J. M. C., *The Hadrianic School*, Cambridge: Cambridge University Press, 1934.

Tsafrir, Yoram, 'A Cave of the Bar Kokhba Period near "Ain Arrub" ', *Qadmoniot* 8 (1975), pp. 24–7 (H).

'Numismatics and the Foundation of Aelia Capitolina' in P. Schäfer (ed.), *The Bar Kokhba War Reconsidered*, Tübingen: Mohr Siebeck, 2003, pp. 31–6.

and Zissu, B., 'A Hiding Complex from the Second Temple Period and the Time of the Bar Kokhba Revolt at Ain-Arrub in the Hebron Hills' in J. Humphrey (ed.), *The Roman And Byzantine Near East, Journal of Roman Archaeology* Supplementary Series 49, Portsmouth, RI: 2002, vol. 3, pp. 6–36.

Ussushkin, D., 'Betar: The Last Stronghold of Bar Kochba', *Bulletin of the Anglo-Israel Archaeological Society* 6 (1986/87), pp. 49–50.

Yadin, Yigael, *Bar-Kokhba. The Rediscovery of the Legendary Hero of the Last Jewish Revolt Against Rome*, New York: Random House, 1971.

'Expedition D' in *The Expedition to the Judaean Desert*, 1960, *IEJ* 11, 1 (1961), pp. 41–52.

Judaean Desert Studies. The Finds from the Bar Kokhba Period in the Cave of Letters, Jerusalem: Israel Exploration Society, 1963.

Yeivin, Shmuel, *The War of Bar Kokhba,* Jerusalem: Mosad Byalik, 1946 (H).

Zeitlin, Solomon, 'The Fiction of the Bar Kokhba Letters', *JQR* 51 (1960/61), pp. 265–74.

Zerubavel, Yael, 'Bar Kokhba's Image in Modern Israeli Culture' in P. Schäfer (ed.), *The Bar Kokhba War Reconsidered*, Tübingen: Mohr Siebeck, 2003, pp. 279–97.

Zissu, Boaz, 'The Geographical Distribution of Coins from the Bar Kokhba War', *INJ* 14 (2002), pp. 157–67.

INTELLIGENCE GLOSSARY

Clandestine operations – An operation sponsored or conducted by governmental departments or agencies in such a way as to assure secrecy or concealment. A clandestine operation differs from a covert operation (q.v.) in that emphasis is placed on concealment of the operation rather than on concealment of the identity of the sponsor. In special operations, an activity may be both covert and clandestine and may focus equally on operational considerations and intelligence-related activities.*

Counterintelligence (CI) – Information gathered and activities conducted to protect against espionage, other intelligence activities, sabotage or assassinations conducted by or on behalf of foreign governments or elements thereof, foreign organisations or foreign persons, or international terrorist activities.*

Covert operation – An operation that is so planned and executed as to conceal the identity of or permit plausible denial by the sponsor. A covert operation differs from a clandestine operation (q.v.) in that the emphasis is placed on concealment of identity of the sponsor rather than on concealment of the operation itself.*

Disinformation – Deliberately misleading information announced publicly or leaked by a government, intelligence agency, corporation or other entity for the purpose of influencing opinions or perceptions. Unlike misinformation, which is also a form of wrong information, disinformation is produced by people who intend to deceive their audience.

Force multiplier – A capability that, when added to and employed by a combat force, significantly increases the combat potential of that force and thus enhances the probability of successful mission accomplishment.§

HUMINT (human intelligence) – A category of intelligence derived from information collected and provided by human sources.*§ See US Army field manuals FM 34-2 and FM 34-3.

Intelligence – A body of evidence and the conclusions drawn therefrom that is acquired and furnished in response to the known or perceived requirements of consumers. It is often, but not always, derived from information that is concealed or not intended to be available for use by the acquirer.

Intelligence cycle – The steps by which information is converted into intelligence and made available to users. In the modern version, there are five steps in the process: (1) planning and direction; (2) collection; (3) processing; (4) production; and (5) dissemination. The ancient version is scaled down to four: (1) targeting; (2) collection; (3) analysis; and (4) dissemination.

Reconnaissance – A mission undertaken to obtain, by visual observation or other detection methods, information about the activities and resources of an enemy or potential enemy or to secure data concerning the meteorological, hydrographic or geographic characteristics of a particular area.*§

Reconnaissance in force – An offensive operation designed to discover and/or test the enemy's strength or to obtain other information.*§

Safe house – An innocent-appearing house or premises established by an organisation for the purpose of conducting clandestine or covert activity in relative security.*

Strategic intelligence – Intelligence that is required for the formulation of military strategy, policy and plans and operations at national and theatre levels.

Tactical intelligence – Intelligence that is required for planning and conducting tactical operations.*

Tradecraft – An intelligence term for the skills taught to field agents in the espionage business. Running spy networks, using dead drops, the techniques of secret writing, flaps and seals, and escape and evasion. Except for our technical advances, examples of most of these techniques, or at least primitive versions of them, are found in the ancient world.

SOURCES

* *Department of Defense Dictionary of Military and Associated Terms* (Washington, DC: Government Reprints Press, 2001)

§ US Army field manuals FM 101–5–1/MCRP 5–2A, *Operational Terms and Graphics*, 30 September 1997, Headquarters, Department of the Army, US Marine Corps

INDEX

Aaron 22
Abdullam 92–3
Abigail 115
Abimelech 74–5
Abner, son of Ner 89–90
Abraham (patriarch) 34
Absalom 90–1
Acco Ptolemais 132
Achan 51
Achior 115
Achish of Gath 85
Achor, Valley of 51
Acre 189
Aelia Capitolina 180–1, 198
Afghanistan 151
Africa 124
agents 22, 46–7, 60, 64, 67,
    75–6, 99, 103, 115, 153,
    155, 174–5
  disinformation 113
  double 90, 123, 164
  female 47, 76, 123
  intelligence 183
  Roman 164, 173–4
  secret 75–6, 115, 163
  undercover 112, 171
Agrippa 132
Agrippa II, King of Judaea
    134
Ahitophel 90–1
Ai, city of 25, 48, 50–2,
    59–62, 87, 207, 226
  Battle of 53
Aijalon, valley of 57, 97,
    104–5
Albinus, Roman prefect 161
Albright, William F. 15,
    24–5, 28, 54, 118
Alexandria 139, 150
Algeria 195
Allenby, Field Marshall
    E. H. H. 20
Alt, Albrecht 26, 58
Amalekites 70, 73, 91
Amarna letters 28
ambushes 36, 61–2, 85–6, 90,
    97, 102–8, 124, 136, 138,
    144, 147, 177, 195–6,

204–7, 242
Americans 195
Amman, Jordan 45, 95
Ammonites 84, 94–5, 115,
    236
  Ammonite war 94
  King Hanun 94
  Syrian coalition with 95
Amorites 46, 53–4, 227
amphictyony 79
Ananias, high priest 134
Ananus 133
anarchists 155
anthropology 15
anti-semitism 170
Antioch 108
Antiochus III 99
Antiochus IV Epiphanes 99,
    103–5, 240
Antonia fortress 134, 144–5,
    161
Apelles 100
Aphek 58
Aphek Gezer 26
apiru 28, 221
Apocrypha 112
Apollodorus of Damascus 189
  Poliorketika 189
Apollonius 103–5, 241
apostles 162
Arabia 184, 188, 191
Aramaeans 84
archaeology, archaeologists
    25–7, 29, 42, 52, 57–60,
    69, 118, 121, 124, 209
  biblical 15, 24–5
  discoveries 23, 29, 31–6
  evidence 20–4, 36, 41,
    48–9, 58, 69, 81–2,
    84, 95–6, 124–5, 146,
    179–82, 209, 219, 225–6
  techniques 23
archers and archery 73, 90,
    136, 204–5
aristocratic party, Jewish
    134, 141
Ark of the Covenant 49
Armageddon 14

Armenia 151
Arminius 182
armour 102, 205
Ashdod 26
Asher, tribe of 67, 71, 73
Ashkelon 107
assassination 90, 115–16,
    130, 141, 151, 200, 237
  assassins 68, 123, 130–1,
    133, 149, 155
  political assassination 64
Assyria and Assyrians 18,
    26, 33, 35, 49–50, 53,
    55, 57–60, 69, 80, 92,
    112–16, 120
  Assyrian camp (Jerusalem)
    144
  royal inscriptions 59–60
Astrologers 17
Augustan history 152, 179
auxiliary troops 136
Aviezer, tribe of 71
Avvim 55
Azaezel 82

Baal 74
Bab el-Wad 106
Babylon 33, 35
  Babylonian Jews 142
  Babylonians 33, 35, 69, 92,
    112, 121, 192
  exile of Jews in 120–1
Bagoas 115–16
ballistas 103
bandits 130, 132, 165
Bar Kokhba 179, 181–5, 188,
    196–8
  letters of 182–3
Bar Kokhba Revolt 15, 19,
    148, 179–99, 261–8
  Babatha archive 191
  Bar Kokhba letters 191,
    266
  coinage of 179, 185–6, 188,
    194, 261–3
  papyri 188, 198
Barabbas, Jesus 169, 173, 175
Barak 65, 67–9, 81, 122, 203

Basques 201
Bassus, Roman governor of
    Syria 146
battering rams 103, 140, 145
battles, set-piece 103
Bedouin 27, 72, 191, 201
Beeroth 54
Beersheba 202
Benjamin, tribe of 85
Beth haven 87
Beth Horon 54, 86, 104–5,
    138, 238, 250
  Upper 137
Beth Shemesh 82
Beth Zechariah 108
Beth Zur 107–8, 243
Bethany 157
Bethar 192
Bethel 24, 50, 52–3, 55, 63,
    227–8
Bethlehem 108
Bethulia 112–13, 115–16,
    244–5
betrayal 211
Bible, Hebrew 13–16, 18–24,
    30–3, 36, 41, 45, 47, 51,
    59, 64, 68, 71, 85–6, 92,
    95–6, 107, 109, 112, 114,
    116–17, 120–1, 124, 179,
    201, 205–6, 208–9, 211,
    217–18
Bible, Hebrew and Christian
    15–17, 22, 24, 29, 174,
    200
Bimson, John 53
Bittir *see* Bethar
blasphemy 166, 170
Bloch, Marc 210
boiling oil 140
Book of Jashar 205
Book of Wars of the Lord 205
Bosnia 151
Boudicca 182
bows, bowmen 65, 76, 103,
    136, 144, 205, 228
Brandon, S. G. F. 156
brigands 132, 139, 155, 165
Bright, John 24, 118, 210

Britain 194
Bronze Age 14, 33, 42, 49
  Early 52
  Late 16, 18, 25, 2728, 33,
    49, 52, 54–5, 60–1, 81,
    95, 220–1, 235
  Late II 25, 28, 52, 55, 225
  Middle 54, 96, 227

Caesarea 154
Caiaphas 167, 171
Caleb 22
Caligula, Roman emperor 170
Callaway, Joseph 52
Cambridge History of Judaism
  210
camels 70–1, 92, 232
camouflage 140
Canaan 15, 18, 21–4, 26–7,
  33–4, 37, 48, 52, 59–61,
  80, 83, 118, 123
  kings of 41
Canaanites 33–5, 45, 50–1,
  56, 61–3, 65, 67–8, 70,
  80, 82–3, 119, 122–3,
  200–1, 220, 222
  armies 61
  cities 25–27, 36, 42, 58,
    65, 81, 124
  coalition 58
  conquest of 50
  gods on 50
  idolatry 82
  infantry 56
  inhabitants of lowlands 35
  kingdoms 57
  kings 97
  literature 49–50
  peasants 28
  shrines and worship 35, 82
  society 56
Cargill, Jack 211
Carmel pass 97, 184
Carmichael, Joel 156
catapults 139
cavalry 86, 106–7, 138
Cave of Horrors 194
Cave of Letters 191, 195
Cestius Gallus 136–8
chariots and chariotry 24, 28,
  35–6, 56, 58, 61–2, 65,
  67–8, 82, 86, 89, 95, 97,
  103, 204–5, 231, 235
Charlemagne 201
Chemosh 82
Chepirah 54–5; see also
  Khirbet Kefire
Christians and Christianity
  162, 169–71, 174, 176–7
  Christian scriptures 173
circumcision 99, 109, 181
citadel 99
Civilis 182
clandestine operations 64, 99,
  102, 182, 186
Clausewitz, 73–4, 150, 197

Clement of Rome 81
Cline, Eric 14, 19–20
collaborators 130, 139
colonial occupation 195
  anti-colonial wars 199
combat 17
  hand-to-hand 204
  long-weapon 205
command structure 203–4
commando units 140
communications 96–7, 102,
  118, 136, 203
Conquest Model 14, 24, 27,
  41, 53, 58, 117, 121, 125,
  217, 222
counterinsurgency 105
counterintelligence 186
Covenant, Laws of 50
covert operations 61–2, 70,
  119, 123, 200, 232
Craigie, P. C. 79
Creveld, Martin van 13
criminal justice, Roman 168
Crossan, John Dominic 170
crucifixion 154, 156, 160,
  166, 170–2, 175–8, 199
Cyprus 197, 199
Cyrenaica 197

Dacia 189
Dagon, god of the Philistines
  77
Damascus 112, 115
Damiyah bridge 45
Dan, tribe of 67, 202
Daniel, Book of 100
Danube river 189
David, King 34, 55, 58,
  84–5, 90–6, 98, 116,
  157–8, 204, 236–8
  army of 96
  house of 84, 96
  kingdom of 95
Davies, Philip R. 30, 95
Dead Sea 183
  caves 188
Debir 24–25
Deborah 57, 64–70, 78, 81–2,
  112, 115, 203, 230–1,
  234
  Song of 64, 67
deception, deception
  operations 13, 17, 36,
  49–51, 64, 67, 80, 92,
  115–16, 119, 124, 139,
  147, 205–6
decoys 36, 205
defection 67
delatores 169
Delilah 75–8, 115, 123,
  233–5
democracies 19
deserters 140, 144
Deuteronomist (history,
  historian) 32–3, 35,
  42–3, 49, 53, 55, 58–61,

63, 69, 74, 80, 82, 94,
  96–8, 118–22, 202.
  210, 220
Deuteronomy, Book of 32–3,
  60, 120
Dever, William G. 15,
Dibon 24
Dio Cassius Cocceianus 179,
  181–2, 185, 188, 194–5,
  197, 207
  Epitome 179
diplomacy 19, 167, 207
disciples 155, 164–5, 176
disinformation 22, 112–15,
  244
diversionary manoeuvres
  36, 205
Donaldson, T. L. 133
double agent 90
drought 70
Dulles, Allen 17

Eck, Werner 188, 192
eclipse, solar 57
Edomites 84
Eglon, king of Moab 64, 79
Egypt and Egyptians 20, 23,
  25–6, 33–6, 42, 69, 84,
  91, 96, 99, 124, 139, 184,
  186, 197, 209
  Roman Egypt 124
Ehud, son of Gera the
  Benjaminite 64, 79
Eisler, Robert 156
Eleazar ben Simon 131,
  134, 142
Eleazar ben Yair, the *sicarius*
  130, 146
Eleazar Maccabeus 108
elephants 103
Emmaus 105–6
Endor, Spring of 71
engineering warfare 142, 189
England 189
Ephraim, tribe of 73, 79, 87
espionage 16, 34, 47, 61, 99,
  112, 116, 123, 206, 210
Essenes 130, 150
Euphrates 84
Eusebius 192
evangelists 157, 166, 173,
  177
executions 167, 170
Exodus 21, 23–4, 33–4,
  122, 209
exorcists and exorcism 156,
  175

fanaticism, religious 169
feints 36, 205
feigned retreat 205
Finkelstein, Israel 32–4, 36,
  53, 57–8, 60, 98, 120
The Bible Unearthed 32
Finley, Moses 209
force multiplier 36, 56, 62,

116, 152, 188
Foucault, Michel 29
Frankel, Raphael 81
Fritz, Volkmar 26
Fronto, M. Cornelius 192, 194
  De Bello Parthico 192
  Letter to Marcus Aurelius
  194
frumentarii 183

Ga'al ben Ebed 75
Gabao 137–8
Gabriel, Richard A. 14, 75,
  118, 123, 209–10, 229
Gad, tribe of 67
Gale, General Sir Richard
  13–14,
Galilee (ha Galil) 25,
  55–6, 81–2, 129–30, 132,
  136–7, 139–41, 147,
  154–7, 160, 162, 171,
  173, 179–80, 182, 184,
  186, 188–9, 193, 197,
  203, 249
  Sea of 155
  Upper 25, 56, 81
Gamala 140, 147
Gamaliel 183
Garstang, John 25
Gaul 151
Gaza 78, 186
Geba 86–7
Genesis, Book of 27, 33
genocide 191, 201
gentiles 156
Gerasa 141, 189
Germany and Germans 26–7,
  149, 199
Gessius Florus 133
Gethsemane 164–5
Gezer 26, 49, 90, 96
Gibeah 87, 227
Gibeon 25, 41, 53–4, 57,
  98, 227
  Battle of 55, 57
  Gibeonites 53–5
Gibeon's Pool 98
Gichon, Mordechai 14–15,
  49, 54, 57, 68, 118, 123,
  186, 188, 210
Gideon 70–5, 78, 122, 203,
  235
Gilboa, Mount 72, 89, 97
Gilead 71
Gilgal 53, 86
Gischala 140
gnostics 170
God, a well-known deity 17,
  22, 24, 28, 33, 35, 47–8,
  54, 57, 64–5, 74, 81–2,
  87, 89, 91, 98, 112–16,
  123, 130, 150, 151, 158,
  162, 171, 198, 201, 208
Goethe, Johann Wolfgang von
  125
Goliath 98, 116, 148, 241

Goodman, Martin 180
Gophna 100, 102–4, 242
Gorgias 105–6
gospels and gospel writers
  154, 156–7, 160, 162–8,
  170–2, 175–6
  John 155, 158, 165, 167,
    169–70, 173–4
  Luke 157–8, 162–5, 175
  Mark 157, 160, 163–5,
    169, 172
  Matthew 156–8, 164,
    169–70
  synoptic 160, 164, 172
Gottwald, Norman K. 28–30,
  119
Greeks 109, 125, 182, 189,
  200–1, 205, 241
  historians 121
  historiography 121
  myth 78
guerrilla warfare 13, 18, 36,
  62, 85, 90, 99, 100, 102,
  105, 107–9, 111, 116,
  129, 132–3, 138–40, 142,
  147–9, 151–2, 176, 182,
  184, 189, 191, 195–7,
  202, 204–5
  guerrilla leaders 156, 182
Gunkel, Hermann 74

Hadrian, Roman emperor
  179–81, 185, 188–9, 192,
  194, 198–9
Halpern, Baruch 15, 201
Hanson, J. S. 132–3
Hanukkah 107, 243
Hanun, king of the
  Ammonites 94
Ha-Shomer Watchmen's
  Society 198
Harkabi, Yehoshafat 197–9
  The Bar Kokhba Syndrome
    197
Harod, Spring of 71
Harosheth-ha-goiim 68
Hasidim 100, 241
Hasmonean Dynasty 108, 110
  Hasmonean period 112
Hazor 25, 41, 49, 57–9, 90,
  96, 230
Heber the Kenite 67–8
Hebrews 15
Hebron 89–90, 92–3, 107
Hecataeus of Miletus 121
Hellenistic period 30, 32,
  95, 108–9, 116, 120–1,
  196, 201
  Palestine 30
  writers 32
helmets 102
Hengel, Martin 207
Hermann, 210
Herod and Herodians 122,
  134, 144, 146, 166
  Agrippa II 134

Herod Agrippa 132
Herod Antipas 154–5, 166
  Philip 155
Herodium 146
Herodotus 121
Herzog, Chaim 14, 49, 54,
  57, 68
Heshbon 24
Hezbollah 205
High Priest 163–9
  priestly aristocracy 164–5,
    168, 172–3, 175, 247
Historia Augusta see Augustan
  History
historians, military 14, 36,
  124, 209
Hittites 26, 124
Hivite cities 55
Hobsbawm, Eric 122, 132
Holofernes 18, 113–16, 245
holy war 79–80, 235, 246
hoplites 102, 106, 196
Horsley, Richard A. 132–3,
  156
Human sacrifice 82
HUMINT 13, 19
Hushai 91
Hyksos 25, 228

Idumea 107, 141
Iliad 98, 201
infiltrators 124
informers 161, 164, 167, 174
insurgents and insurgency
  100, 108, 119, 130, 138,
  153, 160, 171, 179–80,
  182, 184, 192, 195–96
  counterinsurgency 105
insurrection 129, 147, 155,
  159, 169, 172, 174–5,
  181, 183
intelligence 19–22, 24, 36–7,
  41–2, 45–8, 50–4, 56,
  59, 60–3, 67, 75, 92–4,
  105–6, 108, 111, 114,
  123, 134, 138, 140, 142,
  147, 150, 152–4, 159,
  167, 171, 173–5, 177,
  182–3, 186, 188, 192,
  195–6, 199, 201, 203,
  206–7, 209
  activities 15, 21
  agents 173–4
  analysts 200
  collection 19
  David's 91, 94
  economic 21
  failure 211
  gathering 61, 84–5, 97,
    102, 104, 107, 123, 147,
    153, 172, 178, 197,
    203–4, 206
  geographic 93
  history 200, 211
  Jewish 184

lessons 83
Maccabean 102
military 20–21
networks 171
officers 206
operations 13, 41–2, 80,
  84–5, 90, 125, 195, 202,
  206, 208, 210
problems 189
professionals 154
religious revelation 16
reports 173
Roman 183, 196
strategic 17, 153, 183–4
tactical 17, 184–5
training 37
transmission 19
war 179, 192
internal security 71, 90–1,
  153–4, 161, 166
intifada 205
Roman 177
Iran 151, 197
Iraq 151, 197
Iron Age 30, 42, 49, 54, 58,
  82, 95–6, 210, 225
  Early 23, 25, 29
  Iron Age 1 (1200–100 BCE)
    18, 25, 42, 75, 81, 225,
    235
  Iron Age II 18
  Late 32
Isaac, Benjamin 181
Isaiah 160
Ishbosheth 89–90, 239
Israel (ancient) 22–37, 59, 80,
  82–3, 89–90, 92, 94, 98,
  112, 118–19, 121, 124–5,
  151, 158, 165, 182, 196,
  200–3, 206, 208–10
  monarchical period 18, 84,
    203–4, 236–9
  northern kingdom 33
  pre-monarchical 203, 209
Israel (modern) 17
  Six Day War 223
  war of independence (1948)
    183, 204–5
Israelites 17, 22–5, 27–9,
  31, 33–4, 36, 41, 46–7,
  49–52, 55–7, 63–71, 73,
  78–9, 83–4, 86–7, 90,
  92, 94, 97, 119, 123–4,
  204–7, 210

Jabin, king of Hazor 56–7,
  65, 68, 70, 230
Jacob, patriarch 34
Jael 65, 67–70, 112, 115–16,
  123, 231–2
Jaffa 104
Jagersma 210
James Boanerges 155, 169
javelin 90, 103, 203
Jeremiah 160
Jericho 25, 41, 45–50, 52–3,

  59, 69, 86, 124, 141, 186,
  189, 227
Jeroboam II 57
Jerusalem 34–5, 45, 82, 84,
  90–3, 95–6, 98, 100,
  104–5, 108, 110, 112,
  129, 131–4, 136–7,
  139–42, 145–7, 149,
  154–6, 160–4, 166–7,
  172, 174, 176, 179–81,
  184–5, 188, 192, 195,
  197–8, 228, 238–9
  citadel of 158
  triumphal entry of Jesus
    156–160, 168, 173
Jesus, son of Ananias 161
Jesus of Nazareth 18, 154–68,
  170–8, 254–61
  arrest of 164–6
  execution of 169–70, 175–6
  Jesus file 156, 162, 168,
    173
  trial before the Sanhedrin
    166–8, 173
  trial before Pontius Pilate
    168–73
Jewish Revolt, First 18, 104,
  129–30, 133, 139–50,
  153, 161, 169, 176–7,
  179–80, 183, 189, 196,
  198, 247–54
Jews 15, 18–21, 23, 49, 99,
  103, 105–15, 129–30,
  132, 134, 136–8, 140–4,
  150–2, 158–9, 164,
  166–9, 171–7, 179–86,
  188–9, 191–2, 194–208
  defeat by Romans 146–50
  defending Jerusalem 144
  escape from Egypt 23
  exile (diaspora) 13, 158,
    180, 196–7, 202
  factional quarrels 141, 202
  Hellenistic and Hellenized
    99–100, 177, 180
  Jewish aristocracy 166
  Jewish factions 137, 145
  Jewish fighters 140
  Jewish history 151, 201
  Jewish law 166, 176
  Jewish leadership 134
  Jewish nationalists 129,
    158, 171, 195, 204
  Jewish priests 139
  Jewish state 156
  Jews in Galilee 155
  return from Babylon 35
  wandering in the wilderness
    23–4
Jezreel valley 14, 63–5, 67,
  70–1
Jib, el 54
Joab 89–92, 94–5
Joakim, High Priest 115
Joan of Arc 64
John Boanerges 155, 169

John Hyrcanus 100, 144
John of Gischala 140–4, 145–6
John the Baptist 154
Jonathan, son of Saul 86–7, 89, 204
Jonathan Maccabeus 100, 110–11
Joppa 202
Jordan (modern country) 14, 17, 202
Jordan river 26–7, 42, 45, 50, 56, 59, 63–4, 72–3, 91
Cis-Jordan 53, 229
trans-Jordan 23–4, 27, 63, 70–1, 141, 189, 192
valley 45, 189
Joseph, tribe of 63
Josephus, Flavius (Jewish historian) 45, 106, 121, 129–33, 137, 139–40, 144, 146, 148–51, 161, 171–2, 179, 201, 204, 207–8
Antiquities 130
Jewish Wars 130–1
Joshua, Book of 14–15, 18, 24–7, 33–4, 36, 41–2, 45–50, 53, 55, 57–61, 63, 68–9, 79–80, 85–6, 97, 117–18, 120, 123, 151, 205, 207, 210, 223–9
Joshua, general 22–7, 34, 45–51, 53–61, 63, 68–9, 73, 80, 82, 97–8, 179
Josiah, King 32–6, 49–50, 53, 58, 74, 80–2, 118, 120
Jotapata 140, 150
Judaea 42, 44, 61, 85, 91, 99, 102–6, 108, 111–12, 129–30, 133, 136, 138–9, 141–2, 146–7, 151, 153, 166, 170–1, 174–5, 177–8, 180, 182–6, 188, 191–2, 194–9, 201
economy of 162
hellenizing of 99
hills of 102, 104, 106–7, 149, 185, 195
Judaean cities 55
Judaean desert 179, 181–2, 184
Judaean mountains 54–5, 184, 186
Judaean resistance to the Romans 144
Judaean wilderness 85
occupied by Seleucids 99
Judah, kingdom of 24, 32–5, 53–5, 58–9, 89, 92, 96, 102
Judaism 166, 176–7, 181, 207–8, 210
rabbinic 182
Judas Iscariot 155–6, 159,

163–4, 254
Judas Maccabeus 100, 102–10, 116, 148, 179, 188
Judas of Galilee 129–30, 156
Judges,
Book of 15, 18, 33, 36, 42, 59, 63–5, 68, 70, 72, 74–5, 77, 79–83, 85, 97, 112, 117, 120, 122–3, 151, 205, 210, 229–35
of Israel (*shophetim*) 63, 74, 80–1, 122
Period of 18, 79, 82
Judith 18, 112–16, 123, 244–5
Book of 112, 115, 244–5
Jugurtha 182
Julius Severus, governor of Britain 189
Jupiter Capitolinus 181

Kedesh in Naphtali 65, 67
Kenyon, Kathleen 25, 53, 239
Keret, King 49
Kerioth 155
Kern, Paul Bentley 13
Ancient Siege Warfare
kerygma 173
Khirbet Beth-heiran 107
Khirbet el-Tell (Ai) 52
Khirbet Kefire (Chefirah) 55
kidnapping 130
kingdom of God 156
Kings, Books of 15, 18, 24, 32–3, 36, 41, 80, 84–6, 97, 120, 210
kings and kingship 156
Kiriath Jeaarim 54
Kishon river 65, 67, 69, 231

Lachish 24, 26, 58
ladders, scaling 140
Lapp, Paul W. 25
Lappidoth, woman of 64, 230
legions, Roman 139, 149, 180, 184–5, 189, 192, 201
II Traiana 183
III Cyrenaica 183, 191
III Gallica 188
VI Ferrata 184
X Fretensis 142, 146, 184
XII 139
XXII Deiotariana 186
vexillationes 192
Lemche, Nils Peter 30, 59, 95, 121
The Israelites in History and Tradition 30
lestai 132, 165, 169, 175
Levites 82
Leviticus 33
Lind, M. C. 61
literacy 96, 119
Livy 16

Lod 104
Longstreth, Edward 13
Loukuas-Andreas 197
low-intensity conflict 204
Lucius Quietus 197, 199
Lucretia 125
Lydda 186
Lysias 105, 107–8

Maccabees 18, 99, 103, 108–10, 125, 151, 158, 240
First Book of 99–100, 104, 110, 158, 205
Maccabean warriors 208
period 208
revolt of 100, 104–5, 110, 148, 179, 183. 196, 207, 240–4
Second Book of 99–100, 106, 110, 121
Maccoby, Hyam 156
Machaerus 141, 146
magic 174–5, 200
Malamat, Abraham 17, 49, 54, 118, 123
Manasseh, tribe of 71, 73
Mao Tse-tung 103
Marisa (Mareshah) 107
Marquet-Krause, Judith 52
Maryannu 56
Masada 134, 141, 146, 150, 197, 199
excavations at 146
Mattathias Maccabeus 100, 102, 110, 241
May, E. C. 20
Mediterranean Sea 13, 112, 124, 148, 198
Megiddo 14, 26, 49, 58, 67, 69, 90, 96, 98
pass at 124
waters of 65
Menachem, leader of the *sicarii* 130, 134
Mendenhall, George 28
The Tribes of Yahweh 28
mercenaries 87, 209
Greek 102
Merom, Mount 56
brook 56
Waters of 56–8, 68
valley of 56
Mesha stele 96, 236
Mesopotamia 96, 120, 124, 175, 180, 197, 224, 260
messengers 96
Messiah (*meshiach*) 154, 158, 162, 165–66, 168, 170, 174, 176, 181
annointing of 158
as liberator 159
messianic kings 134, 157–8, 168–9, 171–4, 198
messianic prophets 130, 155

messianic rebellions 132
mezuzah 183
Michmash, Battle of 85–9, 97–8, 204, 236–7
Midianites 70–4, 97, 203
Mildenberg, Leo 186
military historians 20, 124
minimalists 29–30, 202, 218
miracles and miracle workers 48, 80, 98, 107, 110, 116, 125, 152, 154–5, 174–5, 198
Miriam 115
Mishna 166
Mitanni 26
Moab and Moabites 23, 64, 71, 79, 84, 123
Moabite Stone 96, 236, 239
mob, urban 130
Modi'in 100, 240
Momigliano, Arnaldo 201
Mommsen, Theodor 199
Monarchy, united 14, 18, 26, 30, 37, 80, 84–5, 92–3, 95–7
under King David 80, 89–90
Moors 197
Moreh, Hill of 71
Moses 21–2, 34–5, 45, 60, 123
Mosaic Law 191
Mount Gilboa 97
Mount of Olives 142, 169
Mount Scopus 137–8
Mount Tabor 65, 140

Naaman, Nadav 55, 58
Nahal el-Haramiah 103
Nahal Hever 191, 194–5
Naomi 115
Naphtali, tribe of 67, 71, 73
nasi (prince) 182, 198
Nazarenes 177
Nazirite 77–8, 81
Near East, ancient 14, 17, 23, 95, 117, 121, 123, 151, 210
gods 98
sources 95
Nebuchadrezzer 100, 112, 240
Necho II (pharaoh) 34–6
Negev 21, 70, 188
Neolithic period 45
Neopolitanus, Roman tribune 136
Nero, Roman emperor 139, 141–2, 151, 199
Nerva, Roman emperor 180
Neustadt, Richard E. 20
New Testament 19
Nicanor 105
Niebuhr, Berthold Georg 125
night assemblies (*coetus nocturni*) 169

night attacks and battles 71, 73–4, 89, 124
Nile River 23, 69
Nineveh 112
nomads 23, 25, 27–8, 37, 41–2, 67, 70–2, 74, 85, 123, 207, 209
  Bedouin 72
North Africa 199
Noth, Martin 26, 32, 58, 229
Numbers, Book of 15, 21, 33

Observation platform 189
officium 153
Old Testament 31, 79, 117–18, 123, 182
Ophrah (Afula) 71, 74, 86
oracles 17, 94, 218, 237
Oreb, Midianite general 73
Orthodoxy 100

pacifism 156, 172
Palestine (ancient) 23, 27–30, 59, 70, 82, 89, 99, 117, 119–20, 123–5, 139, 141, 154, 177, 179, 197, 202, 205
  hill country of 18, 21, 29
  literary culture 121
  maritime plain 82
  pre-monarchical period 70
  Roman 15,
  Western 27
Palestinians, modern 15, 221
Parthians 105, 142, 148, 150–1, 185, 192, 199
Passover (*pesach*) 36, 156–7, 159, 163–5
Patriarchs 33
Patriarchy 47
Patton, George C. 209
Paul of Tarsus, Pauline Christianity 170, 177
Pausanias 194
Peaceful infiltration 26–7, 117–18
Pentateuch 36, 117, 120–1
Persians 92, 121
phalanx, hoplite 106
Pharisees 130, 166, 174
Philadelphia 95
Philip 108
Philip (brother of Herod Antipas) 108, 155
Philistines 26, 55, 65, 75–8, 82, 84–9, 91–5, 97, 122, 200, 220, 236–8
  agent 75–6
  city-states 65, 95
Philo of Alexandria 170
police, Temple 161–2, 165, 167
polytheism 74
Pompey 110, 177
Pontius Pilate 153, 165, 167–78

post-modernism 29
Price, Jonathan 133
Pritchard, James B. 54
propaganda 15, 19, 30, 61, 89, 171, 174, 209, 222
  Yahwistic 59, 61
prophets, prophetesses 17, 65, 122, 130, 155–8, 162, 165, 167, 195
prostitution 45, 47, 78, 206, 224
Psalm 203
psychological warfare 49
Ptolemies 99, 110–11
Ptolemy, Syrian general 105
Publius Marcellus, governor of Syria 188
Purah, the armour-bearer 72
Pyrenees 201
Pyrrhic victory 194

qannai 155
quislings 154
Qumran 160, 189

Rabbi Akiva 182, 198
Rabbi Meir 183
Rabbi Simon of Timnah 184
rabbinical sources 183, 192
Rachel 115
Rad, Gerhard von 79
Rahab 45–7, 59, 61–3, 69, 122, 224–5, 228, 232
Ramallah 100
Ramses III 25–6
razzias and raids 70, 92
Rebekah 115
rebels and rebellion 75, 100, 102, 105, 110, 129, 132–4, 136, 139–41, 146, 149, 151, 153, 162, 164, 167, 169–71, 175, 177, 180, 183, 185, 188, 192, 194, 196, 198, 207–8,
  rebel factions 133
  urban rebels 133
reconnaissance 21, 23, 27, 45, 48–50, 54, 59–61, 67, 71–4, 86–7, 89, 91, 93, 97, 99, 104, 106–7, 123, 137–8
Rephaim valley 92–4, 237–9
  campaigns 92
republics 19
resistance movements 100, 134
retreat, feigned 51
Reuben, tribe of 67
revelation, religious 16–17
Revisionists, biblical 15, 29, 222
revolts, 166, 169, 182
  for independence 99, 134
  peasant 28–9, 118
revolutionaries and revolutionary groups 130,

132, 136–7, 139, 150, 155, 160, 162, 164–5, 167, 169, 171, 175, 177, 181. 205
Rhine 199
riots and rioting 161, 166, 176
Romans 18–19, 109, 111, 121, 129, 131–34, 136–9, 141–6, 149–56, 158–9, 162, 165–6, 172–5, 177, 179, 181–200, 202, 205
  agents 173
  army 136, 138, 140, 149, 165, 167, 171, 173, 183, 196
  citizens 168
  colonies of 180–1
  counteroffensive 189
  emperors 129, 153, 171, 174–5, 181
  empire 177–8, 191, 199–200
  generals 140
  jurisdiction 168
  jurisprudence 172, 176
  occupation of Judaea 204
  prefects 161, 166–7, 170–1
  procurators (governors) 129, 133, 157, 163, 166, 168–9, 172, 174, 177–8, 207
  provincial trials 168
  subjects 164
  tribunes (*chiliarchos*) 165
  veteran colonies 132
  violence 133
Rome, city of 141
Roncesvalles pass 201
ruses de guerre 78, 106, 140, 206–7
Ruth 115

Sabbath (*shabbes*) 99–100, 157, 166
Sadducees 130, 159, 170
Safe house 45
Salome Alexandria 110
Samaria 49, 53, 72, 102–3, 136, 184, 188, 191
Samson, judge 75–8, 81–2, 122, 233–5
Samuel, Books of 33, 78, 92, 97–8, 110, 120
Samuel, prophet 63
Sanhedrin 162, 166, 173, 176
Saracens 201
Sarah 115
Sargon 217
Sasson, Jack 95
Saudi Arabia 197
Saul, King 85–7, 89–90, 95–8
saviour 177
Scaevola, Mucius 125
scouts and scouting 45, 50–1,

67, 92, 184
Scriptures, Christian 14,
Scythopolis 188
Sea Peoples 26
secrecy 19, 76, 78, 86, 102, 108, 130–1, 140, 163–5, 167, 183, 185–6, 188, 211
  secret agents 73, 115, 163
  secret army 167
  secret operations 131, 188
  secret passage 64
security risks 154, 173
sedentarization 25, 27
sedition 171, 174–6
seduction 211
Seers 17
Seleucids 18, 99, 102–8, 110–11, 202
Seron 103–5, 242
Sex and espionage 47, 75, 78, 112
  seduction 115
Shaar Hagai 106
Shechem 75
Sheldon, Rose Mary, *Trust in the Gods, But Verify* 19
Shephelah 82, 92, 188
Sherwin-White, A. N. 168
shields 205
Shimon ben Kosiba *see* Bar Kokhba
sicarii 130–1, 133–4, 146–7, 149–50, 155–6, 164, 247, 250
siege warfare 13, 41, 64, 92, 108, 138, 140, 188, 196, 205, 207
  siege engines 144, 149–50
  siege of Jerusalem 142–8
signals and signalling 17, 49, 52, 72–3, 207
  smoke 52
  trumpets 48, 50, 72, 79, 91
Silberman, Neil Asher 32–4
Simon bar Giora 137–8, 141–2, 145–6
Simon bar Jonas (son of Zebedee) 155
Simon Maccabeus 100, 110, 158
Simon Peter, the apostle 164, 169
Simon the Iscariot 155
Simon the Zealot (the freedom fighter) 155–6
Sinai 23, 27, 37, 70
Sisera 65, 67–8, 69, 81
slaves and slavery 20, 106, 209
slings and slingers 90, 103, 136, 204–5
Smithsonian Institution 15
social bandits 132
Soggin, J. Alberto 209–10
Solomon, King 34, 84, 95–6,

98, 158, 204
Song of Roland 201
soothsayers 17
Spartacus 182, 199
spears 20, 52, 65, 90, 103
speculatores 183–4
speed 50, 57, 205–6
spies 16, 19, 21–3, 46, 50,
    60, 63–4, 69, 72–73, 75,
    90, 112, 117, 123–4,
    153, 184, 200, 206, 208,
    210, 226
  Absalom's 90
  David's 90–1
  Israelite 45–9
  Jewish 157
  Maccabean 99, 103–6, 110
  Moses' 21, 45
  Old Testament 117–25,
    245–6
  Roman 157, 159
  Saul's 87
  Seleucid 106
  spy networks 153
Spong, John Shelby 31
spy stories 16, 20, 28, 30–1,
    36, 42, 47–8, 59–60, 78,
    97, 117, 119, 124–5, 211
Stephen, Saint 160
stoning 166
stratagems 17, 63, 75, 123–4,
    205–7, 269
strategy 64
  grand 203
strongholds 182
subterfuge 63
subterranean passages and
    strongholds 186, 188
subversion 153, 168, 184
Suetonius 207
Sun Tzu 206, 211, 218
Supper, The Last 163–4
surprise
  attack 17, 36, 50–1, 56–8,
    61–2, 67, 71–5, 86, 89,
    91–3, 99–100, 104–7,
    109, 115, 124, 136–7,
    139–40, 142, 147, 152,
    183, 186, 188, 196,
    203–7, 211, 243
  in warfare 60–1
  stealth 57
  tactical 56, 92
surveillance 22, 73, 146,
    157, 163
swords and swordsmen 64,
    86–7, 102–4, 115, 140,
    156, 159, 165, 173,

204–5
Syria and Syrians 28, 30,
    95–6, 99, 103–5, 108–9,
    124, 132, 139, 184,
    188–9, 197, 208, 241
  Roman governors of Syria
    136, 146
  Syrian troops 148

Tabernacles, feast of 158
Tabor, Mount 67, 231
Tacitus 207
tactics, military 36, 51, 56,
    61–2, 64, 73, 75, 80,
    84–6, 89–90, 92–4, 97,
    99, 102, 106, 108–9,132,
    136, 139, 140, 142,
    148–9, 184–6, 188–9,
    191, 195–7, 203–5,
    207, 209
  battle 94
  hit and run 92, 102, 108,
    191
  irregular 188
  Jewish 142, 148, 205
  siege 140
  unconventional 99
Talmud 77, 107, 148, 192,
    194, 197
  Midrash 30, 194
  Midrash Rabbah 192
  Talmudic period 77
Tamar 115
Tanaach 65, 67, 69
Tel Masos 220
Tell Damiyah 45
Temple, Second (in Jerusalem)
    96, 98–9, 107, 110, 131,
    133–4, 137, 141–2,
    145–8, 157–62, 165–6,
    168, 171–3, 180–181,
    192, 204–5, 208
  dedication by Judas
    Maccabeus 158
  destruction of 176, 192
  money changers at 161–2,
    167, 174
  Mount 205
  priests 165
  rebuilding of 180
  second temple period 176
  so-called 'cleansing of'
    160–3, 173, 175
  tax 160
  Temple Mount 142
  threats against 160–2
terrorism 109, 119, 130–3,
    147, 151, 200

terrorist acts 13, 36,
    129–30, 147, 149, 247
Teutoberg Forest 149, 199
Thebes 75
theocracy 208
theology 17, 48, 60, 82,
    89, 94, 98, 120–1, 123,
    125, 161, 166–7, 172,
    208, 239
  theological explanations 89,
    94
Thompson, Thomas 30,
    59, 95
  The Mythic Past 30
Thutmose III 20, 98, 228
Tiberius, Roman emperor 207
Tidwell 92
Tinneus Rufus, governor of
    Judaea 188
Titus, Roman emperor
    139–42, 144–6, 151, 180
titulus 172, 259
Tomb of Queen Helena 142
Torah 48
torture 164
tradecraft 16–17, 19, 37
traitors 49
Trajan (Marcus Ulpius
    Traianus), Roman emperor
    180
Trajan (Marcus Ulpius
    Traianus, Sr) 180
trans-Jordan 23–4, 27
transhumance 42
treason trials 141
tribes of Israel 18, 71
tribute payment 66, 168,
    175, 207
Trojan War 201
troublemakers 155–6, 159,
    162
Tsafrir, Yoram 181

Ugarit, Ugaritic tablets 49,
    238
undercover agents 112, 171,
    173
underground movements
    181–2

Van Creveld, Martin 13
Van Seters, John 58–9, 121
Vaux, Roland de 117, 210
Vercingetorix 182
Vespasian, Roman emperor
    139–42, 146, 180, 199
Vietnam 195

Wadi ed-Daliyah 191
Wadi Murabba'at 191
warfare, 13, 203, 206
  ancient 217
  conventional 103, 206
  defensive 203
  irregular 206
  small wars 204
  unconventional 103
weapons, weaponry 14, 28,
    61, 63, 65, 70, 84, 89, 98,
    102–3, 112, 130–1, 136.
    139, 164, 196, 199, 203,
    205, 209–10
Weber 199
Weippert, Manfred 80
West Bank 45
Whitelam, Keith W. 30
  *The Invention of Ancient
    Israel* 30
  *The Silencing of Palestinian
    History* 30
Witch of Endor 17
women in espionage 45–8, 70,
    75–6, 79, 81, 112, 230
Women's Gate 142
Wood, Bryant 53
Wright, G. Ernest 25, 118

Xiphilinus (Byzantine monk)
    179, 182

Yadin, Yigael 14, 25, 54,
    63–4, 71, 183
Yahweh 17, 28, 34–5, 42,
    48, 50–1, 59, 69, 74, 78,
    80–3, 89, 91, 93–4, 97–8,
    100, 112, 120–3, 181,
    200–1, 208
  Yahweh war 57, 79, 121–2,
    246
Yavneh 183

Zadok the Pharisee 129–30
Zakovich, Yair 36
zealots 105, 131, 134, 141,
    149–50, 198, 241, 248
  barjonna 155
  party in First Jewish Revolt
    131–3
  qannai (kannanaios 155
Zeboim 86
Zebul 75
Zebulun, tribe of 67, 71
Zechariah 157
Zeeb, Midianite general 73
Zeus, Olympian 99
Zionists 15, 30, 198